Law and Society in Later Medieval England and Ireland

Law mattered in later medieval England and Ireland. A quick glance at the sources suggests as much. From the charter to the will to the court roll, the majority of the documents which have survived from later medieval England and Ireland, and medieval Europe in general, are legal in nature. Yet despite the fact that law played a prominent role in medieval society, legal history has long been a marginal subject within medieval studies both in Britain and North America. Much good work has been done in this field, but there is much still to do. This volume, a collection of essays in honour of Paul Brand, who has contributed perhaps more than any other historian to our understanding of the legal developments of later medieval England and Ireland, is intended to help fill this gap. The essays collected in this volume, which range from the twelfth to the sixteenth century, offer the latest research on a variety of topics within this field of inquiry. While some consider familiar topics, they do so from new angles, whether by exploring the underlying assumptions behind England's adoption of trial by jury for crime or by assessing the financial aspects of the General Eyre, a core institution of jurisdiction in twelfth- and thirteenth-century England. Most, however, consider topics which have received little attention from scholars, from the significance of judges and lawyers smiling and laughing in the courtroom to the profits and perils of judicial office in English Ireland. The essays provide new insights into how the law developed and functioned within the legal profession and courtroom in late medieval England and Ireland, as well as how it pervaded the society at large.

Travis R. Baker is a private scholar living in San Diego, California.

Law and Society in Later Medieval England and Ireland

Essays in Honour of Paul Brand

Edited by Travis R. Baker

Routledge
Taylor & Francis Group
LONDON AND NEW YORK

First published 2018 by Routledge

2 Park Square, Milton Park, Abingdon, Oxfordshire OX14 4RN
52 Vanderbilt Avenue, New York, NY 10017

Routledge is an imprint of the Taylor & Francis Group, an informa business

First issued in paperback 2020

British Library Cataloguing-in-Publication Data
A catalogue record for this book is available from the British Library

Library of Congress Cataloging-in-Publication Data
A catalog record for this book has been requested

ISBN: 978-1-4724-7738-5 (hbk)
ISBN: 978-0-367-59436-7 (pbk)

Typeset in Sabon
by Apex CoVantage, LLC

Paul Brand

Photo by Susanne Brand

Contents

Contributors

David Crouch is Professor of Medieval History at the University of Hull.

William Eves is a Post-Doctoral Research Fellow at the University of St Andrews.

Áine Foley is an independent researcher.

Robin Frame is Emeritus Professor of History at Durham University.

Thomas A. Green is Emeritus Professor of History and Law at the University of Michigan and Affiliate Scholar at Oberlin College.

Elizabeth Papp Kamali is Assistant Professor of Law at Harvard Law School.

F. Donald Logan is Emeritus Professor of History at Emmanuel College.

Anthony Musson is Professor of Legal History at the University of Exeter.

Jens Röhrkasten is Lecturer in Medieval History at the University of Birmingham.

Ryan Rowberry is Associate Professor of Law at Georgia State University Law School.

Gwen Seabourne is Professor of Law at the University of Bristol Law School.

David J. Seipp is Professor of Law at Boston University Law School.

Karl Shoemaker is Professor of History and Law at the University of Wisconsin-Madison.

Joshua C. Tate is Associate Professor of Law at SMU Dedman School of Law.

Preface

Will the history of English law ever be written? Probably not, at least not any time soon. According to Professor Sir John Baker's calculations in 1971, the editing of the 'Year Books of Edward II will not be completed before the year 2010, and the series will reach Henry VIII somewhere around 2750'.[1] Twenty-seven years later, Professor Baker had to concede that his calculations were 'wildly optimistic'.[2] While there is little hope then that the history of English law as a whole will be written any time this millennium, there is one century whose definitive history should be written and published in the not too distant future: the thirteenth. Why the optimism? The answer of course is Paul Brand, FBA, Emeritus Fellow at All Souls College, Oxford and honourand of this volume. For more than forty years, Paul has been expertly writing and publishing on nearly every aspect of the English medieval common law, including its transplantation to Ireland. Although Paul's scholarship ranges from the twelfth to the sixteenth century, the thirteenth is the one which he 'has made his own',[3] being 'the scholar today who has the best command of the intricacies of thirteenth-century English law'.[4] So extensive in fact is Paul's knowledge of the law of that century that Professor Baker has recently remarked that Paul 'knows everything there is to know about the law of that period'.[5] In the light of these comments, it almost seems invidious not to conclude with Professor Mark Godfrey that Paul is 'the most prominent and distinguished contemporary historian of medieval English law'.[6]

As it stands, Paul's published work consists of three authored books, eight editions of primary-source texts, five jointly edited volumes, eighty-five major articles and seventy dictionary/encyclopedia entries, which, when taken together, total more than 7,500 pages, with thousands more forthcoming, *Deo volente*. The results generated by this massive body of scholarship have been nothing less than transformative. Few historians can honestly claim to have rewritten the history of their chosen field of expertise, but that is exactly what Paul has done for the legal history of thirteenth-century England. He has been able to accomplish this because of his long-standing commitment to reading the original sources, especially the published and unpublished plea rolls of the king's courts and the published and unpublished law reports. As Paul explained at the beginning of his lecture to the Welsh Legal History Society in June 2003, 'it is the evidence of these original sources for English legal history that I have been working on in the confident hope that they will provide the necessary foundations for a rewriting of the legal history of thirteenth-century England'.[7] Perhaps the most striking example of this commitment to reading the original sources is found in his essay 'Family and Inheritance, women and children', published in *An Illustrated History of Late Medieval England*. While the usual practice in such volumes is to write an essay synthesising the current scholarship on the topic under consideration and adding a few primary-source references along the way, Paul's essay is based entirely on *unpublished* primary sources![8] But Paul has not only been an omnivorous animal, reading almost all the primary sources from this period.[9] He has also consistently understood their significance, no small achievement when it comes to medieval legal records. Take for example his paper 'A Working Draft of the Statute of Acton Burnell (1283)'. Here Paul argues that a text of 59 lines found on a badly damaged parchment membrane contains a working draft of the Statute of Acton Burnell, which was 'produced for discussion at parliament or in council, annotated with the deletions and additions that reflected the course of argument there, and perhaps sealed at the end of discussion'. Although we possess other documents which were produced during the drafting process of legislation, none of these 'are the actual original documents and none contain the deletions or insertions which capture the process by which original drafts were amended'.[10] These conclusions would be far from self-evident to most readers of this document, especially since much of its surface has been stained with gall and as result is very difficult even to read much less understand its significance. Yet despite the formidable difficulties presented by this text, Paul's faultless erudition and historical imagination have enabled him to uncover the uniqueness and significance of this seemingly insignificant document.

Almost as remarkable as Paul's profound and encyclopedic knowledge of the legal records of medieval England and Ireland is his willingness to share that knowledge with other scholars. As Professor David Carpenter has put it, 'How often does one come across the footnote "I owe this information to Paul Brand", so much so that he almost seems a primary source in himself'.[11] Paul has also been very generous in the amount of time he has devoted to reading and commenting on entire drafts of books of other scholars. In the preface to his book, *Runaway Religious in Medieval England*, Donald Logan writes that 'To no other scholar do I owe more than to Paul Brand, who read the entire text. He gave the text the benefit of his broad erudition and sound historical judgement, and he gave the author much appreciated words of encouragement'.[12] This would not be the only time that Paul's erudition and generosity would be singled out in the preface of another scholar's book. In the preface to *Select Ecclesiastical Cases from the King's Courts 1272–1307*, David Millon writes that 'I owe a huge debt to Professor Paul Brand, who painstakingly read the entire manuscript and corrected many errors in the transcriptions and translations. He deserves a large measure of credit for any merit this volume might posses'.[13] Many other scholars have undoubtedly felt the same way after Paul has read and commented on their work. I know for certain that the editor of this volume has.

In his memoir on George Osborne Sayles for the British Academy, Paul ends by asserting that Sayles 'is one of the few legal and constitutional historians who have written since Maitland whom it is not wholly inappropriate to compare him with'.[14] I would suggest that it is not 'wholly inappropriate' to add Paul's name to that small group of constitutional and legal historians, for it is hard to think of too many other legal historians, past or present, who have shed as much light on the history of medieval English law as he has.

Since this volume is a collection of essays in Paul's honour, my first thanks must go to each contributor for their willingness to be a part of it and for their patience in seeing it to publication. I am grateful to Routledge for accepting this volume for publication and to Max Novick, Jennifer Morrow and Jennifer Bonnar for making the editorial process such a smooth and enjoyable one. I am thankful to Paul's wife Susanne for providing me with the lovely photograph of Paul. I am also very grateful to my wife Hannah for all her support throughout this project. Finally, I am thankful to my son David for helping me compile the index and for asking me with all sincerity, along with his brothers Alex and Charles, when the book will be finished.

Notes

1 John H. Baker, 'Unprinted Sources of English Legal History', *Law Library Journal* 64 (1971): 302–13, at 309.

2 Idem, *Why the History of English Law Has Not Been Finished*, An Inaugural lecture delivered in the Law School on 14 October 1998 (Cambridge: Cambridge University Press, 1999), 20.

3 This quote comes from Richard H. Helmholz's essay, 'Annuities and Annual Pensions', in *Laws, Lawyers and Texts: Studies in Medieval Legal History in Honour of Paul Brand*, eds. Susanne Jenks, Jonathan Rose and Christopher Whittick, Medieval Law and Its Practice, 13 (Leiden: Brill, 2012), 70.

4 This quote comes from Charles Donahue's essay, 'Whither Legal History', in *Transformations in American Legal History: Essays in Honor of Professor Morton J. Horwitz*, eds. Daniel W. Hamilton and Alfred L. Brophy (Cambridge, MA: Harvard University Press, 2009), 343 n.25.

5 Jenks, Rose and Whittick, *Laws, Lawyers and Texts*, 177.

6 Review of *Laws, Lawyers and Texts: Studies in Medieval Legal History*, edited by Susanne Jenks, Jonathan Rose and Christopher Whittick, *Zeitschrift der Savigny-Stiftung für Rechtsgeschichte Germanistische Abteilung* 132 (2015): 672–5, at 672.

7 Paul A. Brand, 'An English Legal Historian Looks at the Statute of Wales', in *Y Cyfraniad Cymreig (Welsh Contributions to Legal Development)*, ed. Thomas Glyn Watkin (Bangor: The Welsh Legal History Society, 2005), 21.

8 Chris Given-Wilson, ed., *An Illustrated History of Late Medieval England* (Manchester: Manchester University Press, 1996), 280.

9 For legal historians being omnivorous animals, see Paul's recent essay 'The Fine Rolls of Henry III as a Source for the Legal Historian', in *The Growth of Royal Government Under Henry III*, eds. David Crook and Louise J. Wilkinson (Woodbridge: The Boydell Press, 2015), 44: 'Legal historians are omnivorous animals. Almost every kind of official governmental record from thirteenth-century England is something which the legal historian can draw on'.

10 Paul Brand, 'A Working Draft of the Statute of Acton Burnell (1283)', in *Foundations of Medieval Scholarship: Records Edited in Honour of David Crook*, eds. Paul Brand and Sean Cunningham (York: The Borthwick Institute, 2008), 28.

11 Jenks, Rose and Whittick, *Laws, Lawyers and Texts*, 129.

12 F. Donald Logan, *Runaway Religious in medieval England, c.1240 to 1540* (Cambridge: Cambridge University Press, 1996), xiv.

13 David Millon, ed., *Select Ecclesiastical Cases From the King's Court 1272–1307* (London: Selden Society, 2009), Preface.

14 'George Osborne Sayles, 1901–1994', in *1995 Lectures and Memoirs*, Proceedings of the British Academy, 90 (London: Published for the British Academy by Oxford University Press, 1996), 441–63, at 463.

Abbreviations

AALT	Anglo-American Legal Tradition website: http://aalt.law.uh.edu/
Acts and Letters	David Crouch, ed., *The Acts and Letters of the Marshal Family, Marshals of England and Earls of Pembroke, 1145–1248*, Camden Society, 5th ser., vol. 47 (Oxford, 2015)
AHR	*American Historical Review*
AJLH	*American Journal of Legal History*
Annales Monastici	*Annales Monastici*, ed. H.R. Luard, 5 vols. (London, 1866)
BL	British Library
BNB	*Bracton's Note Book: A Collection of Cases decided in the King's Courts during the Reign of Henry the Third, annotated by a lawyer of that Time, seemingly by Henry of Bratton*, ed. F.W. Maitland, 3 vols. (London, 1887)
Bracton	Bracton, *De Legibus et Consuetudinibus Angliae*, ed. G.E. Woodbine and trans., with revision and notes, by Samuel E. Thorne, 4 vols. (Cambridge, MA, 1968–77)
Brand, *MCL*	Paul Brand, *The Making of the Common Law* (London, 1992)
Brand, *OELP*	Paul Brand, *The Origins of the English Legal Profession* (Oxford, 1992)
Britton	*Britton*, ed. and trans. F.M. Nichols, 2 vols. (Oxford, 1865)
BRUC	A.B. Emden, *A Biographical Register of the University of Cambridge to 1500* (Cambridge, 1963)
BRUO	A.B. Emden, *A Biographical Register of the University of Oxford to A.D. 1500*, 3 vols. (Oxford, 1957–59)
CChR	*Calendar of Charter Rolls*, 6 vols. (London, 1903–1927)

CCR	*Calendar of Close Rolls*, 47 vols. (London, 1892–1963)
CDI	*Calendar of Documents relating to Ireland, 1171–1307*, ed. H.S. Sweetman, 5 vols. (London, 1875–86)
CFR	*Calendar of the Fine Rolls*, 22 vols. (London, 1911–63)
CIPM	*Calendar of Inquisitions Post Mortem*, 19 vols. (London, 1904–1992)
CIRCLE	'Calendar of Irish Chancery Letters. *c.*1244–1509' (www.tcd.ie.chancery)
CJCP	Chief Justice of the Court of Common Pleas
CJKB	Chief Justice of the Court of the King's Bench
CJRI	*Calendar of the Justiciary Rolls of Ireland, 1295–1314*, ed. J. Mills et al., 3 vols. (Dublin, 1905–56)
COD	*Conciliorum oecumenicorum decreta*, ed. Giuseppe Alberigo et al., 3rd ed. (Bologna, 1973)
Cod. J.	Codex of Justinian
CP	Records of the Court of Common Pleas
CPR	*Calendar of Patent Rolls*, 72 vols. (London, 1891–1986)
CRR	*Curia Regis Rolls*, 20 vols. (London, 1922–2006)
Dig.	Digest of Justinian
'Dublin Deeds'	J.G. Smyly, 'Old Latin deeds in Trinity College Library, parts I–III', *Hermathena*, 66–8 (1945–7). The deeds are numbered consecutively throughout.
EELR	*The Earliest English Law Reports*, ed. Paul A. Brand, 4 vols., Selden Society 111, 112, 122, 123 (London, 1996–2007)
EETS	Early English Text Society
EHD	*English Historical Documents*, vol. 1, c. 500–1042, ed. D. Whitelock, 2nd ed. (London, 1979); vol. 2, 1049–1189, ed. D.C. Douglas and G.W. Greenway, 2nd ed. (London, 1981)
EHR	*English Historical Review*
Exch. Ch.	Exchequer Chamber
Fleta	*Fleta*, volumes 2, 3, 4 [vol. 1 not published], ed. H.G. Richardson and G.O. Sayles [vol. 4 by Sayles alone], 3 vols., Selden Society, 72, 89 and 99 (London, 1955–1984)
Foedera	*Foedera, conventiones, litterae et cujuscunque generis acta publica*, ed. Thomas Rymer (Record Commission, 1816)

Glanvill	*The Treatise on the Laws and Customs of the Realm of England Commonly Called Glanvill*, ed. and trans. G.D.G. Hall, with a guide to further reading by Michael T. Clanchy (Oxford, 1993)
Green, *Verdict*	Thomas A. Green, *Verdict According to Conscience: Perspectives on the English Criminal Trial Jury, 1200–1800* (Chicago, 1985)
Hand, *English Law*	G.J. Hand, *English Law in Ireland, 1290–1324* (Cambridge, 1967)
HWM	*History of William Marshal*, ed. A. J. Holden and David Crouch, trans. S. Gregory, 3 vols., Anglo-Norman Text Society, Occasional Publication Series, 4–6 (London, 2002–7)
IEP	*Irish Exchequer Payments, 1270–1446*, ed. P. Connolly (Dublin 1998)
IHS	*Irish Historical Studies* (1938–)
JLH	*Journal of Legal History*
KB	Records of the Court of King's Bench
Lawsuits	*English Lawsuits from William I to Richard I* *English Lawsuits from William I to Richard I*, ed. R.C. van Caenegem, 2 vols., Selden Society 106 and 107 (London, 1990–1991)
LHR	*Law and History Review*
LHP	*Leges Henrici Primi*, ed. and trans. L.J. Downer (Oxford, 1972)
Lincs.	*The Earliest Lincolnshire Assize Rolls A.D. 1202–1209*, ed. Doris M.Stenton, Lincoln Record Society, 22 (Lincoln, 1926)
Logan, *Arches*	F. Donald Logan, ed., *The Medieval Court of Arches*, Canterbury and York Society, 95 (Woodbridge, 2005)
LQR	*Law Quarterly Review*
McHardy, *London*	A.K. McHardy, *The Church in London, 1375–1392*, London Record Society, 13 (London, 1977)
Medieval Dublin	*Medieval Dublin* I [etc]: *Proceedings of the Friends of Medieval Dublin,Symposium, Dublin*, ed. Seán Duffy (Dublin, 2000–)
Meekings, *Surrey*	*The 1235 Surrey Eyre*, ed. C.A.F. Meekings, D. Crook, and S. Neal, 3 vols., Surrey Record Society, 31, 32 and 37 (Guildford, 1979–2002)
Mirror of Justices	*The Mirror of Justices*, ed. W.J. Whittaker, Selden Society, 7 (London, 1895)
NAI	National Archives of Ireland
NLI	National Library of Ireland

Northants	*The Earliest Northamptonshire Assize Rolls, A.D. 1202 and 1203*, ed. Doris M. Stenton, Northamptonshire Record Society, 5 (Lincoln, 1930)
ODNB	*Oxford Dictionary of National Biography*, eds. H.C.G. Matthew and Brian Harrison, 61 vols. (Oxford, 2004)
P&M	F. Pollock and F.W. Maitland, *The History of English Law Before the Time of Edward I*, 2nd ed., 2 vols. (Cambridge, 1898)
PBKJ	*Pleas Before the King or His Justices*, ed. Doris M. Stenton, 4 vols., Selden Society 67, 68, 83 and 84 (London, 1952–1967)
PROME	*Parliament Rolls of Medieval England*, 16 vols. (London, 2005)
PRS	Pipe Roll Society
RA	*Registrum Antiquissimum of the Church of Lincoln*, eds. C.W. Foster and K. Major, 12 vols., Lincoln Record Society, 27–29, 32, 34, 41–42, 46,51, 62, 67–68 (Hereford, 1931–1973)
RCh	*Rotuli chartarum in Turri Londinensi asservati*, ed. T. D. Hardy, vol. 1 (London, 1837)
RCR	*Rotuli Curiae Regis: Rolls and Record of the Court Held Before the King's Justiciars or Justices*, ed. F. Palgrave, 2 vols. (London, 1835)
Reg. Sudbury	Register of Simon Sudbury, Archbishop of Canterbury (London, Lambeth Palace Library)
Rep. DKI	*Report of the Deputy Keeper of the Public Records of Ireland* (Dublin, 1869–). Nos. 35–9, 42–5, 47 and 53–4 contain 'Catalogue of Pipe Rolls', a selective calendar of the Irish exchequer Pipe Rolls destroyed in 1922.
RLC	*Rotuli litterarum clausarum in Turri Londinensi asservati*, ed. T. D. Hardy, 2 vols. (London, 1833–4)
RLP	*Rotuli litterarum patentium in Turri Londinensi asservati*, ed. T.D. Hardy, vol. 1 (London, 1835)
ROF	*Rotuli de Oblatis et Finibus in Turri Londinensi asservati tempore regis Johannes*, ed. T.D. Hardy (London, 1835)
Rot. Parl.	*Rotuli Parliamentorum*, 6 vols. (1783)
RS	Rolls Series
Seipp	David Seipp's index: www.bu.edu/law/seipp/
Select Bills in Eyre	*Select Bills in Eyre, 1292–1333*, ed. W.C. Bolland, Selden Society, 30 (London, 1914)

Sext.	*Liber Sextus Decretalium*, in *Corpus Juris Canonici*, vol. 2, ed. A. Friedberg (Leipzig, 1879; repr. Graz, 1959)
Sjt	serjeant at law
SR	*Statutes of the Realm*, ed. A. Luders et al., 11 vols. (London, 1810–28)
SS	Selden Society (annual volumes, 1887–)
Star. Ch.	Star Chamber
Statutes, *Ireland*	*Statutes, Ordinances and Acts of the Parliament of Ireland, King John to Henry V, Ireland*, ed. H.F. Berry (Dublin, 1907)
Stubbs, *Charters*	*Select Charters and other Illustrations of England Constitutional History*, ed. W. Stubbs, 9th ed. revised by H.W.C. Davis (Oxford, 1913)
TNA	The National Archives, Kew
VCH, London	*The Victoria History of London*, ed. William Page (London, 1909)
WH	Walther Holtzmann, *Studies in the Collections of Twelfth-Century Decretals*, edited and revised by C.R. Cheney and Mary Cheney, MIC, Series B, vol. 3 (Città del Vaticano, 1979)
X	*Decretales Gregorii Noni*, in *Corpus Juris Canonici*, vol. 2, ed. A. Friedberg (Leipzig, 1879; repr. Graz, 1959)
YB	Year Book

1 Justice delayed

Absent recognitors and the Angevin legal reforms, *c.* 1200

William Eves

The legal reforms of Henry II's reign laid many of the foundations of the English common law. Royal control over criminal pleas was increased. Likewise, a number of actions were created which allowed disputes concerning land, which might previously have been heard in lords' courts, to be brought directly before royal justices. These actions, known as 'assizes', proved to be extremely popular, a fact illustrated by the large number of cases found in the earliest surviving plea rolls of the royal courts.[1] The procedures followed by each type of assize could differ somewhat, although a common feature was the mode of proof used to decide the case. This was the 'recognition'.[2] Twelve local landholders were empanelled as 'recognitors' to provide a formal answer, on oath, to a question of fact. Recognitions nevertheless differed from a modern jury as the recognitors were asked to swear, at least ostensibly, on what they knew to be true, rather than what they judged to be true after weighing the evidence presented to them.[3]

Although central to the new Angevin procedures, the recognition was not an invention of Henry II's reign. Carolingian royal inquests had relied on the testimony of jurors.[4] Likewise, we have records of Anglo-Saxon disputes which were resolved through sworn neighbourhood testimony.[5] The verdict of groups of neighbours as to a person's *fama* could also be used as proof in a range of Romano-canonical procedures.[6] Nevertheless, as Susan Reynolds has observed, the Angevin reformers built on these procedures and gave recognitions 'precise form and rules of application' in the English royal courts.[7]

F.W. Maitland commented that the recognition 'suited Englishmen well; it became a cherished institution and was connected in their minds with all those liberties that they held dear'.[8] Indeed, no juridical concept has found more widespread and vocal exaltation in the traditionally sombre confines of Anglo-American jurisprudence. Famously described by Lord Devlin as 'the lamp that shows that freedom lives', collective judgment is seen by many as the palladium of liberty.[9]

Despite the importance of the recognition in the early common law, the study of 'civil' recognitions in the late twelfth and early thirteenth centuries has been somewhat neglected, with most scholarly attention focussing on the later medieval criminal jury.[10] The works that have considered the recognition have generally fallen into two categories. A number of historians have investigated the earlier history of juries in the Middle Ages, and have attempted to pinpoint the origins of the English procedure.[11] Others have considered the influence of the recognition on the socio-political development of the medieval state.[12] The conduct of the recognitors themselves has thus been somewhat overlooked. However, discussion on this topic has recently been reinvigorated by Paul Brand's re-examination of the 'Millon thesis', an argument put forward by David Millon in 1989 which suggested that recognitors in the late medieval and early modern periods eschewed legal norms and frequently used their discretion to decide cases.[13]

This chapter examines another aspect of the conduct of recognitors in civil cases. It investigates the extent to which the absence of recognitors from court affected the administration of justice in the earliest years of the common law. Many of the new Angevin procedures were designed to provide swift justice. It will be seen, however, that a significant number of actions suffered postponements because insufficient recognitors turned up on the day of the hearing. Actions heard at the Bench, which commonly sat at Westminster, were particularly susceptible to these delays. Cases brought before the court which travelled with the king, known as the court *coram rege*, were also frequently affected. In contrast, actions heard locally by the justices of eyre were less likely to be affected by recognitor absences.

The first part of this chapter outlines the background to the Angevin reforms and illustrates why swift justice may have been of such concern to the reformers. The new Angevin procedures are then examined. Particular attention is given to the procedural rules which were introduced to ensure that cases proceeded to judgment without undue delay. We then turn to the surviving plea rolls of the royal courts to examine the impact of recognitor absences on these new actions. We begin our survey in 1194, the date of the earliest surviving plea rolls.[14] The period up to *c.* 1208 is considered. This provides a good selection of plea rolls and allows us to end our survey before the activity of the royal courts was disrupted in the tumultuous later years of John's reign.[15]

The background to the Angevin legal reforms

In order to understand the context of the Angevin reforms, it is helpful to consider the nature of English justice in the early years of the twelfth century. A writ of Henry I provides us with an outline, perhaps somewhat idealised, of the court structure in operation in England following the Conquest. Disputes concerning right to land were to be heard in the court of the lord of the fee in which the land in dispute was located. If the jurisdiction of the lord's court was unsuitable, most likely because the litigants claimed to hold the land in dispute of different lords, the case would be heard in the county courts. Disputes between tenants-in-chief would be heard by the king himself, acting in his capacity as immediate lord of the litigants.[16] It was also possible for other well-placed individuals to call upon the king to hear their cases, although such royal intervention occurred on an *ad hoc* basis.[17] In any of the above courts, proof might take various forms, including the use of documents and sworn testimony. When cases could not be resolved through other means, the matter was often decided through trial by battle.[18]

Regardless of the type of court before which the dispute was brought, the path to justice could be slow and frustrating. Richard de Anstey's case against his cousin, Mabel de Francheville, provides a well-known instance of a case beset by delays in both the secular and ecclesiastical courts.[19] Richard brought the case before the king's court in 1158. The first hearing was scheduled to take place at Northampton, so Richard travelled to court with his friends and helpers. However, the matter was postponed and a day was given for a subsequent hearing at Southampton. As Richard alleged that Mabel was illegitimate, the dispute was then transferred to the archbishop of Canterbury's court. The case was then subject to many delays, and both parties made appeals to Rome. Richard, in his appeal, criticised Mabel's 'shiftiness' and made it clear that 'he was aggrieved by the fact that he had now been troubled by a series of postponements for more than two years and had been cheated of his just claim'.[20] Mabel was eventually judged to be illegitimate and the case then returned to the secular courts. The justiciar gave Richard a day for pleading at London in the beginning of March 1163. However, the case was postponed on numerous occasions and it eventually came before the king in July 1163. 'At last', Richard wrote, 'by the grace of God and of the king, and by judgment of his court, my uncle's land was adjudged to me'.[21] The case had cost him £344, 7s, 4d.[22]

Richard de Anstey's case suffered delays in both the secular and ecclesiastical courts. Nevertheless, cases which did not require an intervening ecclesiastical hearing might also suffer long postponements. In the early years of Henry II's reign, for example, Turstin fitz Simon was summoned to the county court to answer a complaint brought by the abbot of Abingdon. The abbot alleged that Turstin had unjustly obtained possession of the church of Marcham and certain other tenements.[23] The Abingdon chronicler tells us that Turstin, 'conscious of his misdeed, cleverly evaded the meetings of the county for two years and more . . . under pretext of the king's service or illness or some other cause'.[24] The abbot met the king at Woodstock in 1157 and 'strenuously begged him to have mercy and put an end to his pain and the case'.[25] Turstin was subsequently summoned to the king's court and, at last, the abbot was able to obtain justice.

A case between Battle Abbey and Gilbert de Balliol, probably from the following year, proceeded in a similar manner. The dispute concerned land which had been granted to the abbey by Gilbert's predecessor, and which Gilbert had then taken back into his own hands.[26] We are told that, once the abbot had managed to become a friend of the king, he obtained a royal writ ordering the case to be heard in the court of John, Count of Eu. Gilbert did not appear, despite many summonses, and is said to have made all manner of excuses to avoid the suit. With the honorial court of the count unable to secure the appearance of the parties, the abbot petitioned the king, both personally and through his friends. At length the case was transferred to the royal court. The case dragged on as the king's other business delayed matters. Eventually a day was set, and 'after many subterfuges . . . many dissimulations . . . [and] much plaguing by the abbot and his men', the case was given a hearing and the land was finally restored to the abbot.[27]

The Angevin reforms

Lawsuits in the early years of Henry II's reign might therefore have suffered long delays, exacerbated by procedural uncertainty and the problem of securing the attendance of litigants at court. Such problems were addressed by the design of the new Angevin procedures. Different types of dispute were sorted into distinct forms of action, and each type of case was regulated by tightly configured procedural rules.

The first actions to be developed were perhaps influenced by the Roman law distinction between *possessio* and *proprietas*. The legal treatise known as *Glanvill*, written *c.* 1188, explains that they concerned an individual's entitlement to 'seisin only'.[28] In this context, seisin was roughly analogous to possession, and was contrasted to 'right' to land, which obtained a more proprietary character.[29] The new procedures therefore became known as the possessory, or petty, assizes. While actions of right might continue to be brought in the seigniorial and county courts, the possessory assizes brought the case directly before the king's justices. *Glanvill* lists a number of procedures concerning seisin, although four examples are discussed in particular detail: the assize *utrum*, *novel disseisin*, *mort d'ancestor* and *darrein presentment*.[30]

An early form of the assize *utrum* can be found in the 1164 Constitutions of Clarendon.[31] The assize led to a recognition as to whether land was held as a lay or an ecclesiastical fee, and thus whether it fell under secular or ecclesiastical jurisdiction.[32] *Novel disseisin*, probably created in 1166, called for a recognition as to whether the defendant had 'unjustly and without judgment' disseised the demandant of their free tenement.[33] *Mort d'ancestor*, established at the 1176 Council of Northampton, was designed to allow the nearest heir of a deceased tenant to claim seisin of their ancestor's land.[34] A recognition was called upon to answer the question of whether the claimant was the next heir of the ancestor, and whether the latter had died seised 'in demesne and as of fee' of the land in question; that is, in direct possession (although possibly with unfree tenants) of land which was capable of descending heritably.[35] *Darrein presentment*, created towards the end of the 1170s, used a recognition to determine the identity of the individual who presented the last parson to a church, and thus who should have seisin of the disputed advowson.[36]

In addition to the new possessory actions, the grand assize was introduced, probably in 1179 at the Council of Windsor, to provide an alternative procedure through which actions of right could be decided.[37] Once the tenant had elected to put himself on the grand assize, the case, if it was being heard in a seigniorial or county court, was put before the king's justices. A recognition was then held to determine which party had the greater right to the tenement in dispute.[38]

Recognitions were perhaps favoured by the Angevin reformers because they resolved cases through human reason.[39] It is possible that confidence in supernatural modes of proof had waned throughout the course of the twelfth century, and *Glanvill* talks about the 'doubtful' outcome of trial by battle.[40] It should be noted, however, that the Angevin reformers retained trial by ordeal as a mode of proof in criminal procedures.[41] The discussion in *Glanvill* may therefore simply reflect the concern that judicial combat favoured the strong, and not amount to a criticism of supernatural proof in general.[42] Recognitions may also have been favoured because they directly involved members of the local community in the case. It was perhaps hoped that community pressure would encourage litigants to settle their disputes rather than drag them through the courts. It may also have been hoped that, when cases did go to judgment, the losing parties would be discouraged from disputing a verdict delivered by their neighbours.

Efficiency and the Angevin legal reforms

The new assizes introduced by the Angevin reformers aimed to ensure that cases proceeded swiftly to judgment. The procedural stages of the actions were carefully designed so that litigants had limited opportunities to delay the case.[43]

The desire for swift justice is particularly apparent in the design of the possessory assizes. Once a writ initiating the action had been obtained from the chancery, the sheriff was instructed to select twelve freemen from the neighbourhood of the tenement in dispute as recognitors. Both the demandant and the tenant (the defendant) could be present when the twelve freemen were elected. However, the election would take place whether or not the tenant appeared.[44] The sheriff then arranged for the recognitors to make a view of the disputed tenement. Again, the tenant would be summoned only once. If he was not present at the first summons, the view would take place in his absence.[45]

Rules concerning the tenant's appearance at court on the day of the recognition were also designed to minimise delays. With the exception of *novel disseisin*, which is discussed separately below, the same basic procedure applied in all the possessory assizes. The sheriff was first to summon the tenant 'to be before the king or his justices on the day stated in the writ'.[46] If the tenant was absent on the day of the hearing, he would be resummoned once. The recognition would take place at the subsequent hearing regardless of whether or not he appeared.[47]

Rather than simply not turning up, the tenant might instead send a formal excuse for non-attendance, known as an *essoin*, in an attempt to secure a postponement. However, restrictions were placed on the type of *essoins* which could be used. The *essoin* which could often cause the longest delays, that concerning 'bed-sickness' (*de malo lecti*), was inadmissible in possessory actions.[48] This *essoin* concerned situations in which an individual was too ill to rise from their sick-bed, and required the case to be postponed for at least a year.[49] Other types of *essoin*, those concerning difficulty in reaching court (*de malo veniendi*), were nevertheless allowed. These concerned other problems encountered by litigants in appearing before the justices and were often sent due to illness on the journey to court, in which case the hearing would be postponed for at least a fortnight.[50] The number of *essoins de malo veniendi* allowed to the tenant was, however, limited. According to *Glanvill*, no more than two successive *essoins* were allowed in a possessory action before appearance was expected at court.[51] If the defendant tried to send a third *essoin*, the recognition would proceed regardless.[52] The number of successive *essoins* available to litigants was further reduced in the years following *Glanvill*. By the time the legal treatise known as *Bracton* was written (predominantly in the 1220s and 1230s), only one *essoin de malo veniendi* was permitted before appearance was expected at court.[53] This rule in fact applied in any type of action for which *essoins* were allowed, and plea roll evidence suggests that it was in place by the end of the twelfth century.[54]

Rules concerning the vouching of a warrantor (an individual called upon to take up the defence of the plea) also reveal how considerations of speed influenced the procedural design of the possessory assizes. The author of *Glanvill*, writing at a time when the tenant was still allowed recourse to two successive *essoins de malo veniendi*, was unsure whether a warrantor should be awaited if they were not present in court, especially if they were vouched after the tenant had sent two *essoins*.[55] However, changes to the number of *essoins* available to the tenant after the treatise was written perhaps alleviated fears about the delay caused by such a voucher to warranty. Evidence from the early plea rolls shows that warrantors were, as a general rule, awaited.[56]

The desire for speed is all the more apparent in the assize of *novel disseisin*, which allowed for even less delay than the other possessory assizes. The action was intended to address recent dispossessions, perhaps before the ejected party resorted to violent self-help, which meant that it was particularly important to resolve the case swiftly.[57] Here, rather than being summoned, the defendant was attached (made to find sureties for attendance at court) and no *essoins* were allowed at all. The assize would proceed on the day appointed for the recognition whether or not the defendant was present.[58] Likewise, the recognition would proceed if the defendant vouched a warrantor who was not present in court. There would be no waiting for the warrantor to be summoned.[59]

The grand assize was also designed with speed in mind. It was certainly intended to provide swifter justice than trial by battle, which might also be used to decide actions of right.[60] The decision of whether to choose the grand assize rested with the tenant. Before this choice could be made, however, the parties had to be convened in court and the demandant had to state his claim. Here, a number of opportunities for delay presented themselves. *Glanvill*, discussing actions of right heard in the king's court, explains that the tenant was allowed recourse to three successive *essoins* before appearing before the justices. Although, as we have seen, the number of successive *essoins de malo veniendi* allowed to litigants in the royal courts was later reduced, the tenant in an action of right could nevertheless delay his appearance before the justices by following his *essoin de malo veniendi* with an *essoin de malo lecti*.[61]

Once he had appeared in court, the tenant could request that certain free men of the county conduct a view of the tenement in dispute, although only if he had other lands in the vill in which the disputed tenement was situated.[62] The tenant might then choose to put the case to the grand assize. Alternatively, the tenant might vouch a warrantor, who also had recourse to *essoins*. Further delay was therefore possible, and *Glanvill* speaks of the warrantor 'eventually' ('*tandem*') appearing in court.[63] Actions of right proceeding in the county and seigniorial courts might have suffered similar delays until the tenant or their warrantor appeared in court and put themselves on the grand assize. It is possible, however, that some procedures of these courts differed from those of the king's court.[64]

The procedure leading to the choice of proof in an action of right was therefore somewhat dilatory. Nevertheless, the procedure of the grand assize itself was designed to minimise postponements. In comparison with the procedure leading to trial by battle, which allowed both the tenant and his champion further *essoins* before the battle was fought, the grand assize offered fewer opportunities for delay.[65] *Glanvill* describes the assize in the following terms:

> This assize is a royal benefit granted to the people by the goodness of the king . . . justice, which is seldom arrived at by battle even after many and long delays, is more easily and quickly attained through its use. Fewer *essoins* are allowed in the assize than in battle . . . and so the people generally are saved trouble and the poor are saved money.[66]

Once the tenant had put himself on the assize, the sheriff was ordered to summon four knights of the neighbourhood to appear before the royal justices. These four knights were then to elect twelve knights of the neighbourhood as recognitors.[67] This more formal process of election, and the fact that the recognitors were required to be of knightly status, reflects the fact that the ultimate issue of right, rather than seisin, was at stake. The procedure was nevertheless streamlined because the tenant could not delay proceedings by *essoining* himself on the day of the election. *Glanvill* explains that the court could direct the four knights to make the election whether or not the tenant was present.[68] Furthermore, it was possible for the election of the recognitors to proceed if some of the four knights appointed to the task were absent. Provided the tenant was present, and both parties consented, the election could be made by the knights who had turned up together with 'other knights of the same county if any such can be found in court'.[69] According to *Glanvill*, 'for greater safety and to avoid all quibbling', six or more knights were often summoned to make the election.[70] Once the knights who were to take the grand assize had been elected, a day was appointed for the recognition to take place. Speed was, again, of the essence. On the day of the recognition the tenant was allowed no *essoin*, and the assize would proceed regardless of whether or not he was present in court.[71]

The reforms in practice

Although careful thought had gone into the design of the new actions, the swift progress of cases to judgment also depended upon the arrival of the recognitors in court on the day of the recognition. This was by no means guaranteed. They too were allowed *essoins*, although in keeping with restrictions placed on the number of successive *essoins de malo veniendi* allowed to litigants, each recognitor was probably allowed only one *essoin* before they were expected to appear before the justices. Those who were incapacitated by a long illness were probably replaced.[72] Recognitors might also default, neither appearing nor sending an *essoin*.

Let us, therefore, examine the extent and impact of these absences. The following analysis considers the effect of recognitor absences on the four possessory assizes discussed above (*utrum*, *novel disseisin*, *mort d'ancestor* and *darrein presentment*) and on actions proceeding to the grand assize.

The majority of assizes were probably heard locally, during visitations to the counties undertaken by the itinerant justices.[73] Many of these visitations took place during a general eyre, when the country would be divided into several circuits and groups of justices would travel along each circuit and hold sessions in the counties through which they passed.[74]

The sessions held at the eyre do not appear to have been severely affected by the non-attendance of recognitors, probably because of the local nature of the hearings. Some recognitors may already have been in court, conducting their own litigation before the justices. Others, if not already in court, would have been able to travel to the location of the hearing without encountering too many difficulties. Nevertheless, some visitations fared better than others, and we find some sessions in which a number of actions were postponed for lack of recognitors.

A sample of plea rolls made at the eyre illustrates this point. Many of the entries contained in the early plea rolls of the royal courts record routine administrative business, such as parties appointing attorneys, litigants sending *essoins*, justices granting the parties permission to reach a settlement and so on. However, a significant number of entries concern cases which had successfully navigated all procedural impediments and were ready to proceed to a recognition.

The plea roll of the 1194 Wiltshire visitation, for example, contains records of 17 assizes ready to proceed to a recognition. All were able to do so. There are no entries which record that an assize was postponed because of absent recognitors.[75] A roll from a Bedford and Buckinghamshire visitation of 1194–5 shows 14 assizes ready to hear the oath of the recognitors. This time, however, 11 assizes proceeded but three actions were postponed because insufficient recognitors appeared at court.[76] The records from a 1198 Hertford, Essex and Middlesex visitation show 26 assizes ready to proceed to a recognition. We find that the recognition proceeded in twenty-five of these cases, whilst one case was postponed because of absent recognitors.[77] The plea roll of the 1201 Cornwall visitation contains records of 43 assizes ready to proceed to a recognition. We find that 42 assizes were able to do so and, again, one case was postponed for lack of recognitors. It is notable that the case which was delayed concerned land in Dorset and nine recognitors sent *essoins*. These recognitors would have been required to undertake a journey outside their home county to reach the location of the hearing, which perhaps explains why so many were absent.[78] Finally, the plea roll of the main 1202 Northamptonshire visitation provides evidence of 33 assizes ready to proceed to a recognition. We find that 30 assizes were able to do so, whilst three were postponed as a result of recognitor absences.[79]

Although a complete survey of eyres from this period is impossible because of the fragmentary nature of the surviving rolls, this sample suggests that recognitors were reasonably diligent in presenting themselves before the itinerant justices on the required day. Nevertheless, a few cases were delayed because insufficient recognitors appeared in court. As shown by the above case from Dorset, 'foreign pleas' – cases from a county other than the one in which the justices were holding their session – were particularly susceptible to such postponements. This is further illustrated by the records of 'outstanding pleas' ('*residua placitorum*') heard by the justices during a short session held at Northampton in August 1202, before the county's main visitation in September. These outstanding pleas were probably cases adjourned from previous sessions held by the justices at Lincoln, Leicester and Coventry.[80] We find seven actions ready to proceed to a recognition. However, five were postponed for lack of recognitors.[81]

The eyre provided convenient, local access to the royal courts. However, visitations of the itinerant justices took place only intermittently. Between 1176 and 1194 there were general eyres, on average, slightly more often than once every two years. Visitations occurred less frequently from 1194 onwards, with general eyres held in 1194–5, 1198–9, 1201–3 and 1208–9.[82] Justices would occasionally travel to certain counties in the intervening years to hear assizes, often those of *novel disseisin*, but these visitations did not occur frequently, nor did they allow a wide range of other pleas to be heard.[83] Litigants who did not wish to wait until the next eyre might instead attempt to have their cases heard at the Bench or before the court *coram rege*. With this in mind, let us now turn to the records of these courts.

When the king was out of the country, cases which were not brought before the itinerant justices would come to the Bench. This meant that a significant number of assizes were heard at Westminster.[84] In contrast to the eyre, hearings at the Bench often suffered postponements as a result of recognitor absences.

A sample of plea rolls illustrates the extent of the problem. By the end of the twelfth century, the Bench divided its annual business into four terms: Hilary, Easter, Trinity and Michaelmas. The earliest surviving plea roll of the court is a roll of seven membranes recording pleas heard in the 1194 Trinity term.[85] This contains records of six assizes ready to proceed to a recognition. However, only two were able to do so, whilst four were postponed as insufficient recognitors arrived at court.[86] Other plea rolls reveal similar results. For example, the two surviving main rolls of the 1198 Easter term, printed as Rolls 8A and 8B in the *Curia Regis Rolls* series, record 11 assizes ready to hear the oath of the recognitors. Of these, only four proceeded to the recognition, whilst seven were postponed as a result of recognitor absences.[87]

The plea rolls of the Bench begin to survive in greater numbers from the first years of the thirteenth century onwards. A precise statistical analysis nevertheless remains impossible as a number of membranes are damaged, missing or of uncertain date. However, the greater availability of evidence further illustrates the extent of the problem. The pleas brought before the Bench in the 1200 Hilary term, for example, are recorded in Rolls 19 and 20 of the *Curia Regis Rolls*.[88] They contain records of 33 assizes ready to proceed to a recognition. However, only 10 were able to do so, whilst the remaining 23 were postponed for lack of recognitors.[89] An examination of one more term of the court is all that is required to illustrate the point. The pleas of the 1200 Michaelmas term are recorded in Roll 24 of the *Curia Regis Rolls* (and duplicated in rolls 22 and 23).[90] We find records of 31 assizes ready to proceed to a recognition. Only eight were able to do so, whilst 23 were postponed because insufficient recognitors appeared in court.[91] Indeed, one assize was postponed twice for lack of recognitors. This case, a grand assize concerning land in Hertfordshire, first came before the justices on the octaves of Michaelmas. It was then put to the octaves of All Saints, later in the same term, where it was again postponed.[92]

It is not, in fact, uncommon to find a case postponed more than once for lack of recognitors. The above case was heard (and postponed) twice in the

Michaelmas term because it first came before the justices at the very beginning of the term. This meant that the next hearing could be scheduled before the vacation which separated the Michaelmas and Hilary terms. However, many actions postponed in one term of the Bench were given a return day in a subsequent term.[93] This meant that cases delayed a number of times for lack of recognitors could drag on for months, if not years.

Perhaps the longest delay is found in the dispute between Henry de Alneto of Cornwall, demandant, and Henry de Alneto of Maidford, tenant, concerning a knight's fee in Maidford, Northamptonshire. The case was brought before the Bench in the 1200 Trinity term.[94] The tenant requested a view of the disputed tenement and, in the 1201 Easter term, put himself on the grand assize.[95] The election of the recognitors for the grand assize took place in the 1201 Michaelmas term.[96] We next find the case in the records of the 1203 Easter term, when an attempt was made to take the recognition on the quindene of Easter (20 April).[97] However, the case had to be postponed to the octaves of Trinity (8 June) in the following Trinity term as only five recognitors appeared and the rest *essoined* themselves.[98] The case is next found in the records of pleas heard on the octaves of Michaelmas (6 October) in the 1203 Michaelmas term, which record another postponement as three recognitors *essoined* themselves, two came and the rest neither appeared nor sent an *essoin*. A day was given for the next hearing on the octaves of Martinmas (18 November).[99] At this hearing, only four recognitors came. The case was rescheduled to appear before the justices three weeks from Easter Sunday (16 May) the following year.[100] We have no record of this hearing and the case is next found in the plea roll of the 1204 Michaelmas term, which records that a hearing took place on the quindene of Michaelmas (13 October). On this day four recognitors came, six sent *essoins* and the remainder were absent without *essoin*. The case was postponed to the octaves of Martinmas (18 November), later in the same term.[101] At the following hearing no recognitor arrived or sent an *essoin*, although we are told that 'afterwards' (*postea*) some attempted to *essoin* themselves. A day was given on the quindene of Hilary (27 January) in the 1205 Hilary term.[102] Again, insufficient recognitors turned up at the hearing and the case was postponed until three weeks from Easter Sunday (1 May).[103] Here, five recognitors were absent, none of whom sent an *essoin*. The case was postponed to be heard before the king at Northampton on the Sunday after the Feast of the Ascension (22 May).[104] At this hearing, perhaps because of the king's presence in their home county, the recognitors all came to deliver their verdict.[105]

The above example concerns a case proceeding to the grand assize. However, possessory actions were just as susceptible to postponements caused by absent recognitors. Even actions of *novel disseisin*, designed to provide an extremely swift remedy for recent, unjust dispossessions, were affected. For example, of the 23 assizes which were postponed for lack of recognitors in the 1200 Hilary term, eight were actions of *novel disseisin*,[106] seven were actions of *mort d'ancestor*,[107] five were grand assizes,[108] one was the assize *utrum*[109] and the nature of the plea is unspecified in the two remaining cases.[110] Possessory assizes could also suffer from multiple postponements. Richard Sillard, for example, brought an assize of *novel disseisin* against Richard son of Peter on the octaves of Trinity (8 June) in the 1203 Bench Trinity term. The case was postponed until the Sunday after the feast of St John the Baptist (27 June), which fell later in the same term, as an unspecified number of recognitors *essoined* themselves and five were absent without sending *essoins*.[111] At this later hearing five of the recognitors did not come or *essoin* themselves. A day was given on the octaves of Michaelmas (6 October) in the following Michaelmas term.[112] Here, the assize was finally able to be taken.[113]

Actions from the more outlying counties appear, quite understandably, to have been particularly affected by recognitor absences. In the 1200 Hilary term, for example, no assize from any county further afield than Suffolk could be taken. Hearings from Dorset, Gloucestershire, Leicestershire, Lincolnshire, Shropshire, Somerset, Staffordshire, Worcestershire and Yorkshire were all postponed for lack of recognitors.[114] This does not mean that actions from counties such as these never progressed to a recognition at Westminster, but they were likely to suffer a significant number of postponements for lack of recognitors before they reached a conclusion.[115] Delays caused by absent recognitors were not, however, solely confined to actions from the more distant counties. At the same 1200 Hilary term, for example, assizes from Bedfordshire, Essex and Sussex were also postponed because insufficient recognitors appeared at court.[116]

Let us now turn to the actions brought before the court *coram rege*. This court heard pleas only when the king was in England. Henry II was frequently abroad during the later years of his reign. Richard, likewise, was seldom in the country.[117] During these years the activity of the court diminished. John, however, spent more time in England than his predecessors, and during his reign a significant number of assizes were heard *coram rege*. Some cases were brought directly before the king, whilst others were transferred from the Bench or the eyre.[118]

The first surviving plea roll of the court dates from 1200 and contains pleas heard during John's brief stay in England from late February until mid-April.[119] However, later rolls cover longer periods of judicial activity and allow us to conduct a more extensive survey of the cases which came before the court. They show that, as with cases heard at Westminster, a large proportion of actions were postponed because of recognitor absences. For example, Roll 21 of the *Curia Regis Rolls* contains the record of the pleas heard by the court in the 1201 Easter term. Here, five assizes were ready to proceed to a recognition. However, only two were able to do so, whilst three were postponed for lack of recognitors.[120] Likewise, we find three assizes ready to proceed to a recognition in the 1204 Easter term (the record of which is scattered amongst Rolls 36, 65 and 67 of the *Curia Regis Rolls*).

Two assizes were concluded successfully, whilst one was postponed because insufficient recognitors appeared in court.[121]

Recognitors probably found it difficult to appear before the court *coram rege* because of the speed with which John travelled around the country.[122] Pleas frequently had to be heard some distance from their county of origin, and recognitors were often faced with a considerable journey to appear before the king.[123] A striking example is the action of *mort d'ancestor* brought by Richard Pikenet against John de Hudebovil concerning a knight's fee in Suffolk. The case was first heard *coram rege* in 1207 on the octaves of Michaelmas (6 October) while John was at Westminster. However, the case was postponed until the quindene of Martinmas (25 November) due to the default of the recognitors.[124] On this date the king was in Wiltshire.[125] Only two recognitors appeared in court, and the assize was again postponed until the octaves of Hilary (20 January) in the following year.[126] The case came before the king at Westminster, although the assize was again postponed because three recognitors were absent.[127] The case is next found in the rolls of pleas heard before the king on the octaves of Trinity (1 June), when the king was probably in Wiltshire.[128] It appears that the parties were present in court but once again the case was postponed as none of the recognitors arrived.[129] The next hearing was scheduled for the quindene of St John the Baptist (8 July), on which date the king was apparently in Buckinghamshire.[130] The next record of the case, however, appears in the roll of pleas heard before the king on the quindene of St Michael (13 October) at Gloucester. By this stage the parties had reached a settlement, having perhaps lost hope of a recognition ever taking place. They were now in pursuit of a chirograph which would record the terms of their agreement. Both parties came to court, although for an unspecified reason the matter was postponed and the parties were instructed to appear before the itinerant justices who had recently set out on eyre.[131]

Attempts to prevent postponements

Delays caused by absent recognitors were therefore common at both the Bench and the court *coram rege*. Attempts were, however, made to prevent such postponements. As advised by *Glanvill*, more than twelve knights were often elected to form the grand assize.[132] It became common to nominate sixteen individuals, although during our period numbers could vary.[133] It was hoped that, even if some failed to arrive, at least twelve would be present in court ready to take the assize. This also meant that, if more than twelve appeared in court, substitutes would be available if the impartiality of a recognitor was challenged.[134] Likewise, additional recognitors were sometimes appointed to possessory assizes, especially if the case had suffered previous delays because of recognitor absences. The plea rolls frequently record that the sheriff was ordered to find so many recognitors that the assize would not stand over due to their absence ('*et tot apponat quod assisa non remaneat*').[135] While it is impossible to determine the number of cases saved from postponements by this approach, the above evidence suggests that such tactics met with limited success. This is shown explicitly in some cases. In 1200, for example, a grand assize was postponed even though sixteen recognitors had been summoned. Five of the knights *essoined* themselves, leaving only eleven in court on the appointed day.[136]

By the time *Bracton* was written, other measures had also been put in place to reduce delays caused by absent recognitors. Actions of *novel disseisin* were allowed to proceed with as few as seven recognitors present.[137] It does not, however, appear that this rule was in operation during our earlier period.[138] Furthermore, it remained essential to secure the presence of twelve recognitors to hear the other assizes.[139] *Bracton* does, however, suggest that absent recognitors might be replaced with other individuals who were present in court on the day of the hearing. The new recognitors could then swear their oath saving the fact that they had not made the view.[140] It is unclear whether this was possible during our earlier period. If so, it could help explain why relatively few cases were postponed for want of recognitors at the eyre. Potential replacements must have been easy to find amongst the county's freeholders who had come to conduct their own business in court. However, it would have been more difficult to find individuals from the neighbourhood who could stand in as recognitors when cases were heard at the Bench or court *coram rege*.

Deliberate absences

Some recognitors may have met with genuine difficulties as they attempted to reach court.[141] However, as Lady Stenton noted, a great number did not even send *essoins* (assuming that the individual charged with delivering the *essoin* had not been waylaid). This may suggest that they had deliberately reneged on their responsibilities.[142] Even those who sent *essoins* may have done so dishonestly, inventing a fictitious excuse to avoid appearing in court.[143]

Serving as a recognitor certainly seems to have been unpopular. Henry II's contemporary Ralph Niger complained bitterly that the king weighed down nearly everyone in the country with recognitions and other duties owed to the royal administrative system.[144] Indeed, many individuals seem to have been eager to avoid serving on a recognition. The chronicler Jocelin of Brakelond, for example, mentions a case from 1187 in which the king summoned twelve knights to Westminster to make a recognition about certain rights of the Liberty of St Edmund. This appears to have been a recognition crafted specially for the dispute at hand. The summons demanded that half the recognitors should be from Norfolk and half from Suffolk. However, Jocelin explains, six knights were found who held land in both counties. Only these six were sent 'to save labour and expense'.[145] Some individuals even went so far as to obtain grants of exemption from serving on recognitions. As A.B. White noted, these exist even on the earliest chancery enrolments.[146] Such exemptions in fact became so common towards the middle of the thirteenth century that there were complaints that too few knights were available in certain counties to take grand assizes.[147]

There are a number of factors which probably contributed to this unpopularity and encouraged those summoned to stay at home rather than play their part in the administration of justice. One of the most significant of these must have been the long journey often required to reach the Bench or the court *coram rege*. Distances of about 25 miles a day were perhaps possible on horseback along good roads, although fewer miles could be covered on foot or with pack horses.[148] This means that many recognitors would have been required to travel for a number of days to reach the location of the hearing. Those from outlying counties such as Northumberland, Yorkshire and Cornwall would have faced a journey of well over a week to reach Westminster. Even if the king's highways were kept in good condition, other roads might have been less well-maintained and journeys could have taken considerably longer.[149] As White commented, these journeys brought sickness and other dangers.[150] They might also lead to considerable financial loss. Richard de Anstey's account of his travels around England in pursuit of his claim against Mabel de Francheville illustrates the ease with which valuable horses could be lost on long journeys. Richard made two journeys to Southampton and lost a palfrey on the first journey and a pack horse on the second. His brother and another helper also each lost a palfrey travelling around the country in support of his claim.[151]

Recognitors perhaps also dwelt on the possibility that, after all their efforts to appear in court, the case might nevertheless be postponed. The action could be delayed by a litigant's *essoin*, a voucher to warranty, or even the absence of other recognitors. The temptation to stay at home and avoid the risk of a wasted journey must have been great, especially if the case was scheduled to be heard many miles away at the Bench or before the court *coram rege*.[152]

It is possible that such concerns were shared amongst the recognitors before the hearing. The view of the disputed tenement, a procedural requirement of the possessory assizes, would have provided an ideal opportunity for the recognitors to discuss the case amongst themselves. Other opportunities for communication would also have been available, especially as all those involved were from the same neighbourhood. If a number of recognitors made it obvious to the others that they intended to avoid the hearing, thus making a postponement inevitable, the remainder would see little reason to attend. This may explain some instances in which all of the recognitors failed to appear at court on the required day.

Other considerations, besides the length of the journey to court, may also have encouraged recognitors to stay at home. Maitland highlighted how recognitions could put the recognitors into conflict with powerful individuals who had an interest in the case.[153] Some may even have been subject to intimidation before the hearing. Absence might therefore have been a method of self-preservation if reprisals were feared following the verdict. Again, the view of the tenement in dispute may have provided the ideal opportunity for communication between those involved in the case. The litigants could meet with the recognitors as a group, and one or both of the parties might use the opportunity to issue threats. The view was not, however, the only opportunity for certain individuals or their supporters to intimidate the recognitors. As those involved in the case probably lived near each other, there would have been many such opportunities in the days or weeks preceding the hearing.

The sanctions which could be imposed upon defaulting recognitors would have done little to deter such absences.[154] A recognitor who was absent and had not sent an *essoin* would often be attached.[155] If they defaulted again they were likely to be reattached and made to find better sureties. On their third default, the sheriff might be issued with an order of *habeas corpus* and made personally responsible for their appearance in court, with the power to seize chattels or perhaps arrest the individual if necessary.[156] Some entries expressly record that the recognitors who defaulted were to be amerced.[157] However, these measures do not appear to have been particularly effective. It is not uncommon to find recognitors who had been attached defaulting again.[158] There is sometimes no acknowledgement in the rolls that absent recognitors had previously been attached, even though this was clearly ordered at the earlier hearing.[159] Likewise, amercements for non-appearance were rarely severe, often probably half a mark or one mark.[160] As James Masschaele has suggested, many recognitors must have viewed them as 'utterly fair trade-offs' for staying at home and shirking the job.[161] Furthermore, the above procedures were designed to apply cumulative coercive pressure on repeat offenders. They were less effective if a different group of recognitors were absent at each hearing. It is true that harsher penalties for non-attendance could have been introduced, but this risked losing whatever goodwill remained in the very people on whom the system depended. The result was that many recognitors were able to avoid court without much thought for the consequences.

Conclusion

Considerable thought had been put into the procedural design of the new Angevin legal procedures. The appearance of the litigants at court was carefully regulated, and efforts were made to ensure that cases progressed swiftly to judgment. However, the careful design of the new actions could do little to prevent delays caused by absent recognitors. Although cases heard locally at the eyre did not often suffer from such postponements, actions brought at Westminster, or before the court *coram rege*, were frequently affected. Significantly, eyres took place only intermittently, and for long periods the Bench and the court *coram rege* were the only courts available to litigants. Even when eyres did occur, they were extremely busy and it was not uncommon for cases to be postponed to Westminster because they could not be concluded in the counties.[162] This meant that the problems caused by absent recognitors at Westminster and the court *coram rege* affected a considerable proportion of litigation in the early years of the common law.[163]

The contrast revealed by this chapter between litigation at the eyre and the Bench or court *coram rege* highlights the importance of local justice in the early years of the common law, and the problems which could arise if this was lacking. Attempts were indeed made to increase the availability of local hearings as the thirteenth century progressed. Magna Carta stated that common pleas were not to follow the king, but were to be heard in a fixed place, and that possessory assizes such as *mort d'ancestor* and *novel disseisin* ought to be heard at first instance in their county of origin.[164] Justices were also ordered to visit the counties four times a year to hear assizes, although this was reduced to once a year in the 1217 reissue of the Charter.[165] These visitations failed to materialise, although other measures were put in place to allow a greater number of assizes to be heard in the counties. Most notably, a system of special commissions emerged, which allowed justices and county knights to hear individual assizes at specially convened local hearings.[166]

Nevertheless, these changes came about too late for the litigants of our period who brought their cases before the Bench or the court *coram rege*. The experience of many would have been similar to that of Richard de Anstey or the abbot of Abingdon, who we found in the early years of Henry's reign lamenting the numerous delays which plagued their cases. It is also worth remembering that many litigants who brought their cases to these courts did so because they regarded the matter as too urgent to wait for the eyre.[167] In such instances the delays caused by absent recognitors would have been particularly frustrating. The Angevin reformers must have been dismayed to find their carefully streamlined procedures undermined time and again by the inability, or unwillingness, of recognitors to fulfil their duties.

Notes

1 See generally Paul Brand, '"Multis Vigiliis Excogitatam et Inventam": Henry II and the Creation of the English Common Law', in Brand, *MCL*, 77–102. See also S.F.C. Milsom, *The Legal Framework of English Feudalism* (Cambridge: Cambridge University Press, 1976); Joseph Biancalana, 'For Want of Justice: Legal Reforms of Henry II', *Columbia Law Review* 88 (1988): 433–536; and John Hudson, *The Formation of the English Common Law: Law and Society in England From the Norman Conquest to Magna Carta* (New York: Routledge, 2016; London: Longman, 1996). I am grateful to Professor John Hudson for comments on an earlier draft of this chapter, and to Professors Paul Brand and William Ian Miller for discussions on the subject at various intervals over the past few years.

2 See generally R.C. van Caenegem, *Royal Writs in England From the Conquest to Glanvill*, SS 77 (London: B. Quaritch, 1959), 51–103.

3 This distinction must often have been difficult to maintain in practice and the recognitors may well have investigated the facts behind the dispute before they appeared in court. See P&M, 2: 624–5.
4 Heinrich Brunner, *Die Entstehung der Schwurgerichte*, summarised in R.C. van Caenegem, *The Birth of the Common Law*, 2nd ed. (Cambridge: Cambridge University Press, 1988), 73–6.
5 van Caenegem, *Writs*, 69–71.
6 Mike McNair, 'Vicinage and the Antecedents of the Jury', *LHR* 17 (1999): 537–90, at 571–8.
7 Susan Reynolds, *Kingdoms and Communities in Western Europe, 900–1300*, 2nd ed. (Oxford: Oxford University Press, 1997), 33–4.
8 P&M, 2: 632.
9 Patrick Devlin, *Trial by Jury*, The Hamlyn Lectures, 8th Series (London: Stevens and Sons, 1956), 164. Also note William Blackstone, *Commentaries on the Laws of England, a Facsimile of the First Edition of 1765–1769* (Chicago and London: University of Chicago Press, 1979), 4: 343. See also C.T. Coleman, 'Origin and Development of Trial by Jury', *Virginian Law Review* 6 (1919): 77–86.
10 A summary of the relevant literature is provided in James Masschaele, *Jury, State, and Society in Medieval England* (New York: Palgrave MacMillan, 2008), 7–8. Note also the discussion in the preface of *'The Dearest Birth Right of the People of England': The Jury in the History of the Common Law*, eds. John W. Cairns and Grant McLeod (Oxford: Hart Publishing, 2002), v–ix. See in particular Green, *Verdict*.
11 See Masschaele, *Jury, State, and Society*, 15–44; McNair, 'Vicinage'; van Caenegem, *Writs*, 57–86; and Doris M. Stenton, *English Justice Between the Norman Conquest and the Great Charter, 1066–1215* (London: George Allen & Unwin Ltd, 1965), 13–17.
12 See A.B. White, *Self-Government at the King's Command: A Study in the Beginnings of English Democracy* (Minneapolis: University of Minnesota, 1933) and Masschaele, *Jury, State, and Society*.
13 David Millon, 'Positivism in the Historiography of the Common Law', *Wisconsin Law Review* 1989 (1989): 669–714; Paul Brand, 'Judges and Juries in Civil Litigation in Later Medieval England: The Millon Thesis Reconsidered', *JLH* 37 (2016): 1–40.
14 It is likely that plea rolls were made by the royal courts before 1194, although none have survived. See Brand, 'Multis Vigiliis', 95.
15 See Stenton, *English Justice*, 101–14.
16 'Charter of Henry I Concerning the Holding of Courts Shire and Hundred (26 July 1108 – August 1111)', in *EHD*, 2: no. 43, at 474–5.
17 Hudson, *Formation*, 27–9.
18 Ibid., 111.
19 *Lawsuits*, 2: no. 408, at 395.
20 Ibid., no. 408, at 395.
21 Ibid., no. 408, at 402.
22 Ibid., no. 408, at 404.
23 Ibid., no. 363, at 325–7.
24 Ibid., no. 363, at 326.
25 Ibid., no. 363, at 326.
26 Ibid., no. 377, at 337–41.
27 Ibid., no. 377, at 339–40. Quotation at 339.
28 *Glanvill*, XIII, 1 (Hall, 149).
29 Ibid., I, 3 (Hall, 4) and ibid., XIII, 1 (Hall, 148).
30 Ibid., XIII, 1–39 (Hall, 148–70).

31 John Hudson, *The Oxford History of the Laws of England, Volume II, 871–1216* (Oxford: Oxford University Press, 2012), 607–8.
32 *Glanvill*, XIII, 23–4 (Hall, 163).
33 Ibid., XIII, 32–7 (Hall, 167–9); Hudson, *Oxford History*, 609–10.
34 Hudson, *Oxford History*, 604–5.
35 *Glanvill*, XIII, 3 (Hall, 150). Alternative writs of *mort d'ancestor* were available for use in specific circumstances, for example if the claimant's ancestor had died on pilgrimage, or entered religion and thus 'died' to the secular world. *Glanvill*, XIII, 4–6 (Hall, 150–1).
36 *Glanvill*, XIII, 18–19 (Hall, 160–1); Hudson, *Oxford History*, 607.
37 Hudson, *Oxford History*, 600.
38 *Glanvill*, II, 6–21 (Hall, 26–37).
39 Donald W. Sutherland, *The Assize of Novel Disseisin* (Oxford: Oxford University Press, 1973), 36–8. See also Masschaele, *Jury, State, and Society*, 68.
40 *Glanvill*, II, 7 (Hall, 28). For a discussion on attitudes to supernatural proof in the twelfth century, see Charles M. Radding, 'Superstition to Science: Nature, Fortune, and the Passing of the Medieval Ordeal', *AHR* 84 (1979): 945–69, and R.C. van Caenegem, *Legal History: A European Perspective* (London: Hambledon, 1990), 73–113. For a contrasting view, see Robert Bartlett, *Trial by Fire and Water: The Medieval Judicial Ordeal* (New York: Oxford University Press, 1986), especially chapter 4.
41 Hudson, *Oxford History*, 533.
42 Ibid., 534.
43 For further discussion about the continuing development of procedural rules designed to minimise delay in the thirteenth and fourteenth centuries, see Paul Brand, 'Delay in the English Common Law Courts (Thirteenth to Fourteenth Centuries)', in *The Law's Delay: Essays on Undue Delay in Civil Litigation*, ed. C.H. van Rhee (Antwerp and Groningen: Intersentia, 2004), 31–45.
44 *Glanvill*, XIII, 7 (Hall, 152).
45 Ibid., XIII, 7 (Hall, 152).
46 Ibid.
47 See Brand, 'Delay in the English Common Law Courts', 32.
48 *Glanvill*, XIII, 25, (Hall, 164).
49 Ibid., I, 19, (Hall, 11–12).
50 Other *essoins*, also classified as *essoins de malo veniendi*, could sometimes lead to longer delays. For example, it was possible for an individual to send an *essoin* on account of being on the king's service, which might see the case postponed until they returned from their service in the king's army. See generally, *Glanvill*, I, 11–29 (Hall, 7–17). See also Meekings, *Surrey*, 1: 36.
51 *Glanvill*, XIII, 7 (Hall, 152).
52 Ibid., XIII, 7 (Hall, 152).
53 *Bracton*, 4: 82.
54 *PBKJ*, 1: 156–7. The plea roll entries found by Lady Stenton to support this view relate to actions of right. However, it is reasonable to suggest that, if the procedure of the more dilatory action of right changed, the procedure of the swifter possessory assizes also changed.
55 *Glanvill*, XIII, 30 (Hall, 166).
56 Hudson, *Oxford History*, 616. See, e.g. *RCR*, 1:19.
57 Sutherland, *Novel Disseisin*, 18–19.
58 *Glanvill*, XIII, 38 (Hall, 169).
59 Ibid., XIII, 38 (Hall, 169).
60 *Glanvill*, II, 7 (Hall, 28).
61 *PBKJ*, 1: 157–8.
62 *Glanvill*, II, 1 (Hall, 22).

63 Ibid., III, 1, (Hall, 38). See also Hudson, *Oxford History*, 596–7.
64 Hudson, *Oxford History*, 588.
65 *Glanvill*, II, 7 (Hall, 28) and II, 12 (Hall, 31). *Glanvill*'s statement concerning the number of *essoins* allowed in trial by battle may be found at *Glanvill*, II, 3 (Hall, 23). Note, however, the above discussion on the limitation of successive *essoins de malo veniendi*, which was in place by the end of the twelfth century.
66 Ibid., II, 7 (Hall, 28).
67 Ibid., II, 10–11 (Hall, 30–1).
68 Ibid., II, 12 (Hall, 31).
69 Ibid., II, 12 (Hall, 32).
70 Ibid., II, 12 (Hall, 32): '*Ad maiorem eciam cautelam et ad omnem cauillationem devitandam*'.
71 Ibid., II, 16 (Hall, 33–4).
72 Although it should be noted that plea roll entries often fail to provide details as to why a recognitor had been removed. See, e.g. *CRR*, 2: 193; *CRR*, 5: 201.
73 Sutherland, *Novel Disseisin*, 60, n.1.
74 For further details, see David Crook, *Records of the General Eyre* (London: H.M.S.O., 1982). See also Meekings, *Surrey*.
75 F.W. Maitland, ed., *Three Rolls of the King's Court in the Reign of King Richard the First A.D. 1194–1195*, Pipe Roll Society, 14 (London: Wyman and Sons, 1891), (henceforth: *Three Rolls of the King's Court*), cases proceeding to recognition (references are to page numbers in this and all following footnotes unless stated otherwise): 65 (two cases), 66, 66–7, 67 (two cases), 67–8, 69 (two cases), 70, 71, 71–2, 72 (two cases), 73, 73–4, 74.
76 *Three Rolls of the King's Court*, cases proceeding to the recognition: 120–121, 126, 129 (two cases), 130 (two cases), 131, 131–132, 132, 134, 134–135; cases postponed: 128, 128–129, 129.
77 *RCR*, 1, cases proceeding to the recognition: 154 (four cases), 155 (three cases), 157, 174, 176 (three cases), 177 (three cases), 188–189, 189, 190, 191 (two cases), 192, 193, 196, 198, 213; case postponed: 194.
78 *PBKJ*, 2, cases proceeding to the recognition: nos. 410, 411, 412, 414, 415, 418, 419, 420, 423, 425, 426, 430, 431, 436, 438, 439, 440, 441, 442, 445, 450, 451, 453, 455, 456, 461, 462, 464, 465, 466, 468, 470, 471, 476, 478, 485, 488, 496, 500, 501, 536, 545; case postponed: no. 427.
79 All pleas for this term are printed in *Northants* except the Lincolnshire pleas heard at Northampton, which are printed in *Lincs*. A compilation of these two publications provides the figures. Cases proceeding to the recognition: *Northants*, nos. 372, 374, 377, 382, 394, 413, 417, 421, 422, 423, 424, 429, 439, 448, 450, 454, 534, and at page 86 (no plea number in printed edition). *Lincs*, nos 1139, 1140, 1141, 1144, 1145, 1162, 1167, 1178, 1179, 1183, 1185, 1186; cases postponed: *Northants*, nos, 525, 544; *Lincs*, no. 1171 (in this last assize the defendant subsequently conceded the case).
80 See Doris M. Stenton's comments in *Lincs*, xxxv.
81 Cases proceeding to the recognition: *Lincs*, no. 1122, *Northants*, no. 290; cases postponed: *Lincs*, nos 1121, 1123, 1124, 1125, 1133.
82 Hudson, *Oxford History*, 545. For dates of the general eyres of this period, see Crook, *Records of the General Eyre*, 56–71.
83 Hudson, *Oxford History*, 548.
84 Sutherland, *Novel Disseisin*, 60, n.1.
85 See Maitland's introductory comments in *Three Rolls of the King's Courts*, xvi–xix.
86 *Three Rolls of the King's Court*, cases proceeding to recognition: 2, 39; cases postponed: 5, 13, 23, 47. Note also a further case at 5, postponed '*pro defectu recti*', where it is recorded that many of the recognitors were absent on the day

of the hearing. This may suggest scribal error, and that the clerk meant to write an abbreviated form of *pro defectu recognitorum* in the roll.

87 Roll 6 also covers this term but contains duplicate entries. The printed membranes of these rolls are scattered between three publications. Roll 8A is printed in *RCR*, 1: 138–48. Half of Roll 8B is printed in *CRR*, 1: 55–68. The other half is printed in *The Memoranda Roll for the Tenth Year of the Reign of King John (1207–8): Together With the Curia Regis Rolls of Hilary 7 Richard I (1196) and Easter 9 Richard I (1198), a Roll of Plate Held by Hugh de Neville in 9 John (1207–8), and Fragments of the Close Rolls of 16 and 17 John (1215–16)*, ed. R.A. Brown, Pipe Roll Society, New Series, 31 (London: J.W. Ruddock, 1957), 96–118. Cases proceeding to the recognition: *CRR*, 1: 57, 58; *RCR*, 1: 139, 141; cases postponed: *Memoranda Roll for the Tenth Year of King John*, 103; *CRR*, 1: 53 (two cases), 63, *RCR*, 1: 139, 141, 142–3.

88 *CRR*, 1: 115–71 (Roll 20); *RCR*, 2: 154–5 (Roll 19).

89 Cases proceeding to the recognition: *CRR*, 1: 117, 119 (two cases), 121, 135, 136, (this entry is, however, left blank after the words '*juratores dicunt*'), 138, 139, 143, 149; cases postponed: *CRR*, 1: 116, 118, 119, 120, 122, 124, 132 (two cases), 133, 134 (two cases), 135, 136, 137 (this entry does not state a reason for the postponement but records that at least five recognitors were absent, which suggests that the case was postponed for this reason), 138, 139, (two cases) 140, 141 (two cases), 158, 159, 161.

90 *CRR*, 1: 269–373.

91 Cases proceeding to the recognition: *CRR*, 1: 271, 286, 287, 308, 320, 325, 332, 350; cases postponed: *CRR*, 1: 271, 272–273, 273, 288 (two cases), 289, 290 (two cases), 292, 295, 300, 305 (three cases), 306 (two cases), 310 (two cases), 321, 325, 326, 330 (subsequent hearing of case at 272–273), 333, 346. Note also 308 in which it appears that the sheriff was at fault for not sending to court a list of the names of the recognitors he had selected for the assize.

92 *CRR*, 1: 272–3 and 330.

93 For a discussion of the schedule of postponements followed at the Bench, see Brand, 'Delay in the English Common Law Courts', 38–9.

94 *CRR*, 1: 205, 244. This case is noted in C.T. Flower, *Introduction to the Curia Regis Rolls, 1199–1230 A.D.*, SS 62 (London: B. Quaritch, 1944), 131–2. It is also discussed in Peter Coss, *The Origins of the English Gentry* (Cambridge: Cambridge University Press, 2003), 48–9.

95 *CRR*, 1: 473.

96 Ibid., 2: 27.

97 Note that this and the subsequent calendar dates provided in this chapter mark the beginning of the legal 'return day', a period which lasted for up to seven calendar days. See Paul Brand, 'Lawyers' Time in England in the Later Middle Ages', in *Time in the Medieval World*, eds. Chris Humphrey and W. Mark Ormrod (York: York Medieval Press, 2001), 73–104, at 78.

98 *CRR*, 2: 199–200.

99 Ibid., 3: 13.

100 Ibid., 3: 67.

101 Ibid., 3: 179.

102 Ibid., 3: 229.

103 Ibid., 3: 254–5.

104 Ibid., 3: 307.

105 Ibid., 3: 341.

106 Ibid., 1: 119, 122, 133, 134, 137, 138, 159–60, 161.

107 Ibid., 1: 116, 118, 124, 132 (two cases), 141 (two cases).

108 Ibid., 1: 120, 134–5, 135, 136, 158.

109 Ibid., 1: 140.

110 Ibid., 1: 139 (two cases).
111 Ibid., 2: 254.
112 Ibid., 2: 287.
113 Ibid., 3: 4.
114 See, e.g. ibid., 1: 122 (Dorset), 132 (Lincolnshire and Gloucestershire), 134 (Yorkshire), 135 (Leicestershire), 138 (Worcestershire), 139 (Staffordshire), 159–60 (Shropshire), 161 (Somerset).
115 See, e.g. ibid., 1: 286 for recognitors finally giving their verdict in the action from Yorkshire, which had been postponed in the 1200 Hilary term.
116 Ibid., 1: 118 (Sussex), 124 (Essex), 134–5 (Bedfordshire).
117 See P&M, 1: 155, and Stenton, *English Justice*, 90.
118 See Stenton, *English Justice*, 91–5.
119 *PBKJ*, 1: 60–1. Roll printed at 296–310.
120 *CRR*, 1: 413–41. Cases proceeding to the recognition: *CRR*, 1: 416, 430; cases postponed: *CRR*, 1: 414, 417, 440.
121 Ibid., 3: 102–20. Cases proceeding to the recognition: ibid., 3: 117, 118; cases postponed: ibid., 3: 108.
122 See the itinerary of King John set out in *RLP*.
123 The phrase '*coram rege ubicumque fuerit in Anglia*' is often found in plea roll entries which record that a case is to come before the king on a certain date 'wherever he should be in England'. See, e.g. *PBKJ*, 1: no. 3289 and *CRR*, 1: 289.
124 *CRR*, 5: 42. For information about the location of the court, see Doris M. Stenton's comments in *PBKJ*, 3: ccl.
125 *PBKJ*, 3: ccl.
126 *CRR*, 5: 68.
127 *PBKJ*, 3: cclvi; *CRR*, 5: 133.
128 See *RLP*, 'June 1208'.
129 *CRR*, 5: 226.
130 *RLP*, 'July 1208', and *PBKJ*, 3: cclviii.
131 *CRR*, 5: 306.
132 *Glanvill*, II, 12 (Hall 31–2).
133 See, e.g. *RCR*, 1: 140–1, 146, 158, 189–90.
134 Meekings, *Surrey*, 52.
135 See, e.g. *CRR*, 1: 141, 287–8, 346, 400.
136 *CRR*, 5: 177.
137 *Bracton*, 3: 71 and 3: 58; Meekings, *Surrey*, 70; Sutherland, *Novel Disseisin*, 67, n.5.
138 See, e.g. *CRR*, 2: 287 (concerning Richard Sillard's case, discussed above. The assize was postponed because five recognitors were absent, despite the fact that, presumably, seven were present in court ready to take their oath).
139 *Bracton*, 3: 254.
140 Ibid., 3: 63 and 3: 254.
141 For a discussion of the difficulties which could be encountered while travelling to court in the later Middle Ages, see Paul Brand, 'The Travails of Travel: The Difficulties of Getting to Court in Later Medieval England', in *Freedom of Movement in the Middle Ages, Proceedings of the 2003 Harlaxton Symposium*, ed. Peregrine Horden (Donington: Shaun Tyas, 2007), 215–28.
142 *PBKJ*, 1: 166.
143 For a similar view on the evident lack of diligence displayed by recognitors, see Coss, *The Origins of the English Gentry*, 49.
144 '*Scutagiis, recognitionibus, et variis angariarum alluvionibus fere omnes depressit*'. Ralph Niger, *Chronicle*, ed. R. Anstruther (London: Caxton Society, 1851), 168.

145 H.E. Butler, ed., *The Chronicle of Jocelin of Brakelond* (London: Nelson, 1949), 65.
146 White, *Self-Government*, 72.
147 *Petition of the Barons* 1258, cap. 28. See Paul Brand, *Kings, Barons and Justices: The Making and Enforcement of Legislation in Thirteenth-Century England* (Cambridge: Cambridge University Press, 2003), 333–4, 421. See also Scott L. Waugh, 'Reluctant Knights and Jurors: Respites, Exemptions and Public Obligations in the Reign of Henry III', *Speculum* 58 (1983): 937–86, at 937.
148 Robert Bartlett, *England Under the Norman and Angevin Kings, 1075–1225* (New York: Oxford University Press, 2000), 363. See also M.N. Boyer, 'A Day's Journey in Medieval France', *Speculum* 26 (1951): 597–608.
149 Bartlett, *England Under the Norman and Angevin Kings*, 363.
150 White, *Self-Government*, 68.
151 *Lawsuits*, 2: no. 408, at 397–404.
152 See Doris M. Stenton's comments in *PBKJ*, 1: 166.
153 P&M, 2: 631.
154 See also Kathryn Faulkner, 'The Transformation of Knighthood in Thirteenth-Century England', *EHR* 111 (1996): 1–23, at 17.
155 See, e.g. *CRR*, 1: 252 and 118.
156 See, e.g. ibid., 1: 292. This was the mesne process followed in personal and mixed actions, although in our period the procedure as concerning recognitors might not have been as clearly structured as the developed mesne process of the later thirteenth century. See Brand, 'Delay in the English Common Law Courts', 33. See also Meekings, *Surrey*, 52 and 78.
157 See, e.g. *PBKJ*, 2: no. 866; *CRR*, 1: 288; and *CRR*, 5: 192. See also Flower, *Introduction*, 453.
158 See, e.g. *CRR*, 1: 254 and *CRR*, 2: 287.
159 See, e.g. ibid., 2: 4 and 51.
160 See, e.g. the amercement roll published in *The Roll of the Shropshire Eyre of 1256*, ed., Alan Harding, SS 96 (London: Selden Society, 1981), 332–43. This roll dates from a slightly later period than the one covered by this chapter, but contains clear examples of amercements for recognitor non-attendance. These are sometimes less easily identifiable in earlier records. It is likely, however, that such amercements were of a similar level in the twelfth century. We often find, for example, amercements of half a mark or one mark exacted for unspecified defaults (which may include recognitor non-attendance) in the earliest plea rolls. See, e.g. the amercements of the 1198 Hertfordshire eyre, *RCR*, 1: 168–70.
161 Masschaele, *Jury, State, and Society*, 205.
162 Hudson, *Oxford History*, 544.
163 The plea roll containing records of the cases postponed from the 1202 East Anglian eyre and heard at Westminster provides a clear illustration of how cases which were moved from the eyre to Westminster could suffer from delays caused by absent recognitors. Only eleven cases proceeded to the recognition, and fourteen were postponed because the recognitors were absent. See *PBJK*, 2: 226–341, cases proceeding to a recognition: nos. 780, 783, 784, 791, 801, 804, 811, 859, 868, 864, 921; cases postponed: nos. 771, 769, 813, 824, 846, 852, 855, 856, 866, 903, 910, 922, 943, 972.
164 *Magna Carta* 1215, caps. 17 and 18.
165 Ibid., 1215, cap. 18; ibid., 1217, cap. 13.
166 Meekings, *Surrey*, 66–7.
167 Note the comments in Stenton, *English Justice*, 92.

2 Testament and inheritance

The lessons of the brief widowhood of Isabel, countess of Pembroke

*David Crouch**

The great Earl William Marshal died on 14 May 1219, leaving ten children and a relatively young widow, Isabel, daughter of Earl Richard Strongbow of Striguil and Aífe of Leinster. Isabel had married Marshal in London in August 1189, when he was already around forty-three. She could not then have been more than nineteen years of age, and was probably rather younger. At her husband's death she would have been in her later forties. Isabel did not live long as a widow; she was herself dead well within a year. Fragments of a Tintern chronicle copied by the sixteenth-century antiquary Thomas Talbot record her death in 1220 and her burial in the same abbey. A list of obits from Tintern Abbey preserved by the fifteenth-century antiquary William Worcestre gives her date of death as 11 March, which agrees with other evidence presented below.[1]

The ten months or so of Isabel's widowhood raise questions which have not had much academic attention paid to them. How did widows of such wealth and power deal with their lands while adult sons waited in the wings? What part did the wishes expressed in her husband's testament play in the transmission of lands which were her patrimony? How binding indeed were deathbed settlements at the beginning of the thirteenth century? What of the developing role of the executor in medieval society? If attention has been given to such issues, it has generally been in the past to the relationship between the king and such women. Issues such as fines to avoid remarriage and the payment to secure delivery of lands have been predominant, not surprisingly in view of the prominence of these issues in Magna Carta. But the attitude of the king, his officers and his courts would only have been the first of the widow's problems; closer to her was her family and its attitudes and expectations.

Isabel's brief widowhood has a surprising amount to say about such questions, for we are better informed on hers than we are about those of many of her contemporaries due to the accidents of documentary survival. To begin with, if the question has ever been considered, it is generally – but erroneously – assumed that Isabel's eldest son came directly into his inheritance on her husband's death.[2] Isabel's inheritance included the lordship of Leinster in Ireland, the county of Pembroke in West Wales, the lordships of

Striguil and Usk in South East Wales, and the lordship of Long Crendon in England. Both Striguil and Crendon included scattered demesne manors and fees across the south of England, including a hall and urban properties in the district of Charing on the road between London and Westminster. Most problematical of all, Isabel's inheritance included several lordships in Normandy, which her late husband had managed to retain in 1204–5, despite the war between the kings of England and France. These were Longueville-sur-Scie and Meulers (Seine-Maritime), ancient castles of her Giffard ancestors, and Orbec (Calvados) from her father's 'Clare' lineage, lands whose possession in her family went back to the time of the count of Brionne, her eleventh-century, pre-Conquest ancestor.[3] Such politically sensitive possessions demanded care in their disposal, and there is evidence that Isabel's husband gave a good deal of thought to it, even though she would be the person who had to deal with the fallout of his death.

Her husband's biography gives a rare first-hand account of how a magnate like her dying husband disposed of his great estate. It draws on the recollections of his son and executors about the council around his bedside which informed the drawing up of his lost testament. But to begin with, we happen to know that Marshal's deathbed testament was not his first. In 1200, probably just before he crossed for the first time to Ireland, he made a testament and nominated executors. We discover this from King John's confirmation of its (unspecified) terms and an apparent codicil Marshal added after his return about founding a Cistercian abbey in Leinster.[4] The reason for his making a testament at the point he did may be no more than he was about to undertake a long and difficult voyage (as it happens he was caught in a near fatal storm at sea en route to Wexford). Just as important however is that it was drafted at a point when he was just about to take the homage of his great new honors of Leinster and Pembroke, and he may well have wanted to establish his wishes as to which of his sons would get them after his death.

In 1219, this former testament was entirely ignored and a new one made, which may reflect Marshal's anxiety as to the expectations of the numerous further children he had fathered over the two decades since 1200. According to his biography, the Marshal first broached the subject of making a 'devis' of his estate on 10 April 1219 as he lay mortally ill at his manor of Caversham on the Thames, opposite Reading, the day after he resigned as 'Rector' of England. He made this declaration after calling together Countess Isabel and his household. He then sketched out a division of his estates between his children, whose terms can be reconstructed from the later dispositions.[5] His council queried the fact that he wanted to leave nothing to the youngest son, Ansel, but rather leave him to make a career as a household knight once he was of age to be knighted. John of Earley, who was to be one of the executors of the 'devis', protested. The Marshal reconsidered and allotted the boy an annual charge of £140 on his estates. He also considered what to do about his unmarried daughter, Joan, and decided on leaving her an annual rent-charge of £30 and a lump sum of 200 marks.[6]

The Marshal example is of enormous importance in illustrating how a father might attempt to dispose of his estates before he died, and has much to say on the developing practice of making such arrangements. Empirical reconstructions have proved that it was the frequent – though not invariable – custom amongst eleventh- and twelfth-century Anglo-Norman families to divide an inheritance amongst multiple sons within a generation, and indeed usually to allot daughters some share also.[7] The Marshal 'devis' of 1219 for once reveals how such an arrangement was executed and documented. The word used, 'devis(e)', Latinised as *divisa*, can be translated as one's 'wish', 'will', 'instruction' or in this context, 'a disposition'. It was the same word used by William Marshal's elder brother, John Marshal II, to describe the ante-mortem grant to Bradenstoke priory of half an estate made by their father, John I (who died in 1165).[8] 'Devis' appears to be the usual twelfth-century French vernacular word for an ante-mortem disposition of estates which would come into effect after the death of the deviser. It might be called in Latin by other writers a *testamentum*.[9] Earl William's 'devis' was doubly conditional as it would come into full effect not on his death, but on the death of his wife.[10] The evidence is not there to tell us whether there was any understanding at the time that its terms were meant to be irrevocable and binding, or that they could be adjusted after his death. The participation of senior clerics in implementing its provisions does give the impression that the Marshal was disposing of what he regarded as his estate. He treats all the lands he held as a unity, whether patrimonial or belonging to his wife and held by him through a husband's right of 'coverture'. The safeguard of testaments was the business of church courts, as the treatise called *Glanvill* already asserts in Henry II's reign, and by entrusting the future of his 'devis' to the Church authorities he was buttressing its future implementation. It is likeliest that the Marshal saw his 'devis' as a mutual compact over the future of their family lands between himself and his wife; he may even have been attempting to extend his tutorship over her beyond his death. He was certainly ensuring that his views influenced the manner in which their lands were distributed between their heirs. Ultimately it is not possible to say how much the terms reflected his or his wife's ideas. It is however doubtful that such dispositions could have had any force unless Isabel herself consented to them, and was willing to promote them after Marshal's death. The elaborate nature of the arrangements perhaps betrays their frailty.

This is a good point to pause and observe how the Marshal 'devis' stands in relation to other examples of arrangements by which a dying man of his time would attempt to dispose of lands that were his, but would soon not be. There are some instances of ante-mortem written dispositions from before his time, though not many.[11] The earliest in England might well be the division of his cross-Channel honors by Count Robert I of Meulan and Leicester datable to 1107 (he died in 1118), which we know of because of its confirmation by King Henry I. It was intended to be binding after Count Robert's death. Indeed it even envisaged that adjustments might be made to the settlement if family circumstances changed, if one of the count's sons died without issue or turned out to be mentally incompetent, or if the count's estates were diminished on one or other side of the Channel.[12] There are other examples. It hardly needs pointing out that Henry II of England divided his domains between his sons in his *testamentum* of 1170.[13] The widow of Earl Hugh Bigod claimed in 1177 that before he died her late husband divided his lands between his sons, giving purchases and acquisitions to a younger one.[14] A particularly relevant example is that of the young baron Roger II de Baalun, whose mother recalled the arrangements he made for his estates on his deathbed (which occurred between 1161 and 1166), which the document calls Roger's *ultimum elogium* (final statement). Roger made in it a grant at Upton, Berkshire, to Bermondsey priory and appointed the earl of Salisbury as *custos* of his lands after his death. The earl (William Marshal's uncle, as it happens) later took responsibility for conveying this grant, and so occupied a role analogous to an executor.[15] Most relevant of all is the division of his lands executed by Ralph, lord of Coucy, in 1190 before his departure on crusade, which commences

> whereas I am ready to set out on my journey, so no disagreement occur between my children as to the portion of their inheritance, I have disposed of my land with all due consideration according to my conscience and the advice of my trusted followers.

Ralph goes on to leave all his patrimony to his eldest son, but reserved particular estates and rents to the younger siblings, including his wife's *maritagium* to Robert, the youngest of them.[16]

It was therefore by no means unprecedented in 1219 for a layman to dispose of his estates well before his death or during his last illness, especially for the good of his soon-to-be-liberated soul. The provident William Marshal at least had not left it too late, as his onetime master King John did while he laboured in his last hours at Newark, too much in pain and confused by his fatal illness to do more in his *testamentum* than name the thirteen men who would 'set in order and dispose of' his kingdom to secure his sons' inheritance and settle his involved spiritual affairs.[17] Such men clearly regarded the lands concerned as at their disposal and may well have been discussing potential arrangements and divisions for decades before they died, as indeed we know Marshal himself had.[18] Another point to make one's wishes known might be before commencing a hazardous venture where death was a strong possibility. Like Ralph de Coucy, Earl Saher de Quincy of Winchester made his *testamentum* before leaving for Crusade in 1219 from which, as it happens, he did not return (see below). Earl William Longespée of Salisbury made his *testamentum* in mid-Lent 1225 as he completed his arrangements to join the king's expedition to Gascony. In this case, the copy of it entered on the Chancery Close Rolls tells us of its provisions and the circumstances of its making. As with William Marshal's last will, Longespée's was widely circulated in ways comparable to the Marshal testaments of both 1200 and 1219 (see below). A master-copy was sealed by the king and others were confided to the protection of supervisors, in this case four bishops. The dean and treasurer of Salisbury cathedral, and no less a person than the younger Earl William Marshal were to be Longespée's effective executors, with a household knight and clerk named as their agents for its implementation. But unlike the Marshal's 1219 'devis', Longespée's dealt only with debts, chattels and a Carthusian monastery he proposed founding. Though Longespée had more than one son, the text we have says nothing of any disposition of estates.[19]

Disposing of chattels and of estates were two separate concerns in will-making and might well have involved two different procedures. It is an open question how much credit we should give to Glanvill's assumption in the 1180s that 'testaments' deal only with the disposal of chattels (as indeed is the case with the Longespée instance).[20] This assumption may owe more to Glanvill's desire to regularise the use of words than to stigmatise bequests in lands, or even to reflect on actual contemporary practice. The several examples of 'devises' we have looked at here are quite clear on the matter. They make plans for estates that would soon not be the possession of its owner, and asserted that the dying man's will still counted after he was dead and beyond the cares of being a landowner.[21] Glanvill may simply have chosen not to interpret a 'devis' as a *testamentum*. Perhaps the best indication that what the Marshal did with his lands in his deathbed 'devis' was normal practice at the time comes from an English formulary of the first decade of the thirteenth century, now in the Walters Art Museum of Johns Hopkins University. The formulary contains some sixty sample documents, amongst which is a model agreement between two men as to the care of four children who had come into their wardship on the death of their father. One of them was to take the two sons and the other the two daughters and provide for them, 'and when the boys come to the age of thirty, A. will give the boys their father's lands, and will share out the land between the boys as their father divided it in his *testamentum* on his deathbed'.[22] The daughters were also to have their predetermined share of their father's estate. The document is only an exemplar of how such an agreement might be drawn up, and its reservation of the land till the sons reach the age of thirty seems eccentric. But it clearly assumes that a father's 'devis' of his lands on his deathbed would in the end determine how much and which lands his children would enjoy, and indeed when. It also calls the instrument concerned a *testamentum*, in apparent defiance of Glanvill.

Most of the lands concerned in the final Marshal 'devis' were not his own patrimony. The countess's presence at his deathbed council in April 1219 was no formality. She was a woman who had conveyed a great inheritance to her husband and in due course would transmit it to her children. Her agreement to her dying husband's disposition of what were in fact largely her lands was therefore a necessity. In the course of events she might live on for as much as several decades after his death and she might very easily subvert its provisions, especially if – as sometimes happened – her sons predeceased her. So her agreement had to be secured. Some time elapsed after the verbal statement of the Marshal's will until the document was actually drawn up, perhaps as long as several days. It was however eventually presented to him and sealed in a 'private meeting' (*priveement*) by his own seal and those of Countess Isabel and their eldest son, the younger William Marshal. It was then taken off to the nearby royal court with a request that the legate Pandulf, the archbishop of Canterbury and the bishops of Salisbury and Winchester should likewise seal it and consent to act as its 'mestre executor', the supervisors of its execution. For good measure the clerics issued an excommunication against anyone who dared contest its provisions. The document was returned to the dying Marshal at Caversham 'for they thought it fitting that he should have sight of it before his death'.[23] From later evidence we know that the men charged with its execution were two of the Marshal's closest household knights, John II of Earley and Henry fitz Gerold, and a senior clerical associate, David Hunderer, Augustinian abbot of Bristol. We hear of the archbishop's steward, Elias of Dereham, later named as one of the co-executors, and it may be he was nominated by the 'mestre executor' to represent their interests.[24]

Countess Isabel continued to play a leading part in the ceremonies of the deathbed. She was summoned along with their five daughters to his council to hear the Marshal declare that he wished to enter the order of Knights Templar before death. His changed status to monk brought him to the point of farewell with the countess, for admission to a monastic order theoretically terminated the state of marriage, as long as the wife consented.[25] It was with this in mind that the old man 'who was generous, gentle and kind towards his wife the countess' asked Isabel to kiss him 'for you will never be able to do it again', as he said. His wife of three decades obliged, and they wept together, as did everyone else in the death chamber, recognising that the Marshal had taken a major step towards his last journey: parting company with his status as a secular magnate and as a husband. In the end it was too much. The inconsolable countess and her daughters had to be taken out of the chamber 'for nobody was able to comfort them'.[26]

The biography does not again mention Countess Isabel as attending on her husband. But since his daughters were allowed in to see him up till a few days before his death, it is likely that the countess was often in the chamber, though the biography consistently portrays the eldest son, William Marshal the younger, as taking the principal part in managing the deathbed. The biography however does indicate another place in the Caversham manor complex where the countess might very well have been usefully engaged as her husband lay dying. It is likely that her own station during her husband's prolonged deathbed had been in the chapel within the precinct with the clergy, hearing the offices, psalters and masses for her dying husband. The biography indicates as much, talking of the ceaseless vigils and exertions she had undertaken over the weeks before her husband died.[27] Professor Vincent has pointed out the evidence that the chapel of the Virgin at Caversham was a major centre of Marian devotion in thirteenth-century England. Its relics and statue were to be much patronised by Henry III throughout his reign.[28] The chapel of the Virgin at Caversham had been built, or rebuilt, on a lavish scale by the Marshal and his countess in the 1190s and endowed to be served by a cell of canons from his Augustinian abbey of Notley. That the chapel was conceived as a particular Marian cult centre is evident from the Marshal's stipulations that the canons must find wax candles to burn in it on Saturdays, the weekday devoted to a celebration dedicated to the Virgin, the Lady Mass.[29]

As he felt his death come upon him, at midday on 14 May 1219, the old Marshal had the strength to order his knight, John of Earley, to open the doors and windows and summon Countess Isabel, his son and knights so as to take a final leave. There was a rush to the chamber to hear the old man's final commendation, delivered as he was supported in his son's arms with a cross placed before him for his adoration and with a plenary absolution sent from the legate being pronounced by two abbots. After his death, the Marshal's body was prepared and placed in a coffin, which was then set up in state 'in the glorious and beautiful chapel which he had built'.[30] His countess was present for the first commemorative mass for his departed soul and the liturgy of the vigil; it was said that she was in such a weakened state that she had to be supported. The question that engages the rest of this article is the extent to which the need for that support continued throughout the widowhood which had now commenced.

The Marshal biography, written in the mid-1220s, several years after Countess Isabel herself had died, heralds the new state of affairs as soon as it begins dealing with the account of the elder Marshal's exequies. It was 'le filz e la mere' who are said to have given an annual rent of 100 shillings to Reading Abbey to secure the intercession of the community for the late earl's soul on its reception of the body on 15 May.[31] The countess's subsequent written act granting lands and rents to Reading Abbey (rather more modest than the biography's claims) echoes the biographer's words. It was granted by Countess Isabel 'with the agreement and advice of my eldest son, William Marshal'.[32] The relationship between mother and son became all-important after the old Marshal's death. It is therefore vital to work out what it might have been. How much freedom of action did the countess now have? To what extent did she control her great inheritance over the next ten months? Was the son to become a surrogate husband figure – her protector yet also heir? Did the younger Marshal exercise any constraint on his mother's movements and actions? We know that the younger William was well aware of what might happen when a wealthy widow finally came into her own. He had been present on 8 May 1216 in London when Isabel, countess of Gloucester and Essex, was finally given charge of her great honor and began issuing confirmations to the tenants who were now directly answerable to her, 'during the first year after the death of my husband, Earl Geoffrey de Mandeville, in my untramelled power (*in ligia potestate mea*)'.[33] The presence of the younger Marshal in his mother's act to Reading and his apparent contemporary confirmation of her grant at Long Crendon to William le Taylour certainly indicate that beneficiaries believed it important to have his consent to her grants recorded.[34] But this was simple good sense. He would inherit her lands, and so securing his consent was politic. In the same way before 1219 beneficiaries in the acts of the elder William occasionally wanted Countess Isabel's consent recorded to grants made by her husband out of her patrimony, for she would likely survive him and assume direct control of her inheritance.[35] Almost all the known instances of this occur in Leinster and the couple's Norman lands, which may be significant. It may be that the Marshal felt less secure in his possession of his lands overseas, and was more likely to reinforce his grants there with his wife's name, and indeed beneficiaries may have insisted on her assent for the same reason. Significantly also perhaps, Leinster produces an example of a grant of a church made by Isabel herself in her husband's lifetime, for which the Marshal's explicit permission was sought and recorded.[36]

There are however other indications that the countess herself had taken control of her inheritance after May 1219 and that the planned division between her sons remained in the future. The grant to William le Taylour in Crendon (Buckinghamshire) is important. To begin with it was clearly accepted within the family as her own to make. Though her eldest son confirmed it, he did not, like his father in the Irish example above, give permission for it to be made. Since we know Crendon was destined to be the lordship of her second son Richard, the confirmation of her grant there by her eldest son William is equally important. It tends to indicate that the 'devis' of the elder Marshal on his deathbed had little bearing on the perception of who had what rights in his former lands during Isabel's widowhood; anything might happen before she in turn died. Richard Marshal did in the end confirm the Taylour grant, but since he did so as *dominus de Longavilla et de Crendon*, it was done after his mother's death.[37] In her widowhood, Isabel's lands were perceived as her own and no one was making any assumptions as to who would eventually get them. This uncertainty as to who ultimately would get what must have often been felt in the disposition of lands. Oddly enough we find a parallel in an act of her husband's late father, John Marshal I (died 1165). In a grant of a manor in Somerset he issued a conditional warranty to the beneficiary, necessary because he had numerous sons and had either not yet decided to which the land in question would go, or was aware that the accidents of mortality would make naming any particular heir pointless, so 'my sons Gilbert and John swore to keep to this with all the power at law they had, as much as was in them, if the land should fall to their lot'.[38]

Countess Isabel certainly secured her patrimony very soon after her husband's death, though we don't know on precisely what terms. There survives her letter to the justiciar, Hubert de Burgh, asking that he send her promptly the necessary writs for the king's sheriffs in England and the justiciar of Ireland which would put her in seisin (that is, formal possession) of her lands (Appendix no. 4). Her letter mentions that she had negotiated the seisin with the legate, who then ordered the justiciar to expedite matters. The response – within five weeks of her husband's death – was a series of writs dated 18 June 1219 to the sheriffs of Gloucester, Oxford, Buckingham and Hertford, at the instance of Hubert and the bishop of Winchester. They notified the sheriffs that the countess had done homage to the king for the lands of her inheritance, and that she was to be given full possession of them: the manors of Bagworth, Caversham, Crendon and Weston were mentioned as, presumably, her chief demesne possessions in each county. This was followed the next day by a more general letter to the justiciar of Ireland to the same effect for her Irish lands.[39]

What is not known are the conditions on which Isabel might have obtained her inheritance. Had she paid for the privilege? Did she offer to pay a fine that she not be remarried?[40] There is no trace of such a fine in the Pipe Rolls. The only inkling is in a letter of Abbot David of Bristol, one of her husband's executors, to the legate datable to February 1220 (Appendix, no. 2) which alludes to a substantial debt the countess owed the legate. This might be part of a fine she had entered into with him for her lands. But her late husband's affairs were so involved at his death, the sum of 200 marks it mentions might be owed for any number of other reasons.

Having promptly and successfully obtained her English and Irish lands, Countess Isabel moved to secure the Norman ones. In 1205 the elder William Marshal had negotiated a settlement with King Philip II of France by which he had retained the lordships of Longueville, Meulers and Orbec, which he held by right of his wife, despite the fall of Normandy to the French.[41] In July 1219 at Pont de l'Arche in Normandy, Countess Isabel acknowledged the terms on which she had received her Norman estates from the king.[42] She was to hold them as her late husband had on the day of his death. As the Norman lands were put in pledge for the agreement, we may assume that a fine had been agreed for their delivery to her. Now in control of her Norman lands, we find the countess making a grant from them (presumably while still in Normandy) to the abbey of Bec-Hellouin.[43] Perhaps most interestingly, the countess's acknowledgement of the settlement with King Philip described the safe conduct granted her two elder sons and their households by the king for their travel to and from France. We know that the second son, Richard Marshal, would one day succeed to the Norman lands, and presumably this would be why his rights to enter Normandy were being safeguarded. He had in fact been at the court of Philip II when he heard news of his father's death, according to the biography, and that may well be because he was cultivating a relationship with the Capetian court necessary to secure his future possession of the Norman lands.

The reason why Isabel's eldest son, William, was given the same safe conduct into France as his younger brother could well be because he was recognised as his mother's agent in her management of her patrimony. There is however another possibility. In a briefing paper in the name of the young King Henry III, probably drawn up for the information of English proctors at Rome late in 1223 or early in 1224, the king recalled the circumstances by which the king had come to agree to his sister's marriage to the younger Earl William Marshal (a ceremony which finally took place in April 1224). Though long known to historians, this document has not to date been fully analysed and its significance in the understanding of the Marshal succession has never been registered. According to what it has to say, the marriage was first proposed between 1219 and 1221, when the younger Marshal was still in possession of the castles of Marlborough and Ludgershall and when Pandulf was legate.[44] Historians have generally assumed that the proposal was therefore made in 1221, the year when Marshal gave up the castles in pledge for the marriage.[45] However this cannot be the case. The text tells us that the marriage proposal was made by the regency to thwart a foreign match being proposed to the younger Marshal, to whom the sister of the count of Dreux had been offered by the French court. The counter-proposal of marriage to the English king's sister was made 'so as not to render England more accessible to foreigners, especially since Richard Marshal, the brother of the earl, *might* obtain (*haberet*) all his lands in Normandy'.[46] Since Richard did in fact go on to obtain those French lands on his mother's death in March 1220, the Angevin and Capetian marriages suggested to the younger William Marshal have to have been proposed *during* the period of Countess Isabel's widowhood, not after it, as has been too readily assumed. Indeed the document also says the marriage of the younger Marshal to Eleanor was proposed while the earl of Chester was in the Holy Land. Since Chester left England in 1218 and did not return till July 1220, this fact supports the deduction that the Capetian marriage proposal was made during Isabel's widowhood.[47] The Dreux children were in the wardship of their cousin the king in 1219, and so the offer to the younger Marshal might very well have come from King Philip himself at the time the Marshal family was together in Normandy in July of that year.

It is difficult to say what part the countess played in these marriage negotiations. But it seems clear enough that she and her sons found themselves very much at the centre of Capetian and Angevin machinations in July 1219. The alarm that the Capetian offer inspired when the regency council in England got to hear of it is striking, a panic which inspired the prompt counter-offer of marriage to the English king's younger sister, Eleanor.[48] It indicates the vital importance to the regency of the young earl (who attained his thirtieth birthday in the summer of 1219), despite the fact that his mother occupied the greater part of his eventual inheritance. The younger Marshal did however have lands in his own right, including continued enjoyment of the Béthune fees he had in Kent and elsewhere from his ill-starred marriage to the late Alice, daughter of Count Baldwin. These included the large manors of Luton (Bedfordshire), Wantage (Berkshire) and Greens Norton (Northamptonshire), which appear in his hands as *terrae datae* in the 1218 pipe roll. His father's own modest patrimony of the honor of Hamstead Marshal, with its Berkshire castle, and the port of Bosham in Sussex (held at farm), would have come to William directly on his father's death, as would his father's acquisitions in England. He already held the castles of Marlborough and Ludgershall in Wiltshire, which had been the long-term object of Marshal family ambitions since the period between 1138 and 1158 when John Marshal, grandfather of William Marshal II, had held them.[49] In February 1218 the younger William had been given, 'for my support' as he put it, a huge annual charge of a thousand marks from the revenues of the exchange, the agency which re-coined foreign currency into sterling at the ports of entry to England, which he was not to surrender until some months after his mother's death in 1220.[50] He had also held during the civil war the custody of the confiscated honors of Huntingdon and Gant, continuing to hold on to the Huntingdon castle of Fotheringhay after the restoration of the honor to Earl David in March 1218. William did not surrender the castle until after his mother's death in 1220.[51] According to Henry III himself, it was the young earl's continued possession of Marlborough and Ludgershall which was the royal council's main concern in the summer of 1219. Nonetheless, it was the inheritance his mother's death would bring him that made the younger William Marshal so important, and the indications that she allowed him some influence in her lands during her widowhood would simply confirm this. He was certainly exerting himself on behalf of the burgesses of the Marshal towns of New Ross and Wexford in his mother's lordship of Leinster in August 1219.[52]

The letter of Abbot David of Bristol to Pandulf, datable to the countess's last weeks on earth (Appendix, no. 2), reveals something of the complications involved in Isabel's widowhood. The role of the old earl's executors, of which the abbot was one, was a difficult one.[53] Many of the terms of the 'devis' could not be carried out in her lifetime, but the executors were nonetheless responsible for the elder Marshal's debts and legacies, which, according to his son, were still more than he could cope with financially even when he had finally secured his inheritance.[54] Indeed, we happen to know that William was being harassed before and at the time of his father's death to meet the debts in Flanders on the estate of his late wife, Alice de Béthune, which he had to compound for in order to recover her marriage-portion.[55] Abbot David was forced into an adversarial relationship with Isabel as debt collector for the legate, who was himself a supervisor of the terms of the 'devis'. It may be that Abbot David was in February 1219 harrassing Isabel for part payment of her husband's debts. The countess's refusal to pay up as her son was not present rather hints that mother and son were able to use the situation to their advantage, each shifting responsibility for debts to the other. The death of the countess in March 1219 and the succession of her sons to her lands seems in the end to have triggered a demand for a full account, which cannot have been easy to produce.[56] Indeed the surviving exhaustive account of the elder Marshal's debts and moveable property at his death by his executors, dating from mid-1224, may indicate that it took several years to produce any convincing document. The full complications of the Marshal's financial position at his death are staggeringly revealed by this account.[57] The executors and their heirs were still being chased for the elder Marshal's debts as late as 1244, when, of the original group, only Henry fitz Gerold and Elias of Dereham were still alive and the Marshal earldom was about to become extinct. Elias tells us that the late Marshal's entire movable wealth was used up (*functi sunt*) by the process of execution, and that by January 1227 there was not a penny left to meet further royal demands.[58]

By late February 1220, it was clear that Countess Isabel had been afflicted by a terminal illness. She settled down to her own deathbed at Chepstow, seat of her father's earldom of Striguil in the southern March of Wales. It was there that Abbot David of Bristol sought her out to no good effect, and it was from there that she sent letters urging her eldest son to join her before it was too late. The younger Marshal was at Cirencester en route to his mother on 2 March 1220 when messengers from the regency council reached him urging his attendance at a meeting in London. He sent his apologies and headed on into the March.[59] He would therefore have been with his mother for over a week before her death on 11 March 1220, attending his second parent out of this world in the space of less than a year. She determined on burial at the Cistercian abbey her great-uncle Walter fitz Gilbert had founded at Tintern, upriver on the Wye from Chepstow. And there she rested with others of her lineage, after a brief widowhood of only ten months. Her son, we know, then moved from Chepstow to Marlborough, where he was in late March or April. He put the castle in defence, perhaps with the intention of increasing pressure on the regency council to carry through its end of the bargain over the promised marriage to Eleanor, before embarking for Normandy to settle promptly with King Philip II his younger brother's entry into their mother's Norman lands.[60] It may be at that point that the younger Marshal further increased the pressure on the regency by putting out feelers to propose other marriage alliances with the daughter of the duke of Brabant or sister of King Alexander II of Scotland, which Henry III was to mention later.[61] His apparent willingness in 1220–1 to consider surrendering Marlborough to the regency in return for marriage to the king's sister can only have been a consequence of coming into real possession of his late mother's great patrimony. Marlborough was a lot less important to him now.

It is necessary to keep it clearly in mind that Isabel was of the élite class of widows who were themselves heiresses to great estates. She was not a widow whose precarious welfare depended on securing a third share of her late husband's lands, a 'doweress'. This was the sort of widow whose tribulations generated a large amount of the litigation in the various English courts of the thirteenth century.[62] Isabel's type of widow was far more important to the rulers of England. Such widows as her were themselves influential and came from powerful families. They represented a source both of political danger and opportunity, while their fate deeply concerned the king, as we can see here. What does this account of the brief widowhood of Countess Isabel of Pembroke then tell us about such successions? For several reasons, not least the identity of her late husband, Isabel's seisin of her lands appear to have been managed with due reference to the principles of the version of Magna Carta issued under her husband's own seal in 1217. She had prompt delivery of her lands, as we know, within the term of forty days Magna Carta laid down for delivery of dower lands and inheritance to a widow.[63] She was not obliged to remarry, and so far as we know she did not make a fine to secure her freedom, though she may have had to offer security against her marrying without the king's consent (cc. 7–8). Isabel was not subject to the exploitation of noble widows that had been characteristic of the reigns of the first three Angevin kings, which had informed the aristocratic agenda against the king in 1214.[64]

It was the marriage of Isabel's eldest son which concerned the regency council in 1219, not her own availability for remarriage. She was just as promptly dealt with by the Capetian court, and secured her Norman estates with apparently little trouble. However, Isabel seems not to have wished to manage her considerable patrimony by herself. Her eldest son was being called an 'earl' even before his father had died, and was 'earl of Pembroke' throughout the period of his mother's widowhood, even though he himself technically held none of her lands. An act of his dated 8 September 1219 at Chepstow confirms – without citing it – his father's charter for 'my' burgesses of Haverfordwest, which indicates that his tenants were already perhaps looking to him as the source of privileges and authority during his mother's widowhood.[65] The indications are therefore that the younger William Marshal took on the role of adviser and manager of her estates and interests between May 1219 and March 1220. This may account for a historical note, ultimately deriving from a family of lost annals of Tintern Abbey, that in 1219 the younger Marshal came into his office and lands on his father's death, 'his mother still living and soliciting it'.[66] In fact the young earl might quite conceivably have had a relaxed attitude to this state of affairs, as he had sufficient lands and income in his own right to support his status; there was no initial complicating issue of his dependence on his mother's charity. The overwhelming size of his mother's withheld inheritance might in the end have caused trouble had her widowhood gone on for decades, but this did not happen.

How does Isabel's experience compare with others of her contemporaries and predecessors? We must first bring up the subject of her mother. Countess Aífe survived her husband, the conquistador of Ireland, by several years. She was certainly alive in 1184, and she may have lived on for many more years after that.[67] Between 1189 and 1199 Archbishop John of Dublin apparently secured from her an act as *Eva comitissa heres regis Deremitii*, which implies that she certainly regarded herself as being the true possessor of the lordship of that great province. If that was not enough of an indicator, Aífe's act gave a sweeping confirmation to the archbishop and his successors of 'all the possessions and alms, ecclesiastical or secular which Count John and the other decent folk of Leinster conferred on them in pious liberality' (Appendix no. 1). In her own mind therefore, and indeed in those of the archbishop's household, the grant of the overlordship of Ireland in 1177 to Count John, the king's son, had by no means extinguished the reality of the lordship of Leinster and the claims ultimately deriving from King Diarmait mac Murchada, her father. Indeed, one could go so far as to suggest that for many years between 1176 and 1199, Aífe was regarded as the lady of Leinster, as her daughter would go on to be in 1219–20.

We have contemporary comparisons to Isabel to offer. The management of her widowhood was by no means unique. When news reached England in July 1220 of the death of Saher de Quincy, earl of Winchester, in the Holy Land, his widow Margaret, one of the co-heirs of the earldom of Leicester, received prompt seisin of her great inheritance in ten counties, after her performance of homage to the young Henry III. For good measure she was assigned one of her late husband's patrimonial demesne manors until her dower for his lands should be assigned. The provident Earl Saher had made his testament before he left England, and his executors, like the Marshal's, were left to secure what they could of his mobile wealth to pay his debts.[68] Unlike Isabel, however, Countess Margaret was to have a profitable and influential widowhood which lasted for fifteen years.

Perhaps most significant in this analysis of Isabel's widowhood is the use of her sons as protectors. Discussion of this strategy has not been much in evidence in scholarship on widowhood, though there are some earlier parallels. When Countess Margaret of Warwick became a widow in 1119, she determined on not remarrying and moved to Normandy to live with a younger son for nearly three decades, while using her children to administer her substantial dower lands.[69] The parallel with Countess Isabel of Pembroke is not exact, for she was a 'doweress', not a great heiress, even though the Marcher lordship of Gower was part of her dower third. But there is an exact parallel in the case of Mabel countess of Gloucester, the heiress of Robert fitz Hamo and wife of Earl Robert, who came into control of her great inheritance on her distinguished husband's death in 1147. Mabel's eventual control of her lands was already being anticipated in the treaty reached in 1142 between her husband and the earl of Hereford, and when the earl was dying he took care to get the assent of his wife 'of whose inheritance the land is', for his deathbed foundation of Margam Abbey.[70] In a parallel to the case of Isabel of Pembroke and her son, Mabel's adult son (another William) took the title of earl after his father's death. Mother and son either issued joint charters or his consent to his mother's grants were noted. Her active part in administration is indicated by the young earl's writ to his mother and their Norman officers, which indicates she may have – like Countess Margaret of Warwick – eventually retired to Normandy to leave her son free rein in England.[71] Mabel survived her husband by nearly ten years, so the arrangement with her son had to last.

Another instructive comparison is with Isabel's older contemporary, Petronilla de Grandmesnil, countess of Leicester, whose widowhood lasted from 1190 to 1212. The comparison here is significant as Countess Petronilla had brought her husband, Earl Robert III of Leicester, the large Central Norman honor of Grandmesnil, which was her inheritance from her father William.[72] Petronilla too became a widow while possessing an adult son, Earl Robert IV. She set herself up in her widowhood in a residence at Ware in Hertfordshire, a Grandmesnil centre in England at the time of Domesday Book, from where she controlled an estate called the 'honor of Grandmesnil'. Here we find her pursuing pleas, sponsoring a market in the town, and exercising advocacy over the priory her Grandmesnil ancestors had founded. It may even be that she lived in the priory precinct, a practice not unknown amongst royal and aristocratic women in the twelfth century. It seems clear that she was perfectly capable of assuming a political role. On her son's death in October 1204 she even made an expensive bid to wrest control of the earldom of Leicester from his sisters and heirs.[73] Her charter to the abbey of St-Evroult confirms that she took control of her Grandmesnil patrimony in Normandy after 1190, though her control may not have survived the separation of England and Normandy in 1204.[74] She issued numerous charters in her own right as widow. But as with Isabel of Pembroke, Countess Petronilla relied on her eldest son for support in the period before his premature death. He is found managing her debts to Aaron of Lincoln. The fact that he customarily styled himself *Robertus comes de Leicestria filius Petronille comitisse* (or some variant) in his acts more than hints at a very strong affective link between mother and son which was being evoked here, as also indicating the source of his Norman wealth.

The use of sons as agents by widows plainly depended as a strategy on trust between them and their mothers. The Marshal biography portrays the Marshal family in the early thirteenth century as affective, functional and supportive, and there is no reason to doubt its picture. Even when Marshals were on opposite sides in civil struggles, as the Marshal brothers were in 1192–94, and the elder and younger William were in 1215–16, it is clear that they were acting in concert to protect the family interests.[75] Sometimes relations were not so happy between mothers and sons. There was the case of Countess Alice of Eu, who rivalled Isabel of Pembroke as the greatest international heiress of her day, controlling considerable lands in England, Normandy and Poitou in her widowhood. Alice spent many years excluding her son, Ralph d'Issoudun, from his inheritance, and he seems not to have appreciated the delay. In the testament she drew up in March 1245, she appointed the three great abbots of her ancestral county as her executors, 'advising them on these matters to call in my venerable lord and father the lord archbishop of Rouen to coerce my son if they find him recalcitrant in any matter'.[76] Sons – dutiful or undutiful – were not always to be had. If that were the case, other close male relatives would have to do. Countess Isabel of Northampton, widow of Earl Simon II (died 1153) and subsequently of Gervase Paganel (died 1194), chose to commit her dower estates for the remainder of her lifetime 'and my own self' to her nephew Earl Robert IV of Leicester (1190–1204), to whom, she added, her marriage portion would revert after her death as her heir (Appendix, no. 3). This was the same Earl Robert who was collaborating with his mother, Countess Petronilla, in the affairs of her widowhood. The protection of Isabel's son, Earl Simon III de Senlis, had ended with his childless death in 1184 and in her old age she seems in Earl Robert to have sought out the assistance of her most powerful surviving younger male relative.

The widowhood of Isabel, countess of Pembroke, though brief, has considerable significance for our understanding of the place of female inheritance in twelfth- and thirteenth-century England and France, and indeed for the history of testamentary dispositions of estates. The insight into the complications of the interrelationship between king, widow, children and executors unveils something of the intimidating and unresolved complexity of the inheritance custom of her day. In the end it was resolved by an informal admission of Isabel's son into a role as administrator of her estate, even though seisin was undoubtedly hers. The terms of her late husband's deathbed disposition were put in suspense, and the work of his executors in discharging his debts and obligations apparently discouraged. Isabel was certainly keen to assume control over her large and widespread inheritance, but the personalities and practicalities meant that – even though her right was contested in neither England nor France – she felt she had to accommodate and work with her sons to make it effective. Other examples show that Isabel's case was not unique amongst the greatest women of her day. Taken together they argue against too legalistic an understanding of female inheritance and the exercise of power by widows in Anglo-Norman society. Glanvill's was but one voice among many in his day, and other opinions than his might hold sway in the tribunals and debates of his customary world.

Notes

* I would like to record my deep thanks for the help of Paul Brand, Martha Carlin, Lynley Herbert, Janet Loengard, Jean-François Nieus, Richard Sharpe and Louise Wilkinson in the preparation of this paper. They are in no way responsible for the views it contains.

1 William Worcestre, *Itineraries*, ed. and trans. J.H. Harvey (Oxford: Clarendon Press, 1969), 54; Julian Harrison, 'The Tintern Abbey Chronicles', *Monmouthshire Antiquary* 16 (2000): 95: a similar notice of death and burial comes from Dublin, *Chartularies of St Mary's Abbey, Dublin*, ed. J.T. Gilbert, 2 vols. (London: Longman, 1884), 1: 142, and from fifteenth-century historical memoranda in both the (now lost) 'Liber Rubeus' and the extant 'Liber Primus' of Kilkenny, relating to the Marshal family descent, which themselves drew on

Tintern sources, British Library (BL), Additional MSS 4791, fol. 64v; 4792, fol. 81r; 4793, fol. 109v; Charles McNeill, ed., *Liber Primus Kilkenniensis* (Dublin: Irish Manuscripts Commission, 1931), 64–5. A sixteenth-century copy of an epitaph purportedly carved on the tomb of Isabel and her daughter at Tintern Abbey, which records the year of her death as 1220, is to be found in London, College of Arms, MS Philipot 12.80, fol. 60r.

2 As in, Vickary Gibbs et al., eds., *Complete Peerage of England, Scotland, Ireland and Great Britain*, 13 vols. in 14 (London: St Catherine Press, 1910–59), 10: 366 and n. (d).

3 Daniel Power, 'The French Interests of the Marshal Earls of Striguil and Pembroke, 1189–1234', in *Anglo-Norman Studies 25*, ed. John Gillingham (Woodbridge: Boydell and Brewer Press, 2003), 202–5. See Appendix no. 3 below.

4 *Acts and Letters*, Appendix 1, no. 11.

5 David Crouch, *William Marshal*, 3rd ed. (London: Routledge, 2016), 174–5.

6 *HWM*, 2: lines 18119–68. We later hear of other clauses of the Marshal's will: he left fifty marks to each abbey on his lands, and a further ten marks to an unspecified number of other distinguished ecclesiastical chapters, *HWM*, 2: lines 18647–66.

7 For such divisions, J.C. Holt, 'Politics and Property in Early Medieval England', *Past and Present* 57 (1972): 3–52.

8 BL, MS Cotton Vitellius A xi (Cartulary of Bradenstoke priory), fol. 104r: 'Notum uobis facio me concessisse et confirmasse diuisam patris mei scilicet medietatem uille de Estona cum omnibus pertinentiis suis. sicut carta patris mei testatur' (*Acts and Letters*, no. 2, 54). 'Devise' was also the word used to translate a Mosaic commandment, Paul Meyer, 'Les manuscrits français de Cambridge', *Romania* 32 (1903): 71.

9 M.M. Sheehan, *The Will in Medieval England*, Pontifical Institute of Medieval Studies and Texts, 6 (Toronto: Pontifical Institute of Mediaeval Studies, 1963), 139. Sheehan points out that the mid-twelfth-century *Leis Willelmi* talks of an intestate man dying *senz devise*, which in the Latin version becomes *sine testamento*, see *Leis Willelme*, c. 34, in *Die Gesetze der Angelsachsen*, ed. Felix Liebermann, 3 vols. (Halle: M. Niemeyer, 1903–16), 1: 514. For another use of the word 'devis' in this context, see Wace's account of the ante-mortem dispositions of Richard II of Normandy between his sons, *Le Roman de Rou*, ed. A.J. Holden, 3 vols. (Paris: A & J Picard, 1970–3), 1/3: lines 2213–46. For an exact fictional parallel (*c.*1240) to the Marshal's final division of his estates, Philip de Remy, *Jehan et Blonde*, ed. Sylvie Lécuyer (Paris: Libr. H. Champion, 1984) lines 2087–9, where the dying count of Dammartin debates the division of his lands with his eldest son and council, and a division is effected which favours the younger sons.

10 However, note that in June 1231 his fourth son, Walter Marshal, newly come to adult status, was given seisin of the manor of Sturminster Marshall, which it was said his late father had given him, *in vita sua*, which could indicate that the dispositions of the Marshal 'devis' were perceived to have immediate authority on its sealing for at the time of his father's death Walter was a child, *Close Rolls of the Reign of Henry III*, 14 vols. (London: H.M.S.O, 1902–38), 2: 527.

11 A number datable to before 1216 are considered in Stephen D. Church, 'King John's Testament and the Last Days of his Reign', *EHR* 125 (2010): 505–28, at 509–15, which adds one more to those listed in Michael M. Sheehan, 'A List of Thirteenth-Century English Wills', *Genealogists Magazine* 13 (1961): 259–65, reprinted in his *Marriage, Family, and Law in Medieval Europe: Collected Studies*, ed. J.K. Farge (Toronto: University of Toronto Press, 1997), 8–15.

12 H.W.C. Davis et al., eds., *Regesta Regum Anglo-Normannorum*, 4 vols. (Oxford: Clarendon Press, 1913–69), 2: 319, the arrangement between the sons is called a *divisio* by the king. The distinction between the Latin words *divisio* and *divisa* needs to be emphasised here even though both ultimately derive from the same

Latin verb *dividere*; *divisio* is the classical Latin for the act of division while *divisa* re-Latinises the French 'devis', meaning a 'disposition'. The potential for confusion I think leads Glanvill (*c*.1180) to substitute *testamentum* for *divisio* for the disposition of estates and use *divisa* for the allotment between heirs, *Glanvill*, 79 and n. 6.

13 William Stubbs, ed., *Gesta Henrici secundi*, 2 vols. (London: Longmans, 1867), 1: 6–7. Church does not consider this example, but only Henry's division of his movable wealth in 1182, Church, 'King John's Testament', 511–12. It may be that the later document did not consider the distribution of lands since that of 1170 was still perceived as valid, for all his sons still survived at that point.

14 Stubbs, *Gesta Henrici secundi*, 1: 143. See also a charter of Archbishop John Cumin of Dublin *c*.1190 which confirms to Geoffrey de Marisco the castle and fee Walter his brother *ei in testimonio legavit*, London, Lambeth Palace Library, MS 608, fol. 10r. E.A. Bond, *Chronica monasterii de Melsa*, 3 vols. (London: Longmans, 1866–8), 1: 356–8, depicts a Yorkshire knight in the 1210s withholding a copy of his father's *testamentum* in which the monks claimed the father had granted them a portion of moorland.

15 London, College of Arms, Glover MS 2, fol. 111r (extracts from a lost Bermondsey cartulary): 'Notum est uniuersis etc quod ego Haawis de Gornai interfui ubi Rogerus de Baalun filius meus cum ultimum conderet elogium monasterio de Bermondes 100 solidatas terre de hereditate sua in Upton in perpetuam elemosinam legauit etc. Huius rei etiam testes sunt vir illustris comes Patricius qui custos terre sue rogatu eius hoc legatum optulit super altare sancti Saluatoris de Bermondes fuit . . . '. For Roger's date of death, see John Horace Round 'The Family of Ballon and the Conquest of South Wales', in his *Studies in Peerage and Family History* (Westminster: Archibald Constable, 1901), 197–198.

16 François de l'Alouëtte, *Traité des Nobles et des vertus dont ils sont formés . . . avec une histoire . . . de la . . . Maison de Couci, et de ses alliances* (Paris: Robert le Manier, 1577), 121–3, a reference I owe to R.A. Leson. Ralph's testament actually uses the word *divisio*.

17 Church, 'King John's Testament', 516: 'ut quod ipsi fideliter ordinauerint et disposuerint de rebus meis'.

18 Take the further case of Robert II count of Meulan: he devised his county of Meulan (Yvelines) and lordship of Beaumont-le-Roger (Eure) on his adult eldest son Waleran III in 1183. Before Waleran predeceased him around 1197 his father had already allotted various lands outside these lordships to his remaining sons and daughters. In 1189 he reserved certain estates in Normandy outside Beaumont for marriage portions for his daughters and as shares for his several other sons, which Waleran was obliged to accept, *Cartulaire de l'église de la Sainte-Trinité de Beaumont-le-Roger*, ed. Étienne Deville (Paris: Champion, 1912), 209, 214. Before 1202 he had promised their mother's Cornish dower lands to two younger sons, BL, Harley charter 45 I 29. In 1201 he was planning to devise a third of all his lands on his grandaughter Mary, wife of Peter des Préaux, College of Arms, Vincent MS 59, p. 84; Taunton, Somerset Record Office, DD/WO (Trevelyan Papers) Box 10, Bundle 3.

19 *RLC*, 1: 71. Of the nominated household executors, the clerk John Bonet is named elsewhere as the earl's seneschal and under-sheriff of Wiltshire, BL, MS Stowe 925 (Cartulary of Bradenstoke) fols 111r, 111v. It might be noted that the will Louis VIII of France made in June 1225 did divide his lands between his many sons, *Layettes du Trésor des chartes*, ed. Alexandre Teulet, 5 vols. (Paris: Henri Plon, 1863–1909), 2: no. 1710.

20 *Glanvill*, 79–80. The Assize of Northampton of 1176 (c. 4) mentions in passing the right of heirs of a deceased free tenant to his chattels according to his *divisa*, which parallels (or possibly informs) Glanvill's standpoint, Stubbs, *Charters*, 179.

21 Sheehan, *The Will in Medieval England*, ch. 4; idem, 'The Bequest of Land in England in the High Middle Ages: Testaments and the Law', in *Marriage, Property and Succession*, ed. Lloyd Bonfield (Berlin: Duncker & Humblot, 1992), 327–38.

22 'Et cum illi fuerint .xxx. annorum; predictus .A. dabit pueris terram que fuit patris eorum. Et dividet terram illam inter eos prout pater eorum moriens in testamento suo eam divisit', Baltimore, MD, Walters Art Museum MS W. 15, fol. 81r (see Appendix, no. 4, below). My thanks to Martha Carlin for this reference.

23 *HWM*, 2, lines 18321–50.

24 F.A. Cazel Jr, ed., *Roll of Divers Accounts* (London: Pipe Roll Society, 1982), 32. For Elias of Dereham as executor, mentioned in 1244, TNA, E.368/15 m. 12d.

25 As noted in Sheehan, *The Will in Medieval England*, 147 and n.164.

26 *HWM*, 2, lines 18367–87.

27 *HWM*, 2, lines 18991–6.

28 Nicholas Vincent, 'King Henry III and the Blessed Virgin Mary', in *The Church and Mary*, ed. R.N. Swanson, Studies in Church History, 39 (Woodbridge: Boydell and Brewer, 2004), 135, 143.

29 Oxford, Christchurch muniments DY13a (Charter roll of Notley abbey), m. 3.

30 *HWM*, 2, lines 18987–90.

31 *HWM*, 2, lines 18997–19000.

32 *Acts and Letters*, no. 107, 192.

33 London, Lincoln's Inn Library, MS Hale 100, fol. 4r. The charter was issued just after her second husband's death in a tournament, with the sanction of the assembled rebel barons, whose Magna Carta had promised such power to women. The charter was overlooked in Patterson's edition of the Gloucester acta.

34 *Acts and Letters*, nos. 108 (p. 194), 176 (p. 295).

35 Note that in 1219 the royal justices advised two barons making a concord to have the wife of one of them present at the drawing up of the document concerning a contested office, 'because it is her inheritance', *CRR, 3–4 Henry III*: 93. For the tutorship in which husbands held wives and their lands, see observations in S.F.C. Milsom, 'Inheritance by Women in the Twelfth and Thirteenth Centuries', in *Studies in the History of the Common Law* (London: Hambledon Press, 1985), 250–60. For an example of a solemn act of the elder Marshal recording his wife's assent, see *Acts and Letters*, no 32, 90.

36 *Acts and Letters*, no. 54, 122–3.

37 *Acts and Letters*, no. 176, 295. Power, 'The French Interests of the Marshal Earls', 210, on the basis of William Marshal the younger's confirmation to Taylour, suggests that Richard and William shared the Crendon lordship, but this assumption takes no account of the circumstances of the widowhood in which the grant was made. There is no evidence that William Marshal the younger exercised rights in Crendon between 1220 and his death in 1231. The fact that William owed a half of the scutage payments for the former Giffard honour can be accounted for by the fact that William, as his mother's heir, shared the responsibility for scutage with the earls of Hertford and Gloucester – with whom the elder Marshal had divided the honor in 1189, *Pipe Roll of 14 Henry III*, 131; *Cartae Antiquae Rolls, 11–20*, ed. J.C. Davies (London: Pipe Roll Society, 1957), no. 564. William Marshal the younger inherited the major Giffard demesne manor of Caversham, and that explains his responsibility for half the scutage not, as Power suggests, that he shared Crendon with his brother Richard. For other grants of *Ricardus Marescallus filius comitis Willelmi marescalli* in Crendon between 1220 and 1231, *Acts and Letters*, nos. 185 (pp. 317–8), 194 (pp. 330–2).

38 'Et hoc affidavit Gilleb(er)tus filius meus et Joh(anne)s filius meus ad tenendum ad suum legale posse. quantum ad eos, si terra in manus eorum ceciderit', *Acts and Letters*, no. 5, 57.

39 *RLC*, 1: 392.

40 For some observations on the continuing prevalence of such fines in Henry III's England, Janet Loengard, 'What Did Magna Carta Mean to Widows', in *Magna Carta and the England of King John*, ed. Janet Loengard (Woodbridge: Boydell and Brewer, 2010), 147.

41 Crouch, *William Marshal*, 110–13; Power, 'The French Interests of the Marshal Earls', 211–13.

42 *Acts and Letters*, no. 106, 191.

43 *Acts and Letters*, no. 101, 185.

44 For text and analysis, see *Acts and Letters*, 485–91. William Marshal the younger was a widower by 1215. His earlier childless marriage to Alice, daughter of his father's old ally, Baldwin de Béthune, had ended with her premature death around 1215. For the biography's discussion of the marriage – arranged between William Marshal I and Baldwin – HWM, 2: lines 14965–15022. Before 1219 the younger William confirmed a chantry she had asked in her will to be set up at St Pauls for her soul, *Acts and Letters*, nos. 164–5, 280–3. For further details of the marriage, see below.

45 David Carpenter, *The Minority of Henry III* (London: Methuen, 1990), 239, 243–4, discusses the political circumstances of Marlborough's surrender by Marshal to the crown in April 1221. However, within a year Marshal was claiming at the papal curia that despite oath-taking on both sides, 'some jealous persons' had obstructed the marriage, and secured a mandate from Honorius III for the oath taken by Hubert de Burgh and Pandulf to be honoured, *Calendar of Entries in the Papal Registers Relating to Great Britain and Ireland, 1198–1304*, ed. W.H. Bliss (London: Eyre and Spottiswoode, 1893), 88. Carpenter's reasoning needs to be qualified in seeing the surrender of Marlborough as the opening of marriage negotiations for they had begun two years before then, Carpenter, *Minority of Henry III*, 245. It was to be April 1224 before the marriage took place, by which time Eleanor was still only nine years of age at most, and Marshal was thirty-three.

46 *Acts and Letters*, 488: 'presertim cum Ricardus marescallus frater ipsius marescalli omnes terras suas haberet in Normannia'.

47 *Annales de Dunstaplia*, in *Annales Monastici*, 3: 54, 60, which confirms the early date of the betrothal.

48 Eleanor in 1219 was in the keeping of Bishop Peter des Roches, housed with her nurses and knights at his castle of Taunton in Somerset. She was not much more than an infant in 1219, having been born in 1215; for her custody, Nicholas Vincent, *Peter des Roches: An Alien in English Politics* (Cambridge: Cambridge Univeristy Press, 1996), 153 and n.93.

49 *Pipe Roll of 2 Henry III*, 31, 56, 57 (referring to his tenure of Norton in 1216), 61. William Marshal was to grant Wantage onwards to Fulk fitz Warin for one knight's service, *Acts and Letters*, no. 141. By 1225 he had granted Norton to his cousin, John Marshal of Hockering, *Luffield Priory Charters*, ed. G.R. Elvey, 2 vols., Northamptonshire Record Society, 22, 36 (Welwyn Garden City: Buckinghamshire Record Society and the Northamptonshire Record Society, 1968–75), 1: 163–5, 166–7. William also made a grant in the manor of Severn Stoke before his father's death, though it is not known on what terms, *Acts and Letters*, no. 142, 241–2. All these manors had been acquisitions of his late father-in-law, Count Baldwin, in England, and had been assigned to the younger Marshal in the marriage settlement of 1203, *RCh*, 112–13.

50 Carpenter, *Minority of Henry III*, 73, 200; W.W. Shirley, ed., *Royal and Other Historical Letters Illustrative of the Reign of Henry III From the Originals in the Public Record Office*, 2 vols. (London: Longman, 1862–66), 1: 70–1.

51 TNA, E.368/3 m. 3d, copies a writ of the elder William Marshal instructing the sheriff of Lincolnshire to assist his son's collection of scutage from the honors of Earl David and Gilbert de Gant 'which are in his hands'; see for other references,

Keith Stringer, *Earl David of Huntingdon: A Study in Anglo-Scottish History* (Edinburgh: Edinburgh University Press, 1985), 52–3.

52 *RLC*, 1: 399, 408.

53 The Marshal executors can be glimpsed at work retrieving his movable assets in Gloucestershire in August 1219, *RLC*, 1: 399. For some exotic differences between the marginalisation of the testament in the case of Isabel – who owed her rights to her father – and its importance in the case of a countess in Catalonia – who owed her rights to her husband – see the case of Ermessende of Carcassone, Martin Aurell, *Les noces du comte: mariage et pouvoir en Catalogne, 785–1213* (Paris: Publications de la Sorbonne, 1995), 223–35.

54 *Acts and Letters*, no. 151, 254–6. For the responsibility by this time of the executors for the deceased's debts, under pressure from the king for prompt payment of what was owed to him by the deceased, see Sheehan, *The Will in Medieval England*, 152–8.

55 Lille, Archives départmentales du Nord, B 1007 n° 311, settlement between Earl William Marshal the younger and Daniel de Béthune, advocate of Arras, Alice's first cousin, with deep thanks to Jean-François Nieus for his generosity in communicating this (see *Acts and Letters*, no. 110, 196–7).

56 TNA, E.368/3 m. 2, which records a writ sent around October 1220 to the executors for the delivery of their account of the Marshal's debts at the exchequer on 3 February 1221, and another which records an apparent postponement till mid-October 1221, ibid., m.3.

57 Cazel, ed., *Roll of Divers Accounts*, 32. For a suggested date of May 1224 for this account, ibid., x.

58 TNA, E.368/15 m. 12d.

59 *Acts and Letters*, no. 149, 251–2.

60 There is evidence of a relief payment made by Richard for his French lands, see Vincent, *Peter des Roches*, 324 and n.55. For William's presence in Marlborough at the beginning of April 1220, *Receipt Rolls, 4, 5, 6 Henry III*, ed. Nick Barratt (London: Pipe Roll Society, 2003), 11; *Royal and Other Letters*, 1: 100–1. For the Norman agreement, dated June 1220, *Acts and Letters*, no. 172, 290–1.

61 *Acts and Letters*, 489.

62 On the 'doweress', Janet Loengard, 'English Dower in the Year 1200', in *Women of the Medieval World*, eds. Julius Kirshner and S.F. Wemple (Oxford: Blackwell, 1985), 215–55; eadem, '*Rationabilis Dos*: Magna Carta and the Widow's 'Fair Share' in the Earlier Thirteenth Century', in *Wife and Widow in Medieval England*, ed. S.S. Walker (Ann Arbor: University of Michigan Press, 1993), 59–80, where she points out (p. 69) that Earl William Marshal I had not been too particular in applying the clauses of Magna Carta to the rights of widows during his period of regency. See also her recent, 'What Did Magna Carta Mean to Widows?', 134–50.

63 This term is referred to as the *quarantena* by Bracton, who says that within it widows might claim from the estate all their expenses until they get seisin, *Bracton*, 2: 180.

64 S.L. Waugh, *The Lordship of England: Royal Wardships and Marriages in English Society and Politics, 1217–1327* (Princeton: Princeton University Press, 1988), 158–61. The nuanced, numerical study by R.C. DeAragon, 'Dowager Countesses, 1069–1230', in *Anglo-Norman Studies* 17, ed. Christopher Harper-Bill (Woodbridge: Boydell Press, 1994), 96–9, points out that the exploitation of widows in Henry II's and Richard's reigns in general happened lower down the social scale than countesses, even if she judges John's reputation for harshness to widows is deserved. She finds the remarriage rate of widows early in Henry III's reign declined to what it had been in Henry II's, presumably as a result of Magna Carta's strictures.

65 TNA, C.53/118 (Charter Roll of 5 Edw III, inspeximus dated 4 June 1332) m. 15. For William Marshal the younger as 'earl' before his father's death, David Crouch, *The Image of Aristocracy in Britain, 1000–1300* (London: Routledge, 1992), 69. However, there is a valid argument that the younger William could have received Pembrokeshire on his father's death as a Marshal acquisition, rather than as his mother's inheritance, see R.F. Walker, 'The Earls of Pembroke, 1138–1389', in *Pembrokeshire County History* 2, *Medieval Pembrokeshire*, ed. R.F. Walker (Haverfordwest: The Pembrokeshire Historical Society, 2002), 42. It might be added that his mother did not receive writs to give her seisin of the county. The parallel between the Marshal and Longespée successions drawn by Vincent, *Peter des Roches*, 383 and n.93, may not therefore be clear-cut.

66 'Willelmus mariscallus obiit . . . et sepultus est apud London in Novo Templo et eodem anno Willelmus filius eius primogenitus successit in hereditatem et mariscalciam patris sui (matre adhuc vivente et petente)', *Liber Primus Kilkenniensis*, ed. McNeill, 65.

67 I follow here the reasoning of M.T. Flanagan, 'Strongbow, Henry II and Anglo-Norman Intervention in Ireland', in *War and Government in the Middle Ages*, eds. John Gillingham and J.C. Holt (Woodbridge: Boydell and Brewer, 1984), 72–7.

68 *RLC*, 1: 424. Her homage for her inheritance to the boy king in 1220 'in her untrammelled widowhood' is recorded in a number of her charters, Oxford, Magdalen College MSS Syresham 46, Brackley C 87; BL, MS Cotton Faustina A iv (Cartulary of St Neots) fol. 89r; BL, MS Harley 1400, fol. 35v; A.M. Leys, ed., *Sandford Cartulary*, 2 vols., Oxfordshire Record Society, 19, 22 (Oxford: Oxfordshire Record Society, 1938–41), 1: 67–8.

69 David Crouch, 'Oddities in the Early History of the Marcher Lordship of Gower', *Bulletin of the Board of Celtic Studies* 31 (1984): 133–40.

70 R.B. Patterson, ed., *Earldom of Gloucester Charters* (Oxford: Clarendon Press, 1973), nos. 95, 119; K.R. Potter, ed., *Historia Novella* (London: Thomas Nelson, 1955), 67.

71 *Earldom of Gloucester Charters*, nos. 86, 167, 171, 172.

72 David Crouch, *The Beaumont Twins: The Roots and Branches of Power in the Twelfth Century* (Cambridge: Cambridge University Press, 1986), 90–1, 91 and n.140.

73 *Pipe Roll of 7 John*, 32, 265; *RLP*, 69; BL, MS Cotton Otho B xiv (Inventory of deeds of Ware priory) fol. 115v ('Item, carta Petronille comitisse Leyc' de homagio recepto'). For her political machinations, see now David Crouch, 'The Battle of the Countesses: The Division of the Honor of Leicester, March–December 1207', in *Rulership and Rebellion in the Anglo-Norman World*, eds. Paul Dalton and D.E. Luscombe (Farnham: Ashgate, 2015), 179–211.

74 BnF, MS latin 11055 (Cartulary of St Evroult), fols 33v–35v. In 1207 the king of France had control of the fees of Breteuil and Grandmesnil, *Recueil des historiens des Gaules et de la France*, eds. Martin Bouquet et al., 24 vols. (Paris: V. Palmé, 1864–1904), 23: 705. Her charters are listed in S.M. Johns, *Noblewomen, Aristocracy and Power in the Twelfth-Century Anglo-Norman Realm* (Manchester: Manchester University Press, 2003), 79.

75 Crouch, *William Marshal*, 152.

76 Rouen, Archives départementales de la Seine-Maritime 8 H 9, 'et super illos ad illos consulendos et filium meum si eis in aliquo rebellus esset compellandum venerabilem patrem et dominum meum archiepiscopum Rothomagensem'.

Appendix

1

Countess Eve the heir of King Diarmait notifies that for her soul and that of her husband, Earl Richard and those of her ancestors, she has conceded to the church of Dublin and J(ohn) its archbishop and his successors all the possessions and alms in ecclesiastical or worldly holdings which Count John and the other good folk of Leinster conferred in pious liberality [1189 × 1199].

B = Dublin, Representative Church Body Library, ms C.6.1 (Crede Mihi), fol. 11v (s.xiii). C = Dublin, Representative Church Body Library, ms C.6.3 ((Registrum Alani), fol. 94v (copy of *c.*1530). D = Dublin, Trinity College ms 554, fol. 172v (s xviii) from C.

Printed (from B), *Crede Mihi*, ed. John T. Gilbert (Dublin, 1897), 50

B

Omnibus tam presentibus quam futuris ad quos presens carta peruenerit, Eua comitissa heres regis Deremicii, salutem. Nouerit vniuersitas vestra me pro salute anime mee et domini mei comitis Ric(ard)i. et antecessorum meorum concessisse et presenti carta confirmasse deo et ecclesie Dublinien(si). et.J. eiusdem ecclesie archiepiscopo et successoribus suis omnes possessiones et elemosinas tam in ecclesiasticis quam in mundanis tenementis quas eis comes Joh(anne)s et alii boni viri de Lagenia pia largitione contulerunt. Et uolo quod prefata ecclesia et eiusdem ecclesie archiepiscopi eas teneant et habeant libere. quiete. et honorifice. et integre cum omnibus pertinentiis suis in perpetuam elemosinam sicut carte donatorum testantur. Hiis t(estibus) etc.

The charter would at first sight appear to have been issued when John was count of Mortain, that is, between 1189 and 1199.

2

Abbot David of Bristol to the legate [Pandulf]. On hearing that the countess of Pembroke might be in her final illness he has gone himself to her to collect two hundred marks according to the instruction he has had from the legate. But since she delayed the payment with the excuse that the earl was away, it was so arranged that the countess's part of the sum should continue to be in pledge, so that the earl should come all the sooner to his mother to arrange the payment to the legate. It was done in a way that the countess could not deny the debt. He asks that for this reason the legate should not hold him culpable should he miss the council in London [1220, late February].

B = Letter Book of Abbot David Hunderer of Bristol, British Library, Cotton Roll IV 58, m. 2. s.xiiii
Printed, Ecclesiastical Letter Books of the Thirteenth Century, ed. R. Hill (Oxford, 1936), 224.

B

Domino legato [David abbas etc. nos] audientes[a] quod comitissa de Pembroch laboraret in extremis accessimus ad eam personaliter .cc. marcis [in] nomine uestro iuxta tenorem litterarum uestrarum exigentibus ab eadem. et cum earundem numeracio pretextu absencie domini comitis Pembr[ochie] caperet dilationem tantum elaboratum est quod quicquid de comitissa contingat dicta pecunia in tuto consistit. quam citius memoratus com[es] ad matrem suam uenerit uobis fideliter destinanda. Hoc etiam actum est quod et si comitissa uellet dictam pecuniam reuocaret non posset. Hinc est quod sanctitati uestre humili supplicamus deuotione quatinus absenciam nostram habentes excusatam non ducatis pro malo si sacro concilio uestro London' celebrando non potuerimus interesse. Valete.

[a] audito *ms.*

There is a reference in a letter of Pandulf dated 31 January 1220 to a council he proposes to attend fairly soon in London, which would seem also to be the council referred to in this letter, *Royal and other Historical Letters*, 1: 80. The 'sacrum concilium' referred to here may be a gathering of prelates to be held simultaneously before the legate, rather than a fully fledged church council. No such church council is listed in reference works. The continuator of William of Newburgh talks of Pandulf and King Henry with Stephen Langton and almost all the bishops, earls and barons at a council at Westminster early in 1220, which debated the peace of the realm, *Continuatio Chronici Willelmi de Novoburgo*, in *Chronicles of the Reigns of Stephen, Henry II and Richard I*, ed. Richard Howlett (Rolls Series, 1885), 2: 527. This would apparently be the same council which considered the renewal of the truce with the king of France late in February, concluding on 3 March 1220, Carpenter, *Minority of Henry III*, 177.

3

Isabel, countess of Northampton, notifies the king and all his justices that she has conceded her land of Bradefeld, Botindon, Norfeld *and* Watham *to her nephew, Earl Robert of Leicester for her lifetime and has committed herself to his protection and safeguard. After her death, the village of Waltham which is her marriage portion will revert to the earl as her heir. They should allow the earl to do with the lands as he wishes because that which suits the earl, as far as herself and the land is concerned, will be acceptable to her* [1184 × 1204].

B = Kew, National Archives (PRO), DL42/2 (Cartulary of the Duchy of Lancaster) fol. 47r (s. xv.). C = BL, MS Lansdowne 229, fol. 106r (s. xvi) *ex magno registro ducatui Lancastriae spectante.*

B

Illustri regi Anglie et omnibus iusticiariis suis .I. comitissa Norhamthon', salutem. Ad sublimitatis vestre notitiam perueniat me omnem terram meam de Bradefeld' et de Botindon' et Norfeld' et Watham .R. comiti Legr(ecestrie) nepoti meo quamdiu vixero concessisse et dedisse. ac mea carta confirmasse et me ipsam in manu sua. protectione et tutela commisisse. Postquam autem decessero, villa de Watham cum omnibus pertinentiis suis que est mariagium meum ad predictum comitem sicut heredem reuertetur. Quare vos precor vt hanc meam concessionem sigillo et scripto meo confirmatam firmam habeatis. et predictum comitem predictas terras bene et in pace possidere. et pro voluntate sua tractare permittatis. quia quicquid prefatus comes de me et de terris fecerit vel facere placuerit, ego semper gratum habebo et acceptum.

4

Settlement between A. and B. over the children and heirs of N. A. will have wardship of the two boys along with eleven acres of land and the capital messuage of the tenement, finding them all necessaries in clothing and food till they are thirty years of age, and then he will give them their father's land as the father devised it in his testament. B. will have the two girls in wardship with seven acres of land and the stone buildings, and provide for them till they are twenty years of age; when they are of childbearing age and wish to marry he will give them to whichever men seems best by the advice of their friends, or if they had rather enter a monastery as nuns or be anchorites, then he will deliver the land to the right heirs and give the girls ten marks each in return [1204 × 1209].

B = Baltimore MD, Walters Art Gallery ms W. 13, fo. 81r (s. xiii^{fin}) copy of an ecclesiastical formulary copied within a glossed gospel.

B

Hec est facta conventio inter A. et B. super causa que uentilabatur inter illos pro filiis et filiabus .N. scilicet quod predictus A. habebit duos pueros .N. in custodia sua cum .xi. acris terre et cum principali mesuagio. Et inueniet predictis pueris omnia necessaria usque dum sint .xxx^{ta}. annorum. videlicet sic. predictus .A. exibebit predictos pueros in omnibus usque ad .xxx^{ta}. annos. tam in pannis quam in cibis. Et cum illi fuerint .xxx. annorum, predictus .A. dabit pueris terram que fuit patris eorum. Et diuidet terram illam inter eos prout pater eorum moriens in testamento suo eam diuisit. Predictus uero .B. habebit duas filias .N. in custodia sua cum .vii. acris terre. et lapideis edificiis. et ministrabit eis necessaria usque ad .xx. annos. videlicet sic. quousque peruenerint ad annos nubiles tunc si eis uiros sumere placuerit, dabit eas uiris. quousque melius poterit consensu et consilio amicorum suorum. uel si maluerint ad religionem transferre et sanctimoniales vel anacorite fieri, predictus .B. reddet prefatam terra iustis heredibus et heredes dabunt puellis pro terra reddita .x. marcas argenti. Hiis t(estibus). A. B. C. terminis suprascriptis ut prius ab aliquo enotabili facto. vel anno ab incarnatione domini.

3 A crossroads in criminal procedure

The assumptions underlying England's adoption of trial by jury for crime[1]

Elizabeth Papp Kamali and Thomas A. Green

Introduction

According to a tale from York Cathedral dating to the late twelfth or early thirteenth century, two women were arrested upon an accusation of homicide.[2] One died in prison, while the other denied involvement in the alleged homicide and was ordered to undergo trial by hot iron to determine whether she was guilty of the homicide or not (*utrum esset rea ejus homicidii vel non*). She carried the hot iron. When her hand was later unbandaged, a large swelling was found; she was declared guilty and ordered to be burnt to death. All this is unremarkable. What is surprising is that the guilty verdict was handed down by a group of twelve knights who had been designated the judges in her case. The knights, in turn, reported their verdict to the 'principal justices' (*justitiariis principalibus*).

The story is not an official trial narrative from the plea rolls but rather a miracle tale. It continues: prior to her execution, the condemned woman prayed at the tomb of St. William of York, and her swelling immediately disappeared. This miraculous healing was reported to the justices, who sent the knights to inspect the woman's hand again. The knights confirmed that her hand had indeed healed. The justices, in turn, pronounced the woman 'absolved and innocent' (*absolutam et innoxiam*), setting her free. The knights were placed in the king's mercy, presumably fined, for bearing false testimony and handing down 'an iniquitous judgment' (*iniquum judicium*) in the first place.

The story perplexes. It speaks of trial by ordeal, known in its time as the *iudicium dei* or judgment of God, yet the verdict was handed down by a jury, a panel of twelve knights.[3] The knights correctly identified the woman's hand as festering rather than healing. Nevertheless, the justices later condemned the knights for issuing a wrongful judgment despite the fact that the knights could not have foreseen St. William's miraculous intercession. The justices, although initially content to hand over the responsibility of issuing a verdict to the knights, later stepped in heavy-handedly to absolve the woman of guilt and set her free. They appeared to be more comfortable with this post-miracle alteration of judgment than they had been with rendering judgment in the first place. And the tale never resolves the ambiguity about the woman's guilt or innocence of the crime charged: was it a case of wrongful accusation from the outset, or had she committed the homicide but nevertheless secured the saint's intercession and an acquittal due to her piety and, perhaps, remorse?

A tale that raises more questions than answers offers an appropriate starting point for an essay engaging in the most speculative of pursuits, discernment of the assumptions underlying the adoption of trial by jury for felony cases in the wake of the Fourth Lateran Council's effective abolition of the ordeal in 1215. Eight hundred years ago, England faced a crossroads in criminal justice procedure when compelled to abandon the practice of trial by ordeal. This occurred during a tense period of transition from the unpopular reign of King John to that of his nine-year-old son, Henry III. Within a few years of Lateran IV's prohibition of priestly involvement in ordeals, England moved definitively toward a criminal justice system based on trial by jury. In part, this was a natural development in light of the encroachment of jury procedure in more and more areas of common law adjudication, both civil and criminal. Nevertheless, it is one that cannot be taken for granted, as the justices who experimented with procedure in the first post–Lateran IV eyres, and the young king's councilors who gave the justices license to experiment, did not take the transition to jury trial for granted.

This essay will explore the underlying assumptions in the early thirteenth century as to the jury's function within a criminal justice regime that countenanced only capital sanctions for those convicted of felony.[4] To unearth these assumptions, the essay will consider earlier ordeal procedure and other kinds of criminal juries in the late twelfth and early thirteenth centuries, most notably juries of presentment, coroners' inquests, and juries tasked with responding to writs *de odio et atia*, which alleged that an accusation had been made out of hate and spite. It will also situate jury trial within the broader context of felony adjudication with its many escape valves, including pardons, benefit of clergy, sanctuary and abjuration, by means of which a confessed felon entered permanent exile abroad. The essay will rely upon a re-examination of primary source materials and engage with the existing secondary literature to grapple with the broad questions of what constituted serious criminal wrongdoing, what jurors were expected to know and do in adjudicating felony cases, and the extent to which jurors' verdicts were based on knowledge or belief in the guilt of an individual, in addition to such factors as reputation, rumour or expected recidivism. The essay will also examine the question of justice-jury interaction in the early use of trial juries in criminal cases, asking whether justices reached consensus with juries in the issuance of verdicts, or whether alternatively justices merely acquiesced to the high felony acquittal and pardon rate that followed from jury trial. Related to this is the macro-level question of what constituted the law, including the matter of how jurors were to know the law and respond to it. As a think piece, this essay will present several hypotheses regarding problems fundamental to the history of English criminal law, some of which may prove unresolvable.

Nevertheless, this essay does make some confident claims. First, building off recent work by one of us (Kamali) on felony, we argue that the transition from ordeal to jury trial happened swiftly due to the recognition that juries were best suited to provide access to local knowledge, and that such local knowledge included, at its core, information dispositive of a defendant's state of mind in allegedly committing a felonious act. Second, this essay contends that scholars of nineteenth-century criminal law, in making claims for the rise of notions of *mens rea* in the Victorian era, have understated the degree to which assessment of mind entered into adjudication of premodern English felony cases. Third, we argue that the initial, post-1215 assumptions about the nature of judge-jury interaction, most notably the expected level of agreement between judges and juries regarding verdicts, would soon come to be cast into doubt in response to juries' inclination toward acquittals and pardons in a broader range of cases than anticipated at the outset. This essay does, therefore, offer some answers, while also raising questions to guide future scholarship on medieval English understandings of criminal responsibility.

A brief timeline of criminal procedure

The turn of the twelfth into the thirteenth century was a time of rapid transformation in medieval English felony procedure. During the reign of Henry II, a push was made to centralise felony procedure and bring such cases before the king's justices. In 1166, Henry regularised the jury of presentment, ancestor of our grand jury, through the Assize of Clarendon. The Assize decreed that inquiries should be made 'through twelve of the more lawful men of the hundred, and through four of the more lawful men of each vill, on oath that they will speak the truth', whether in the hundred or vill there are any men who are 'accused or publicly known' (*rettatus vel publicatus*) to be robbers, murderers, thieves or receivers of them.[5] Those suspected of guilt were to undergo the ordeal of water, swearing that they were not indeed a robber, murderer, thief or receiver. Those found guilty of felony were subject to maiming or abjuration, but not by default capital punishment. Examined within the context of the remaining provisions of the Assize, the clauses were part of a comprehensive program designed to centralise and systematise the prosecution of crime. For example, another clause asserted that all accused through the presentment process should be tried by the king's justices, and that in instances when a royal justice was not scheduled to come to the locality for some time, the sheriffs should send word to the next closest justice to determine how best to proceed. Moreover, the Assize declared that gaols should be built at the king's expense in any county not yet equipped with such a facility.

The scope of crimes subject to presentment expanded with the Assize of Northampton in 1176, which added forgery and arson to the list of felonies. It also specified that twelve knights should ideally present accused criminals, but that the Clarendon-imposed use of twelve lawful men from each hundred and four from each vill might be relied upon when knights were unavailable.[6] Those accused by a presenting jury were to go to the ordeal of water and, if found guilty, would lose a foot and a hand in addition to abjuring the realm within forty days. Those cleared by the ordeal would nevertheless have to provide sureties, and, in some instances, might still have to abjure the realm. This was true for those who had been accused of murder – referring in this context to unlawful homicide generally – or some other shameful felony (*turpi felonia*), by the community of the county (*per commune comitatus*), and by lawful knights of the country.

Richard I, a king renowned more for his exploits abroad than for his domestic policy initiatives, firmly established the office of coroner in 1194, thereby placing a royal officer in the role of first investigator in cases of suspected homicide. This was early in the justiciarship of Hubert Walter, who also reinforced the system of eyres to bring royal justice systematically to the counties. From the outset, coroners were heavily dependent upon local juries, insofar as they were obliged to summon inquests to assist them in the examination of the bodies of those who appeared to have died under unnatural circumstances.[7] To round out the important dates, 1215 marked the Fourth Lateran Council, which instituted a series of reforms, most notably for our purposes a ban on priestly involvement in the administration of trial by ordeal.

During the minority of John's son and successor, Henry III, England experimented with alternatives to the ordeal. Such experimentation was in fact encouraged by royal fiat, in the form of a set of instructions sent to the justices in eyre in 1219. In a letter patent entitled 'On doing justice in place of [trial by] fire and water' (*De justicia facienda loco ignis et aquae* [sic]), the king and his inner circle provided tentative directions to the itinerant justices of several counties on how to deal with those accused of the most serious crimes of theft, murder and arson in the wake of the Roman church's withdrawal from involvement in administering trial by ordeal.[8] In short, if the justices suspected that an accused individual was actually guilty and might commit further crimes if allowed to abjure the realm, they were to place him or her in prison. Those accused of medium-level crimes were to be permitted abjuration if this did not pose a clear threat of recidivism. Finally, those accused of minor crimes and not generally suspected of evildoing were to be released upon securing pledges.[9] The letter patent gave leeway to the justices to apply their own discretion and conscience, which might indicate a lack of consensus among the king's councilors about how best to proceed in a post-ordeal world. The absence of the death penalty from the menu of possible punishments likely reflects discomfort with the use of the capital sanction in the absence of the *iudicium dei*, which had placed some cognitive distance between the person pronouncing judgment and the judgment itself. As late as 1219, there is evidence of reluctance to accept final verdicts from juries in the absence of manifest guilt, such as a confession or being caught in possession of stolen goods, suggesting that juries were not yet viewed as an adequate substitute for the *iudicium dei*.[10] Nevertheless, by the early 1220s, juries were the chosen mechanism for issuing felony verdicts, with trial juries being drawn from the ranks of presenting juries.[11] While it is possible that jury verdicts were understood, by that time, to be a new form of *iudicium dei*, with God's judgment mediated by a group of twelve men, the requirement that defendants consent to jury trial suggests instead that the jury was understood to be a distinct substitute, and a potentially inferior one at that.[12]

Themes in the history of criminal responsibility

But what were these early trial juries doing? What were they evaluating as they sorted the guilty from the innocent? How much did issues of mind factor into their analysis? While understandings of *mens rea* have not historically been a major focus of scholarship on medieval English law, several prominent scholars of common-law criminal responsibility, working on a much later period, have used the premodern period as a foil for what they see to be modern developments in criminal law doctrine.[13] In doing so, we argue, they have mischaracterized the premodern era as a time in which issues of mind were not yet affecting criminal adjudication, or at least not in any meaningful way.

Namely, scholars of criminal responsibility have described a transition from more primitive modes of assessing criminal behaviour toward a comparatively sophisticated interest in issues of mind and intentionality. In *Rethinking Criminal Law*, George Fletcher drew a distinction between manifest and subjective criminality, a distinction that he limited primarily to the realm of larceny but which has since been extended by others to the development of felony law more generally.[14] Fletcher argued that the common law of larceny up until the time of Blackstone – a sweeping expanse of time, it bears noting – reflected what he describes as a pattern of manifest criminality, while the modern law of larceny, which emerged in the late eighteenth century, reflected instead a pattern of subjective criminality.[15] Under Fletcher's rubric of manifest criminality, the basic feature of liability required 'that the commission of the crime be objectively discernible at the time that it occurs'.[16] Crime was such that a third-party observer could recognise the act as criminal without knowing the intention of the actor. Not imposed upon a community by legislation, crime was 'the product of community experience' in the manifest criminality regime.[17] Rather than requiring proof of intentionality to inculpate an individual, manifest criminality looked to intent only if the issue was raised 'as a challenge to the authenticity of appearances', i.e., to argue in favour of exculpation.[18]

According to Fletcher's model, intentionality could not yet stand on its own as a distinct category of legal analysis: 'It is not thought of as some mysterious inner dimension of experience that exists independently from acting in the external world'.[19]

In describing a paradigm shift in understandings of subjectivity in the late eighteenth century, Fletcher suggests that what came before was markedly different in kind. His theory of manifest and subjective criminality, however, fails to account for the sophisticated theories of mind apparent in Christian theology and popular piety at the time when jury trial was adopted for felony cases in the early thirteenth century.[20] Analysis of a jury-based system of adjudication necessarily must consider popular understandings of criminality, rather than relying solely on what legal treatises or even trial records have to say on the subject, particularly in light of the fact that jury verdicts then, like jury verdicts today, were typically recorded without any detail as to how the verdict was reached. To determine whether Fletcher is correct in describing pre-nineteenth-century criminal law as based on a notion of manifest criminality would require, in turn, combing through legal and cultural evidence alike across the centuries to test his sweeping hypothesis. Presumably notions of criminal responsibility were not static over time, particularly taking into account sweeping changes in England's religious foundations during the pre- and post-Reformation eras. We contend, at the very least, that the theory of manifest criminality fails to describe accurately the state of criminal responsibility at the turn of the thirteenth century, even if the theory might more adequately describe early eighteenth-century understandings, about which we remain doubtful.

Influenced by Fletcher but modifying the manifest criminality paradigm to account for juries' interest in internal states, Lindsay Farmer has argued that, prior to the early nineteenth century, the doctrines of malice aforethought or implied malice in homicide 'did not operate in a way that we would recognise, for rather than looking to the intention of the accused, they looked to the circumstances surrounding the killing to judge whether these indicated wickedness or a malignant spirit'.[21] Farmer contends: 'The state of an individual's mind was not regarded as something that could be factually determined'.[22] Farmer appears to be suggesting that there did not yet exist a notion of *mens rea* or intentionality vis à vis the pre-nineteenth-century criminal law, which instead fell back on notions of wickedness. This leaves open the question of the relationship, if any, between the concept of wickedness and understandings of mental states. Presumably wickedness could be analysed separately from the underlying act itself, but whether or not it constituted a state of mind is unclear in Farmer's framework. According to Farmer, discomfort with judging mind would fade by the nineteenth century. Discussing 'the outright invention' of a new form of liability in homicide – recklessness – Farmer argues that it was the Criminal Law Commissioners of Victorian England who perceived that the presence of recklessness as a state of mind could be factually determined by examining the circumstances surrounding an act.[23] Yet it is noteworthy that reliance on analysis of the circumstances, which continues to inform how we determine the presence or absence of criminal intent today, can be traced back to the medieval period, when the circumstances were the focus of analysis for confessors and coroners alike in assessing guilt.[24] In fact, examination of the circumstances of a crime for insight into a defendant's state of mind can be traced to the earliest days of criminal trial juries, and even further back in time given the fact that coroners' juries were already undertaking a sophisticated inquiry into the circumstances of alleged homicides before the transition from ordeal to jury trial. [25]

Once the transition was made in the post-Blackstone world toward a paradigm of subjective criminality, Fletcher asserts, the underlying assumption changed such that 'the core of criminal conduct is the intention to violate a legally protected interest'.[26] Farmer, too, describes 'the emergence of a new type of legal subjectivity where the state of mind of the individual was paramount'.[27] Rather than being raised only as an exculpatory factor, intent came to stand front and center. Reflecting a dualistic understanding of body versus mind and act versus intent, intentionality was now treated, according to Fletcher, 'as a dimension of experience totally distinct from external behavior'.[28] While Fletcher sees homicide's development as distinct from that of larceny, he argues that there is nonetheless a similar shift in both from use of intent as a means of excuse and toward intent as an element of crime. However, while the transition from manifest to subjective criminality in larceny led to an expansion of liability, such that even some takings that appeared innocent might be condemned as unlawful, the restructuring of homicide law to require intent as an element of an offense may have led to a narrowing of the scope of the crime.[29] Yet during the medieval period, when according to Fletcher's rubric homicide was broadly defined, acquittal rates for felony were exceedingly high.[30] Whether Fletcher would suggest that this reflects a disconnect between the actual law and the law as applied remains unclear.

Drawing in part upon Fletcher, Nicola Lacey has described a shift in the criminal trial from operating on something like a presumption of guilt up to the early nineteenth century to a presumption of innocence thereafter.[31] In eighteenth-century trials, Lacey relates, most evidence involved either eyewitness testimony or character and reputational evidence.[32] Lacey acknowledges that eighteenth-century culpability requirements, including actions done maliciously, wickedly, feloniously or *animus furandi*, were discussed by treatise authors and judges, but she argues that 'these were very far from equating to the psychological and capacity-based requirements of '*mens rea*' with which we are familiar today'.[33] Lacey concedes that the writings of Aristotle and Christian theologians demonstrate a long-standing engagement with ideas of individual responsibility, but nevertheless contends that 'most contemporary philosophical analyses of responsibility are grounded in notions of human agency that emerged in Europe in the philosophy of the Enlightenment.'[34] Arguing against those who might be inclined 'to read the past backwards' and claim *mens rea* as a central feature of criminal law prior to the period of her analysis, Lacey contends that three factors – 'speed of trial, lack of legal argumentation, predominance of lay justice' – made it unlikely that typical eighteenth-century trial process dealt with evidence of *mens rea* in any sophisticated way. As we discuss below, we believe that Lacey's focus on the trial in isolation fails to account for the more extensive inquiries that occurred pre-trial.[35]

Taken together, the work of Fletcher, Farmer and Lacey raises provocative questions about the evolution of criminal justice over a broad expanse of time. Our examination of likely assumptions as of 1215–20 about adoption of the trial jury is premised, in part, upon our view that medieval English evidence points toward a more sophisticated understanding of mind as it pertains to both official understandings and lay determinations of criminal responsibility than the above-cited literature suggests. While Farmer might be correct in arguing that *gradations* of intent 'emerged blinking into the legal daylight' in Victorian England,[36] it would be manifestly inaccurate to suppose that medieval English juries adjudicated felony cases in a pre–*mens rea* dark ages.

Assumptions underlying the adoption of trial by jury for felony

Upon first examination, it might appear that Fletcher's framework fits medieval English felony law, insofar as the substantive law of crime was only very rudimentarily mapped out: we have no criminal statutes defining the boundaries of substantive offenses, or even any treatises laying out in systematic fashion the general and special parts of the criminal law. Yet to suggest that intentionality therefore played a secondary role in the analysis engaged in by justices and jurors, or that felony was conceived of as a mere act without any presumed mental component, would be to assume too much on the basis of an admittedly terse legal record. In the absence of a distinct prosecutorial office, expecting any overt grounds for inculpation, whether based on acts or states of mind, would also be to expect too much. Indeed, as one of us has argued elsewhere, we must look to the factors used to exculpate in order to perceive what was essential to inculpate.[37] Where the plea rolls most often tell us merely that a defendant was acquitted or convicted, we necessarily must rely upon the narratives driving acquittals and recommendations for pardon, where some kind of explanation was added to the record, to enable us to perceive what was required for the purposes of inculpation and, therefore, to perceive the boundaries of the paradigmatic felonies of homicide, theft, arson, etc. Studying these narratives gives us insight into the factors that led jurors, in some cases, to believe a person should not hang for felony.

For instance, in recommendations of pardon based on insanity, juries sometimes reported that the defendant had been labouring under a mental illness for some time and had been in the throes of that illness when they stabbed another or, in more rare circumstances, pilfered goods.[38] To take one example, an early thirteenth-century jury noted that Seger de Chippenham had taken a mare while 'detained by frenzy' (*detinebatur frenesi*) and after having been frenetic (*freneticus*) for seven years, with understanding (*cognicionem*) of neither right nor wrong. In acquitting him, the jurors contended that Seger had not taken the horse in felony and had indeed disavowed the theft when he was of sane memory.[39] In cases of homicide perpetrated by children, the jury narrative might report that the defendant had not acted feloniously but rather out of simplicity in killing a playmate.[40] In cases of self-defense, emphasis was often placed upon the felonious, premeditated nature of the deceased's attack upon the self-defender, thereby justifying the latter's homicidal actions.[41] In fact, descriptions of attacks precipitating an act of self-defense are particularly vivid in relaying societal understandings of the most heinous forms of homicide, typically emphasising the premeditation of the deceased and frequently including aggravating circumstances, such as stealth and housebreaking.[42] The boundaries of felonious theft are more obscure, particularly in the absence of any categories of pardonable theft, but an examination of legal and non-legal textual evidence enables the legal historian to map out some of the societal understandings of the kinds of theft for which a perpetrator merited capital punishment.[43] For example, a person who took another's goods but lacked an unlawful *animus* would not be convicted of felony.[44]

Institutional developments, lay practices and officials' expectations support a series of inferences regarding officials' assumptions about the adoption of the criminal trial jury, particularly when read in light of the importance of mind in general, and intentionality/motivation in particular, to the criminal law and its administration as of the early thirteenth century. We treat a number of partly independent, partly interrelated matters from which such inferences might be drawn. At first we mainly allow relevant developments to speak for themselves, but increasingly we relate them to hypotheses regarding adoption, which we bring into more sustained focus in the final section on justice-jury relations. We concentrate in part on assumptions at the time of adoption of trial by jury for felony, but also take note of features of the criminal law and its administration in the early thirteenth century, both pre- and post-adoption.

The spread of juries in the criminal law arena

With the reforms of Henry II, criminal prosecution came to be more heavily centred in royal hands. For example, royal justices were to try felony cases, and they were to be sent from the centre to the periphery to deliver gaols and officiate over civil and criminal pleas alike at local eyres. The system of presentment enabled the crown to compel local actors to initiate public prosecutions, thereby expanding the reach of criminal justice beyond cases initiated by private citizens bringing appeals of felony. Moreover, royal justices began to intervene with prosecution in private appeals where the appellor chose to abandon his or her suit. This can be seen during the reign of John, but became standard practice under Henry III.[45] As royal power over criminal prosecutions expanded, so did the use of juries to adjudicate medial and final matters. The miracle tale with which we opened this essay suggests that there may have been a third use of juries in criminal cases prior to Lateran IV: alongside juries of presentment and juries to adjudicate writs *de odio et atia*, panels of twelve may sometimes have issued ordeal verdicts. This lends further credence to the idea that juries were a natural choice for adjudicating felony cases in a post–Lateran IV world due to their extensive use in criminal cases before that time. In fact, the mystery for historians may be less why the jury was introduced as an alternative to trial by ordeal after Lateran IV, and more the question why this final frontier in the use of juries in felony cases was so long in coming.

In *Verdict According to Conscience*, Thomas Green describes the introduction of trial juries in felony cases after Lateran IV as 'the final stage of a century-long evolution in the administration of the criminal law', with a shift from private to public prosecution, compensation to capital punishment, and toward the use of trial juries that reflected 'communal attitudes', much as presenting juries had done previously.[46] In fact, well before Lateran IV, the role of juries was expanding in English felony prosecution. Roger Groot has highlighted the extensive use of juries in private criminal prosecutions before 1215, most notably through writs *de odio et atia*, which triggered the use of a local inquest to determine whether an appellor's accusation had been motivated by hate and spite.[47] Groot convincingly demonstrates that such inquests must have gotten to the merits of an accusation rather than simply attesting to the appellor's motivation, a theory supported by the phrasing of the writ *de odio et atia* as it appears in later registers of writs.[48] Medial jury verdicts came into play before 1215 in accusations by presentment and by appeal, a pattern that suggests to Groot that jury verdicts were a preferred means for resolving felony cases prior to Lateran IV, although juries could not yet convict.[49] In some instances, it has been asserted, defendants were paying for a trial jury before 1215.[50] More commonly they specifically paid for a jury to testify as to their character in response to an accusation of criminal behaviour.[51] Moreover, whether or not an accused individual faced trial by ordeal was itself determined by a jury. Thus, by the time of Lateran IV, not only were juries routinely being employed in criminal cases, but their scope of use was actively expanding beyond their initial role as presenters. As a result, officials in a post-ordeal England may have viewed trial juries as a natural extension of the use of juries in other aspects of criminal adjudication. This may help to explain not only the decision to experiment with juries issuing final verdicts in post–Lateran IV eyres, but also the rapid extension of this new guilt/innocence jury from appeals to prosecutions initiated by presentment.[52]

Knowing neighbors: juries as a source of local facts

This expanding use of juries can be attributed in part to the fact that they were perceived to be a reliable source for local information. In fact, one static assumption between the reigns of Henry II and Henry III was the notion that local juries were peculiarly well suited for serving as witnesses and fact finders in criminal matters.[53] The Assize of Clarendon was based upon the idea that local individuals were capable of identifying those within their community suspected of serious crime. When the trial jury was introduced, this principle of local knowledge was extended to the issuance of verdicts, with trial jury pools drawn from presenters. In fact, it was not uncommon for there to be overlap between presenting and trial juries even as late as the early fourteenth century.[54] This supports the findings of Daniel Klerman that the thirteenth-century criminal jury was self-informing, even if it occasionally heard testimony from defendants, victims or others in court.[55] This arrangement might well have disincentivized courts from engaging in extensive evidence gathering and in-court testimony, and justices were viewed to be comparatively ignorant of the facts of the cases tried before them and therefore greatly dependent upon the judgment of jurors, an issue to be explored further below.[56]

Written shortly after the transitional phase to trial by jury, the *Bracton* treatise provides some insight into early understandings of the criminal trial jury. For example, the treatise describes the oaths taken by jurors, who raised their hands and swore, 'Hear this, ye justices, that we will speak the truth about what is asked of us on the king's behalf, nor will we for any reason fail to tell the truth, so help us God, etc'.[57] Evidence from trial records supports the fact that juries, even those tasked only with adjudicating claims of *odio et atia*, were indeed questioned as to the specifics of an allegation. At the Yorkshire Eyre in 1218–19, for example, in a private prosecution for housebreaking, robbery and homicide, the defendant paid for the privilege of having a jury determine whether he was guilty or had been accused out of hate and spite.[58] The jury, questioned by the presiding justice, had to respond as to: a) whether the house had been broken into, b) whether the householder had indeed been wounded, c) whether the householder had brought an action for this wounding, and d) whether the person bringing the private prosecution on behalf of the now-deceased householder had been 'in the land after that deed in time of peace', in which case his delay in prosecuting would not be tolerated.[59] From the line of questioning, the justices in eyre reveal their dependence upon the jury for details of an alleged crime said to have taken place roughly a decade earlier, as well as insight into subsequent procedural developments in the case. In this particular instance, the jury's responses to the questions led to an acquittal of the accused.

In fact, it was in the very nature of eyre jurisdiction that local juries were essential to the process, insofar as traveling justices would be ill-equipped to familiarise themselves with the facts of a given case without the help of local witnesses, particularly when the events had occurred years earlier. At the 1221 eyre in Coventry, for example, a case was adjourned to be heard in the county of Staffordshire because the jurors in Coventry were not familiar with the truth (*isti juratores nullam veritatem inde sciunt*) surrounding a quarrel between the accused and the deceased.[60] In a later case arising in the 1248 Berkshire eyre, several justices were reprimanded for allowing an alleged forger of coinage, William le Locker, to be tried by a jury of outsiders (*de forinseco*) rather than the local jurors of the vill of Reading on whose verdict the accused had placed himself.[61] *Bracton*, written sometime between these two cases, relates the words to be spoken by the justices once the jurors have sworn an oath to tell the truth: 'Such a one, who is here present', the justices are to say, 'charged with the death of such a one (or some other crime) comes and denies the death and everything else and on this matter puts himself for good and ill upon the words of your mouth (*super linguas vestras*)'.[62] This phrasing helps to clarify what was so troubling about William le Locker's case: when William 'put himself for good and ill upon a jury of the vill of Reading' (*posuit se de bono et malo super juratam ville de Rading*), he had specifically consented to judgment by the spoken words of that particular jury, not a jury of outsiders. Local knowledge was central to adjudicating felony in medieval England, and the assumption at the outset of the adoption of jury trial was that jurors were best suited to serve as sources of information about neighborhood events and personalities. Moreover, local juries were perceived to be the most fair alternative for defendants once the *iudicium dei* was no longer available. Defendants were nevertheless required to consent to trial by jury, sometimes under duress, in recognition of the marked shift from divine to human judgment.

Fama to facts: what juries were judging

By broadening the scope of analysis to the decades preceding Lateran IV, particularly the crucial decades between the Assize of Clarendon and the formalisation of the office of coroner in 1194, another pattern emerges that suggests a shift in emphasis from matters of reputation toward more scientifically discernible facts in the adjudication of crime. Reputation and rumor, or bad *fama*, lay at the heart of the Assize of Clarendon. In a clause reminiscent of Fletcher's manifest criminality theory, the Assize stated that anyone captured red-handed with stolen goods might be deprived of their law (i.e., not allowed to proceed to trial by ordeal). However, in a move that perhaps calls into doubt the aptness of Fletcher's principle in describing medieval law, such outlawry was predicated upon the apparent thief also being of bad repute (*diffamatus*) and having bad public testimony against him or her (*habeat malum testimonium de publicamento*).[63] Depending upon the nature of the assessment of the suspect's being of bad repute, there might well have been a broadening of the inquiry beyond the derivative question of whether or not a particular act was manifestly criminal in nature. This inquiry possibly extended to inferences regarding the mind of the manifest thief. For those men and women caught red-handed but not publicly infamous, further process was called for, namely the ordeal of water. Yet even for a person who passed the ordeal, reputation (in accordance with an assessment that might or might not be mind-related) could have further consequences. A person cleared by the ordeal might still be required to abjure the realm within forty days if found to be 'of the worst repute, and publicly and shamefully defamed by the testimony of many lawful men' (*de pessimo testimonio, et publice et turpiter diffamati testimonio multorum et legalium hominum*).[64] In extreme cases, reputation might be held dispositive if shared by a large enough number of lawful men. It is unlikely that the ordeal verdict was deemed incorrect as to the alleged crime; more likely, public safety nevertheless demanded extreme measures due to the accused's known reputation within the community. It must be admitted, however, that in some instances where evil mind was deemed relevant, it might not have attached to the specific act that generated the prosecution.

The goal of abjuration, applied here to a person acquitted by the ordeal, was purgation not of the accused individual, as was typical under ecclesiastical criminal procedure, but rather of the entire realm, which was to be cleansed of all those of condemnable *fama* who came into contact with the royal system of criminal justice. This realm-purging use of abjuration in fact continued in the years after Lateran IV, when it was used in doubtful cases where the gallows might have been too severe. At Warwick in 1222, for example, a jury acquitted Celestia of Hatton of robbery but asserted that Richard of Newnham, who was taken for the same crime, was 'a robber rather than a lawful man' (*latro sit quam legalis*).[65] The phrasing suggests some ambiguity as to whether he was known to be guilty of a specific robbery, as opposed to simply bearing a bad reputation for engagement in crime. Rather than sending Richard to the gallows, the court determined that Richard should abjure the realm 'because [the jurors] spoke uncertainly' (*quia incerte locuntur*). The jurors' ambivalence perhaps made both release and the gallows unreasonable, while abjuration ensured that if Richard were indeed an unredeemable criminal, he would no longer pose a threat within the realm.

While *fama* was greatly emphasised by the Assize of Clarendon and maintained some measure of importance in succeeding decades, other factors were given greater emphasis by the innovation of the coroner's inquest, most recently described by Sara Butler in her book *Forensic Medicine and Death Investigation in Medieval England*.[66] In cases of homicide, the coroner asked the local bailiff to summon a jury to examine the body with him and determine the probable cause of death. The coroner and inquest jurors systematically described the circumstances surrounding the death, including who had been present at the homicide, what weapon, if any, had been employed, where and when the death took place, and, if known, any possible motive for the killing. Where the Assize of Clarendon had placed reputation at the forefront of the presenting jury's obligations to report suspicious behaviour and wrongdoing, the procedure of the coroner's inquest focused instead on a factual determination related to the specific alleged crime at hand, a factual determination that might, in turn, elucidate the underlying intention of the allegedly homicidal actor.[67]

In many instances, evidence of motive was enough to raise suspicion, particularly if coupled with circumstantial evidence connecting an individual to a crime scene. In Worcester in 1221, for example, the presenting jury suspected one Robert le Bret of the homicide of Hugh of Adlestrop because of a quarrel between Robert and Hugh's brother over a church, as well as due to the fact that Robert's horses were found near the site where Hugh was killed.[68] Both motive and circumstantial evidence brought Robert under suspicion. He was ordered to be attached, but his fate at trial, if there ever was one, is unknown. In another 1221 Worcester case, a jury confidently convicted Osbert Alfolc of the death of Nicholas of Hagley, determining that he was both a robber and receiver of robbers, including the deceased, and also determining that he killed Nicholas 'so that thus he might conceal his wickedness' (*ut sic celaret iniquitatem suam*).[69] Osbert's brother, John, was also arrested for ill fame (*malo retto*) but refused a jury. Perhaps because there was nothing more than reputation to go upon, John was permitted to abjure the realm. While *fama* might suffice to bring a person of ill repute within the reach of the criminal justice system through the actions of the jury of presentment, *fama* alone does not appear to have been sufficient for a jury to convict a person of felony. Some other indicia of guilt might have been necessary, and the relatively high acquittal rate may be a testament to the typical outcome in uncertain cases.

More recently, one of us (Kamali) has explored the issue of just what the community's concept of liability for felony might have been, and most importantly, how crucial the issue of guilty mind was in that assessment.[70] She argues that mind was central to how jurors determined whether a particular defendant should be convicted, pardoned or acquitted outright. Analysing the meaning of 'felony' in medieval England's three primary languages, Kamali relates that the word was often used interchangeably with such concepts as malice, iniquity, treason and evil. Furthermore, by examining the narrative justifications for pardon recommendations, Kamali describes a default understanding of felony (applicable, she argues, to all felonies, not simply to homicide) that involved, in its paradigmatic form, three essential elements: an act that was reasoned, willed in a way not constrained by necessity, and evil or wicked in its essence. Although the law of felony was not theorised in the period under examination,[71] patterns in the plea rolls give some insight into jurors' understanding of the meaning and nature of felony. For example, jurors sometimes emphasised a defendant's lack of deliberation or premeditation, particularly when a defendant was a child or known in the community to be suffering from mental illness. In cases of accidental homicide, jurors tended to highlight the defendant's lack of felony aforethought. And in acquitting some women of crimes committed in company with their husbands, juries were inclined to focus on the husband's coercive power over his wife.[72] An examination of contemporary literature, including hortatory texts designed for the use of parish priests in instructing the laity, lends further support to the notion that understandings of guilt centred upon a person's state of mind in this period.[73]

As noted, Nicola Lacey suggests that the factors of speed in the administration of trials, the lack of argumentation by prosecution and defense, and the use of lay justice all worked against the possibility of taking *mens rea* seriously in premodern English trials. Her points have at least surface plausibility, insofar as trials were brief, courtroom argumentation appears to have been perfunctory, and indeed lay jurors were handing down verdicts from the 1220s onward. But trials were, as understood from the outset, the final step in a criminal process wherein earlier stages were brought to a culmination against the background of a possible death sentence. In cases of homicide, for example, a more sophisticated exploration of the circumstances of an alleged crime occurred earlier, through the use of a different kind of jury, the coroners' inquest. In these instances, a jury closer to the facts of the alleged crime was gathered speedily to examine the body. Combining that physical postmortem with knowledge gained either first-hand or through gossip channels within the neighborhood, the coroner's inquest produced a narrative that could in turn be read to the court if a case later proceeded to trial. Rarely do these coroners' narratives deal directly with questions of intentionality, but then it was understood, as it is still understood today, that states of mind can normally only be inferred obliquely by examining the circumstances of an allegedly criminal act. Moreover, insofar as reputation and character can provide some insight into the *likely* state of mind of an individual committing a particular act – in the way that we can assume that a person who habitually pilfers from his neighbors might be assumed to have taken a sheep with wrongful intent, and not mistakenly – then the very use of local lay jurors may have facilitated taking into account issues of mind at trial. In trials for all kinds of felonies, jurors were understood to bring with them knowledge about the defendant gained from their participation in pre-trial proceedings and informal conversations, including long-standing settled beliefs about the defendant's intent specific to the time of the act in question and/or more generally.[74] Precisely this local aspect of 'lay justice' could as easily have allowed for rough analogues to modern assessments of criminal responsibility as cut against them. Moreover, it is conceivable that this aspect of jury trial made the jury verdict more administratively attractive than judge-issued verdicts, as the latter would likely have been dependent upon an investigatory body to furnish the judge with facts, a role more efficiently filled by self-informing jurors.[75] Without the assistance of a trial jury, justices riding circuit would have only the inferences they could gain by observing the defendant in court and perhaps by reading the coroners' record to try to ascertain intentionality.

We are not compelled to assume that sheer character or reputation was core to the determination of guilt or innocence, or that mind was only evaluated as a long-term aspect of an individual's character or reputation: self-defense cases provide clear evidence that a person's state of mind at the moment of an alleged criminal act was – and was from the outset expected to be – central to jury decision-making. In fact, in self-defense cases, juries frequently made a disposition as to the accused's state of mind, i.e., whether or not he or she feared imminent death, as well as to the mind of the homicide victim, i.e., whether he or she intended to kill, or whether they harbored anger or hatred toward the self-defender. This interest in mind at the time of an act's commission comes through as well in insanity cases, which are sometimes explicit in distinguishing between long-term affliction and acute illness at the time of the alleged felony. Lindsay Farmer has alluded to the new presence of gradations of intent in the Victorian era, and it is true that in medieval England juries had nothing approaching the detail of a Victorian treatise expounding the special part of the criminal law, not to mention the Model Penal Code's differentiation of purposeful, knowing, reckless and negligent conduct today, yet this level of gradation is itself problematic, with blurring between categories intended to offer bright-line gradations of culpability.[76] At the very least, medieval English juries were well equipped to differentiate between the accidental and the deliberate, the knowing and the illness- or immaturity-induced, the deed that was (as conventionally conceived) freely willed and the act driven by exigencies that pitted a life against a life in self-defense cases. We believe that mind was generally a factor, a central one, and that this helps explain the decision to rely on local juries rather than itinerant justices to issue felony verdicts in a post-ordeal England.

Misericordia et veritas, iustitia et pax: competing criminal law priorities

Mercy and truth, justice and peace[77] were all purportedly goals of the medieval English church and the criminal justice system.[78] In the decades leading up to the transition from ordeal to trial by jury, England appears to have experienced a punitive turn while maintaining a consistent emphasis on the tempering of the severity of justice with the gift of mercy. With regard to punishment, the England of 1166 was not the England of 1220. Although capital punishment had long been one of the possible outcomes upon conviction of a serious crime, the reforms of Henry II envisioned a combination of maiming and abjuration for those convicted. Maitland notes that Henry I reintroduced the practice of hanging thieves caught in the act and observes that maiming 'became fashionable' under Henry II, although he also hanged killers and exiled traitors.[79] By the time of Henry III, a more punitive turn had occurred, resulting in capital punishment, typically death by hanging, as the sole punishment for felony. In this regard, the young Henry and his councilors were part of a broader trend in western Christendom toward a more unforgiving stance on serious crime. Like continental Europe, England was affected by the reforming ethos of Pope Innocent III (r. 1198–1216), who famously observed that it was in the interest of public utility that crimes not remain unpunished.[80] While Innocent's concern was with crime-committing clerics, his exhortation to take crime seriously had broader effects, and England's shift toward single-minded emphasis on capital punishment for felony may be one of them, or at the very least part of the same western European trend.

This is not to suggest, however, that the England of Henry III was a gruesome landscape punctuated by gallows scenes. Rather, one constant from the time of Henry II was that trial by jury, much like trial by ordeal before it,[81] was employed in a small percentage of cases, with most alleged felonies followed instead by flight leading to outlawry, abjuration or a claim of benefit of clergy. While trials were not unusual, the majority of suspected felons both in the time of Henry II and that of Henry III never stood trial. In the twelfth century, when trial by ordeal, compurgation and trial by battle predominated, and in the early thirteenth when trial by jury first took hold, only a small minority of cases proceeded to trial. If one examines any given coroner's roll, for example, one will find repeated descriptions of homicides in which the alleged perpetrator immediately fled the vicinity or took sanctuary in a nearby church. Comparing this with a typical eyre roll, produced when the royal justices finally made it through town, one finds again an enumeration of criminal accusations with the note that a person had fled and should therefore be outlawed, as well as indications that others had taken sanctuary and in many instances abjured the realm. William Chester Jordan's recent book on abjuration reveals a France and broader continental Europe that was a world of exiles, with thousands of English abjurors living in coastal France, as well as countless intracontinental exiles biding their time and waiting for word of reconciliation as a prelude to repatriation once passions had cooled.[82]

Indeed, by the time that jury trial was adopted, it had already long been the case that most of those accused or suspected of crime completely eluded prosecution through flight. Without anything like a system of policing, aside from night watch in cities and towns and the informal system of hue and cry elsewhere, many individuals might commit thefts and homicide and evade detection altogether. In other instances, having had witnesses to the event, or perhaps fearing suspicion due to a past history of wrongdoing or disrepute in the community, an individual might flee the locality altogether. Many of these flights were never resolved, as far as we can tell from the surviving record. In rare instances, a jury might determine that a person who had fled was not actually guilty or even suspected of complicity in an alleged crime, in which case the surviving record might note that the former suspect could return to the community, only forfeiting his or her movable goods as a consequence of taking flight in the first place. The existence of these invitations to return suggests that in some cases where accused individuals fled, they managed to maintain lines of communication with relatives or friends in the locality.

As noted, in some instances of flight, an accused or suspected individual might take sanctuary in the nearest church. Within forty days, they had the option of agreeing to stand trial, or alternatively of confessing their crime to the local coroner, who would then make arrangements for the confessed felon to walk barefoot to an assigned port of departure to abjure the English realm entirely. In yet other cases, individuals might claim benefit of clergy, alleging that due to their clerical status, they could not rightfully be prosecuted in a royal court but should instead be handed over to ecclesiastical authorities. This removed the case from the royal into the ecclesiastical courts where, subject to ecclesiastical sanctions, such individuals escaped the threat of the death penalty. Before handing a cleric over to his ordinary, however, the royal court would subject him to a form of perfunctory trial in which a jury would issue a verdict as to his guilt or innocence. This may be a holdover from the jurisdictional tensions dating back to the Henry II-Becket controversy, reflecting a twelfth-century compromise that held fast straight through to the expansion of clergy in the fifteenth century. Alternatively, or perhaps in addition, it may reflect something about the understanding of the role of trial juries within the community. Insisting that a cleric be handed over as guilty or acquitted, as opposed to entirely untried, enabled representatives of the community to reach their own determination of his guilt or innocence and to have this recorded officially on the plea roll. What mattered was the communicative aspect of this mini-trial, both with regard to the practicalities of recidivism (i.e., having a record of a past conviction if a cleric should reoffend)[83] and with regard to bringing an accusation to a resolution satisfactory to the community, even if it could not be followed up with the imposition of punishment for those found guilty.

When trial by ordeal was still a primary means of adjudicating felony cases prior to Lateran IV, these were all available 'escape valves' enabling suspects to avoid or mitigate the consequences of a felony conviction. When trial by jury replaced trial by ordeal, there was no discussion of closing off these escape valves. Rather, the presumption seems to have been, at the outset, that only a small subset of suspects would ever stand trial. Albeit to a lesser extent, jury trial, just like trial by fire or water, was the exception rather than the norm. This is not to imply that the adoption of trial by jury therefore raised few concerns, but rather that it was situated in a context of escape valves that existed prior to the ordeal's abolition, and that were expected to continue following the post-ordeal transition.

Justices as presiders, not deciders

For those cases that did proceed to trial, a defendant appeared before justices and jurors alike, who determined his or her fate. A remaining question is how justices and jurors interacted with each other, an issue regarding which we can turn to the honourand of this festschrift for guidance. In a 2016 article, Paul Brand revisited the provocative argument made by David

Millon in 1989 that the outcome of medieval and early modern civil litigation was driven by the normative, discretionary leanings of juries as opposed to the comparatively 'official' legal doctrine reflected in the law reports and readings from the Inns of Court.[84] Millon had argued that civil procedure minimized the involvement of justices in the resolution of legal controversies, placing instead great discretionary power in the hands of the jurors.[85] Examining the evidence, Brand concluded that Millon's model greatly underestimated the extent of judicial control over juries in the period around 1300, and likely in later times as well.[86] The questions posed by Millon and Brand regarding the civil jury might easily be extended to the criminal trial jury, but the answers are likely to be quite different, as Brand himself acknowledges. Brand sketches a few reasons for thinking that criminal juries might have had greater control of judicial outcomes than their civil counterparts: the jury verdict was more centrally important in criminal cases, there was no real preliminary pleading stage, professional lawyers typically did not participate, and there existed a greater urgency in criminal than in civil cases for jurors to engage in 'bending the facts to achieve a "just" result'.[87] Lives, rather than simply property interests, were at stake.

The question of justice-jury interaction also stands at the fore of the ordeal story with which we opened this essay. The twelve knights in that tale were reprimanded by the justices for issuing a wrongful judgment when they condemned a woman accused of homicide to death. In fact, the justices fined the knights, despite the fact that the woman's hand healed after the initial verdict thanks to the intervention of a local saint, an intervention that the knights could not have anticipated when they first examined the woman's hand after administration of the hot iron. The story suggests that justices might be heavy-handed in intervening when they believed that a jury had issued a wrongful felony verdict. Some Year Book evidence supports – at least for a later date – such a vision of justice-jury relations: occasionally the Year Books record justices reacting with hostility toward a jury that had decided to acquit, demanding that the jurors name the actual guilty party in light of the manifest nature of the underlying crime.[88] However, these seem to be outlier cases, perhaps recorded in the Year Books because they were noteworthy. Closer to our own moment of interest, the *Bracton* treatise describes the practice of justices questioning the jurors separately to discern the truth, but this is intended to be an extreme measure undertaken, for example, 'where a serious crime is being concealed and the jurors intend to hide the truth through love, hatred or fear'.[89] Evidence of consistent intervention by justices to affect the outcome of jury decision-making, or to try to modify a verdict after the fact, is scant. Similarly, the process of attaint was unavailable in felony cases. The assumption at the outset appears to have been that juries were typically to hand down felony verdicts without interference and without fear of reprisals should the justices disagree with the outcome.

Even if justices did not manhandle jurors, they may have sometimes used their persuasive powers directly against defendants, particularly before a jury had been tasked with issuing a verdict. *Placita Corone*, a thirteenth-century treatise on private appeals of felony, describes justices compelling poorly advised defendants to confess to felony.[90] The Year Books also provide some evidence of judicial heavy-handedness directed toward recalcitrant defendants rather than jurors: when Isabel of Bury was accused of homicide in the 1321 London Eyre, for example, she stood mute before the justices. A jury of twelve was sworn to testify as to whether or not she was mute of malice. Upon taking the oath, the jurors left the room to deliberate. Justice Passeley, in the meanwhile, advised Isabel: 'You would do better to speak, for if we hold an inquest and find that you can speak you will not be permitted to challenge the jurors'. He continued, 'So speak and put yourself on a jury and you will be acquitted'. Moved, no doubt, by the promise of an acquittal, Isabel responded, 'Sir, mercy for God's sake!' The jurors were immediately recalled. After a brief trial, Isabel was hanged.[91] In these examples from a later date, we have significant evidence of justices occasionally interacting forcefully with criminal defendants. This stands in contrast to the comparably thin evidence across the entire period of justices manipulating juries to reach desired verdicts. In line with Brand's speculation, we conclude that judges indeed allowed criminal trial juries more freedom in issuing verdicts than civil juries.

Justice-jury consensus or acquiescence

We turn finally to a related and culminating question, namely, the extent to which justices agreed with or merely acquiesced to the high rate of felony acquittals and recommendations for pardon that proceeded from jury trials for felony. Examining this issue has heretofore involved looking beyond the initial post–Lateran IV years and into the later thirteenth and fourteenth centuries. In *Verdict According to Conscience*, Green compared coroners' indictments with trial records for self-defense cases, finding evidence of trial jury manipulation of facts to place some defendants in a sympathetic light, ultimately resulting in a self-defense verdict and access to a royal pardon.[92] By modifying the narrative at trial, jurors manufactured a distinction (generally including an assessment of the nature of intentionality) between 'simple' homicide, or manslaughter, and murder, a distinction not yet made formally in the law.[93] In this way, the jury imposed 'the community's – or the communities' – concepts of liability for felony' upon the courts.[94] Green further argues that justices, already dependent on juries for information on an alleged crime and on the credibility of witnesses, seemed ready to (or had little choice but to) acquiesce to nullification.[95] John Bellamy suggests thinking of this as justice-jury 'consensus' rather than acquiescence by justices to jury nullification.[96] Favouring the consensus model is the idea that justices and jurors, while not of equivalent social standing, nevertheless were consumers of the same kinds of cultural messages about the dangers of judging and the importance of mercy. Conceivably, the lack of consistent intervention by justices to rein in merciful jury verdicts may reflect shared values and may also have been exacerbated by the exigencies of felony, most notably the fact that a conviction led to the gallows.

The distinction between 'consensus' and 'acquiescence' bears further consideration, for it has possible ramifications with regard to original assumptions both about the role of the trial jury as a mechanism for guilt assessment and about the very nature of the law of felony. In exploring this distinction, we engage in some speculation, and we are well aware that it might not accord at points with the intuitions of the honourand, who will have the opportunity to set matters straight in his forthcoming volume on the law in thirteenth-century England.

As noted, Bellamy drew a distinction between consensus and nullification. In fact, he might have considered consensus and acquiescence as at least roughly the same in nature, both standing in contradistinction to the concept of nullification. In some instances, the bench might fully agree with the jury's verdict of acquittal or pardonable circumstances (consensus), while in others the bench might disagree with the jury's verdict but nevertheless acquiesce to it with relative equanimity. In Bellamy's view, we infer, the term 'nullification' would not apply in either of these situations, nor in those that lay between them. This, in turn, would leave a (possibly small) number of instances in which the bench strongly disagreed with a verdict but could do nothing about the matter, finally accepting the verdict, but with disquietude rather than equanimity, and possibly after having first tried to induce the defendant to confess or the jury to reconsider. We suppose that these select and likely rare instances would amount to nullification in Bellamy's view.

We view the matter somewhat differently, but readily admit that much depends both upon the proportions of the varying instances of consensus, acquiescence and nullification as we have defined them, and – perhaps more importantly – upon how the historian views the question of what constituted 'the law'. To take the latter issue first: it might be the case that the operative law was not in fact the 'black letter' law as reflected in either the seemingly all-encompassing law of theft or, in homicide, as implied by the strict language employed in what became pardons *de cursu*, or in the passages from *Bracton* that Green focused on in his own work of four decades ago.[97] Rather, the true – or operative – law was, on this view, the gloss that juries put on that language, at least up to the point that the bench found minimally acceptable, even though it lacked the power to enforce its view. Beyond that point – and only beyond it – lay true nullification.

We think there is something to this view, at least so far as true consensus was involved. Though even then, one might say that the law was the black letter, and that instances of consensus represented nullification undertaken jointly by juries and justices. It is possible that such joint nullification was expected and deemed appropriate from the outset of the adoption of trial by jury, or that actual experience with jury trial in its first decades forced a need to confront a matter not anticipated at the outset. On this view, the many instances of juries exercising mercy contrary to the wishes of the justices, but to which the justices nevertheless acquiesced, would *a fortiori* qualify as nullifications, just as would, of course, those instances in which judges strongly disagreed and did not truly acquiesce, but could do little more than record the verdict and move on to the next case. Green referred to many such nullifications as mere nullification of sanction, not nullification of the underlying law. This would be especially true in theft, whereas homicide presents a more complicated picture: with homicide, it is difficult to determine whether, in particular instances, a jury was consciously invoking a socially accepted distinction between what we would call 'manslaughter' and what we would call 'murder' (not yet an official legal distinction) or merely exercising mercy as a simple nullification of sanction. Assuming these two motivations are truly distinct, then at the outset, the crown and bench might have consented or acquiesced to simple mercy while not recognizing in law the lay distinction between manslaughter and murder.

Bellamy briefly but lucidly reviews the process by which 'murder' and 'simple homicide', formerly separate species of felony (the former being unemendable, the latter not), came to be conjoined and equally unemendable in the later twelfth century and remained capital felonies at the time of the adoption of the trial jury and for centuries thereafter.[98] As Bellamy's pioneering research demonstrates, a distinction between the two re-emerged by the late thirteenth century by way of the language – various forms of 'murder' – employed to describe particularly heinous slayings and, more crucially, in the mid-fourteenth century, by way of language – various forms of '*impetuose*' – employed with respect to slayings in the nature of what had been 'simple homicide', for which the king could grant a pardon of grace. As Bellamy notes, the crown insisted upon treating the two anciently separate forms as one for purposes of indictment (at least before 1390), culpability at trial and (absent a pardon) punishment. We believe (and Bellamy might agree) that early as well as subsequent jury verdicts often in fact reflected an ongoing social distinction in tension with the formal law of homicide. We think it possible that, as of the time of adoption of the trial jury, the crown and bench anticipated something of this sort. Quite possibly they were prepared to tolerate it up to a point, that is, as a matter of social assessment of death-worthiness alongside other bases for mercy, but not as an instantiation of anything that might have the appearance, especially to prospective offenders, of a rule of law. This assessment of death-worthiness was reflected as well in theft, although without a comparable historical tradition of a legal recognition of different categories to lean on.

Kamali's study of the meaning of felony has significant bearing on historians' best guesses about the crown and bench's understanding of the role of the jury in applying the criminal law. One might hypothesise that the law was meant to be interpreted and applied in a manner consistent with the threshold meaning of felony, as outlined above,[99] and not more broadly. This would likely mean that some slayers and some thieves who seemed to be culpable under the formal law[100] were not in fact meant to be held liable, but that only a jury could make such a determination, case by case. Only juries, on this view, were empowered to decide life or death based upon an assessment of the mind and heart of someone it believed had committed a certain act. Taken to its logical conclusion, this might leave no room for the idea of nullification, the very definition of lawful/unlawful (as opposed to the question of death-worthiness in particular cases) being ultimately in the hands of the jury. Juries, in other words, (on this view) virtually determined the bounds of the law of felony.

We do not believe that contemporaries, whether officials or lay persons, thought about the standing law in this fashion, even if they did recognise that jurors imported a more flexible reading and application of the formal law. First, we doubt that all 'merciful' verdicts reflected a conclusion that the defendant lacked the necessary felonious intent: there were many other reasons for the exoneration of defendants, some being squarely outside any interpretation of the meaning of 'law'. Second, jurors were bound to have their own (e.g., contrary to the formal law) views regarding death-worthiness, even with respect to those they believed had acted unlawfully to the level of felony. One might suppose, of course, that the crown and bench expected – and accepted – some leeway for juries, for they might well have worried about whether the life or death question formerly put to God could, under God, be put to fellow humans, even though, as we have noted, doing so was not entirely novel. They likely worried as well, however, whether it was safe from a law and order perspective to generalise the practice: could limits be placed reliably on such 'leeway'? Both of these cross-cutting considerations might explain the hesitancy implicit in the crown's initial guidance to itinerant justices in the wake of Lateran IV. The use of presenters (knights and/or 'lawful men') as trial jurors – the *modus operandi* at the outset – probably seemed the least novel and most safe replacement for ordeal. This arrangement might in fact have resulted in relatively substantial justice-jury consensus in the first decades after 1219–20. Here, we move away from the question of what the operative law was, to the interrelated question of the proportions of consensus versus acquiescence to nullification of the capital sanction.

James Whitman has set forth an innovative theory that sheds further possible light on the decision to employ lay jurors: doing so relieved the bench of the responsibility for determining guilt in cases involving blood sanctions.[101] This might also explain jurors' merciful verdicts, or at least some measure of them: the hypothesis would be that jurors demanded a high standard of proof to avoid condemning themselves before God by issuing a false verdict of guilty and, in light of Kamali's work, that standard often turned on the state of a defendant's mind and heart. If one accepts the latter side – the jury side – of this hypothesis as reasonable for the historian to entertain, that acceptance carries with it the implication that crown and bench likely anticipated (and accepted) it at the outset. Assuming justices shared this anticipation (and acceptance), this might also condition one's understanding of the proportion of true judicial consensus versus mere judicial acquiescence in the earliest period of the criminal trial jury. Finally, while we are inclined to think that such anticipation (and acceptance) indeed expanded the domain of consensus, we concede that the historian might conclude alternatively that, in the face of this anticipation (but without much acceptance), the bench was both glad to be relieved of responsibility in blood-sanction cases and insistent upon jurors fearlessly bearing that burden alone.

Conclusion

Medieval English jurors exercised some measure of de facto independence in issuing felony verdicts. They did not have the benefit of a prosecutor outlining the elements of a particular offense and demonstrating the various ways in which the defendant before them met those elements through his or her behaviour and state of mind. They may not have had even the benefit of much guidance from the bench, although observations of appellors stating their cases in private appeals and of justices interrogating defendants, in addition to contemplation of questions directed by the bench toward the jury, may have helped clarify for jurors the bounds of the formal law, what little law there was. Aside from this, jurors engaged their own moral compasses, including their sense of the boundaries of guilt and innocence, and of the boundaries between guilt that made one liable to the exigencies of undergoing the criminal trial process, as compared with the level of guilt that sufficed to make someone deserving of the gallows. For these understandings of the boundaries, the gradations of guilt, the legal historian must necessarily assess the broader cultural and social milieu in which notions of guilt and innocence were constructed. This implies, of course, a daunting endeavor, albeit a rewarding one as it promises a recovery of the law in its fullest sense: what criminal responsibility actually amounted to in medieval England. It requires venturing into the world of sermons, morality tales, vernacular poetry and popular literature, all central components of Kamali's recent study of felony. The age in which the criminal trial jury came into its own was the age of confession in medieval England and Europe more broadly, an age of confessors' manuals, of sermon exempla to assist parish priests in teaching the faithful, of vernacular literature focused on personification of the virtues and vices and tales of fictional persons whose lives might exemplify how – or how not (those were the more entertaining tales) – to live a virtuous Christian life. It was, of course, the age of Thomas Aquinas and his morality of intention, although Aquinas, who was born just as England was adopting trial by jury for felony, was part of a much older and larger movement of theologians dedicated to the adaptation of Aristotelian principles to the mission of understanding human subjectivity and the nature of intellect, emotion and will. It was an age in which mind mattered.

To summarise some of this essay's conclusions, we note first that the step toward using trial juries was an almost natural extension of the use of juries elsewhere in the English criminal justice system. Replacing God with man as the source of a final verdict was significant, thereby requiring defendants' consent, but nevertheless was not necessarily viewed as a revolutionary move in the minds of governing authorities. Local jurors were perceived to be essential to the information-gathering required to try alleged felons, and the use of high-status presenters eased concerns over the trustworthiness and reliability of participants in the criminal trial process. The leeway afforded to presenters in sorting out which suspects should face trial by ordeal suggests that two primary factors were at play: 'the law', and the issue of trial-worthiness. The latter, in turn, involved an assessment of the degree of evidence against the accused, including the state of his or her mind and heart, *fama*, and perceived threat to the community.

Allowing presenting jurors to issue verdicts at trial added a further twist: now humans were pronouncing definitive guilt – rather than leaving that to the ordeal – and doing so against the backdrop of the death penalty.[102] At the outset, the expectation was likely that jurors would legitimately be granted some leeway, without necessarily calling into question the state of 'the law' itself. However, verdicts very soon shaded into patterns falling outside the bounds of the expected range of leeway, resulting in what we would call nullification. For example, generous application of the strict rules of self-defense was one matter, while allowing something that looked more like a hot-blooded homicide (what would later be called 'manslaughter') to qualify as pardonable self-defense was another. Merciful acquittals of suspected thieves who appropriated stolen goods *animus furandi* was also nullification (at least of the legal sanction), although here, too, the facts of mind and heart were matters of degree. A shift from mercy within the law to mercy outside the law might have played havoc with the assumption that consensus between justices and jurors would dominate, resulting instead in what appears to have been forced acquiescence.

From the outset, the jury trial system exhibited a fundamental potential for instability. This potential was initially mitigated by the use of high-status presenters, and appears to have been partly accepted as a cost of placing the weighty responsibility for pronouncements of guilt upon laymen. One cannot be certain, but this is our best guess based on the surviving evidence c. 1220. Of course, what ensued across the remainder of the thirteenth and into the fourteenth centuries – increasing social mobility, men returning from military service, formation of household retainers, etc., alongside institutional developments occasioning change in the composition of trial juries – produced a situation that cannot be read back into the original assumptions.

Why authorities stayed with the trial jury in those later times remains an important question. Kamali's current research adds an account of the cultural factors that held jury trial in place to the social, institutional and 'constitutional' factors identified by Green forty years ago. For our purposes in this essay, the various factors provide a framework for thinking about the perhaps unthinkable: just what did authorities have in mind (if anything much) at the time of the trial jury's adoption?

For us, this essay is less a forum for the expression of our own tentative suppositions than an opportunity to set an agenda for further work – by ourselves and others – on one of the fundamental problems in the early history of common-law criminal justice. We are by no means confident that the problem of 'original assumptions' regarding the adoption of trial by jury will ever move from the status of a subject for best guesses and multiple plausible hypotheses to a settled matter. We believe, however (and hope our beliefs will pass the *iudicium Pauli*), that banging one's head against an impenetrable wall is an important and enjoyable part of doing history, and that merely posing questions and generating hypotheses can in this instance, as in others, contribute to historical understanding, albeit an understanding viewed only through a glass darkly.

Notes

1 The authors would like to thank Andrew Crespo, Christine Desan, Charles Donahue, John Goldberg, Richard Helmholz, Genevieve Lakier, Adriaan Lanni, Thomas McSweeney, Daphna Renan, John Rappoport, Jonathan Rose, Jocelyn Simonson, Henry Smith, Matthew Stephenson and Crystal Yang for their comments on an earlier draft. Some of the historiography to follow has been borrowed from Elizabeth Papp Kamali, 'A Felonious State of Mind: Mens Rea in Thirteenth- and Fourteenth-Century England', PhD diss., University of Michigan, 2015.

2 *Lawsuits*, 2: 558–9. Van Caenegem dates the tale to 1177, but it may possibly reflect events from as late as 1208 or 1210, the dates of two York eyres. See Christopher Norton, *St. William of York* (Woodbridge, Suffolk: York Medieval Press, 2006), 168–9. In either case, the ordeal miracle purportedly predates Lateran IV. It is recorded in a miracle collection copied from a fourteenth-century tryptich by seventeenth-century antiquarian Roger Dodsworth. See James Raine, ed., *The Historians of the Church of York and Its Archbishops* (London: Longman, 1886), 2: xxxi. For an extended analysis of this story and its implications for the history of the transition from ordeal to jury trial, see Elizabeth Papp Kamali, 'Trial by Ordeal by Jury In Medieval England, or Saints and Sinners in Literature and Law', in *Emotion, Violence, Vengeance and Law in the Middle Ages: Essays in Honour of William Ian Miller*, eds. Kate Gilbert and Stephen D. White (forthcoming).

3 As opposed to a priest or other officials. On the issuance of ordeal verdicts, see Robert Bartlett, *Trial by Fire and Water: The Medieval Judicial Ordeal* (Oxford: Oxford University Press, 1986; repr. Brattleboro, VT: Echo Point, 2014), 23 (describing, in a twelfth-century French case, how angry crowds might issue an immediate 'verdict' in trial by cold water, lynching the accused immediately rather than waiting for the bishop's council to finish conferring), 41 (relaying how ordeals were generally presided over 'by ecclesiastics, royal officials, and lords, not by the small face-to-face communities from which plaintiffs or accused might emerge'.) For an important, recent analysis of the ordeal, arguing for the efficiency of ordeal procedure in societies with widespread belief in the

iudicium dei, see Peter T. Leeson, 'Ordeals', *Journal of Law and Economics* 55 (2012): 691–714.

4 With some limited exceptions. Mayhem, or serious wounding, might be prosecuted privately as a felony but would not be subject to a capital sanction in the early decades of the criminal trial jury, even as late as the mid-thirteenth century. See, e.g., JUST1/565 AALT 7590 (1250), http://aalt.law.uh.edu/AALT4/JUST1/JUST1no565/bJUST1no565dorses/IMG_7590.htm. This case from the 1250 Norfolk eyre relates a private accusation of wounding and mayhem brought by Ralph Chevre against Philip de Verly. Although the initial appeal failed, a jury was called upon to issue a verdict. It found Philip guilty of the accusations brought in the appeal, and he was compelled to pay a fine of two marks. For Bellamy's discussion of mayhem, see J.G. Bellamy, *The Criminal Trial in Later Medieval England* (Toronto: University of Toronto Press, 1998), 189. Rape, too, at times was subject to corporal but not capital punishment. See, e.g., J.M. Kaye, ed., *Placita Corone, or La Corone Pledee devant Justices* (London: Bernard Quaritch, 1966), 9 (describing blinding, castration or both as possible punishments for a conviction of felonious rape, with the actual punishment left to the justice's discretion). See also P&M, 2: 488 (arguing that those appealed of wounding or mayhem 'seldom, if ever, lost life and seldom lost member').

5 Stubbs, *Charters*, 170.

6 Ibid., 179.

7 For a recent study of the office of coroner, see Sara M. Butler, *Forensic Medicine and Death Investigation in Medieval England* (New York: Routledge, 2014).

8 H.C. Maxwell Lyte, ed., *Patent Rolls of the Reign of Henry III, A.D. 1216–1225* (London: Mackie & Co., 1901), 186.

9 The letter oddly fails to cover several bases. As Tom McSweeney pointed out to us, it is unclear what would happen to a person suspected of a serious crime but believed to be innocent, or of a minor crime and believed to be manifestly guilty. The use of the conjunctive may by symptomatic of sloppy drafting, or may instead reflect a lack of attention to detail driven by the fact that justices were expected to exercise discretion during the transition from trial by ordeal. Other possibilities, of course, exist as well; for example, perhaps there was an earlier order via oral directive to the justices, or even an earlier written order that has since been lost.

10 See *CRR*, 8: 80–1. See also Roger D. Groot, 'The Early Thirteenth-Century Criminal Jury', in *Twelve Good Men and True: The Criminal Trial Jury in England, 1200–1800*, eds. J.S. Cockburn and Thomas A. Green (Princeton: Princeton University Press, 1988), 16–17.

11 For as detailed a study of the earliest use of trial juries to determine guilt or innocence as we now have, see Roger D. Groot, 'Teaching Each Other: Judges, Clerks, Jurors and Malefactors Define the Guilt/Innocence Jury', in *Learning the Law: Teaching and the Transmission of Law in England, 1150–1900*, eds. Jonathan A. Bush and Alain Wijffels (London: Hambledon Press, 1999), 17–32.

12 We do not entirely rule out the possibility that the jury verdict was viewed, in some sense, as a new form of *iudicium dei*. However, the church's proscription of clerical involvement in the ordeal, and the arguments against the ordeal leading up to its abolition, push in favour of the idea that jury verdicts were understood as categorically different from the controversial method of proof that had preceded them. Admittedly, theological arguments against the ordeal would not have been as well known to society at large. Nonetheless, society was exposed to anti-ordeal sentiment through the medium of literature, including literary tales of manipulated ordeals and hagiographical stories of saints intervening to correct ordeal outcomes. See Kamali, Trial by Ordeal by Jury.

13 This is not to suggest that scholarship does not exist on the topic of medieval *mens rea*. See, e.g., Francis Bowes Sayre, 'Mens Rea', *Harvard Law Review* 45 (1932): 974–87. By and large, however, accounts of the medieval English criminal law have tended to be more focused on institutional and procedural developments, such as jury trial and the royal pardon, as opposed to the nature of criminal responsibility itself.

14 George Fletcher, *Rethinking Criminal Law* (Boston: Little, Brown, 1978), 121–2. Fletcher argues that homicide does not necessarily follow the manifest to subjective criminality pattern because the focus for the analysis of liability is on the existence of the harm itself, not merely a dangerous act or an intent to harm. See also ibid., 235. Nicola Lacey has adopted and adapted Fletcher's model, making the case for an intermediate stage of development between manifest and subjective criminality in which a jury's judgments of character were used to compensate for increasingly indirect knowledge of the underlying conduct at issue in a case. See Nicola Lacey, 'In Search of the Responsible Subject: History, Philosophy and Social Sciences in Criminal Law Theory', *Modern Law Review* 64 (2001): 361. See also Nicola Lacey, *In Search of Criminal Responsibility: Ideas, Interests, and Institutions* (Oxford: Oxford University Press, 2016), 37–9.

15 Fletcher, *Rethinking*, 115.

16 Ibid., 115–16.

17 Ibid., 117.

18 Ibid., 117.

19 Ibid., 117.

20 On this issue, see, generally, Kamali, 'A Felonious State of Mind'.

21 Lindsay Farmer, 'Bringing Cinderella to the Ball: Teaching Criminal Law in Context', Review of Alan Norrie, *Crime Reason and History: A Critical Introduction to Criminal Law* (London: Weidenfeld & Nicolson, 1993), in *Modern Law Review* 58 (1995): 762.

22 Farmer, 'Bringing Cinderella', 762.

23 Ibid., 762.

24 See, generally, Kamali, 'A Felonious State of Mind', 294–323.

25 See, generally, ibid., 317–23.

26 Fletcher, *Rethinking*, 118.

27 Farmer, 'Bringing Cinderella', 762.

28 Fletcher, *Rethinking*, 118. This dualistic understanding of mind and body, of course, has ancient roots. See, e.g., Cicero, *Tusculan Disputations*, trans. C.D. Yonge (New York: Harper, 1890), 91–3.

29 See ibid., 240.

30 On acquittal and conviction rates in ordeals and in later jury trials, see, respectively, Margaret H. Kerr, Richard D. Forsyth and Michael J. Plysley, 'Cold Water and Hot Iron: Trial by Ordeal in England', *The Journal of Interdisciplinary History* 22 (1992): 580, 588–9; Bellamy, *Criminal Trial in Later Medieval England*, 95–8.

31 Nicola Lacey, *Women, Crime, and Character* (Oxford: Oxford University Press, 2008), 13.

32 Ibid., 14.

33 Ibid., 17–18. On the meaning of *animus furandi*, which did not refer to a subjective state of mind in Lacey's view, see also Lacey, *In Search of Criminal Responsibility*, 93–9. Focusing on Blackstone's *Commentaries*, Simon Stern is similarly inclined to downplay the centrality of *mens rea* in eighteenth-century thought, although he emphasises Blackstone's focus on issues of capacity, not character. See Simon Stern, 'Blackstone's Criminal Law: Common-Law Harmonization and Legislative Reform', in *Foundational Texts in Modern Criminal Law*, ed. Markus D. Dubber (Oxford: Oxford University Press, 2014), 65–9.

34 See Lacey, *Women, Crime, and Character*, 5.
35 See infra, 65–6.
36 Farmer, 'Bringing Cinderella', 762 (emphasis ours).
37 See, generally, chapter two of Kamali, 'A Felonious State of Mind'.
38 See, e.g., Elizabeth Papp Kamali, '*Felonia Felonice Facta:* Felony and Intentionality in Medieval England', *Criminal Law and Philosophy* 9 (2015): 405–6.
39 See Ralph B. Pugh, *Wiltshire Gaol Delivery and Trailbaston Trials, 1275–1306* (Devizes: Wiltshire Record Society, 1978), 84–5.
40 See, e.g., Kamali, '*Felonia Felonice Facta*', 404–5.
41 See, e.g., Green, *Verdict*, 53–5.
42 See, e.g., ibid., 53–5.
43 See, e.g., ibid., 59–64. For broader cultural evidence of attitudes toward theft, see Kamali, 'A Felonious State of Mind', 265–88.
44 See, e.g., the acquittal of several men for robbery, when it was found by the jury that they had been trying to distrain the allegedly stolen goods, and did not act with the intention of committing robbery (*non animo ipsum robandi*). Henry Summerson, ed., *Crown Pleas of the Devon Eyre of 1238* (Torquay: Devonshire Press, 1985), 87 (discussed in Kamali, 'A Felonious State of Mind', 266).
45 See Margaret H. Kerr, 'Angevin Reform of the Appeal of Felony', *LHR* 13 (1995): 383. See also Daniel Klerman, 'Settlement and the Decline of Private Prosecution in Thirteenth-Century England', *LHR* 19 (2001): 1–65 (describing decreasing rates of private prosecutions following periods in which justices declined to respect settlements, and positing canon law influence on the shift toward prosecuting crimes despite a previous settlement).
46 See Green, *Verdict*, 4. See also Green, 'A Retrospective on the Criminal Trial Jury, 1200–1800', in *Twelve Good Men and True*, 359.
47 See, generally, Roger D. Groot, 'The Jury in Private Criminal Prosecutions Before 1215', *AJLH* 27 (1983): 113–41. See also Groot, 'The Jury of Presentment Before 1215', *AJLH* 26 (1982): 1–24.
48 Groot, 'Jury in Private Criminal Prosecutions', 125. See also Elsa de Haas and G.D.G. Hall, eds., *Early Registers of Writs* (London: Bernard Quaritch, 1970), 190 (writ instructing the sheriff to assemble an inquest to determine whether an accused individual was accused 'by hate and spite or because he is guilty thereof' (*odio et atya an eo quod inde culpabilis sit*), suggesting that juries might be called upon to speak to actual guilt as opposed to simply the motivation of the accuser, although one found guilty would still stand trial.
49 Groot, 'Jury in Private Criminal Prosecutions', 141. See also Alan Harding, *Medieval Law and the Foundations of the State* (Oxford: Oxford University Press, 2002), 136–7. On juries not convicting, see Groot, 'Early Thirteenth-Century Criminal Jury', 9. For the extension of jury use to the issuance of final verdicts of guilt or innocence, see Groot, 'Teaching Each Other', 18–30.
50 See James Fitzjames Stephen, *A History of the Criminal Law of England* (London: Macmillan, 1883), 1: 256–7. Stephen cites, in turn, Francis Palgrave, who provides an example from the ninth year of John's reign. See Francis Palgrave, *The Rise and Progress of the English Commonwealth*, Part II (Proofs and Illustrations) (London: John Murray, 1832), clxxxvi.
51 See, e.g., cases 81 through 84 from the 1202 Assize of Northamptonshire. *Northants*, 18 (describing payment of fines 'to have an inquest regarding what repute he is (*pro habenda inquisitione de quo testimonio sit*)').
52 See Groot, 'Teaching Each Other', 25–9.
53 See James Masschaele, *Jury, State, and Society in Medieval England* (New York: Palgrave Macmillan, 2008), 207. For the argument that jurors can more accurately be described as witnesses than judges, see Mike Macnair, 'Vicinage and the Antecedents of the Jury', *LHR* 17 (1999): 538, 540.

54 Anthony Musson, 'Twelve Good Men and True? The Character of Early Fourteenth-Century Juries', *LHR* 15 (1997): 135–7. This would change by statute in 1352. See, Daniel Klerman, 'Was the Jury Ever Self Informing?', in *Judicial Tribunals in England and Europe, 1200–1700*, eds. Maureen Mulholland and Brian Pullan (Manchester: Manchester University Press, 2003), 75.

55 Klerman, 'Was the Jury Ever Self Informing?', 59–60.

56 Ibid., 60.

57 *Bracton*, 2: 405.

58 The record relates that the defendant paid the king 'half a mark to have the verdict of the country whether he was guilty or appealed through hate and spite' (*dimidiam marcam pro habendo veredicto patrie si ipse sit inde culpabilis vel appellatus per odium et atyam predictam*). Doris M. Stenton, ed., *Rolls of the Justices in Eyre, 3 Henry III, 1218–1219* (London: Bernard Quaritch, 1937), 224.

59 Stenton, *Rolls of the Justices in Eyre, 1218–1219*, 224–5.

60 Doris M. Stenton, ed., *Rolls of the Justices in Eyre for Gloucestershire, Warwickshire and Staffordshire, 1221, 1222* (London: Bernard Quaritch, 1940), 373.

61 M.T. Clanchy, ed., *The Roll and Writ File of the Berkshire Eyre of 1248* (London: Selden Society, 1973), 394.

62 *Bracton*, 2: 405.

63 Stubbs, *Charters*, 171.

64 Ibid., 172.

65 Stenton, ed., *Rolls of the Justices in Eyre for Gloucestershire, Warwickshire and Staffordshire, 1221, 1222*, 623–4.

66 See, generally, Butler, *Forensic Medicine and Death Investigation*, 125–75, for a discussion of the investigatory process undertaken by coroners and their juries.

67 This issue is the subject of chapter 4 in Kamali, 'A Felonious State of Mind'.

68 Doris M. Stenton, ed., *Rolls of the Justices in Eyre for Lincolnshire 1218–9 and Worcestershire 1221* (London: Bernard Quaritch, 1934), 548.

69 Stenton, ed., *Lincolnshire 1218–9 and Worcestershire 1221*, no. 1208, 588–9. For the MS image, see JUST1/1021 AALT 1793 (1221), http://aalt.law.uh.edu/AALT4/JUST1/JUST1no1021/aJUST1no1021fronts/IMG_1793.htm.

70 See, generally, Kamali, 'A Felonious State of Mind'. See also Kamali, '*Felonia Felonice Facta*', 397–421.

71 See, e.g., the cursory treatment of categories of crime in the late twelfth-century treatise known as *Glanvill*, which divides homicide into two varieties, murder (*murdrum*) and simple homicide (*simplex homicidium*) and states that 'the crime of robbery need not be discussed, for it raises no special problems'. *Glanvill*, 174–5.

72 See Kamali, 'A Felonious State of Mind', 87–99.

73 See, generally, chapter 4 in Kamali, 'A Felonious State of Mind'.

74 On this self-informing nature of criminal juries, see Daniel Klerman, 'Was the Jury Ever Self Informing?'.

75 This, of course, leaves open the related question, which lies beyond the scope of this paper, as to why England did not follow the continental European (and ecclesiastical) example by hiring notaries and having them, in turn, question local individuals on oath to create a body of testimony for use by judges.

76 See Matthew R. Ginther et al., 'The Language of Mens Rea', *Vanderbilt Law Review* 67 (2014): 1327–64.

77 A reference to the Vulgate Psalm 84:11 (*misericordia et veritas occurrerunt/iustitia et pax deosculatae sunt*).

78 See *Bracton*, 2: 306 ('A king ought not only to be wise but merciful, his justice tempered with wisdom and mercy'.) Thanks to Charles Donahue for this reference.

79 P&M, 2: 461.
80 See Richard M. Fraher, 'The Theoretical Justification for the New Criminal Law of the High Middle Ages', *University of Illinois Law Review* 1984 (1984): 579 ('*publicae utilitatis intersit, ne crimina remaneant impunita*').
81 On trial by ordeal as a last resort, see Bartlett, *Trial by Fire and Water*, 67.
82 See, generally, William Chester Jordan, *From England to France: Felony and Exile in the High Middle Ages* (Princeton: Princeton University Press, 2015).
83 Not until the sixteenth century would the criminal law provide specific guidance for prosecuting recidivist clerics, but conceivably these records of informal jury verdicts could have served a similar purpose in earlier centuries, enabling the community to mark offending clerics as convicted to prevent recidivists from taking a second bite of the benefit of clergy apple.
84 Paul Brand, 'Judges and Juries in Civil Litigation in Later Medieval England: The Millon Thesis Reconsidered', *JLH* 37 (2016): 1–40.
85 David Millon, 'Positivism in the Historiography of the Common Law', *Wisconsin Law Review* 1989 (1989): 669–714.
86 Brand, 'Judges and Juries', 6.
87 Ibid., 40.
88 See, e.g., Lib. Ass. 22 Edw. 3, fol. 94a, no. 39 (KB 1348), *Seipp*, no. 1348.247 (jury being told, after acquitting a person of homicide, that they should name the actual felon since the crime was notorious).
89 *Bracton*, 2: 406.
90 See, e.g., Kaye, *Placita Corone*, 16–17 (justice cajoling an illiterate alleged horse thief into confessing, which he does, and is promptly hanged); 17–18 (justice trying to persuade an alleged cattle thief to consent to jury trial).
91 Helen M. Cam, ed., *Year Books of Edward II: The Eyre of London, 14 Edward II, A.D. 1321* (London: Bernard Quaritch, 1968), 1: 73–4. It is possible that Justice Passeley misread the jury's disposition toward the defendant when he encouraged Isabel to plead, but his bare statement that she would be acquitted lends itself to the inference that he did not have her best interests in mind.
92 Green, *Verdict*, 31, 36–46.
93 Ibid., 46. See also Green, 'Societal Concepts of Criminal Liability for Homicide in Medieval England', *Speculum* 47 (1972): 669–94.
94 Green, *Verdict*, 28.
95 Ibid., 65. See also Green, 'Retrospective on the Criminal Trial Jury', 359–60.
96 Bellamy, *Criminal Trial in Later Medieval England*, 14. For Green's reply, see his review of Bellamy's book in *AHR* 105 (2000): 266–7.
97 See, generally, Green, 'The Jury and the English Law of Homicide, 1200–1800', *Michigan Law Review* 74 (1975–1976): 413–99. See also chapter three in Green, *Verdict*.
98 See Bellamy, *Criminal Trial in Later Medieval England*, 57–63.
99 *Supra*, 64–5.
100 We employ the phrase 'formal law' to encapsulate the rules generally known by justices. Treatises like *Bracton* and the plea rolls themselves offer insight into settled understandings about the law, understandings likely shared among justices. While jurors were responsible for issuing verdicts, they were not creating the rules upon which their verdicts were theoretically based.
101 See, generally, James Q. Whitman, *The Origins of Reasonable Doubt: Theological Roots of the Criminal Trial* (New Haven: Yale University Press, 2008), 125–58.
102 It bears noting that even with trial by ordeal, a human ultimately had to issue the verdict, announcing, for example, whether the accused had floated (in trial by water) or failed to heal (in trial by hot iron).

4 The general eyre and royal finance[1]

Jens Röhrkasten

The significance of itinerant justices as an instrument of royal control in medieval England is undisputed and the importance of the eyre in the enforcement of royal authority in the counties and as an occasion for the application of the king's jurisdiction was highlighted when English legal history began to emerge as a modern discipline in the nineteenth century.[2] Whereas the legal and administrative mechanisms of this process, which has been traced back to the commissioners who compiled Domesday Book, have received much attention,[3] other aspects of the eyre remain elusive. The eyre was an important tool for the enforcement of royal law for more than a century and its political dimension as an institution which projected royal authority into the localities, affecting a wide social range of county society as well as all elements of the local administration by investigating and cataloguing its failings, imposing usually financial penalties in the process, still remains to be assessed.[4] The conduct in office of sheriffs, coroners and other local office holders came under scrutiny, note was taken of the responses of villagers to all incidents which led to the hue and cry and their attempts to arrest suspects which had occurred since the last eyre, and the proceedings in areas of private jurisdiction were also monitored.[5] The process had its own historical dynamism because the scope of duties entrusted to the eyre justices increased throughout the thirteenth century. This is indicated by the development of the 'Articles of the Eyre', the list of tasks which defined the justices' duties. This list consisted of five articles in 1176 and amounted to seventy clauses within a century, still extending in the reign of Edward II when the institution was already coming to an end.[6]

This wide remit of the eyre 'ad omnia placita' created a number of problems. Local society found itself confronted with the demands and procedures of a highly efficient central government and this presented a high potential for tension. This tension between locality and central government was probably mitigated by the fact that the eyre involved more complex processes of negotiation between different groups within the counties, allowing the members of an emerging gentry to level complaints about encroachments by large landholders whose power could not be checked by the county community without external assistance. This means that the sessions did not only offer potential benefits to individual claimants but also to groups. The general eyre was not merely an effective method to enforce royal authority in the counties, the interaction between the localities and central government potentially also had advantages for freeholders and for towns and villages if they were oppressed by royal officials or even by magnates.[7] But even though the eyre also acted as forum where the county community could voice complaints to the king's representatives about encroachments by both lay and clerical magnates, the requirements for large numbers of jurors to travel often considerable distances, its intrusive procedures and the large number of amercements which were imposed by the justices on the county, as well as on the hundreds, vills and on individuals, made it an unpopular and sometimes feared institution. The discontinuation of country-wide eyre visitations after 1294 were due to the political problems encountered by Edward I's government from the mid-1290s onwards and the 1321 London Eyre had to be abandoned because of the political crisis facing Edward II. After his deposition there were only intermittent attempts to revive the eyre and eventually it was abandoned in the middle of the fourteenth century.[8]

The judicial and political functions of the eyre were not regarded as central elements by all historians. There were those to whom the visitations were merely a form of taxation. T.F.T. Plucknett regarded the eyre as 'a source of great financial profit to the Crown' and to F. Hamil it was 'primarily a financial iter'.[9] Most of the judicial revenue in 1130 was produced by the work of itinerant justices.[10] Plucknett and Hamil were not the first to hold this view. In the 'Dialogus de Scaccario' Richard Fitz Neal lets his 'magister' explain that cash as one of the kingdom's sources for revenue came from 'placitis regni'.[11] Matthew Paris put it even stronger, recording under the year 1240 that the king sent his itinerant justices through the counties who corrected excesses and amassed immense wealth under the pretext of serving justice.[12] According to Helen Maud Cam the Articles of the Eyre and the amercements they generated were the characteristic feature of this form of royal jurisdiction.[13] Given the inconvenience and expenses which inevitably accompanied the beginning of a new eyre, it is not surprising that the people of Cornwall fled into the woods when the justices arrived in 1233.[14] Undoubtedly the royal administration of the law was a source of profit and it may be plausible to conclude that the general eyre at the time of its greatest development generated significant contributions to the royal income. This all the more so since the counties visited were liable to a common fine, the scale of which depending on their size and wealth.[15] Robin Stacey could show that revenues from general eyres generated income also in those years when the justices were not sitting, since amercements continued to be collected, and that in the 1240s the financial contribution from these courts represented the largest share of the crown's income from justice, since the Bench was not in session during the eyre.[16] The fiscal significance of the eyre seems to be highlighted in fourteenth-century petitions when county communities were prepared to offer significant amounts of money in order to avoid a visit by the itinerant justices.[17]

It will not be possible here to take into account the incomes from the central royal courts, the forest eyres and those generated by justices under other commissions. Instead an attempt will be made to focus on the fiscal importance of the general eyre in the thirteenth century using data generated between 1194 and 1294, the time when its judicial and administrative role reached its highest point. Even though the visits of eyre justices to the counties occurred only rarely as part of large, county-wide visitations, they were noted for the thoroughness of their approach.[18] The proceedings during the general eyre included a control of all aspects of the county administration and the justices also revisited all incidents affecting the king's peace. They were not limited in their power to impose amercements for procedural failures they discovered and their jurisdiction extended to all judicial proceedings held since the last visit by justices in eyre.[19] The amounts of money owed by landholders, royal officials, former office holders, villages and towns were noted in the margins of the plea rolls and it was the sheriff's duty to collect the money and account for it at the Exchequer. The amounts of money levied following an eyre could be considerable and it is easy to see why some historians questioned the nature of the general eyre, asking whether it was primarily a legal institution or a fiscal instrument.

Amercements imposed by the justices, the chattels of fugitives and of those convicted of felony and payments for encroachments on crown lands were noted in the margins of the plea rolls and this information had two components: the identity of the person or group responsible for payment and the amount owed. After the end of the eyre the rolls were handed in at the Exchequer and the debts were set out in the Pipe Rolls.[20] After the end of an eyre, information would be recorded in the Pipe Rolls on the money that had been received and on the sums which were still being owed. These are the figures on which this study, which covers the years between 1194 and 1294, is based.[21]

This seemingly transparent system was not as clear as it may seem at first sight and attention needs to be drawn to some of the problems with the sources before the data is analysed. The first problem consists of the calculation of annual royal revenues overall. It has been pointed out before that 'Pipe rolls are records of audit, not of receipt' and that they relate to the Exchequer year rather than to the calendar year, whereas the accounting period may extend beyond the 'official' period, the months from Michaelmas (29 September) to the end of the same month in the following year. The second problem concerns the calculation of revenues from the general eyre. Apart from the mistakes a researcher might easily make among the large number of often relatively small sums copied from the plea rolls, it is sometimes impossible to arrive at clear figures because not all sums are defined as paid or owed; instead the scribes simply left a space for this information to be entered later and it never was.[22] A less common source for inaccuracies is the recording of amercements in kind rather than in cash. Among the debts recorded for the 1236 Hampshire Eyre are 'tres palefridos'.[23] In addition there is another factor which might distort the totals worked out for any given year, the possible discrepancies between the times when payments were made and when they were recorded in the records. The lack of precise information has its parallel in the assessment of royal income overall. Ramsey, the first to provide a comprehensive survey, was criticised for the incomplete data in his work, although he was aware that his figures did not represent the total, the revenues from Normandy and from other non-English territories held by the Plantagenets being excluded.[24] Despite these inaccuracies the available data is sufficient to reveal the fiscal significance of the eyre because it permits a comparison of the scale of income provided by this type of court with an assumed total of royal revenue.

The visitation of 1194–95 is best known for the introduction of keepers of the crown pleas who were to be elected in every county; however, there was a wider context with financial implications.[25] Following his crusade and the subsequent captivity in Germany, Richard I had arrived in England in March 1194, when the collection of his ransom had already been under way for about a year while his younger brother John, in alliance with king Philip II of France, was challenging royal authority. A second coronation at Winchester on Sunday 17 April symbolised his personal control of government after his power had already been established with the capture of Nottingham in the previous month. However, Richard I departed soon afterwards and the government of England was left to Hubert Walter, archbishop of Canterbury and justiciar.[26] The eyre visitation which began in the autumn of 1194 was part of a bundle of measures designed to demonstrate the administration's efficiency and to consolidate royal finance after the payment of the one hundred thousand marks ransom. Hubert Walter himself acted as justice for the eastern circuit. The revenue collected from the thirty-two eyres held in these two years until September 1195 amounted to more than £1299; another £911 were recorded as debts. If it were possible to collect these, the visitation would have brought in about as much as the scutage where revenues amounted to just over £2000 until Michaelmas 1194.[27] The equally well-prepared visitation of 1198–99 even yielded more than £2942 up to Michaelmas 1200.[28] These figures confirm the assessment by Gerald Harriss that 'under Richard I the eyre became more burdensome'.[29] Nevertheless, when compared to the total income of 1194, calculated as either £22,632 or £25,292, it is obvious that the eyre revenue of this year represented only a fraction, in any case less than a tenth of the total amount.[30] The even larger amount for the 1198–99 visitation is to be seen in the context of a total revenue of more than £54,000 over two years.[31] Clearly, other sources of income were more important.

There were only two visitations in King John's reign, extending over the years 1201 to 1203 and 1208 to 1209. Royal revenue from the twenty eyres of the first visitation, recorded in the Pipe Rolls between 1202 and 1205, amounted to over £5290 with another £2386 recorded as debts.[32] Overall royal revenue in these years amounted to more than £108,238.[33] If all debts had actually been collected, the income from this visitation would have represented 7.1 per cent of the total; if none of the debts had been paid, the contribution from this type of jurisdiction would have amounted to 4.8 per cent. Since neither of the extremes is likely, the contribution of the eyre was somewhere between 5.0 per cent and 7.0 per cent. The second visitation in King John's reign consisted only of fourteen eyres and the yield was lower. However, since the amount collected was accounted for only in one year, 1209, the proportion of the £3579 eyre revenue of total revenue (£36086) was higher, being between 9.9 per cent and 12.5 per cent of the year's royal income.[34]

It took almost a decade before another eyre visitation was begun. After the threat posed by the French invasion had been averted and the civil war had ended in 1217, Henry III's minority government was eager to reestablish administrative processes and royal authority. David Carpenter, presumably including the sums that were recorded as debts on the Pipe Rolls, has been able to show that the revenue of the 1218–22 visitation amounted to £2345, representing a significant proportion of the royal cash income at the time.[35] However, Carpenter's figure of c. £5000 differs significantly from the data produced by Ramsay, whose data adds up to four, five or almost eight times this amount.[36] This means that it is difficult to contextualise the income from this visitation. However, it may be worth pointing out that the revenue of these thirty-four eyres was significantly lower than that of the fourteen eyres visited in 1208–09 (£3579).

The second eyre visitation in Henry III's reign brought a very different financial result. More than thirty eyres between the summer of 1226 and spring 1230 yielded a revenue of more than £7200 with a further £2000 of debts recorded in the Pipe Rolls of these years. According to Ramsay, royal income in these five years up to Michaelmas 1230 was just under £160,000 and if the underlying figures are accurate, the eyre would have produced between 4.5 per cent and 5.8 per cent of total revenue, depending on the effectiveness of the administration in the collection of debts. However, already at this stage it is clear that not all incoming payments were paid into the exchequer. Often the salaries of the justices were deducted from the proceeds straight away and cash was also used for other purposes. From the money collected after the 1227 Oxford eyre, 52 marks were allocated by the king for the completion of the town wall of Oxford.[37]

Given the rigour with which the eyre controlled the local administration and the effects it had on county society, it is not surprising to find that the institution was susceptible to political influence. Its political character emerged in the early phase of Henry III's reign but it was also sensitive to political turmoil. Following the capture of Poitou by Louis VIII of France in 1224, Henry III made a series of expensive military efforts to recover territories and his influence in the French kingdom. The financial gain derived from the visitation of 1226 to 1229 is likely to have contributed to meet the expenses of these campaigns, whose modest success stood in no relation to their cost.[38] This background was undoubtedly relevant for the preparations of the next visitation in 1231, following Henry III's campaign to Brittany in 1230; however, the eyres between 1231 and 1233 yielded only a small revenue. Even if the outstanding amercements and other debts are included, the income from this source barely amounted to £3000 because the visitation was not completed and only a dozen eyres were held. The political crisis which caused this change saw the justiciar, Hubert de Burgh, replaced by Stephen of Seagrave, who in the previous year had visited Yorkshire and Lincolnshire as eyre justice but did not complete his circuit in 1232 when he took on his new role. Following a lack of success in France and failure in Wales coupled with a lack of funds, the king had been persuaded by Hubert de Burgh's enemies that the justiciar was behind attacks on Italian clerics who had been provided with English benefices by Gregory IX. Probably at the end of July the justiciar was dismissed from the royal court, the actual reason being his inability to raise more funds for the king.[39] However, the transition to a new government was not smooth and almost led to an armed internal conflict in 1233 when the bishop of Winchester, who had been behind the move against Hubert de Burgh, lost power himself soon afterwards. The eyre visitation was not resumed.[40] If one uses Ramsay's figures of the royal revenue between 1231 and 1233, £101,985, the share of the general eyre amounted to 2.9 per cent.[41]

Following the overthrow of the bishop of Winchester's government in April 1234 a new eyre visitation was planned. This began in the autumn of 1234 and ended with the eyres of Cornwall and Devon in the summer of 1238. Thirty-five individual eyres were held, bringing in a total revenue of £19,000.[42] The income appears to have been particularly high in the first two years, the accounting period up to Michaelmas 1236, declining after that to rally again in 1238–39.[43] The figure produced by Stacey indicates that the total revenue of this visitation amounted to 9.8 per cent of the total revenue over the years 1235–39, which amounted to £194,152 according to Ramsay's estimate. This was a significant share, just under the £22,540 (11.6 per cent of total income) yielded by the Thirtieth of 1237–38.[44]

Royal revenue was even increased in the visitation of 1239 to 1241 and the following eyres between 1242 and 1244. The cash collected in these years, £13,624, amounted to more than 65 per cent of all judicial revenue in the period 1240–45. Given that cases from counties visited by eyre justices were not heard in the Bench, this alignment of judicial income may not be surprising. When the eyre revenue is seen in the context of total royal revenues in these years, its proportion ranges from 6.1 per cent to 7.4 per cent, depending on the inclusion or exclusion of the sums marked as debts.[45]

So far eyre visitations had been sporadic but this was to change: eyres were held every year in the period 1246 to 1258. This began with the visitation of

1246 to 1249, when thirty-two eyres were held. A further eight eyres were organised in the period 1250 to 1252.[46] Royal revenue from eyres between 1246 and 1252 amounted to £11,669 with recorded debts of £2781.[47] This represented a share of between 4.5 per cent and 5.5 per cent of total income, depending on the administration's ability to call in the debts.[48] It is important to point out that in this phase of intensive use of the general eyre the relationship between the sums collected during or immediately after the proceedings and the debts recorded in the Pipe Rolls began to change. Up to this point the cash generated for the Treasury had always been clearly in excess of the sums which were owed. The situation was going to be different for the rest of Henry III's reign.

The fact that the justices followed standardised procedures does not mean that the sessions shared an identical format. Although cooperation with the justices was strictly enforced, there were also instances of resistance, of absence from the proceedings, of behaviours which the royal representatives interpreted as contempt of court. It is not clear whether this extended to the refusal to make the demanded payments, normally perhaps hidden behind the claim of an inability to pay. The debts incurred during the eyres had always been substantial, usually amounting to several thousand pounds.[49] From the 1250s into the 1270s the cash revenue collected during or immediately after the eyres was almost consistenly below the sums which were recorded as debts. This is certainly true for the visitation extending over the years 1252 to 1258, which brought in £5910 while £9491 remained unpaid. The cash receipts amounted to 3.7 per cent of total royal income in the years when the king's financial liabilities led to a serious political crisis.[50] It is true that the uncompleted visitation of 1261 to 1263 does not quite fit into this pattern because the collected revenue exceeded the sum owed, however, with £3880 the amount collected was not much higher than the £3333 which were recorded as debts.[51] Following the end of the Movement of Baronial Reform and Rebellion, another visit by eyre justices to the counties was planned. This last visitation of Henry III's reign, which consisted of thirty-two eyres between 1268 and 1272, produced a cash revenue of more than £3400 in six years. More than £8350 remained unpaid at the time.[52] In the same period it became very common to allocate funds to their ultimate destination immediately after collection rather than having them delivered to the Treasury first, although the accounts were kept in the Pipe Roll. Often the justices took their wages from the proceeds and Peter Chaceporc, treasurer of the wardrobe, sometimes also received lump sums. The queen's wardrobe could be supplied with cash in a similar way.[53] According to the accounts in the Pipe Rolls William de Longespee received £100 of the king's gift from the proceeds of the 1249 Wiltshire eyre, probably as a royal contribution to his crusading plans.[54] Geoffrey of Lusignan, one of the king's half-brothers, also received a gift of £100, in his case from the proceedings of the 1251 Yorkshire eyre.[55] The king's nephew, Hugh of Lusignan, received 250 marks in the crisis year 1258.[56] Arrears of his pensions and wardships were paid to Guy of Lusignan from eyre revenues in 1257 and again in 1271.[57] Wider knowledge of this allocation of funds would not have improved the debtors' willingness to pay. The discrepancy between eyre revenues recorded as paid and the amercements still owed continued into the early years of Edward I's reign. The eyres held between 1274 and 1277 brought in a cash income of only £338 while more than £1257 were recorded as debts to the crown.[58]

The share of revenue generated by the general eyre in relation to the total of royal income may have been as high as 9.8 per cent in the years 1252 to 1258 – if all debts were collected.[59] In the years of the abandoned visitation of 1261 to 1263 royal revenue fell and its share produced by the eyre stood at between 2.5 per cent and 4.9 per cent.[60] This proportion fell still further in the last years of Henry III's reign, the visitation of 1268 to 1272 only bringing in between 1.7 per cent and 6.2 per cent of the total revenue of these years. The last eyres before the addition of the Quo Warranto proceedings were even less significant in financial terms.

The visitation of 1278 to 1289 brought in a cash revenue of at least £13,864, the sum of this and the recorded debts amounting to £21,896. This exceeded the income from the 1230s, however, royal revenue overall was very different at this time. Although the eyre was a financial success its contribution to the overall royal income was between 2.6 per cent and 4.1 per cent.[61] A similar result emerges when the data of the interrupted visitation of 1292 to 1294 is analysed.[62] The income from the general eyre for the three years amounted to £7334 with a possible total of £11,000.[63] In relation to the total royal income, the share derived from this source of revenue was little changed, standing at between 2.8 per cent and 4.2 per cent.

The revenue from the general eyre could be considerable. On the basis of the available data it seems that the visitation of 1208 to 1209 was the most significant in relative terms because it provided the greatest contribution to the royal revenue overall, standing at betwee 9.9 per cent and 12.5 per cent. However, in real terms this visitation yielded far less income than the eyres of the 1230s, 1240s, 1280s and 1290s. Eyre incomes were never stable and the share of the revenue from this source in the total royal income fluctuated as well. There can be little doubt that during visitations the cash income from individual eyres could be of great significance at times when there was an acute cash shortage in the treasury. This was certainly the case in 1219 when the financial administration was still being reconstituted after the end of the civil war.[64] The £3036 in eyre revenues collected in 1257 represented 23.7 per cent of the total revenue calculated by Ramsay (£12,777) and still 13.9 per cent of his admittedly conservative estimate of total royal revenue in the Exchequer year 1256 to 1257.[65] However, such years are not representative because the overall trend saw the share of eyre revenue in total royal income drop in the middle of the thirteenth century, and a levelling out after 1278 despite the clear increase in cash collected after the two eyre visitations before 1294.

Table 4.1 Share of eyre revenue in total royal income

Share of eyre revenue in total royal income	*Minimum*	*Maximum*
1252 to 1294		
Visitation 1252–58	3.70%	9.80%
Visitation 1261–63	2.50%	4.90%
Visitation 1268–72	1.70%	6.20%
Eyres of 1274–77	0.46%	2.20%
Visitation 1278–89	2.60%	4.10%
Visitation 1292–94	2.80%	4.20%

The fact that individual eyres provided welcome cash in times of crisis is no proof that medieval administrators and politicians viewed the general eyre primarily as a fiscal device. There is no sign of them trying to calculate the eyre's financial contribution to the royal income overall as was attempted here. If the eyre had been seen primarily as a tool for taxation, it would have made sense to establish it as a regular institution with annual visits of the justices to all counties rather than letting it remain an extraordinary feature of the legal system, used only after a political decision had been made. Visits by eyre justices to individual counties were rare, even in the thirteenth century when one visitation extended over a decade.[66] This political decision was of an administrative nature and did not require wider consent, in constrast to the later fractional taxes. Instead a tax on movables was created in 1207 and following this a distinctive taxation system was developed in the thirteenth century which – like the eyre visitation – was sporadic but was based on political consent. The general eyre was no part of a taxation system which became ever more sophisticated in the thirteenth century. It consisted of the traditional sources of income, e.g. wardships, scutages, tallages as well as the fractional subsidies, including those from the clergy and income from taxes on trade, leading to a gradual increase in royal revenue.[67]

The eyre was a judicial device with a strong political element. It was a demonstration of royal power to all sections of society and it offered effective control of the tiers of local administration both royal and private. In addition it provided an opportunity for towns as well as for minor freeholders to draw the justices' attention to arbitrary actions by the great lords, both lay and ecclesiastical. Eyre justices had to give an oath to adhere to the Articles of the Eyre and to deal with all legal issues and the rights belonging to the king's crown. Following this oath they were instructed to promote the king's interests. This was not further specified and there is no indication that this interest was fiscal.[68] This focus on judicial and administrative activities defined the justices' tasks in the documentation related to the organisation of the general eyre. A key function of the eyre was to deal with the crown pleas and this remained a central aspect until the breakdown of the system at the end of the thirteenth century.[69] The crown pleas in particular were a standard element of the instructions sent to the sheriffs in preparation of the hearings.[70] Before the beginning of the eyre the justices received their instructions in the form of the Articles of the Eyre. Already the early Articles address economic issues like the control of weights and measures or the infringement of royal rights which have financial implications, however, the objective is legal and political rather than financial.[71] Even when the Articles of the Eyre were further extended, the legal business was always given as the justices' primary objective.[72]

Although the eyre's share in total royal income decreased in significance there remains an important argument for its fiscal character which needs to be considered. In the fourteenth century, after a number of the eyre's functions had been taken over by justices operating under new commissions, there were petitions by county communities with offers of large payments in return for the cancellation of a planned eyre. Such offers were accepted by the government. At face value this looks like a confirmation of the theory that the main purpose of the eyre was fiscal, i.e. these offers were part of negotiations in which a lump sum was offered by those liable to pay tax, thus saving the administration the considerable work of collecting the funds. When an eyre was summoned for the county of Durham after the death of Bishop Beaumont in 1333, the men of the liberty objected and eventually offered the king one thousand marks. Of these, 900 marks were paid and negotiations concerning the remaining sum continued beyond 1338. A similar amount was offered by the county of Kent, Archbishop Mepham of Canterbury having died in the same year.[73] In these and similar instances the eyre has been seen as a mechanism to levy funds from individual counties. However, these attempts to raise income for the crown through the general eyre occurred only in a few instances and they were not a part of a country-wide visitation. Resistance to contribute to the payments offered by those who had not agreed the terms with the Crown made it difficult to collect the money. At a time when many functions of the general eyre had been taken over by other administrative devices, the reduction of the old institution to an item over which bargains could be struck can only have contributed to its disappearance. In the twelfth and thirteenth centuries the eyre was an important part in the way the English government exerted control over the king's subjects and his local administrators. This changed in the fourteenth century when the distant memory of the general eyre could serve as a threat to be averted by county communities in negotiated financial settlements with the crown.

Notes

1 I should like to thank Dr Henry Summerson for his advice and for his permission to use his unpublished notes.

2 Charles Gross, ed., *Select Cases From the Coroners' Roll, A.D. 1265–1413* (London: B. Quaritch, 1896), xxviii; R.B. Pugh, *Itinerant Justices in English History* (Exeter: Exeter University, 1967), 7; P&M, 1: 644–8; W.C. Bolland, *The General*

Eyre (Cambridge: Cambridge University Press, 1922), 64; John Bellamy, *Crime and Public Order in England in the Later Middle Ages* (London: Routledge, 1973), 17, 121.

3 Alan Harding, *The Law Courts of Medieval England* (London: George Allen & Unwin, 1973), 38, 53, 65.

4 S.B. Chrimes, 'Introductory Essay', in *A History of English Law*, ed. Sir William Holdsworth, 7th ed. (London: Methuen, 1966), 1: 43; Harding, *The Law Courts*, 63.

5 H.R.T. Summerson, 'The Structure of Law Enforcement in Thirteenth Century England', *AJLH* 23 (1979): 316.

6 P&M, 2: 521; Chrimes, 'Introductory Essay', 43.

7 Jens Röhrkasten, 'The Role of Minor Freeholders in the General Eyre in Thirteenth-Century England', in *Von Nowgorod bis London. Studien zu Handel, Wirtschaft und Gesellschaft im mittelalterlichen Europa. Festschrift für Stuart Jenks zum 60. Geburtstag*, eds. M. Heckmann, Marie-Luise and Jens Röhrkasten (Göttingen: V&R unipress, 2008), 387–407.

8 G.O. Sayles, ed., *Select Cases in the Court of King's Bench Under Edward I*, 3 vols. (London: B. Quaritch, 1938), 2: xxxvii, xlvi–xlvii. David Crook, *Records of the General Eyre* (London: H.M.S.O., 1982), 171; Michael Prestwich, *Edward I* (London: Methuen, 1988), 289; Seymour Phillips, *Edward II* (New Haven and London: Yale University Press, 2010), 379, 386.

9 F.C. Hamil, 'Presentment of Englishry and the Murder Fine', *Speculum* 12 (1937): 297; T.F.T. Plucknett, *A Concise History of the Common Law*, 3rd ed. (London: Butterworth, 1940), 100. Eyres are listed under 'Finance, royal' in David Carpenter, *The Minority of Henry III* (London: Methuen, 1990), 452.

10 David Carpenter, *The Struggle for Mastery – Britain 1066–1284* (St Ives: Penguin, 2004), 157.

11 Charles Johnson, ed. and trans., *De Necessariis Observantiis Scaccarii Dialogus qui vulgo dicitur Dialogus de Scaccario* (London: Nelson, 1950), 40.

12 'Temporibus sub eisdem misit rex justitiarios itinerantes, qui per totam Angliam omnes comitatus regni spectantes peragrantes, multorumque excessus corrigentes, sub praetextu justitiae infinitam pecuniam ad opus regis omnia dispergentis collegerunt'. H.R. Luard, ed., *Matthaei Parisiensis, Monachi Sancti Albani Chronica Majora* (London: Longman, 1877), 4: 34.

13 H.M. Cam, *Studies in the Hundred Rolls: Some Aspects of Thirteenth-Century Administration* (Oxford: Clarendon Press, 1921), 10.

14 'Eodem anno fuerunt itinerantes justiciarii in Cornubia; quorum metu, omnes ad sylvas fugerunt. Et ideo bannitum fuit, ut omnes redirent ad pacem regis: ita tamen, quod addiscerent et viverent secundum leges regni Angliae. Excepti sunt soli homicidae quorum appellatores in promtu fuerunt'. In *Annales Monastici*, 3:135.

15 Meekings, *Surrey*, 136–9.

16 R.C. Stacey, *Politics, Policy, and Finance Under Henry III, 1216–1245* (Oxford: Clarendon Press, 1987), 213.

17 Crook, *Records*, 187. See also below.

18 R.B. Pugh, *Imprisonment in Medieval England* (Cambridge: Cambridge University Press, 1968), 255, 277.

19 Bolland, *The General Eyre*, f 64; J.H. Ramsay, *A History of the Revenues of the Kings of England, 1066–1399* (Oxford: Clarendon Press, 1925), 1: 88.

20 Johnson, ed., *De Necessariis Observantiis Scaccarii Dialogus*, 77–8, 113.

21 For this study only those sums were used which were recorded as received. It was not possible to follow up the gradual collection of arrears, a process which could extend over years and usually saw sharply declining yields.

22 TNA, E.372/71 rot. 10d.

23 TNA, E.372/80 rot. 9d.; Doris M. Stenton, ed., *The Great Roll of the Pipe for the Fifth Year of the Reign of King John: Michaelmas 1203* (London: J.W. Ruddock & Sons, 1938), 234.

24 Ramsay, *A History of the Revenues*, vii.; Robert Fawtier, 'L'histoire financière de l'Angleterre au moyen âge', *Le Moyen Âge*, 2nd ser., 29 (1928): 48–67. J.C. Holt, *The Northerners* (Oxford: Clarendon Press, 1961), 96; Nick Barratt, 'The Revenue of King John', *EHR* 111 (1996): 836.

25 R.F. Hunnisett, 'The Origins of the Office of Coroner', *Transactions of the Royal Historical Society*, 5th ser., 8 (1958): 86; Harding, *The Law Courts*, 74.

26 C.R. Cheney, *Hubert Walter* (London: Nelson, 1967), 78.

27 Crook, *Records*, 56–9; John Gillingham, *Richard I* (London: Yale University Press, 1999), 271. Doris M. Stenton, *The Great Roll of the Pipe for the Seventh Year of the Reign of King Richard the First: Michaelmas 1195* (London: J.W. Ruddock & Sons, 1929), 6–7, 11–12, 18–20, 26, 73–9, 92–8, 103–5, 110, 118, 121–3, 130–1, 134–5, 146–8, 150, 166–73, 179–82, 191–7, 210–1, 214–6, 223–5, 236–7, 241–2, 245, 249, 253–4, 256–7; eadem, *The Chancellor's Roll for the Eighth Year of the Reign of King Richard the First: Michaelmas 1196* (London: J.W. Ruddock & Sons, 1930), 156–9.

28 A further £1793 were recorded as debts. *PBKJ*, 2: 143. Doris M. Stenton, ed., *The Great Roll of the Pipe for the First Year of the Reign of King John: Michaelmas 1199* (London: J.W. Ruddock & Sons, 1933), 13–16, 20–1, 29–30, 58, 67–8, 77–8, 84–5, 98–102, 111–6, 157–60, 167, 175–8, 193–9, 217–8, 226–7, 258–9, 275–82, 283–7; eadem, ed., *The Great Roll of the Pipe for the Second Year of King John, Michaelmas 1200* (London: J.W. Ruddock & Sons, 1934), 15–18, 73–85, 111–7, 152–3, 181–3, 196–9, 247.

29 G.L. Harriss, *King, Parliament and Public Finance in Medieval England to 1369* (Oxford: Clarendon Press, 1975), 7.

30 Gillingham, *Richard I*, 271; Ramsay, *A History of the Revenues*, 1: 217.

31 Ramsay, *A History of the Revenues*, 1: 228, 231.

32 Doris M. Stenton, ed., *The Great Roll of the Pipe for the Fourth Year of the Reign of King John: Michaelmas 1202* (London: J.W. Ruddock & Sons, 1937), 10–1, 92–4,100–2, 156–8, 168–70, 216–22, 232–6, 240, 242–3, 257–8; eadem, ed., *The Great Roll of the Pipe for the Fifth Year of the Reign of King John*, 5, 26–7, 34–9, 88, 94–5, 130–2, 146–8, 182–3, 187, 196, 216–22, 226–7,232–4, 244, 246–8; eadem, ed., *The Great Roll of the Pipe for the Sixth Year of the Reign of King John: Michaelmas 1204* (London: J.W. Ruddock & Sons, 1940), 18, 91, 110–1, 151–3, 160, 157–8; Sidney Smith, ed., *The Great Roll of the Pipe for the Seventh Year of the Reign of King John: Michaelmas 1205* (London: J.W. Ruddock & Sons, 1941), 148.

33 Barratt, 'The Revenue of King John', 839.

34 Ibid.: The debts recorded in 1209 amounted to just over £934. Doris M. Stenton, ed., *The Great Roll of the Pipe for the Eleventh Year of the Reign of King John: Michaelmas 1209* (London: J.W. Ruddock & Sons, 1949), 15, 22–3, 30–5, 37, 51–4, 76–80, 106, 119–20, 139, 148, 150–1, 160–2, 176.

35 Carpenter, *The Minority of Henry III*, 99, 255. In these years this type of judicial income was on the same scale as the income from Jewish taxation, Stacey, *Politics, Policy, and Finance*, 143.

36 Ramsay, *A History of the Revenues*, 1: 271–5, 1218–19: £21,506; 1219–20: £27,144; 1220–1: £19851; 1221–2: £38433.

37 TNA, E.372/72 rot. 10d.

38 'Expensive expeditions were made, but very little happened'. F.M. Powicke, *The Thirteenth Century, 1216–1307* (Oxford: Clarendon Press, 1953), 84. Élie Berger, 'Les préparations d'une invasion anglaise et la descente de Henri III en Bretagne', *Bibliothèque de l'École des Chartes* 54 (1893): 25: 'Dans toute cette guerre, les Anglais ont beaucoup dépensé pour faire peu de chose'.

39 David Carpenter, 'The Fall of Hubert de Burgh', *Journal of British Studies* 19 (1980): 7.
40 Nicholas Vincent, *Peter des Roches: An Alien in English Politics, 1205–1238* (Cambridge: Cambridge University Press, 1996), 429–38.
41 Ramsay, *A History of the Revenues*, 1: 286–90.
42 Stacey, *Politics, Policy, and Finance*, 42.
43 My figures of collected cash for the period up to Michaelmas 1235 are: £5825; 1236: £2038; 1237: £962; 1238: £409; 1239: £1000; TNA, E.372/79 rot. 1d, 2d, 4d, 6d, 7d, 8, 9d, 12d, 13d, 14d, 15, 16; TNA, E.372/80 rot. 5, 6, 8d, 9d, 10, 12d, 15d, 16d; E.372/81 rot. 6d; E.372/82 rot. 9d; E.372/83 rot. 10.
44 Ramsay, *A History of the Revenues*, 1: 291–5.
45 Sir William Holdsworth, *A History of English Law* (London: Methuen, 1923), 1: 266–7. Stacey, *Politics, Policy, and Finance*, 232. If the total sum had been collected, it would have amounted to £16,496, TNA, E.372/84 rot. 6d, 8d, 9, 11d, 12d; E.372/85 rot. 1, 1d, 2d, 5, 7, 7d, 8d, 9, 11d, 12d, 13, 14d; E.372/87 rot. 6d; E.372/88 rot. 10, 11d, 13; E.372/89 rot 3, 4, 10d, 11d.; H.L. Cannon, ed., *The Great Roll of the Pipe for the Twenty-Sixth Year of the Reign of King Henry the Third: A.D. 1241–1242* (New Haven: Yale University Press, 1918), 20–1, 49, 106–7, 154–8; S.K. Mitchell, *Studies in Taxation Under John and Henry III* (New Haven: Yale University Press, 1914), 238, calculated the revenue for 1242 from the Issue Rolls at £38,606.
46 The accounts for the Yorkshire eyre of 1251 and the eyre held in Nottinghamshire and Derbyshire in 1252 were only drawn up in 1253 and are included in the figures for the period 1252 to 1258.
47 These figures represent the sums of accounts in: TNA, E.372/90 rot. 4d, 10d; E.372/91 rot. 1, 1d, 8; E.372/92 rot. 3, 3d, 4d, 5d, 8d, 11d; E.372/93 rot 4d, 5d, 7d, 8d, 10d, 13d, 16d; E.372/94 rot. 2, 2d, 11d; E.372/95 rot. 1d, 10d; E.372/96 rot. 6, 7d.
48 Total royal revenue between 1246 and 1252 amounted to £261,049 according to Ramsay, *A History of the Revenues*, 1: 304–12.
49 An exception is the visitation of 1231 to 1233 when only £489 were recorded as debts.
50 The total sum of £15,401 would have represented 9.8 per cent of total income (£157,401), Ramsay, *A History of the Revenues*, 1: 314–25. TNA, E.372/96 rot. 6, 7d, 17d; E.372/97 rot. 2d, 11d, 16d, E.372/99 rot. 3, 11, 12, 15, 15d, 16, 16d; E.372/100 rot. 5, 5d, 9, 11d, 15d, 16d, 17d; E.372/101 rot. 6, 12d, 13d, 16, 17, 18, 18d; E.372/102 rot. 3d, 20.
51 TNA, E.372/105 rot. 8d, 11, 12d; E.372/106 rot. 8d, 11, 11d, 12d, 13d, 16d, 18d; E.372/107 rot. 6d, 8d.
52 TNA, E.372/112 rot. 16d, 17d; E.372/113 rot. 3, 4d, 11, 16; E.372/114 rot. 9, 10d, 12, 15; E.372/115 rot. 6d, 18d; E.372/116 rot. 5, 7, 9d, 12, 16d, 23, 26, 27d; E.372/117 rot. 10d.
53 An example is in TNA, E.372/94 rot. 11d. Brand, *OLEP*, 27–9.
54 The accounts were only recorded in 1251, TNA, E.372/95 rot 1d.
55 TNA, E.372/97 rot. 11d.
56 TNA, E.372/102 rot. 20.
57 TNA, E.372/101 rot. 6: £200 'Gwydoni de Lezynan fratri regis de arreragio annui feodi'; TNA, E.372/115 rot. 18d: £165 11 shillings 8 pence 'ad opus Gwydonis de Lezinan fratris regis in partem solutionis mille marcarum tam pro remissione feodi sui quam pro omnibus arreragiis eiusdem feodi'.
58 These figures include the income from the 1272 Shropshire eyre for which its chief justice, Ralph Hengham, only accounted in 1277, TNA E.372/121 rot. 14d. Without the revenue from this eyre the figures stand only as £248 received and £1106 recorded as debts; however, the financial data for the 1276 Bedfordshire eyre is lost, TNA, E.372/121 rot. 15d. The overall figures would certainly have

been higher. The Bedfordshire eyre of 1232 brought a revenue of £88, TNA, E.372/76 rot 7.

59 The money recorded as actually collected in this period amounted only to 3.7 per cent of total revenue.

60 Ramsay, *A History of the Revenues*, 1: 334–49; T.F. Tout, *Chapters in the Administrative History of Mediaeval England: The Wardrobe, the Chamber and the Small Seals* (Manchester: Manchester University Press, 1920), 1: 297.

61 Tout, *Chapters in the Administrative History of Mediaeval England*, 2: 14–31. TNA, E.372/123 rot. 11d, 20, 20d; E.372/124 rot. 6, 8, 8d, 17d; E.372/125 rot. 6d, 7d; E.372/126 rot. 8d, 13d; E.372/127 rot. 9d, 20d; E.372/128 rot. 26d; E.372/130 rot. 15, 26d, 27, 28; E.372/131 rot. 9, 14d, 15d, 17; E.372/132 rot. 7d, 16d; E.372/133 rot. 7d, 11d, 16d, 23d, 27d; E.372/134 rot. 7d, 12d; E.372/135 rot. 24d.

62 Crook, *Records*, 170–8.

63 TNA, E.372/137 rot. 38; E.372/138 rot. 7d, 10, 10d, 11, 17; E.372/139 rot. 10d, 23, 23d, 31d.

64 The contribution of eyre revenue in 1218–19 stood at £990, 4.6 per cent of the annual revenue, Carpenter, *The Minority of Henry III*, 99; Ramsay, *A History of the Revenues*, 1: 271.

65 Ramsay, *A History of the Revenues*, 1: 324; TNA E.372/101 rot. 3d, 6, 12d, 13d, 16, 17, 18, 18d.

66 Pugh, *Imprisonment*, 255, 277. The visitation of 1278 to 1289.

67 Harriss, *King, Parliament and Public Finance*, 9–10, 27. Maureen Jurkowski, Carrie L. Smith and David Crook, *Lay Taxes in England and Wales 1188–1688* (Richmond: PRO Publications, 1998), xxvi, 6–24.

68 *Bracton*, 2: 309.

69 William Stubbs, ed., *Chronica Magistri Rogeri de Houedene* (London: Longmans, 1871), 4: 61. *RLC*, 2: 90.

70 'Facias etiam venire coram eis omnia placita corone que placitata non sunt et que emerserunt postquam assisa ultimo fuit in partibus illis coram Justiciariis itinerantibus . . .', *RLC*, 1: 380 (Yorkshire), 473 (Hertfordshire).

71 'Capitula autem itineris vestri et formam sacramenti quod facere debetis commisimus . . .', *RLC*, 1: 476.

72 Thomas Stapleton, ed., *Chronicon Petroburgense* (London: Camden Society, 1849), 102–3.

73 *Rotuli Parliamentorum ut et petitiones et placita in Parliamenta*, Record Commission (London, 1777), 2:99. W.N. Bryant, 'The Financial Dealings of Edward III with the County Communities, 1330–1360', *EHR* 83 (1968): 761.

5 Royal privilege and episcopal rights in the later thirteenth century

The case of the Ashbourne advowson, 1270–89

*Joshua C. Tate**

Among the many subjects concerning which Professor Paul Brand has made an invaluable contribution to knowledge is the history of English legislation in the thirteenth century. From an American perspective, one of the most important English statutes from that period is the Statute of Mortmain (1279), by which King Edward I prohibited the alienation of land to the church, a ban that was soon afterward circumvented by royal licensing. As Professor Brand has noted, scholars have disagreed on the motives for the statute and the licensing system that followed it, in particular whether Edward's primary motivations were financial, political or some combination of both.[1]

In attempting to resolve the motives of Edward I in partially restricting alienation of land to churches, it is worth considering the history of the one monastery that he personally founded, Vale Royal Abbey, and a related dispute over the church of Ashbourne, whose advowson had been one of Edward's most significant gifts to the abbey.[2] Although the patronage of churches was not the subject of the Statute of Mortmain, Edward's complex and creative dealings with respect to the Ashbourne advowson might help to contextualise the later attitude he took toward the alienation of land to the church by others. I will begin by summarising the principles of canon law with regard to gifts of advowsons of churches, which offer important context for the dispute over Ashbourne. I will then discuss the dispute over Ashbourne, which involved Edward, his abbey and the dean of Lincoln, and was followed by another dispute involving a different and more valuable advowson.

I

Canon law imposed restrictions on the ability of a lay patron to receive income from the church of which he had the advowson. Laymen were not allowed to appropriate tithes to their own use,[3] and clerks who paid money for ecclesiastical office committed the grave sin of simony, for which they could be deprived of their benefice.[4] Canon law did allow a patron to receive 'tribute' from the church; however, the tribute had to have been established by long custom and (in the view of some canonists) the bishop had to have approved.[5] Apart from this limited right to tribute, the patron could not receive any income from the church. However, patronage rights could be used to reward a clerk who had served the patron faithfully in the past, or to encourage such a clerk to provide service in the future.

The administration of a great estate required a private civil service,[6] and some of those who served wealthy lords were clerks who had taken holy orders.[7] Lay magnates needed literate men to keep track of the expenditures, income and debts of their manors. Holding out the prospect of a lucrative appointment to a parsonage was a good way to persuade bright, motivated clerks to enter one's service. Thus, while the value of the benefice ultimately lay in the tithes, the lay patron did not have to keep the tithes himself in order to benefit from the right of patronage.

One question that greatly interested canonists in the late twelfth and early thirteenth centuries was whether an advowson could be transferred from one patron to another. The answer depended on the circumstances, such as whether the advowson was to be transferred as a separate item or as an appurtenance to an estate; whether the transfer was by sale or donation; and whether the bishop had given his approval. Some of these scenarios gave rise to controversy among the canonists.

From the 1180s onward, it was generally accepted that an advowson could be transferred as an appurtenance to a whole property (*universitas*). Although there was some early disagreement on the issue, two decretals of Alexander III dating to the late 1170s established that an advowson could be acquired through the purchase of an estate to which the advowson was appurtenant.[8] Huguccio emphasised that in any transfer of a whole property, whether by sale, gift or enfeoffment, the advowson would be included unless specifically excepted.[9] There was no requirement that the bishop approve the transfer, nor did it matter whether the transfer was to or from a layman or a religious house. Notably, in Roman law, when one estate was servient to another, the servitude was held to follow the sale of either estate, as did a building on either property.[10] It is not surprising that canon law applied this basic principle to advowsons.

On the other hand, when the advowson was transferred by itself, not as an appurtenance, the permissibility of the transfer depended on the circumstances. At the death of Alexander III (1181), the decretal law on the subject of whether an advowson could be transferred by gift was unclear and provided rich material for controversies among the canonists.[11] One point of contention was whether the bishop's consent was required for the transfer. Alanus Anglicus, who taught and wrote ca. 1190–1215, thought that a gift to a layman required episcopal consent but not a gift to a monastery, while the author of the apparatus *Ecce vicit Leo* (1202/1210) believed that episcopal consent was necessary for a gift to a monastery but not for a gift to a layman.[12] By contrast, Huguccio reasoned that the consent of the bishop was never necessary.[13] In the thirteenth century, Tancred (ca. 1185–1236), Vincentius Hispanus (fl. ca. 1210–1248) and Innocent IV (jurist and pope, lived ca. 1200–1254) followed the view of Huguccio, while Johannes Teutonicus (ca. 1170–1245) followed the apparatus *Ecce vicit Leo*.[14] The ordinary gloss to the *Liber Extra*, edited by Bernard of Parma (ca. 1200–66), expressed the view that episcopal consent was always necessary for any gift.[15] Not until the second half of the thirteenth century did the view of Alanus Anglicus gradually prevail.[16]

One type of transfer was always considered impermissible. Under canon law, an advowson could not be sold as independent property; only when the advowson was appurtenant to an estate and sold with the estate was a sale permissible.[17] Peter the Chanter (d. 1197) was the lone dissenter on this point, and his view was summarily rejected by other authors who discussed it.[18] For the most part, debates of the canonists on this topic concerned what would happen to the advowson after an illegal sale, with some offering the view that the patronage would come to an end and others allowing the seller or his heirs to reclaim the advowson.[19]

The plea rolls from the late twelfth and early thirteenth centuries contain scores of references to gifts of advowsons. Gifts were made to both laymen and religious houses. As a general rule, however, an advowson was given to a layman only as an appurtenance to an estate (which was also given to the donee), while advowsons were given to religious houses separately from the land. A survey of the published royal court records from 1194 to 1250 revealed more than four dozen gifts to laymen of land with an advowson, but only half a dozen gifts to laymen of an advowson where land was not mentioned. In none of the latter six cases was judgment given for the donee.[20] On the other hand, a survey of the same records revealed only twenty-six gifts to religious houses of land with an advowson, but close to two hundred advowson gifts to religious houses that do not mention land. It seems to have been customary, when making a gift to a religious house, to give the advowson separately from the land, whereas lay donees usually acquired the advowson as part of some estate.

It is not a coincidence that gifts were frequently the subject of litigation in the late twelfth and early thirteenth centuries. In the twelfth century, before the proprietary church system had been eradicated and while hereditary benefices were still common, laymen frequently gave their churches to religious houses, encouraged by the reform-minded policies of the church. This practice continued through the early decades of the thirteenth century, but then became less common as advowsons became more valuable due to the end of the hereditary benefice and the expansion of seignorial administration.[21] Thus, the late twelfth and early thirteenth centuries were a period of transition. Religious houses saw fewer gifts of advowsons come their way as laymen came to covet this form of patronage. There were still many laymen who wanted to make gifts to religious houses, especially if the patron had a younger son whom he wanted to send to the religious house as a monk or canon,[22] or if he wanted to become a monk or canon himself.[23] But there are also clear signs of a less favourable attitude toward the monasteries. One patron allowed a priest to make one presentation to a church, 'provided that he not confer it on any religious house and do nothing to the prejudice of the right of his heirs'.[24] Many laymen in the thirteenth century wished to repudiate gifts of advowsons made to religious houses by their ancestors in an earlier period, when the advowson was less valuable. This often resulted in litigation.

Religious houses that acquired advowsons by gift were often careful to secure the approval or at least the acknowledgement of the bishop. The records reveal over sixty instances in which a religious house offered a confirmatory charter of the bishop to support its gift, and more than a dozen instances in which a charter of institution or other acknowledgement was offered. Nonetheless, one also finds over a hundred instances in which a religious house claimed a gift and the record includes no reference to an episcopal charter. In twenty-two of these cases, the royal courts gave judgment for the religious house claiming by gift despite the lack of recorded episcopal confirmation.[25] The reasons why the donees prevailed in these cases were various, but it seems clear that the royal courts did not require a confirmatory charter from the bishop.

Donees also sometimes offered confirmatory charters of popes as well as bishops,[26] even though nothing in canon law required papal confirmation for the gift of an advowson. It was also very common to offer confirmatory charters of kings, regardless of whether the king had a special interest in the advowson in question.[27] Such confirmatory charters were generally optional as far as the royal courts were concerned, but they offered important evidence of authenticity in a world where forgery was common and difficult to detect.

While the canon law rules concerning gifts do not seem to have been of much consequence for litigants in the royal courts, the canonical prohibition on sale does not appear to have been violated regularly, if at all. Disregarding cases where an advowson is alleged to have been sold with some land, the plea rolls from the late twelfth and early thirteenth centuries contain only one instance in which an advowson or moiety thereof is adjudged to a party who acquired it by virtue of a sale. In 1227, Thomas of Burgh claimed a moiety of the advowson of Penistone (Yorks) from Richard de Alencun. The jurors reported that a moiety of the advowson had been sold to William de Neville, father of Sarah, who was Thomas's mother and whose heir Thomas was; the other moiety had been sold to Roger de Munbegun, whose heirs were Eudes de Lungvillers and Geoffrey de Neville.[28] The court awarded Thomas the presentation of the moiety in question and Richard was amerced.[29]

The case between Thomas and Richard does suggest that the royal courts might overlook the canonical prohibition on sale. It is worth noting, however, that the sale is referenced only in the jury's verdict, and was not alleged by either of the parties. It is possible that the sale had included land as well as a moiety of the advowson, and the jury simply neglected to mention this fact (or it was not reported on the roll). In any event, one contrary instance does not mean that the royal judges generally failed to respect the canonical prohibition. It must be emphasised, on the other hand, that the standard language for charters did not distinguish between sales and gratuitous transfers. Unless the charter mentioned the consideration, or it came up during the litigation, a sale could be mistaken for a gift. Nevertheless, the surviving evidence gives no reason to think that advowsons were being sold in violation of canon law.

II

With this background in mind, let us now turn to the complex advowson dispute from the late thirteenth century between King Edward I and the Dean and Chapter of Lincoln over the advowson of the church of Ashbourne. The town of Ashbourne lies in the Derbyshire Dales at the southern edge of the Peak District. The current parish church, dedicated to St Oswald of Northumbria, dominates the town. George Eliot once referred to it as 'the finest mere parish church in the kingdom'.[30] Although the present building was dedicated in 1241, it has a Norman crypt, and there has been a church on the site since Saxon times.

The church of Ashbourne is mentioned several times in the *Registrum Antiquissimum* of the Cathedral Church of Lincoln. The first reference to the church is in a writ of William Rufus from the year 1093, stating that he had given the church of Ashbourne, along with three others, to the church of Lincoln and its bishop.[31] At the time of the charter, Lincoln had been a see for only two decades. The cathedral had just been finished the year before, having been consecrated two days after the death of Remigius, the first bishop of Lincoln. The gift was made around the time William named Anselm as archbishop of Canterbury. One assumes that the gift of Ashbourne was intended as a goodwill gesture to the church in general and the new see of Lincoln in particular, during a short period of reconciliation between William and the church. William's gift of Ashbourne was confirmed by Henry II in a charter made at Windsor between 1162 and 1165, also recorded in the *Registrum Antiquissimum*.[32]

The church of Ashbourne was not actually situated in the diocese of Lincoln. Rather, it was in the diocese of Coventry and Lichfield. The *Registrum Antiquissimum* includes a charter of the bishop of Coventry and Lichfield from 1241, providing that the revenues from Ashbourne would go to a vicar, who would then pay fifty marks to the dean of Lincoln as a pension.[33] This arrangement was evidently unacceptable to the dean of Lincoln. In 1258, the dean of Lincoln obtained a bull from Pope Alexander IV deeming the perpetual vicarage to be void and allowing the deanery to recover the church when the vicar died, reserving a portion to be paid to the vicar.[34]

The importance of Ashbourne to Lincoln is also illustrated by a final concord, preserved in the *Registrum Antiquissimum* and arising out of a writ of *utrum*, in which three laymen recognised that certain tofts of land belonged to Lincoln as parson.[35]

At some point around the year 1260, Lincoln lost its claim on Ashbourne when King Henry III recovered it in his court by a writ of *darrein presentment*. This judgment is referred to in a later entry in the Charter Rolls,[36] and the Patent Rolls from 1260 and 1261 refer to the king's presentation of a clerk to the church of Ashbourne.[37] The fact of the king's claim is also noted in a charter from 1262 in the *Registrum Antiquissimum*. The charter reflects the admission of William Lexington, dean of Lincoln, to all his benefices 'excepting . . . the church of Ashbourne which was in the possession of another on the presentation of the king', and one other church which was the subject of an inquest.[38] The dean of Lincoln still did not recognise the validity of the king's claim, as shown by a note that 'the dean protested before the bishop that he should have the church of Ashbourne by reason of his deanery, or at least fifty marks a year in the name of a parsonage or pension'.[39]

Henry III was in a desperate financial situation in the late 1250s and early 1260s, as he quarreled with Simon de Montfort and other magnates during a time of famine and military setbacks. Whatever might have been Henry's basis for claiming Ashbourne, by 1270 he had decided to pass the claim along to someone else, specifically his son Edward, soon to be King Edward I. The Charter Rolls reflect a gift from Henry to his son in May 1270 of 'the advowson of the church of [Ashbourne] and all the chapels thereof'.[40]

Edward did not hold on to the advowson of Ashbourne for long. In August 1270, he included it with three other advowsons in the foundation charter for Vale Royal, the only monastery Edward founded. Lord Edward is said to have founded the new monastery in fulfillment of a vow he made while fearing a shipwreck crossing the channel.[41] He set sail on crusade shortly after making the donation.[42] The records do not indicate that Edward was aware of the dean of Lincoln's claim to the advowson of Ashbourne, but it seems likely that his father or someone else would have advised him about it.

If Edward was aware of the dispute, giving the advowson to his newly founded monastery might have seemed risky at the time, but it led to an amicable settlement eight years later. The dean and chapter of Lincoln brought their claim to the advowson of Ashbourne to the king's council. The dispute was resolved in the summer of 1278 in a three-way settlement recorded in the chancery rolls.

In the first part of the settlement, the abbot and convent of Vale Royal quitclaimed the advowson of Ashbourne and its chapels back to King Edward I. This donation is recorded as having occurred on May 26.[43] A separate entry in the close rolls indicates that the dean of Lincoln 'acknowledges in chancery, for himself and the chapter of Lincoln, that he owes to the abbot and convent of Vale Royal 400 pounds; to be levied, in default of payment, of their lands and chatttels'.[44]

The final entry, from June 1278, recites the facts of the dispute over Ashbourne, including the quitclaim of the advowson back to the king, the initial gift by William Rufus, and the dispute with Henry III, but without any reference to the 400 pounds to be paid to Vale Royal. The entry records that Edward restored the advowson 'to the bishop, dean and chapter to hold as their predecessors held it, in order to make good any diminution of vigor in the charter of the said King William, for the soul of King Henry III'.[45]

In essence, the settlement amounted to a payment of 400 pounds by the dean of Lincoln to Vale Royal in return for the release of all claims to the advowson by the king and his monastery. This settlement prompts the question of why it would be worth 400 pounds to Lincoln Cathedral to have the advowson of Ashbourne back. In the *Taxatio Ecclesiastica* of 1291–92, the church's great tithes were valued at sixty-six pounds, thirteen shillings and fourpence, with the lesser vicarage valued at five pounds.[46]

In rough terms, setting aside inflation and the expenses of litigation, it would have taken the dean and chapter of Lincoln between six and seven years to recoup the 400 pounds paid to Vale Royal. After that point, they would continue to hold onto the advowson indefinitely, so long as the king and his successors upheld their promise. From that perspective, the settlement might have seemed unusually generous to the dean and chapter.

Why, then, did Edward make this deal? The answer may lie in the subsequent steps he took to secure an even more valuable advowson for Vale Royal, the church of Kirkham in York.[47] During the twelfth century, the advowson of Kirkham had belonged to the abbey of Shrewsbury. However, in 1196, the advowson was acquired by Theobald Walter, brother of the archbishop of Canterbury Hubert Walter, after a dispute in the king's court.[48] For several decades afterward, the lands that had belonged to Theobald were often in royal custody, and successive kings presented clerks to Kirkham.

Edward I wanted to compensate Vale Royal with the advowson of Kirkham following their loss of Ashbourne. Despite the evidence that the presentations by the king's ancestors were by reason of wardship, Edward claimed that the presentations were made by full royal right. Theobald Butler, the great-grandson of Theobald Walter, testified in favour of the king's claim. Apparently Theobald Butler was deeply in debt, and Edward granted him 400 marks and a young sparrow hawk for supporting the king's claim.[49]

Kirkham was more than twice as valuable as Ashbourne, and was assessed at 160 pounds in the *Taxatio Ecclesiastica*.[50] It was one of the five most valuable benefices in England. Thus, the abbey of Vale Royal came out very well in the end, controlling Kirkham while receiving payments from Lincoln to compensate them for the loss of Ashbourne. In light of this, agreeing to settle the dispute over Ashbourne could be seen as a shrewd way for Edward to preempt any possible criticism that he was acting unjustly with respect to the more valuable advowson of Kirkham. Perhaps Edward was learning how to manipulate the system in subtle ways that would serve his interests more effectively in the long run.

III

The dispute over the advowson of Ashbourne has no direct relevance to Edward I's famous Statute of Mortmain. It does show, however, that when it came to a religious foundation for which King Edward was directly responsible, his willingness to negotiate with the dean of Lincoln proved to be in the long-term interest of his foundation. It is at least possible that this experience led Edward to develop a flexible system of licensing to allow some alienations to the church despite the outright ban in the Statute of Mortmain. As noted by Professor Brand, 'in practice what the king got [in the Statute of Mortmain] was a share in the control of amortization with the lord of whom the land to be amortized was held'.[51] For an astute and experienced ruler, shared control can sometimes be more beneficial than absolute power.

Notes

* It is an honour to have the opportunity to contribute to this second Festschrift for Paul Brand, who has graciously shared much wisdom with me over the course of my career, as he has done with so many other scholars.

1 Paul Brand, 'The Control of Mortmain Alienations in England, 1200–1300', in Brand, *MCL*, 242–3 (discussing J.M.W. Bean, *The Decline of English Feudalism 1215–1240* (Manchester: Manchester University Press, 1968), 53, 64, and T.F.T. Plucknett, *Legislation of Edward I* (Oxford: Clarendon Press, 1949), 98–9).

2 On the founding of the abbey, see Jeffrey Denton, 'From the Foundation of Vale Royal Abbey to the Statute of Carlisle: Edward I and Ecclesiastical Patronage', in *Thirteenth Century England IV: Proceedings of the Newcastle Upon Tyne Conference*, eds. Peter R. Coss and Simon D. Lloyd (Woodbridge: Boydell Press, 1991).

3 3 Conc. Lat., c. 14 (1179), *COD* 219 = X 3.30.19; 4 Conc. Lat., c. 44 (1215), *COD* 254 = X 3.13.12.

4 2 Conc. Lat., c. 1–2 (1139), *COD* 197. The term 'simony' comes from Simon the sorcerer, who tried to buy the power of the Holy Spirit from the apostles. Acts 8: 9–21.

5 Peter Landau, *Jus Patronatus: Studien zur Entwicklung des Patronats im Dekretalenrecht und der Kanonistik des 12. und 13. Jahrhunderts* (Cologne: Böhlau Verlag, 1975), 130–6.

6 Noël Denholm-Young, *Seignorial Administration in England* (Oxford: Oxford University Press, 1937), 2–3.

7 See J.E. Newman, 'Greater and Lesser Landowners and Parochial Patronage: Yorkshire in the Thirteenth Century', *EHR* 92 (1977): 281.

8 In the first decretal, *Cum seculum*, the pope prohibited the Templars and Hospitallers from making inappropriate use of advowsons they had acquired 'as purchasers or other acquirers of fiefs' (*ratione feudorum emptorum aliterve acquisitorum*), thus implying that it was possible to purchase an advowson. WH 302, 1 Comp. 3.33.16 = X 3.38.13 (1175). The second decretal, *Ex litteris*, involved a lease of a particular vill by a convent to a layman; the pope determined that the advowson appurtenant to the vill was included in the lease because it was not specifically excepted. WH 422, 1 Comp. 3.33.9 = X 3.38.7 (1175–80). These decretals settled the previous dispute among the decretists, although it took some time for their significance to be appreciated. See Landau, *Jus Patronatus*, 111–13.

9 *Item transfertur [ius patronatus] ratione universitatis, sive illa universitas vendatur sive donetur sive infeudetur, vel alio modo aliter, nisi specialiter excipiatur, ut Alexander III Ex litteris, Cum seculum.* Huguccio, *Summa decretorum*, gloss to C.16 q.7 c.26, v. *Pie mentis.* (Admont, Stiftsbibliothek, MS 7, fol.289va).

10 Dig. 8.4.12 (*Cum fundus fundo servit, vendito quoque fundo servitutes sequuntur. aedificia quoque fundis et fundi aedificiis eadem condicione serviunt.*).

11 Landau, *Jus Patronatus*, 79–80. Several decretals of Alexander, for example, suggested that a bishop must consent in order for a gift of an advowson to be valid. See, e.g., WH 880, 1 Comp. 3.33.7 = X 3.38.5 (1179–81); WH 329, 1 Comp. 3.33.13 = X 3.38.11 (1160–76); WH 689, 1 Comp. 3.33.21 = X 3.38.17 (1159–81); WH 998, 1 Comp. 3.33.25 = X 3.38.20 (1177). In one decretal, however, Alexander suggested that a donation to a religious house might be valid even without episcopal authority (although a reference to episcopal authority was interpolated in the *Liber Extra* by Raymond of Peñafort). WH 184, 1 Comp. 3.33.23 = X 3.24.4 (1173–76). Another decretal of Alexander distinguished between the church, which could not be given without lay approval, and the advowson, which could freely be given to a religious house. WH 761, 1 Comp. 3.33.10 = X 3.38.8 (1177) (*laicus sine auctoritate episcopi nemini potest ecclesias dare, licet religioso loco ius patronatus conferendi liberam habeat facultatem*). Later canonists seized on actual or perceived inconsistencies in the decretals to defend their own views as to the requirements for gifts. Landau, *Jus Patronatus*, 80–93.

12 Landau, *Jus Patronatus*, 86; http://legalhistorysources.com/1140a-z.htm.

13 *[P]ossit donari etiam private persone, arg. in extra continebatur, et etiam sine consensus et auctoritate episcopi, quod Alexander innuit in illo decreto Quamvis simus.* Huguccio, *Summa decretorum*, gloss to C.16 q.7 c.26, v. *Pie mentis.* (Admont, Stiftsbibliothek, MS 7, fol.289va).

14 Landau, *Jus Patronatus*, 89–90. For the dates of these canonists, see http://legalhistorysources.com/1140a-z.htm.

15 Bernard of Parma, *Glossa ordinaria* to X 3.38.8, v. *religioso* (*sive concedat ecclesiam, sive ius patronatus, necessaria est auctoritas episcopi*). The *Glossa ordinaria* was rewritten and revised several times between 1241 and Bernard's death in 1266. See http://legalhistorysources.com/1140a-z.htm.

16 Landau, *Jus Patronatus*, 90.

17 Ibid., at 94. The prohibition on sale may be found in the first recension of Gratian's *Decretum* as well as in the decretals of Alexander III. See *Dictum post* C.16, q.7, c.30 (*fundatores ecclesiarum . . . non habent ius uendendi, uel donandi, uel utendi tamquam propriis*); WH 1061, 1 Comp. 3.33.20 = X 3.38.16 (1174–81) (*quum inconveniens sit et penitus inhonestum vendi ius patronatus, quod est spirituali annexum, contractum illum . . . irritum esse decernas*); Anders Winroth, *The Making of Gratian's Decretum* (Cambridge: Cambridge University Press, 2000), 216.

18 In Peter's view, because the advowson was a *ius corporale*, there was no reason why it could not be sold or mortgaged, provided that no creditor exercised the advowson without the patron's consent. Peter the Chanter, *Summa de Sacramentis et animae consiliis*, ed. Jean-Albert Dugauquier, 3 vols. (Louvain: Nauwelaerts, 1954–67), 3/2b: 706–7 (*Credimus . . . quod ius patronatus merum sit corporale et vendi potest, et in perpetuum et ad tempus, et obligari pignori; tamen, si interim uacauerit beneficium aliquod, non debet creditor dare illud sine licentia patroni, quia illud accederet preter sortem et esset usura.*). Peter acknowledged, however, that others did not share his view, and he offered no textual support for his position, which was rejected by later canonists. Landau, *Jus Patronatus*, 98. On the intellectual approach of Peter the Chanter and its context, see Marcia L. Colish, *Medieval Foundations of the Western Intellectual Tradition, 400–1400* (New Haven: Yale University Press, 1997), 287.

19 Landau, *Jus Patronatus*, 99–101. For the latter view, see Bernard of Parma, *Glossa ordinaria* to X 3.38.6, v. *spoliando* (*eo ipso quod imponitur pena emptori, et non venditori, videtur remanere penes ipsum patronum ius patronatus; quia si voluisset privari, hoc dixisset*).

20 See PRS, 14, 122–3 (Sept. 1194) (no judgment); *CRR*, 7: 280 (Mich. 1214) (no judgment); *CRR*, 9: 15–16 (Trin. 1220) (case settled); *BNB*, 3: 452–3, no. 1570 (Mich. 1222); *CRR*, 11: 509–10, no. 2567 (Mich. 1224) (case settled); *BNB*, 2: 495–6, no. 644 (Mich. 1231) (donee loses).

21 Susan Wood, *The Proprietary Church in the Medieval West* (Oxford: Oxford Univervisty Press, 2006), 682–3; Newman, 'Greater and Lesser Landowners', at 281.

22 *CRR*, 9: 11 (Trin. 1220).

23 *CRR*, 4: 126 (Pas. 1206); *CRR*, 6: 348 (Trin. 1212); *CRR*, 11: 78, no. 417 (Hil. 1223).

24 *CRR*, 7: 138 (Trin. 1214) (*ita tamen quod nulli domui religiose predictam ecclesiam conferat et ne aliquid fiat in preiudicium iuris heredum suorum*).

25 For the entries referencing the gifts, see *RCR*, 2: 99 (Mich. 1199); *CRR*, 2: 231–2 (Pas. 1203); *CRR*, 3: 3 (Mich. 1203); *CRR*, 3: 94 (Hil. 1204); *CRR*, 5: 54 (Mich. 1207); *CRR*, 7: 294–5 (Mich. 1214); Yorks. no. 1151, 425–6 (1218–19); *CRR*, 8: 241–2 (Hil. 1220); *CRR*, 8: 287–8 (Pas. 1220); *CRR*, 9: 26–7 (Trin. 1220); *CRR*, 9: 107–8 (Trin. 1220); *BNB*, 2: 139–40, no. 172 (Pas. 1222); *BNB*, 2: 148–9, no. 182 (Pas. 1222); *CRR*, 11: 153, no. 768 (Mich. 1223); *CRR*, 11: 549, no. 2733 (Mich. 1224); *CRR*, 12: 527, no. 2641 (Pas. 1226); *BNB*, 3: 621–2, no. 1813 (Norf. 1227); *BNB*, 3: 632–3, no. 1831 (Norf. 1227); *CRR*, 14: 7, no. 48 (Trin. 1230); *CRR*, 16: 394, no. 1931 (Pas. 1242); *CRR*, 19: 168–9, no. 1058 (Mich. 1249); *CRR*, 19: 173, no. 1079 (Mich. 1249).

26 See, e.g., *Lincs.*: 39, no. 239 (1202) (confirmatory charters of the bishop of Lincoln, the archbishop of Canterbury, and popes Lucius and Alexander); *BNB*, 2: 28–9, no. 34 (Pas./Trin. 1219) (confirmatory charter of Pope Alexander as well as bishop of Ely); *CRR*, 9: 21 (Trin. 1220) (confirmatory charter of Pope Honorius offered along with confirmation of bishop of Lincoln).

27 A search of the published plea rolls for the period under discussion revealed thirty-nine instances of royal charters being offered to confirm a gift.

28 *CRR*, 13: 85, no. 370 (Trin. 1227) (*quidam Johannes filius Suani, qui habuit advocacionem tocius ecclesie, vendidit medietatem illius advocacionis Willelmo de Nevill', patri Sarre que fuit mater predicti Thome et cuius heres predictus Thomas est, et racione illius empcionis presentavit predictus Simon quondam vir ipsius Sarre; et aliam medietatem vendidit predictus Johannes Rogero de Montebegon', cuius heredes uxores Eudonis de Lungvillers et Gaufridi de Nevill' sunt*).

29 Ibid.

30 Letter to Miss Lewis, 23d June 1840, in *George Eliot's Life, as Related in Her Letters and Journals*, ed. J.W. Cross (New York: Harper & Brothers, 1885), 1: 68.

31 *RA*, 27: 17, no. 14.

32 *RA*, 1: 116–17, no. 186.

33 *RA*, 3: 41–3, no. 677.

34 *RA*, 3: 43–4, no. 678.

35 *RA*, 3: 45–7, no. 680.

36 *CChR*, 1257–300, 208.

37 *CPR*, 1258–66, 67, 143.

38 *RA*, 3:110–11, no. 758.

39 Ibid.

40 *CChR*, 1257–300, 143.

41 Denton, 'From the Foundation of Vale Royal Abbey', 124.

42 Ibid.

43 *CChR*, 1257–300, 207.

44 *CCR*, 1272–9, 497.
45 *CChR*, 1257–300, 208.
46 See www.hrionline.ac.uk/taxatio/benkey?benkey=CL.DE.AS.01.
47 On the dispute over Kirkham, see Denton, 'From the Foundation of Vale Royal Abbey', 131–3.
48 Ibid.
49 Ibid.
50 See www.hrionline.ac.uk/taxatio/benkey?benkey=YK.RC.AM.06.
51 Brand, 'The Control of Mortmain Alienations', 243.

6 The clerk William Tyssyngton and the pursuit of fugitives in the late thirteenth century

Karl Shoemaker

Introduction

Sometime in the early 1290s a felon named William Heywode was hanged before royal justices in the county of Staffordshire, England. In the years prior to his execution, Heywode had not made things particularly easy on the local officials responsible for his capture, confinement and conveyance to trial. Before he was finally convicted and executed, he had managed to escape from custody in Tuttebury castle on at least two separate occasions. Each time, he remained at large for a year. Each time, his capture was accomplished by the same man, a clerk named William Tyssyngton who was in service to Thomas de Bray, seneschal of Staffordshire.

The crown pleas for the Staffordshire eyre of 1293 offer a somewhat laconic account of events that were presumably acutely distressing for Heywode, and no doubt annoying and costly to those responsible for his custody. According to the jurors' testimony recorded in the roll, William Heywode 'was captured and imprisoned in Tuttebury castle in the time of Thomas de Bray, Seneschal, and from the custody of the same Thomas, William escaped'. William Heywode then enjoyed a year at large, after which 'he was recaptured by William Tyssyngton, a clerk of the aforesaid Thomas, and returned to Tuttebury Castle'. Upon his recapture, Heywode was held again at Tuttebury Castle until it was time to be delivered to trial. Thomas de Bray again enlisted the assistance of his clerk, William Tyssyngton, and together they took Heywode from Tuttebury Castle, 'wishing to lead him to Northbridge Castle' for trial. Presumably they took other prisoners awaiting gaol delivery as well. Northbridge was not quite fifteen miles north from Tuttebury, perhaps a little more than half a day's walk – even for two men leading a band of unenthusiastic prisoners. Assisting in gaol delivery may have been one of Tyssyngton's regular responsibilities, though such is not specified in the record. We might assume, given Heywode's history of escape, that Tyssyngton and de Bray were alert for further escape attempts. Nonetheless, Heywode successfully escaped from their custody again. After another year at large, Heywode was finally recaptured – still in Staffordshire and again by the cleric William Tyssyngton. Heywode's surname indicates he was from western Staffordshire – modern Haywood. His limited range after his escapes suggest that he was more comfortable near home than roaming far. He would have had ample time, had he chose, to seek sanctuary and abjure the realm under royal protection. Thousands of other English men and women in similar straights made such a choice in late-medieval England. Whatever kept Heywode so near his home ultimately cost him his life. After his recapture, Heywode was led once again to the castle at Northbridge 'and there before the justices at gaol delivery, he was hanged'. The marginal notations on the plea roll indicate that seneschal Thomas de Bray dutifully paid the two fines *de evasione* for which he was personally liable on account of allowing Heywode to escape.[1]

Despite his evident skill at escaping, there is much that is mundane about Heywode's case. Prisoner escapes in thirteenth century England were legion. Fines *de evasione* were routinely imposed upon the officials responsible for custody of escaped prisoners. Convicted felons were usually sentenced to death. Hanging, while not the only method of execution known to English law, was the typical method of imposing the sentence. In short, Heywode's case was replicated thousands of times in the crown pleas of late medieval English royal justice. More interesting is the persistence of the cleric William Tyssyngton, whose sustained activities in pursuit of Heywode are of a sort typically less visible in the plea rolls.

The strange career of William Tyssyngton, clerk

In fact, the plea rolls suggest William Tyssyngton had made something of a career pursuing escaped fugitives. Unusually, at least for these sources, we find Tyssyngton named in a separate plea roll entry pursuing another fugitive. In this instance, he was performing essentially the same service, chasing a prison escapee. This time the events took an improbable and tragic turn. According to the roll, 'William Tyssyngton, a cleric, struck William de Lenton, the caretaker of Tuttebury Castle, in the head with a Danish hatchet, from which he quickly died . . . [and] William quickly put himself in the church of St. Mary de Tuttebury'. But rather than abjuring the realm, as typically occurred in such a case, William 'waited in the church for three weeks'. He then 'put himself on the country and returned himself to the prison at the castle at Northbridge in the time of Bogo de Knoxville, sheriff'.[2]

By the time the royal justices arrived in 1293, however, William Tyssyngton was no longer being held at Northbridge, a fact that would shortly cause some inconvenience for sheriff Bogo. Even so, the jurors knew where Tyssyngton was, testifying 'that William was now staying in Derbyshire'. The town of Tyssyngton (modern Tissington) sits about twenty miles north of Tuttebury, just across the Derbyshire border. There were close ties between Tuttebury and Tyssyngton. The town of Tyssyngton was one of several within the extensive Derbyshire holdings of Staffordshire's Tuttebury priory. Tuttebury Priory was itself an alien priory, founded as a dependent of the Benedictine abbey of St. Pierre-sur-Dives in Normandy.[3] By going to Derbyshire, William had gone home, but he had stayed within an area that was within the ambit of Tuttebury priory. The crown justices ordered that the sheriff of Derbyshire bring William Tyssyngton to appear 'by Saturday'. To indicate that Tyssyngton must appear by a designated day, the word 'Saturday' was entered on the left margin of the roll entry and a small amount of space was left in the roll for further text. Tyssyngton duly appeared, accompanied by sheriff Bogo. The testimony that would be recorded when Tyssyngton and Bogo appeared was longer than the scribe anticipated when he left space next to the marginal notation 'Saturday'. Hence, the record that follows was written on a flap of vellum and sewn into the roll.

Upon his appearance before the eyre court, the justices asked Tyssyngton how he wanted to answer concerning the death of William of Lenton, the porter of Tuttebury Castle. Tyssyngton claimed 'he had already been acquitted of the death before Odo de Hodynet and his fellow justices at the gaol delivery of Northbridge'. To verify this, the justices sent for the rolls of Justice Odo de Hodynet. Consultation of Odo's roll, however, did not quite confirm Tyssyngton's story. Rather, the roll offered a tangled set of events that hinged upon two cases of mistaken identity and resulted in a ruling of 'homicide by misfortune'.

The circumstances of the 'homicide by misfortune' were rather remarkable. As Odo's roll explained, 'it happened that a certain thief was imprisoned in Tuttebury Castle and escaped'. The jailer, 'William le Porter,' who is given as 'William of Lenton, janitor' in the first sentence of the entry, but appeared as 'William le Porter' in Odo's roll, 'ran to the church in order to prevent the thief from entering it'. William le Porter was trying to prevent the escaped fugitive from claiming sanctuary, a claim that would have made him immune to prosecution for his thefts or his escapes, but which also would have required him to abjure the realm of England.[4]

Tyssyngton had the same idea as le Porter. He also ran to the church to prevent the thief from entering and claiming sanctuary. At this point, however, things went seriously awry. Upon 'seeing Tyssyngton coming to the Church, and believing him to be the escaped thief, le Porter struck Tyssyngton under the ear on the left side of his jaw'. Despite suffering a sword blow to his face, Tyssyngton fought back ferociously. According to Odo's roll,

> the cleric, injured and gravely wounded, believed le Porter to be the same escaped thief. He quickly hit back and struck le Porter in the head with his hatchet. Le Porter lived until he had last rites, then died, and was buried in the presence of Hugh Weston, the coroner.

Here we can see with additional clarity why Thomas de Bray relied on Tyssyngton for the rough work of chasing escaped felons and assisting with gaol deliveries. The clerk appears to have been skilled at hand-to-hand combat and rather stout.

Because le Porter's death was ruled 'by misfortune', Tyssyngton was alleviated from immediate liability for felony, but he still needed to obtain a royal pardon for the death. Thus, Tyssyngton was 'returned to prison in order to await the grace of the Lord King'. This was standard practice in medieval English law because an acquittal was not available for those who killed another by mistake. A royal pardon was required.[5] In such cases, defendants were remanded to prison until a royal pardon was granted. As Thomas A. Green has shown, well into the fourteenth century juries were reluctant to acquit defendants even in clear cases of homicide by misfortune. In the medieval common law, self-defense was grounds for receiving a pardon, but it was not an affirmative defense for homicide.[6]

At this point, a difficulty arose for sheriff Bogo. Tyssyngton was no longer in custody. But he had not yet been pardoned or otherwise granted a lawful release from prison. Because the sheriff was responsible for his custody at Northbridge Castle, Bogo was now summoned to answer for his part in the tangled affair. 'Sheriff Bogo came and was not able to say who had William Tyssyngton in his custody and showed nothing concerning his delivery nor how he exited prison'. Bogo was assessed a fine.[7] It is possible that the sheriff released William Tyssyngton because he mistakenly thought Tyssynton had been acquitted. It is also possible that the sheriff knew Tyssyngton had not been acquitted, but released him anyway because of Tyssyngton's ties to seneschal Thomas de Bray and his prominent role in local law enforcement. Perhaps Tyssyngton had even agreed to indemnify Bogo for the fines he might incur for his release. Any such arrangement, if it existed, is submerged beneath the surface of the economy of crown pleas.

Local law enforcement in thirteenth-century England

Tyssyngton's activities bring some interesting details into relief. First, a hatchet-wielding cleric in the employ of the seneschal of Staffordshire appears to have specialised in pursuing and capturing escaped thieves. Tyssyngton's adventures and misadventures offer us a unique view of the texture of local law enforcement in late thirteenth-century England, one that is often occluded in the records of royal justice. Tyssyngton's legal adventures also show us interesting details about the production and use of legal records in late thirteenth-century English law. The documentary practices made it relatively easy for royal justices to summon Tyssyngton to the eyre court from a neighboring county, to adjudge his erroneous claim of prior acquittal, to discipline the sheriff who unlawfully released him from custody, and to insist on a royal pardon for the accidental death before allowing Tyssyngton his freedom. From this, we can also assess the maze of royal law, church privileges, local social networks and official responsibilities that someone like Tyssyngton might have to navigate, if imperfectly, when caught within the processes of medieval English royal law.

As we saw, the cleric Tyssyngton had a knack for catching escapees. He was well prepared and well armed. The 'Danish hatchet' he carried was a close combat weapon. Typically, a Danish hatchet had a wooden handle and a thin, wide, forged blade that curved backward into pointed horns at both ends, forming an effective, rounded cutting edge. The haft of the hatchet might be as long as three feet, or even more. Shorter handled axes were often used by mounted warriors, and might be utilised with one hand. They could be used to strike quickly with devastating effect. As the name suggests, this style of hatchet was originally brought to England by Norse invaders. In the eleventh century, the Danish hatchet, or Danish axe, was still associated with warrior elites. Because of its great utility, by the thirteenth century, the Danish hatchet had spread throughout Europe, becoming a very popular hand weapon.[8]

William Tyssyngton used his hatchet in the service of the seneschal of Staffordshire. The tasks we find Tyssyngton performing fell under the broader peace-keeping responsibilities Edward I had increasingly given to magnates in the late thirteenth century. In Staffordshire, peace-keeping responsibilities had been given to Thomas de Bray. Descended from one of the great Norman families that had fought alongside William at the Conquest, de Bray had been given wide and significant responsibilities by the crown. In 1290, Thomas de Bray had been appointed to oversee the return of lands and castles in Wales that Edward I had taken from Gilbert de Clare, the Earl of Gloucester. Gilbert had enjoyed a tumultuous relationship with King Edward. An early ally of Simon de Montfort, Gilbert later defected and sided with Edward while he was still prince, offering crucial service to him during the Barons' War. For this he was rewarded with additional lands in Wales. Gilbert was also instrumental in solidifying support for Prince Edward when King Henry III died in 1272, swearing fealty to Edward while Edward was still in Sicily on his way back from crusade. By the 1280s Gilbert had been given a military command against the Welsh, though he was relieved of this position after his humiliating defeat at the Battle of Llandeilo Fawr in June of 1282. In the 1290s, Gilbert displayed the independent streak characteristic of marcher lords, waging a private war against the Earl of Hereford. In a test of the customary rights to private war claimed by marcher lords, Edward I summoned both earls to his court, then imprisoned them, confiscated their lands, and fined them. In the wake of this assertion of royal prerogative by Edward, it was Thomas de Bray that was tasked with returning the land and castles to Gilbert, minus a handful of castles that were gifted by Edward to others, when the king released him from captivity a short time later.[9] De Bray's main orbit of activity, however, was in Staffordshire, where his responsibilities as seneschal required him to administer the county on behalf of the king. It was in this setting that men like de Bray relied upon men like William Tyssyngton for gaol delivery and capture of escaped fugitives in the county.

The larger picture, as scholars began to show several decades ago, was one of a growing and widespread perception of increased violence and illegality in late thirteenth-century England. Focusing on a period beginning in the 1290s, scholars discerned an emergent crisis of law and order.[10] The evidence for this emergent crisis of law and order was found largely in the preambles of royal legislation and trailbaston commissions, as well as in a perceived uptick in crimes coming before royal courts. Royal legislation had embraced a declension narrative of social disorder already by the 1270s. The preamble to the 1275 Statute of Westminster lamented 'the peace less kept and the laws less used, and offenders less punished than they ought to be'. Trailbaston commissions were justified by claims that 'large numbers of evildoers' were threatening the countryside and that there were bands of marauders bent on breaking the king's peace and terrorising his people. However we choose to read the alarmist language that formed the rhetorical array of thirteenth preambles and trailbaston commissions, the evidence of the criminal cases coming before the courts themselves is, despite the large number of extant records, too incomplete to support quantitative claims about rising crime.[11]

While it may be impossible to prove whether there was an increase in crime and disorder in the 1290s, the contemporary perception that there was is easy enough to demonstrate. Such perceptions seem to have lent momentum to the institutional reforms that ended the eyre and paved the way for the trailbaston and *oyer* and *terminer* proceedings that emerged in the fourteenth century. As Richard Kaeuper showed, the proliferation of special commissions may have actually contributed to the perception of lawlessness and disorder. Alongside the growth of special commissions, workloads at the eyre courts were increasing, driven as Paul Brand has shown, by the increased production of royal legislation in the second half of the thirteenth century.[12] Against this backdrop, Edward I appears to have been acting in partnership with nobles, seeking to reinforce their common interest in maintaining peace locally.[13] Indeed, this re-centring of law enforcement at the local level may have contributed to the rise of justices of the peace in the fourteenth century.

Tyssyngton was not yet disentangled from the web of legalities that he was caught within after mistakenly killing William le Porter. His claim that he had acquitted was not true. It had been disproved when the eyre justices were able to easily retrieve the rolls of justice Odo Hodynet and read of Tyssyngton's homicide by misfortune. It was a strange misstep for Tyssyngton, who otherwise demonstrated an astute grasp of how to navigate the legalities of the situation in which he found himself once he mistakenly killed le Porter. His first step was to claim sanctuary in the church of St. Mary, situated very near to Tuttebury Castle. Presumably, this was the same church the escaped prisoner was expected to try to reach. Le Porter lived long enough to receive last rites, and was quite likely still alive when Tyssyngton took sanctuary. It was not uncommon for sanctuary seekers to run to the church in anticipation that someone they had wounded would die. Tyssyngton did not, however, abjure the realm after claiming sanctuary. After three weeks, he exited the church and agreed 'to put himself on the country' – that is go before the jury. It is likely, but not conclusive, that Tyssyngton used the three weeks he stayed within the church to apprise himself of his legal options. A letter Tyssyngton wrote in Norman French to his 'very dear cousin and friend' regarding the king's pardon may well have been written from within sanctuary. The letter survives, though it is badly damaged and illegible in crucial respects.[14] There are instances of other sanctuary seekers using their time in sanctuary to secure pardons, or to arrange their affairs. Like Tyssyngton, individuals taking such steps tended to enjoy the support of robust networks of friends and benefactors.[15]

Conclusion

Tyssyngton did not have to wait long. His pardon was issued in February of 1293. It read: Pardon

> to William de Tyssyngton, clerk, for the death of William de Lenton, porter of Tuttebury castle, as it appears by the record of John de Berewyk and his fellow justices in eyre in the county of Stafford, that a thief imprisoned in the said castle, having escaped in the night, the porter, as soon as he became aware of it, went immediately to the church to prevent the thief from entering, and believing the said clerk, who had also gone to the church for the said purpose, to be the thief, struck and wounded him; and the said clerk, likewise believing the porter to be the thief, struck him back upon the head and so killed him by misadventure.[16]

It is not clear why William Tyssyngton did not plead clergy, a step that would have removed him from royal jurisdiction and alleviated the need for a pardon. It may be that he was not tonsured and dressed in clerical habit.[17] That William le Porter did not recognise Tyssyngton as a cleric may be explained by this. Tyssyngton may also have married a widow, an act that would have prevented him from claiming the privilege because he would be a bigamist. Unlike the fifteenth and sixteenth centuries, when the rules concerning claiming benefit of clergy had relaxed to the point that women could claim the privilege, bishops closely regulated the privilege in the late thirteenth century. A plea of clergy would have initiated a process in which Tyssyngton would not have been granted the privilege and handed over to ecclesiastical jurisdiction until he had demonstrated himself to be a cleric before his ordinary in the presence of a royal justice. Perhaps Tyssyngton did not want to risk ecclesiastical discipline, assessing that he was likely to receive a pardon based on the facts of the homicide. Had he plead clergy, he may have faced such discipline on a number of grounds. He shed blood, an act forbidden to clergy. In principle, carrying a weapon was forbidden to clergy. According to the *Liber Extra*, 'clerics carrying arms and usurers were to be excommunicated'.[18] No distinction appears to have been drawn between secular clergy and regular clergy in regard to this prohibition. The gloss made allowances for carrying arms 'through a dangerous place' in order to give 'terror to thieves', though it added somewhat unhelpfully that even armed clerics 'should not strike'.[19] After a third admonition for carrying weapons, a cleric could be deprived of canonical privileges.[20] Whether Tyssyngton wished to avoid such sanctions is not clear. No records that might shed light on this question survive. In any event, he had a royal pardon, necessitated by the vicissitudes of his role chasing and capturing fugitives in late thirteenth-century Staffordshire.

Notes

1 TNA, JUST 1/806 3d. (under sewn vellum flap). See transcription in Appendix 1. This record can be accessed at http://aalt.law.uh.edu/AALT4/JUST1/JUST1no806/bJUST1no806dorses/IMG_2945.htm (last accessed May 19, 2017). I would like to thank Charlotte Whatley and Travis Baker for their suggestions about this record.

2 TNA, JUST 1/806 3d (under sewn flap). See Appendix 2 for transcription. The record is available at http://aalt.law.uh.edu/AALT4/JUST1/JUST1no806/bJUST1no806dorses/IMG_2945.htm.

3 G.C. Baugh et al., 'Alien Houses: The Priory of Tutbury', in *A History of the County of Stafford*, eds. M.W. Greenslade and R.B. Pugh, vol. 3 (London: Victoria County History, 1970), 331–40. *British History Online*, www.british-history.ac.uk/vch/staffs/vol3/pp331-340.

4 Typically, but not always, abjurers went to France. See, William C. Jordan, *From England to France: Felony and Exile in the High Middle Ages* (Princeton: Princeton University Press, 2015). Also, Karl Shoemaker, *Sanctuary and Crime in the Middle Ages, 400–1500* (New York: Fordham University Press, 2011), especially chapter 7.

5 Naomi Hurnard, *The King's Pardon for Homicide Before A.D. 1307* (Oxford: Clarendon Press, 1969).

6 Green, *Verdict.*

7 TNA, JUST 1/806 3d.

8 R.E. Oakeshott, *The Archeology of Weapons, Arms, and Armor From Prehistory to the Age of Chivalry* (Mineola, NY: Dover Publications, 1996). For a later case of a cleric with an axe, see Torstein Jørgensen, '"He Grabbed His Axe and Gave Thore a Blow to His Head": Late Medieval Clerical Violence in Norway According to Canon and Civil Law', in *Medieval Christianity in the North: New Studies*, eds. Kirsi Salonen, Kurt Villads Jensen and Torstein Jørgensen (Turnhout: Brepols, 2013), 209–36.

9 *CPR*, 1281–92, 359.

10 The classic works are: G.O. Sayles, *The Court of King's Bench in Law and History* (London: B. Quaritch, 1959), chapter 3; Alan Harding, *The Law Courts of Medieval England* (London: George Allen & Unwin, 1973); Alan Harding, 'Early Trailbaston Proceedings From the Lincol Roll of 1305', in *Medieval Legal Records*: Edited in Memory of C.A.F. Meekings, eds. R.F. Hunnisett and J.B. Post (London: H.M.S.O, 1978); Michael Prestwich, *War, Politics, and Finance Under Edward I* (Totowa, NJ: Rowman and Littlefield, 1972), 287–90; Ralph

Pugh, 'Some Reflections of a Medieval Criminologist', *Proceedings of the British Academy* 59 (1973): 83–104.

11 For a discussion of the methodological problems involved here, see Richard Kaeuper, 'Law and Order in Fourteenth-Century England: The Evidence of Special Commissions of *Oyer* and *Terminer*', *Speculum* 54 (1979): 734–84, at 735–8.

12 Paul Brand, *Kings, Barons and Justices: The Making and Enforcement of Legislation in Thirteenth-Century England* (Cambridge: Cambridge University Press, 2003).

13 Caroline Burt, *Edward I and the Governance of England, 1272–1307* (Cambridge: Cambridge University Press, 2013), 125.

14 TNA, SC 1/29.

15 See Shoemaker, *Sanctuary and Crime*, 133–8.

16 *CPR*, 1292–301, 6.

17 This requirement was iterated by Pope Boniface VIII, probably between 1295 and 1297. See, Sext. 3.2. On the benefit of clergy, see L.C. Gabel, *Benefit of Clergy in England in the Later Middle Ages* (New York: Octagon Books, 1969) and David Millon, *Select Ecclesiastical Cases From the King's Courts 1272–1307* (London: Selden Society 2009) cxviii–cxviii. I would like to thank Paul Brand and Travis Baker for their insights on this aspect of Tyssyngton's case.

18 X.3.1.2.

19 *Glossa ordinarium* ad "*arma*" X.3.1.2.

20 Ibid.

Appendix 1

TNA, just 1/806 3d

Juratores presentant quod quidem Willelmus de Heywode captus fuit et imprisonatus in Castro de Tuttebury tempore Thomas de Bray Senescallis qui a custode eiusdem Thome evasit. Ideo ad iudicium de evasione eiusdem Willelmi super predictum Thomam. Et predictus Willelmus postquam evasit fugit et per unum annum postea captus fuit apud Leyton per quondam Willelmum de Tyssyngton clericum predicti Thome et reduratus ad castrum de Tuttebury et postea cum predictus Thomam [melius: Thomam] et Willelmus ipsum duxisse voluissent ad Castrum de Bruges idem Willelmus de Heywode tertium evasit a custode eiusdem Thome in villa de Wulverhampton. Ideo ad iudicium de evasione eiusdem Willelmi de Hewode super predictum Thomam. Et predictus Willelmus de Heywode per unum annum postquam reevasit recaptus fuit per predictum Willelmum de Tyssyngton et ductus ad Castrum de Bruges et ibi coram Justiciariis ad Gaol deliberando et supensus nulla habuit cattalam.

Appendix 2

TNA, just 1/806 3d.

Willelmus de Tyssyngton clericus percussit Willelmum de Lenton, ianitor de Tuttebury cum quadam hachia Denesch in capite in burgo de Tuttebury unde statim obit. Primus inventor venit et non malecreditur et Willelmus de Tyssyngton statim posuit se in ecclesiam Sanctae Mariae de Tuttbury et ibi morabatur per tres septimana et postea venit ad pacem et reddit se prisone ad Castrum de Bruges tempore Bogoni de Knoxville vicecomiti. Ideo respondeat de eo. Postea testatum est quod predictus Willelmus manens est in comitatu Derbeie. Ito praeceptum vicecomiti Derbeie quod habeat corpus eius hic die Sabbati. Postea venit predictus Willelmus et quesitur qualiter se velit acquietare dicit quod ipse alias coram Odone de Hodynet et sociis suis Justiciariis ad gayol de Bruges deliberando assignatus acquietatus fuit de predicta morte et de hoc verdictum recordatum rotolorum predictorum Justiciarii et querens suae rotuli in quibus compertum est tale recordum in hec verba. Willelmus clericus de Tyssyngton captus et imprisonatus per morte Willelmi le Porter de Totteburye ponit se de bono et malo super xii juratores qui dicunt per eorum sacramentum quod contigit quod quidam latro imprisonatus fuit in Castro de Tottebury dictus latro evasit de prisona [illegible] de causa ut impediret latronem nec intrare ecclesiam. Willelmus clericus de Tyssyngton ob eandem causam adivit ecclesiam. Willelmus le Porter videns Willelmum clericum venire versus ecclesiam credebat ipsum esse latronem evasum et statim eum percussit cum quodam gladio sub aure in fauce sinistra. Willelmus clericus ab eo insultus et graviter vulnatus ex hoc credebat ipsum esse latronem evasum et ipsum Willelmum le Porter repercussit statim eum quadam hachia in capite quoddam vulnus. Ita quod vixit quousque habuit iura ecclesiae mortuus et sepultus per Hugonem de Weston coronatorem. Unde per casu fortunito dictus Willelmus clericus reversus est ad prisonam ad gratiam domini Regi expectando. Ideo venitur in primus postea venit predictus Bogo et non potest dedire qui habuit predictum Willelmum de Tyssyngton in custode sua et nichil ostendit de deliberatione eius nec qualiter exivit. Ideo ad iudicium. Postea dominus Rex mandavit pro predicto recordo et ei mittatur.

7 Profits and perils of an Irish legal career

Sir Elias Ashbourne (d. 1356), chief justice and marcher lord

Robin Frame

The idea that Ireland should be seen as 'England's first colony' has become familiar in recent years.[1] The term 'colony' seems particularly apt for the student of law and institutions. The laws of England were explicitly extended to Ireland (though in effect mainly to the settler population living there) from 1210. And in the later thirteenth and fourteenth centuries many English lawyers, like many English exchequer clerks, spent parts of their careers in Dublin.[2] The judiciary was not, however, wholly drawn from the metropolis. By the fourteenth century, the lordship of Ireland was developing its own legal profession. The two Irish benches – the sedentary court of common pleas (or Dublin Bench) and the itinerant court of the 'pleas that follow the justiciar of Ireland', which dealt with both civil and criminal cases and also transacted miscellaneous governmental business[3] – were venues where men born on either side of the sea sat together, though not always harmoniously. In the mid-fourteenth century incoming ministers from England sometimes expressed unease about the ties they perceived to exist between local members of the judiciary and the magnates of Ireland.[4] In 1341, when extending to Ireland his recent assault on his judges and other ministers in England, Edward III was moved to insist that his leading ministers in Ireland should have backgrounds and property in England.[5] From such episodes sprang a political rhetoric on the Irish side of the sea that highlighted tensions between 'the English born in Ireland' and 'the English born in England', and asserted that the former had the same rights as the latter.

The ideas encapsulated in such phrases are, of course, worth exploring in their own right. But such neat sub-national distinctions are a poor guide to the complexities of individual lives and political situations.[6] Elias Ashbourne, who was prominent among the judges dismissed in the purge of 1341, is a good example of the finer shadings and the ambiguities that the headlined categories obscure. Ashbourne was a Dubliner, but for upwards of thirty years he had been a regular commuter across the Irish Sea; he had connections with men close to the king; and he held property in England as well as in Ireland. His changing fortunes highlight the close affinity of the politics and government of colony and metropolis, but they also bring into sharp focus the distinctiveness of the colonial society in which English law was administered.

By the standards of the Irish benches, Ashbourne had a long career.[7] In May 1327 he took office as second justice of the justiciar's court. He was appointed chief justice in June 1329 and went on to serve for a total of eight years between that date and May 1344.[8] The year 1341 was not the only occasion when he was removed from office. He had already been displaced in 1331. His return to the bench in 1337 had encountered challenges. And while his career quickly recovered from the setback of 1341, he was again dismissed in 1344, and then imprisoned. This time there was no way back. The circumstances of his final dismissal were such that, while he recovered his freedom and at least some of his property in 1346, he never held office again. In Trinity Term 1344, while Parliament was in session at Westminster, Edward III had sent to his judges of the King's Bench for examination a set of petitions from Ireland laying grave accusations against Ashbourne. There were five main charges.[9] The final one accused him of judicial malpractices. Disregarding his oath to uphold the law, he had sold justice, taking gifts from both sides in a case, and behaved so that honest folk had lost their lands through his misdeeds. When he coveted somebody's lands or goods, he had had them falsely indicted so that out of fear of prison or outlawry they did a financial deal with him, in return for which he arranged their acquittal. Similarly, when men were indicted of homicide, he took payments from them to hand-pick a jury, so that the law did not take its course and justice was denied. These were serious accusations, but of a sort that might have arisen on either side of the Irish Sea. The remaining four charges were of a different order: they alleged that Ashbourne had entered into treasonable conspiracies with the king's 'enemies', the Irish chiefs of south Dublin and Wicklow.

All the accusations, needless to say, raise questions of credibility. Were the charges true? Should they be regarded as exaggerated or tendentious, but with some basis in fact? Or were they fabrications by Elias's rivals and enemies? It is not possible to give firm answers to these questions, though investigation of the background suggests that the charges should not be taken wholly at face value. But the matter of truth or falsehood may be less significant than the window they open on the complexities and tensions of the colonial world. Some of these are apparent in Ashbourne's arguments in the King's Bench in 1344. His accusers wished him to be kept in custody in England until the veracity of the allegations was enquired into by the justiciar of Ireland and reported to the king. If he were permitted to go to Ireland, they claimed, such was his malign influence that nobody would dare plead against him or speak the truth. Elias in response stressed his entitlement to a jury of twelve 'according to the law and custom of the realm of the king of England used in times past'. Taking his stand on a familiar constitutional point, which had for instance been explicitly accepted by Edward I in 1305,[10] he argued that in Ireland the king had his justices and his chancery; it was in Ireland and nowhere else that all cases alleging misdeeds committed there should be heard and determined. This claim echoes a collective petition from Ireland in 1341, protesting against writs of the English chancery summoning people indicted in Ireland to stand trial in England. But by mentioning '*seditions* and felonies', Ashbourne may have pushed his case too far. Edward III's answer in 1342 had been broadly favourable, but had specifically excepted 'treasons and anything that touches the king's person'.[11] Dogged attachment to English rights and liberties, especially when allied to a measure of jurisdictional separateness, was not, however, the most striking feature of the colonial scene. The more spectacular charges against Elias Ashbourne arose from a career that combined, uneasily in the end, the roles of royal justice and marcher lord.

I

Elias Ashbourne was a member of a prolific Dublin family, presumably originating from Ashbourne in Derbyshire, with a long record of office-holding and career-building.[12] His grandfather, Roger Ashbourne, had been a provost of Dublin city in 1256–7 and then mayor from 1261 to 1263 and again in 1268–9. His father, also Roger, was a provost in 1286–7.[13] Roger II's prominence is illustrated by the fact that he acted as a general attorney in Ireland for Richard Burgh, the Red Earl of Ulster, the greatest of the magnates, while Richard was absent in England in 1298–9.[14] Among his other roles was that of steward to the archbishop of Dublin, whose great liberty of St Sepulchre lay immediately to the south of the city and whose estates occupied much prime land in Co. Dublin both north and south of the River Liffey.[15] Such stewardships were often a gateway to legal careers. As Paul Brand has shown, Roger frequently acted as a pleader (*narrator*) for litigants in the Dublin Bench. In 1307, towards the end of his life, described as a serjeant pleader, he travelled with the justiciar's court on its eyre in the south-western counties, earning a considerable income from his share in the damages awarded in the cases with which he was involved.[16]

Elias followed in his father's footsteps in several respects: his prominence in the city of Dublin (though it is not certain that he held high civic office[17]); his links with the archbishopric, where he too was steward in 1325–6; and of course his career in the law. Unlike Roger II, however, he does not seem to have practised as a serjeant. Nor is there evidence that he had formal legal training, though the same could be said of some other judges in Ireland in the early decades of the fourteenth century. But his background and associations meant that he had at the very least relevant practical experience, and probably some familiarity with the legal literature that was in circulation in Ireland as well as England.[18] An early appearance in the record in Ireland sheds light on the company he kept. In 1311 he was one of a group of nine men and one woman pardoned at the request of the magnate Edmund Butler in a session of gaol delivery held at Dublin by John Wogan, the justiciar. Their offence was the castration of a man named Ralph Petybon.[19] Elias stands second in the list of those indicted, after Richard le Blond of Arklow. Richard le Blond served in the courts as a king's serjeant from 1297 to 1322, and was a colleague of Roger Ashbourne II.[20] So, ironically, this unsavoury episode shows Elias moving in legal circles – a milieu where, it would seem, self-help was not unknown.

The career of Roger Ashbourne II had a further dimension: long experience in conducting business on both sides of the Irish Sea. In 1290 he appointed attorneys in Ireland for two years, suggesting that he intended a lengthy stay across the water.[21] In 1307 he was entrusted by the city of Dublin with an important mission to England concerning the common seal of the city, and was sufficiently confident to hold out for extra expenses when his journey was delayed.[22] And it was in England that Elias Ashbourne made his earliest significant appearance in the record, in a dispute that illustrates the interweaving of events in the two countries. In 1309–10 he was accused by Alan son of Sir William fitz Warin of burning his houses at Mears Ashby, near Wellingborough in Northamptonshire.[23] William fitz Warin had been a household knight of Edward I. During the 1270s he spent a stormy period as royal seneschal of Ulster, where he had inherited some property, while the earldom was in the king's hand.[24] Among his English possessions in 1285 was one-third of Mears Ashby, held of the king of Scots, who held it of the king of England.[25] The origins of the dispute between Alan and Elias are not clear, but they appear to have had rival claims to property at Mears Ashby. Victory in the first round may have gone to fitz Warin, for in 1312 Ashbourne required a pardon for felonies committed in Northamptonshire.[26] Rancour crossed the sea to Dublin, where in August 1314 Alan with several others had to make fine for breaking into Elias's houses in the city and seizing goods valued at twenty marks.[27] The dispute then became entangled with affairs of state. The invasion of Ireland by Edward Bruce in May 1315 and his rapid occupation of eastern Ulster faced landholders in the north with hard choices. Alan fitz Warin was at least suspected of having flirted with the enemy, for in 1319 he figured in a list of those pardoned for adherence to the Scots.[28] Possibly it was the need to re-establish his credentials with the authorities that explains a deed he executed at Drogheda in October 1317, surrendering to Elias Ashbourne, his son Thomas and their heirs all his rights in Mears Ashby.[29] From that point on, the Ashbournes appear to have had secure possession.[30]

By this time, Ashbourne's prospects had been advanced through service to one of the more effective careerists of Edward II's reign, John Hotham, bishop of Ely (1316–37), who was to become treasurer (1317–18) and then chancellor (1318–20, 1327–8) of England.[31] Hotham was a nephew of the English Dominican William Hotham, archbishop of Dublin from 1296 to 1298. It is possible that Hotham's link with the Ashbournes went back a generation, since Roger Ashbourne was seneschal of the archiepiscopal demesnes in William Hotham's time and pleaded for the archbishop in the Irish courts. By 1301 John Hotham was a clerk in the Dublin exchequer, where between 1305 and 1310 he rose to become a baron, chancellor and finally deputy treasurer. His reputation as a safe pair of hands and as an expert on Ireland was evident in 1315, when he was dispatched to the lordship as Edward II's special emissary after the king had grasped the seriousness of the Scottish invasion. In 1316 Elias was said to be returning to Ireland with Hotham, and in 1318 the king referred to him as Hotham's yeoman (*valettus*).[32]

Time spent in England, together with the link with Hotham, brought Elias into Edward II's service. Between 1321 and 1327 he is repeatedly referred to as 'the king's yeoman (*valettus regis*)', implying an association with the royal household.[33] At the same time the first signs appear that he was acquiring a role in the Irish courts. In 1319–20 he had been referred to in passing in the Irish exchequer Memoranda roll as 'Elye le mareschal de Asshebourne'.[34] In July 1322 he was given the office of marshal before the justices in eyre in Ireland.[35] He may or may not have participated in the punitive eyre in Meath between January and November 1322, which seized Roger Mortimer's liberty of Trim into the king's hands.[36] He certainly played a leading part in a later *cause célèbre*. In 1325–6 he commended himself to the regime by acting as its agent in an assault on the interests of Walter Islip, a former baron of the exchequer and recently treasurer of Ireland. Islip was an associate of the archbishop of Dublin, Alexander Bicknor, who had been treasurer of Ireland early in Edward II's reign. Bicknor had defected to Queen Isabella and Mortimer during a mission to France in 1325. His account had been under audit at Westminster since 1320; now accusations of false accounting and misappropriation of funds gathered force, no doubt for political reasons. Islip was implicated, along with Robert Cotgrave, an exchequer chamberlain.[37] Ashbourne was made steward of the archbishop's forfeited temporalities, from which he received the substantial gratuity of fifty marks 'for expediting the king's business'.[38] The ensuing dispute between Islip and Ashbourne was rough and bitter. Ashbourne, on his own testimony, had been charged to take the goods of the three miscreants into the king's hands; while going about this business in the city of Dublin, he had been attacked by William Weston, one of Islip's attorneys in Ireland.[39] In 1328 Islip in turn was to claim that the charges against him had been put forward in England by 'his enemies', among whom he named Elias Ashbourne.[40]

Despite his employment by the Despenser regime, Ashbourne's career seems to have been unaffected by the political upheaval of 1326–7. The government of Isabella and Mortimer acknowledged his good service both to the king (now Edward III) and to his father, and in April 1327 appointed him to the justiciar's bench in Ireland.[41] Later evidence suggests that Ashbourne's time around the English court may have brought him a connection with a figure rather more distinguished than John Hotham. This was Richard of Bury, noted bibliophile and bishop of Durham (1333–45), who numbered among his circle Richard FitzRalph of Dundalk, the future archbishop of Armagh.[42] In May 1332, Ashbourne was given royal permission to endow a chantry in Dublin to pray for his soul and those of three other named persons: Bury stood first in the list.[43] Bury may not have been, as once thought, tutor to Edward III, but he was very close to the king, serving as cofferer and keeper of the Wardrobe, and keeper of the privy seal. In the dying days of Mortimer rule, he had helped to establish a clandestine link between Edward and the papal curia.[44]

Elias Ashbourne's early career should serve as a caution against interpreting the ups and downs that followed along a supposed fault-line between 'the English born in Ireland' and newcomers from England. Although his roots lay in Ireland and his mature career was spent there, Ashbourne was no mere provincial figure. He had metropolitan interests, experience and contacts. It was through networking between Ireland and England that he had achieved high office. His resilience in the face of accusations and rivalries during the 1330s and early 1340s is explicable only in the light of his ability to mobilise his defences in England. His reappointment as chief justice in March 1337 was followed by changes of mind on the part of the authorities, which saw him removed from office (in theory at least) in August but restored in September only to be removed once more in May 1338 and again restored the following September. It comes as no surprise to find that he had been in England in the spring of 1337, when he received as a stream of grants from the crown,[45] and that he had returned there in the summer of 1338.[46] Throughout his career, he seems to have been able to draw upon reserves of royal favour, which he had banked from the 1320s onwards.

II

The justiciar's court, where Ashbourne sat for the best part of a decade, never had more than two judges and was probably less significant as a seat of legal knowledge and training than the Dublin Bench – just as in England the Westminster Bench, not the King's Bench, was the chief focus of the legal profession.[47] But its judges carried special weight through their proximity to the governor of Ireland, with whom they travelled around those parts of the lordship of Ireland that were subject to the routines of direct administration. The presence of the judges in parliaments and great councils was, as in England, taken for granted: they were among the 'skilled councillors' whose attendance, according to an ordinance of 1357, was expected.[48] The rolls of the justiciar's court contain, besides the routine of civil and criminal pleas, a great deal of what Geoffrey Hand described, a little dismissively, as 'the residue of non-legal administrative business'.[49] That business might, however, be exceedingly important, giving the record of the court, at times, the character of a council roll.[50] Matters of note could include responses to petitions from leading magnates, arrangements for the defence of castles or border country, agreements with Irish chiefs, and the delivery of hostages from lineage-heads.[51] Unfortunately, almost all the original justiciary rolls were lost in the destruction of the Public Record Office of Ireland in 1922, at a point when their calendaring had not reached beyond 1318. We have nothing beyond a few partial transcripts and antiquarian excerpts from the time when Ashbourne was in office. He can, however, be glimpsed in a political role of the utmost significance. In the summer of 1329, still apparently a puisne judge, he was appointed by John Darcy of Knayth, the justiciar, along with the two chief justices, Nicholas Fastolf and John Grantchester, as an arbitrator 'to hold a day' at Kilkenny between William Burgh, earl of Ulster and Maurice fitz Thomas, earl of Desmond, whose quarrels constantly disturbed the peace of Ireland between 1328 and 1331.[52]

The experience of judges in Ireland might encompass war as well as high politics. The justiciar's eyre often grew into a small-scale military campaign, aimed at countering Irish raids, disciplining English marcher lineages or (more rarely) responding to magnate unrest. Between August and December 1329, for instance, Ashbourne was among those who accompanied John Darcy on four brief expeditions, in Wicklow against the O'Byrnes (twice), in Laois against the O'Dempseys and O'Mores, and in Meath against the MacGeoghegans.[53] There was nothing unusual in this: for instance, Godfrey Folejambe, who began a career in the justiciar's court at the time of Ashbourne's final ousting in 1344, was rewarded for military service against the O'Byrnes in 1354–5.[54] But there are indications that Ashbourne's military involvement went beyond the routine. Between July and November 1331, when he was out of office, he accompanied the justiciar, Anthony Lucy, on an expedition into Munster with six men-at-arms and six hobelars.[55] He received several rewards for other military services during the 1330s and 1340s, not all when he was on the bench.[56] Nor was his martial role confined to Ireland. In May 1335, while still out of office, he was summoned to Scotland with other gentry of Dublin, Kildare and Meath.[57] It is not clear whether he served on the Irish expedition that sailed to the Clyde in August (though he may well have done).[58] But he was certainly involved in the preparations that began the previous April. On 8 June he was described as returning to Ireland after having recently travelled to England; and orders in his favour dated at Northallerton and Durham suggest his presence at court in the run-up to the campaign.[59]

Ashbourne's shifting fortunes during the 1330s and early 1340s may be explained, in part, by two related influences. The first was the impact of changes of governor. The appointment of new justiciars from England tended to be accompanied by other changes in the top stratum of Irish administration. Although appointment of judges of the two benches was reserved to the king and normally made under the great seal of England, a convention existed by which an incoming governor could suggest possible names, from whom the king and council might (or might not) make a choice.[60] In 1331, when Anthony Lucy, lord of Cockermouth, was appointed justiciar, Ashbourne and his fellow judge Roger Preston were removed from office in favour of Peter Tilliol and John Skelton, two members of the Cumbrian retinue that accompanied Lucy to Ireland.[61] Ashbourne's dismissal in 1344 made room for Godfrey Folejambe, who came to Ireland with Ralph Ufford and his wife Maud of Lancaster, countess of Ulster, whose daughter Elizabeth Burgh had been given in marriage to Lionel of Antwerp, Edward III's second surviving son. Folejambe was to have a long career in royal service, first with Queen Philippa (to whom the guardianship of Lionel and Elizabeth had been granted) and later with John of Gaunt, whose chief steward he became.[62]

The swings and roundabouts of judicial careers were not, however, propelled solely by the arrival of new administrative groups. There was also frequent royal disquiet about the state of the Irish administration. This became more persistent and overt from the mid-1330s,[63] when the financial demands of the Scottish and French wars fed dissatisfaction in England with the low level of the Irish revenues, which had shrunk drastically since the time of Edward I.[64] Enquiries undertaken by the treasurer, John Ellerker the Younger, in 1335–6 led to the first of many reforming ordinances, which rightly or wrongly placed much of the blame on the incompetence and venality of royal ministers, who were suspected of siphoning off profits the king might otherwise have received. New administrations from England were commissioned to investigate the misdeeds of their predecessors and of lesser ministers who were still in office. Such bouts of 'reform' created a toxic atmosphere, in which malice, denunciation and blame-shifting flourished, with claims and counter-claims making their way to the king and council in England through both official and back channels.

The administrative purge of 1341 was in addition a by-product of a wider crisis, extending to Ireland the king's attacks on his English ministers and judges in 1340, when he came back in anger from his expensive and indecisive early campaigns in France. His actions had a good deal in common with those of Edward I on his return from a three-year sojourn in Gascony in 1289. As Mark Ormrod has commented, 'it was a commonplace of medieval politics that kings returning from lengthy stays abroad made gestures of good intent by dismissing corrupt officials and taking an interest in the better maintenance of public order'.[65] Irish government, it may be suggested, was subject to repeated low-key versions of the same phenomenon, when it was galvanised (or disturbed) by the arrival of new brooms from England. It also shared a further characteristic of the English upheavals, in that denunciations and waves of dismissals ended up producing less evidence of malpractice than the initial rhetoric suggested, and many of those targeted were fairly quickly re-employed. This was the case in 1342 in Ireland, when Edward – whose priority was now to restore good feelings to assist recruitment for his planned Breton campaign – backed away from the full implications of his actions, and Elias Ashbourne, along with other recent casualties, soon regained office.[66] In 1344, however, Ralph Ufford's actions were to have a sharper edge. As well as possessing strong court connections, he arrived at the head of a substantial military retinue; the vigour with which he set about cleansing Dublin's Augean Stables possibly owed something to the wish to pass offices and custodies to his own people.[67] Ashbourne and others suffered as a result.

III

Whereas files of charges against treasurers and other exchequer officers survive,[68] there is a frustrating lack of equivalent evidence regarding judges who were dismissed. The 1344 allegations of judicial malpractice against Elias Ashbourne are wholly unspecific; only the charges of conspiracy with the Irish name names and cite particular (though undated) episodes. So there is no direct way of assessing his behaviour on the bench. In the absence of such material, the most promising approach is to explore his activities and the sources of his wealth across his time in royal service. There are undoubtedly signs that he made advantageous deals, though no more so, perhaps, than many other ministers. But the character and location of certain of his acquisitions help to make sense of the accusations of closeness to the Irish enemies of the king.

In Ireland as in England, high judicial office was a route towards status and wealth. Knighthood was an accolade aspired to and usually attained by lay members of the English judiciary under Edward III. We do not know when, or by whom, Elias Ashbourne was knighted, but he had achieved the rank by the spring of 1335 at the latest.[69] His standing is also reflected in his presence in 1337 alongside John Darcy as a guarantor for a 1,000-mark pledge for future good behaviour given by the Irish magnate Walter Bermingham, who was seeking full restoration to the lands of his father, William Bermingham, who had been executed in 1332.[70] His prosperity did not come from his salary as a judge. Annual judicial salaries were the same in Ireland as in England: sixty marks (£40) for the chief justice and forty marks for the second justice. These sums were far from princely, and there was no expectation that judges should subsist on them. Lay judges lacked the advantages available to the dying breed of clerical judges, who could be quietly rewarded with canonries and other ecclesiastical preferments in the king's gift. Their bonuses (so to speak) were more visible. The acceptance by judges in England of fees and retainers from lay and ecclesiastical lords was common practice; only in the mid-fourteenth century was it coming to be viewed as incompatible with service to the Crown.[71] Judges in Ireland were certainly in receipt of fees. In 1342–3 Elias himself can be glimpsed receiving an annual fee of one mark from the cathedral priory of the Holy Trinity, Dublin (Christ Church Cathedral).[72] Nor was Christ Church the only Dublin house to retain lawyers who were in the Crown's employ.[73] The accounts of Elizabeth Burgh, lady of Clare, one of the greatest of the non-resident proprietors, confirm the picture: they show, for instance, that she paid Robert Scarborough, the English chief justice of the Dublin Bench, £40 a year to be 'chief keeper' of her Irish lands and gave lesser fees and tips to various ministers of the Irish government.[74]

It is difficult to believe that were not similar associations between the judiciary and resident lay nobles. In 1346 the justiciar, chancellor and treasurer complained to Edward III that 'the men of law who are with us are of the country and retained by all the magnates here'.[75] Unfortunately, such ties are impossible to identify because household and ministerial accounts of lay aristocrats, scarce in England, are virtually non-existent in Ireland. It is tempting to wonder whether Ashbourne's vicissitudes were connected with Irish factional politics, and in particular whether he may have had an attachment to Maurice fitz Thomas, the turbulent first earl of Desmond. Desmond was the prime target of the English governors Anthony Lucy and Ralph Ufford. Although Ashbourne served in Munster with Lucy in 1331, at some point he was convicted before him of an undisclosed trespass, for which he owed a fine of eighty marks.[76] Ufford likewise treated him harshly. By contrast, his career seems to have proceeded with little incident under John Darcy (governor for several spells between 1329 and 1336) and Thomas Charlton, bishop of Hereford (keeper of Ireland in 1338–40), both of whom had a more relaxed relationship with Desmond. But this can be no more than speculation.

Judges in fourteenth-century England cultivated associations and built up property portfolios in their home regions, as for instance Sir William Shareshull, chief justice of the King's Bench, did in the west midlands.[77] The lordship of Ireland was a much smaller world. In Ashbourne's time, direct government still reached deep into south Leinster and Munster. But recruitment to the emerging legal profession was primarily from the four eastern counties of Dublin, Kildare, Meath and Louth, the area that in early Tudor times was to become known as the Pale.[78] The focus of Ashbourne's interests was in Dublin city and its extensive hinterland. He inherited or acquired a considerable scattering of property within the city and county of Dublin and the contiguous area of south-east Meath.[79] His holdings may be roughly grouped into three categories. He owned houses, shops, mills and small parcels of land within the city walls and just outside them, in the pool of Dublin, together with two mills in the southern suburb of Donnybrook.[80] Secondly, he had significant holdings on the estates of the archbishopric, mostly, though not entirely, in north Co. Dublin, which was insulated from the Irish raids that affected the archiepiscopal manors to the south. These lands included one-and-a-half carucates and 265 acres on the prosperous manor of Swords, where the archbishops had a palatial residence.[81] Thirdly, he held some 190 acres, together with various rents, of the barons of Dunboyne and Skreen in Meath.[82] Ashbourne's government service brought useful, but scarcely extravagant, additions to his landed wealth within the same region. The most significant was custody of the north Dublin manors of Dunbro and Huntstown, valued at ten librates, which was transferred to him from Walter Islip, and remained in his hands from 1329, despite Islip's pardon, at the light rent of two marks a year.[83] Besides Dunbro and Huntstown, his rewards within the core area of governmental power appear to have been limited to a handful of other routine custodies, which were not specially remunerative.[84]

The heartlands of the four counties were encircled by border zones, which were agriculturally marginal and dominated by Irish and English stock-rearing lineages. It was in such a milieu – south Dublin and Wicklow, an area of uplands, deep valleys and woodland – that Ashbourne made his more striking and unusual gains and developed an additional dimension to his career. His accumulation of property in the region during the late 1320s and 1330s looks like a considered strategy. There were three main acquisitions. A grant in December 1328 under the Irish seal, later confirmed in England, gave him custody of Ballygunnar, Co. Dublin, which was in royal hands because of the debts owed by Albert Kenley, a former sheriff of Kildare.[85] In 1332 the custody was converted into a heritable grant at an annual rent of 15s.[86] 'Ballygunnar' represents an area in the parish of Delgany, Co. Wicklow, in the hinterland of the modern coastal village of Greystones. It gave Ashbourne control of Kindlestown, a stone castle of the settlement period which Albert Kenley had reconstructed as a hall house, to which his surname became attached.[87] Ashbourne's presence in the area was more than nominal: shortly before his death he was pardoned £10 of his accumulated debts for having maintained troops at Ballygunnar.[88]

The other two acquisitions were contiguous and may be considered together. In 1329 Ashbourne received a grant of a substantial block of territory, sometimes referred to as 'the manor of Bothercolyn', assessed at 760 acres, said to be 'waste', just south of Tallaght in the modern south Dublin suburbs. Tallaght was a notionally huge archiepiscopal manor, many parts of which were alleged in an extent of 1326 to be profitless 'because no tenants will stay as it is near the Irish'.[89] Ashbourne's grant extended for some three miles from east to west. It was first made for a term of twenty years. After an inquisition in 1330 confirmed that the area had lain uncultivated before he received it, the king converted the grant into a heritable fee-farm.[90] Later, he was freed from rent for seven years, upon petitioning that he could not profit from the land without building a stone house from which to control it. This he may have done.[91] After a petition in 1335, his interest in this region was expanded by a twenty-year grant of additional lands also said to be 'waste'.[92] These, in the vicinity of Ballinteer and Killinardan in the parishes of Taney and Whitechurch, have been identified, along with Bothercolyn, as component parts of the early thirteenth-century royal manor of Okelli, which had long ceased to function as a fiscal unit.[93] Between them, the two grants made Ashbourne, potentially at least, the possessor of a substantial, fairly compact lordship on the south Dublin frontiers. The repeated claims that the lands were unprofitable sit uneasily with the fact that such a shrewd and experienced Dubliner thought he could make something of them. Ashbourne's view was evidently shared by Robert Holywood, an acquisitive exchequer official, who took them over in the late 1350s.[94] It is also striking that when some of the properties were re-granted during Ashbourne's forfeiture of 1344–6, the recipient was charged double the farm that Elias had paid.[95]

Ashbourne's involvement in the marches went beyond landed proprietorship. In 1333 he was appointed constable of the coastal castle of Arklow, at the southern tip of the later county Wicklow. Arklow belonged to the Butler earls of Ormond, but it was in the king's hands for three years after its recapture from the Irish and rebuilding by Anthony Lucy in 1332, and it returned to the Crown once more in 1338 owing to a Butler minority. Elias had its keeping from March 1333 to August 1335, and again from June 1339 to June 1341. During his second term his fee was a princely eighty marks a year.[96] Complaints against Irish treasurers in the mid-fourteenth century present constableships as perquisites that were sometimes exploited collusively: the defence of a castle, when not wholly neglected, was entrusted to ill-paid deputies; or the fee for its custody was shared between exchequer officials and the constable, who 'remitted' part of it as the price for being paid the remainder.[97] The size of Ashbourne's fee, which was twice or more the amount allotted to most other constables, and twenty marks higher than that received by Walter Boneville, his successor,[98] may raise suspicions. But there is no hard evidence of malpractice on his part, and a great deal to suggest that he was active in the Leinster marches. For instance, between 1339 and 1341 he was rewarded for supervising the repair and defence of Arklow.[99]

Possession of lands in the march, together with the constableship, involved Ashbourne in dealings both with the chiefs of the fissiparous Irish ruling lineages, who dominated the uplands and regularly raided the shrinking settlements in the lower reaches of the valleys and in the coastal plain, and with the 'English' lineages who competed with them, and with one another, for control of men, livestock and tributes.[100] There is ample testimony to Ashbourne's involvement with both groups. The former ruling dynasty of the O'Tooles, together with the Harolds and Archbolds, were his neighbours in south Dublin. His interests at Ballygunnar involved him primarily with the O'Byrnes of Wicklow and the settler lineage of Lawless (Le Waleys). His position at Arklow brought him into the orbit of the MacMurroughs, descendants of the pre-conquest kings of Leinster, the core of whose power lay in north Wexford. Some examples may illustrate the variety and complexity of his relations with both Irish and English. In 1328 the 'Dublin' chronicle, in the sole annalistic reference to Ashbourne, shows him, together with Nicholas Fastolf, the chief justice of the justiciar's pleas, condemning David O'Toole, the chief of his kin, 'a bold robber, enemy of the king, burner of churches and destroyer of the people', to be drawn at the horse's tail through the middle of the city of Dublin, to the gallows to be hanged.[101] The military expeditions of the following year saw Ashbourne serve alongside leaders of contingents who included Raymond Lawless, Thomas Harold, Thomas Archbold and Murchadh O'Toole, a cousin and possible rival of David.[102] Years later he was rewarded for capturing a felon and raider named Robert 'Rikynesson' Harold and handing him over to the courts, where he received a death sentence.[103] We know too that he employed a messenger with the Irish name Thomas O'Regan, who may possibly have served him as an interpreter, assuming he needed one.[104] The depth of his involvement in this marcher world is apparent in 1335, when he led a delegation including Robert Lawless, the lineage head, and Gerald son of Dúnlaing O'Byrne to meet John Darcy, the archbishop of Dublin and other 'faithful men of the lord king of the marches of Leinster'. An agreement had been brokered that Murchadh, chief of the O'Byrnes, would remain in the Wicklow area at Darcy's order, would accept responsibility for damages caused to the English, would fight disorderly elements till they came to the peace, and would collect in hostages from heads of households within his lineage.[105] It was presumably for his part in negotiating this deal that Ashbourne was granted forty marks for diplomacy in Leinster, bringing Irish who had risen to war to the king's peace.[106]

IV

The more dramatic charges brought against Ashbourne in 1344 must be assessed against this background. First, however, it is important to clarify the circumstances of his fall. As a preliminary to the installation of Ralph Ufford's administration, an order went out in February 1344 forbidding ministers to leave the country before the arrival of justices commissioned to enquire into their conduct; they and any ships' captains and mariners who carried them were threatened with arrest.[107] Payment of Ashbourne's salary as chief justice ceased on 31 May. This may have been the date when he departed to England, perhaps under escort, to face the accusations against him. The ensuing business was transacted while Parliament and its committees were in session at Westminster (10 June to 8 July).[108] Though the king did not explicitly endorse Elias's argument that the case should not proceed in England but should be tried in Ireland, his actions appear to accept it, for on 7 July Edward ordered his release, on the security of six mainpernors who undertook that he would return to Ireland to answer his accusers. The six were headed by John Darcy, now king's chamberlain, John's son Roger Darcy, who was both escheator of Ireland and constable of Dublin castle,[109] and Thomas Ashbourne, Elias's eldest son. By 10 July Elias and Thomas were preparing to return to Ireland, where Ufford and his retinue arrived on 14 July.[110] Silence then falls. We must presume that investigation of the charges went forward in Ireland, though there is no record either of the proceedings or of a verdict. At some point Elias may have broken the terms of his bail, for three of the justiciar's English knights were in possession of chattels that he had forfeited 'for flight'.[111] It was perhaps because of this that he suffered protracted imprisonment, until he was finally released in June 1346, two months after Ralph Ufford's death in office.

The four charges of sedition may be briefly summarized. The first accusation was put forward in the name of the Lawless family, grandly describing themselves as 'the lieges of our lord king of the March of Ireland'. They alleged that Elias had plotted with the Irish and procured O'Byrne to attack and destroy them out of greed to acquire their lands. The ensuing war had lasted for four years, destroying their lands, castles and towns on the Dublin coast. The damage to the king and his people amounted, they claimed, to £1,000. The fourth charge probably came from the same source. It alleged that Elias had provided money, arms and other items to Gerald son of Dúnlaing O'Byrne and Thomas O'Byrne, who in return agreed to kill various loyal marchers at an arranged time. The Irish duly entered the area, killing five named men, four of them Lawlesses, and various others. Since that moment, burnings, destruction and killings had continued, with the damage to the king and his subjects amounting to an improbable £100,000. The third charge was less precise. It claimed that during his time as a judge, when he was duty-bound to act for the king's interests and profit, Ashbourne had summoned the great men of the land to take counsel with the marchers and others to identify ways in which the Irish enemies might be defeated and their destructive activities stopped. The meeting agreed on certain measures. Elias, privy to the details, had given warning to the Irish, so that effective action was prevented. The continuing raids had resulted in damage estimated at a further £10,000.

The remaining accusation came from a different source. Richard de la Sale claimed that Elias, after he had been granted custody of the castle of Arklow, had asked Richard to provide a garrison. This he had done, placing three of his own brothers with other men in the castle. When the town of Arklow was attacked by the Irish, the garrison came to the rescue, killing the leader of the Irish and taking five hostages, whom they lodged in the castle. Elias had then sent emissaries to the castle, demanding its surrender back into his own hands. His agents had proceeded to deliver Richard's brothers to the Irish, while the castle and the hostages within it were yielded to MacMurrough, who occupied the castle until Elias procured the release of seven further hostages from Dublin castle. The upshot, Richard claimed, was continuing war in the area, causing damage amounting to £10,000.

It is impossible either to verify or to disprove these charges, but essential to read them in awareness of the complexities of frontier activity and the shifting alliances that crossed the ethnic boundaries that appear so firm in official phraseology. One of the more familiar complaints made against government representatives in Ireland was that they made truces or peaces that paid too little attention to the local interests that had been damaged by Irish attacks. As recently as 1342, Edward III had responded to a petition on the subject by forbidding the making of agreements that left his lands or those of his loyal subjects in Irish hands, and empowering those who had lost lands to take steps to recover them without fear of punishment for breaching the peace.[112] Such tensions over military policy may partly explain certain of the accusations against Ashbourne. Possibly, too, there were jealousies sparked by the intrusion of an influential new proprietor into the established pecking order of south Dublin and the Wicklow coast. There is evidence of competition between Ashbourne and the Lawlesses over the constableship of Arklow. In October 1338 Edward III had received a petition from 'certain lieges' asking for the office to be awarded to whichever of Elias Ashbourne or John Lawless was fitter for its defence, and had referred the matter back to the justiciar of Ireland.[113] In the following March the king confirmed the appointment of Elias, which had already been made under the Irish seal.[114] In the interim, Arklow had been held by Thomas son of Michael Lawless, whom Elias accordingly displaced.[115]

The lurid allegations put forward by Richard de la Sale also need to be assessed in awareness of the political climate in which they were made. De la Sale's origins are uncertain,[116] but he either already had, or quickly formed, an association with Ralph Ufford, and was a chief beneficiary of Ashbourne's fall. It was Richard who in November 1344 was commissioned to enquire of Elias's goods and chattels and to take them into the king's hand.[117] In January 1345, described as 'the king's esquire', he had a grant of certain of Ashbourne's lands in the Dublin marches.[118] And in the following summer he led a small retinue on Ufford's campaign against the earl of Desmond in Munster.[119] None of this, of course, proves that his allegations were untrue, but it does suggest that at the very least they found a receptive ear in Ralph Ufford. The circumstances of Ashbourne's release and partial rehabilitation are also intriguing. In June 1346 he was given a general pardon under the Irish seal, at the petition of John l'Archer, prior of the Hospitallers, the chancellor of Ireland; John Burnham, the treasurer; Roger Darcy, the escheator; and Hugh Burgh, the chief baron of the exchequer. The pardon referred to the damages he had suffered through his 'long imprisonment'. All these men were English-born; all had been in office under Ufford; Hugh Burgh was, moreover, an old servant of Ufford's wife, Countess Maud of Ulster. The same group of ministers were vocal in lobbying the king to uphold Ufford's actions against the earl of Desmond, alarmed by signs that Edward might offer an olive branch to the outlawed earl (which he did).[120] Their contrasting advocacy of Ashbourne's case may suggest that they thought his treatment since the summer of 1344 unduly harsh.

Elias Ashbourne recovered his standing to some extent. In 1349, for instance, he stood first in the witness-list of a significant Dublin deed, ahead of both Robert Preston, a king's serjeant who was shortly to become a judge of the Dublin Bench, and Nicholas St Lawrence, the lord of Howth.[121] Between 1346 and 1356 he was back in possession of many of his lands and rents, though he appears to have devolved some of them to his three sons, Sir Thomas, Robert and John.[122] During his last decade, he was more than once rewarded for his military and diplomatic efforts in south Dublin and Wicklow.[123] But he never held high office again, and he was burdened with heavy debts. He died on or around 12 May 1356. In the last days of his life he conveyed further property in Dublin city to Robert Ashbourne, and enfeoffed a certain Simon Loterel with a major part of his Meath holdings.[124] Presumably these death-bed transactions were designed to frustrate his creditors, the king among them. They were unsuccessful. His property was soon seized on account of his debts to the crown, and an intervention by the justiciar, the earl of Kildare, was needed to permit Thomas Ashbourne to hold the inheritance as a custody, paying the extent.[125] During 1357 and 1358 Thomas granted much of his property in Dublin city to Walter Passavaunt, to whom the king transferred the custody in December 1358.[126] Thomas, who claimed to be without the means to support himself and his family, was granted ten marks from the issues of the lands for himself and a further twenty marks for his wife and children.[127] At the same period, the weight of Elias's debts was also falling on his younger sons.[128] And by 1364 they had caught up with Walter Passavaunt, from whom the exchequer recovered lead, timber and slates to the value of £33.[129] By then, the Ashbourne family had already faded from the Christ Church deeds and other record sources in which they were once so prominent.

V

Elias Ashbourne was not the only judge to involve himself in marcher affairs. Robert Preston, who from 1358 had a long career as chief justice of the Dublin Bench, married the daughter and eventual heiress of Sir Walter Bermingham (d. 1350). Among the Bermingham interests were the districts of Carbury and Tethmoy in the Kildare-Meath marches, where collateral branches of the family were powerful. In 1367, after the cadet Berminghams had raided Meath, Preston 'placed a large garrison in the castle of Carbury and incurred much expenditure against the king's enemies, defending the right that he held through his wife'.[130] Nor was Elias the only minister to face charges relating to the wars in Leinster. In 1350 the incoming justiciar, Sir Thomas Rokeby, dismissed the treasurer, Robert Embleton, a king's clerk who had once been chamberlain of Berwick, and gathered a spectacular dossier of complaints against him. One was that he had frustrated a defensive campaign in Wicklow by refusing to release funds. In consequence, it was said, the Irish had been able to rustle livestock valued at 400 marks.[131] Among the charges made against the governor, William Windsor, in the 1370s was that he and his retinue wilfully tarried in Dublin castle while the O'Byrnes ran riot.[132] Any Irish ministerial career was likely to be affected, in one way or another, by the existence of march zones, where social conventions, habits of dispute-settlement and patterns of governmental action differed from those familiar in the sheltered heartlands of the colony. Elias Ashbourne stands out because of the large investment he made in the marches and the multiple roles he played there over an extended period.

Ashbourne's career, awkwardly combining life on the judicial bench and life in the marches, might stand as a metaphor for the social context of law and governance in English Ireland. The 'custom of the land of Ireland' was English common law, with some minor local variants.[133] Like Ashbourne in 1344, the settler elites were often vocal on the subject of their entitlement to English law and liberties. So too, substantive changes in the law, from Magna Carta through the statutes of Edward I to the economic and social legislation of the fourteenth century, were received from England, though sometimes with a time-lag, and occasionally a degree of uncertainty or confusion.[134] Yet that is only part of the picture. From at least as early as 1278, statutes and ordinances of local application were enacted in Irish parliaments and great councils, or sent from England in response to collective petitions from Ireland or on the advice of ministers in Dublin.[135] Such legislation has tended to be of limited interest to legal historians. As Geoffrey Hand remarked, 'very seldom . . . did these [statutes] (or those of them that survive) touch upon broad questions of substantive law'.[136] Nor does this local legislation, at least before the promulgation of the Statutes of Kilkenny in 1366, seem to have been much pleaded in the courts.[137] Yet it engaged with subjects that were of fundamental importance to those who sought to prosper in the lordship of Ireland. Official rhetoric, and petitions from those spied profit in victimhood, might present border zones as a remote penumbra, alien and menacing. In reality, they were part of the familiar scene; and enactments that dealt with defence and regulation of the marches, relations with Gaelic lords and with Irish culture, and indeed the very definition of 'peace' and 'war', engaged with matters that helped to give English Ireland its distinctive character. The society of the marches shaped the fortunes of Sir Elias Ashbourne as surely as did the official world of Dublin and Westminster, within which so much of his career was set.

Notes

1 See, e.g., J.A. Watt, 'Approaches to the History of Fourteenth-Century Ireland', in Art Cosgrove, ed., *Medieval Ireland, 1169–1534: A New History of Ireland*, vol. 2 (Oxford: Oxford University Press, 1987), 312–13; Robin Frame, *Ireland and Britain, 1170–1450* (London: Hambledon Press, 1998), 184–5; and Peter Crooks, 'State of the Union: Perspectives on English Imperialism in the Late Middle Ages', *Past and Present* 212 (2011): 12. All argue that the term fits Ireland much better than Gascony, which saw neither substantial settlement from England nor an implantation of English law: cf. M.W. Labarge, *Gascony, England's First Colony, 1204–1453* (London: Hamish Hamilton, 1980). I would like to thank Peter Crooks for helpful comments on a draft of this paper.

2 Classic studies of the law are Hand, *English Law*, and Paul Brand, 'Ireland and the Literature of the Early Common Law', in Brand, *MCL*, 445–63. On lawyers, see two essays by Brand, 'The Early History of the Legal Profession in the Lordship of Ireland, 1250–1350', ibid., 21–56; and 'The Birth and Early Development of a Colonial Judiciary: The Judges of the Lordship of Ireland, 1210–1377', in *Explorations in Law and History: Irish Legal History Discourses, 1988–94*, ed. W.N. Osborough (Dublin: Four Courts Press, 1995), 3–48. More generally, see Robin Frame, 'Exporting State and Nation: Being English in Medieval Ireland', in *Power and the Nation in European History*, eds. Len Scales and Oliver Zimmer (Cambridge: Cambridge University Press, 2005), 143–65.

3 For the justiciar's court, see Hand, *English Law*, ch. 3.

4 *Documents on the Affairs of Ireland before the King's Council*, ed. G.O. Sayles (Dublin: Irish Manuscripts Commission, 1979), nos. 203, 212.

5 *Foedera*, 2, ii, 1171.

6 For the slipperiness of the terminology and the need to set its use in particular political contexts, see Robin Frame, *English Lordship in Ireland, 1318–1361* (Oxford: Clarendon Press, 1982), 246–7; and Peter Crooks, '"Hobbes", "Dogs" and Politics in the Ireland of Lionel of Antwerp, *c.*1361–6', *Haskins Society Journal* 16 (2005): 117–48.

7 Brand, 'Colonial Judiciary', 42–6. For outlines of his life, see Frame, *English Lordship*, 102–4, and R. McKay, *Dictionary of Irish Biography*, eds. James McGuire and James Quinn, 9 vols. (Cambridge: Cambridge University Press, 2009), 1: 174–5; and F.E. Ball, *The Judges in Ireland, 1221–1921*, 2 vols. (London: J. Murray, 1926), 1: 68–9.

8 Ashbourne's periods of service as given in H.G. Richardson and G.O. Sayles, *The Administration of Ireland, 1172–1377* (Dublin: Irish Manuscripts Commission, 1963), 169–70, need to be revised. It seems clear that his initial term as a puisne judge did not end with the appointment of Nicholas Fastolf as chief justice on 29 October 1327; though no record of payment of his salary survives after that date, he is to be found sitting with Fastolf during 1328 (J.T. Gilbert, ed., *Chartularies of St Mary's Abbey, Dublin*, 2 vols. (RS, 1884–6), 2: 366–7). Nor did he finally leave office on 26 February 1343: he continued to be paid as chief justice until 31 May 1344, with writs of *liberate* being issued in his favour in February and May 1344: *IEP*, 412; CIRCLE, Close Roll 18 Edw. III, nos. 7, 43.

9 TNA, KB 27/337, m. 27 Rex. For brief comments on the case, see G.J. Hand, 'English Law in Ireland, 1172–1351', *Northern Ireland Legal Quarterly* 23 (1972): 411–12; Brand, 'Colonial Judiciary', 39. Paul Brand first drew the case to my attention a quarter of a century ago; it has taken me too long to do something with it.

10 *Calendar of Chancery Warrants, 1244–1326* (London: H.M.S.O. 1927), 253–4.

11 Statutes, *Ireland*, 350–1. It is not clear from the record that Ashbourne had been formally indicted in Ireland.

12 Men of that name were members of the Dublin guild merchant in the 1220s and 1230s: Philomena Connolly and Geoffrey Martin, eds., *The Dublin Guild Merchant Roll, c.1190–1265* (Dublin: Dublin Corporation, 1994), 55, 70–1. Ashbourne in Co. Meath (an area where, coincidentally, Elias Ashbourne held lands) is a nineteenth-century place-name.

13 T.W. Moody et al., eds., *A New History of Ireland*, vol. 9 (Oxford: Oxford University Press, 1984), 548; H.F. Berry, 'Catalogue of the Mayors, Provosts and Bailiffs of Dublin City, 1229–1447', reprinted in *Medieval Dublin: The Living City*, ed. Howard Clarke (Dublin: Irish Academic Press, 1990), 157–8. That the two Rogers (whom I mistakenly conflated in *English Lordship*, 102) were father and son is confirmed by the ratification, probably at Elias's request, of an exemption from tolls and tallages granted by the mayor and community of Dublin to Roger son and heir of Roger Ashbourne, and his heirs (*CPR 1327–30*, 128). From 1292, the two provosts elected annually were known by the more familiar term 'bailiffs' (Berry, 'Catalogue', 154).

14 *CDI, 1293–1301*, nos. 580, 685. He had recently acted as a pleader on the earl's behalf in the justiciar's court: *CJRI*, 1: 104.

15 A.J. Otway-Ruthven, 'The Mediaeval Church Lands of Co. Dublin', in *Mediaeval Studies Presented to Aubrey Gwynn, S.J.*, ed. J.A. Watt et al. (Dublin: Colm O Lochlainn, 1961), 55–63, 72–3, and the map at the end of the volume.

16 *CJRI*, 2: 392, 406, 417, 429; and cf. 385, 410, 416, 426, 433, 447, 452. See Brand, 'Legal Profession in Ireland', 36.

17 His name is not included in the standard lists cited above (n. 13); but the compilers refer to 'a TCD deed of *c.* 1324–5' in which he appears as mayor (*New History of Ireland*, 9: 551, n. 10; Berry, 'Catalogue', 222, n. 51). I have not

identified this document, which is not among the deeds calendared in 'Dublin Deeds'. On the basis of the same vague reference, Ashbourne has been included in some other compilations: E.C. Bairéad, 'The Bailiffs, Provosts and Sheriffs of the City of Dublin', *Medieval Dublin* XIV (2015), 262, 284. It is possible that he deputised for John le Decer, who was elected mayor in 1324 and again in 1325.

18 On this topic, see Brand, 'Legal profession in Ireland', 31–2.

19 *CJRI*, 3: 221. As late as 1248, English law permitted a husband (but only him) to take revenge by castrating a man who had committed adultery with his wife (P&M, 2: 484–5).

20 Richardson and Sayles, *Administration*, 174–5; *CJRI*, 1: 309; *CJRI*, 2: 126, 308, 329–30.

21 *CDI, 1285–92*, nos. 718, 727.

22 J.T. Gilbert, ed., *Historic and Municipal Documents of Ireland, A.D.1172–1320* (RS, 1870), 228–30.

23 *CPR, 1307–13*, 247, 252.

24 Beth Hartland, 'The Household Knights of Edward I in Ireland', *Historical Research* 77 (2004): 161–77, at 164–5.

25 *Feudal Aids, 1284–1431*, 6 vols. (London: H.M.S.O, 1899–1920), 4: 16. He also held of the honour of Huntingdon at nearby Wilby. See M.F. Moore, *The Lands of the Scottish Kings in England* (London: Allen and Unwin, 1915), 68, 126.

26 *CPR, 1307–13*, 508.

27 NAI, KB 2/7, m. 2.

28 *CPR, 1317–21*, 313. His reputation had recovered before his death in 1327 (*CCR, 1323–7*, 534–5).

29 NAI, RC 7/12, m. 30d.

30 *CIPM*, vi, no. 588.

31 For his career, see J.R.S. Phillips, 'The Mission of John de Hothum to Ireland, 1315–16', in *England and Ireland in the Later Middle Ages: Essays in Honour of Jocelyn Otway-Ruthven*, ed. J.F. Lydon (Dublin: Irish Academic Press, 1981), 62–85.

32 CIRCLE, Patent Roll 11 Edward II, no. 186. During the 1320s he served as one of Hotham's general attorneys in Ireland (*CPR, 1321–4*, 41; *CPR, 1327–30*, 373).

33 *CPR, 1321–4*, 41; *CFR, 1319–27*, 144; *CPR, 1324–7*, 311; *CCR, 1323–7*, 603; *CPR, 1327–30*, 125.

34 NAI, EX 1/2, m. 13. It is not clear whether he was serving in the exchequer itself or in another court.

35 *CPR, 1321–4*, 41.

36 H. Wood, 'The Muniments of Edmund de Mortimer, Third Earl of March, Concerning His Liberty of Trim', *Proceedings of the Royal Irish Academy* 40C (1932): 339–40. Ashbourne appears to have been in England in December 1321 (*CPR, 1321–4*, 41).

37 J.F. Lydon, 'The Enrolled Account of Alexander Bicknor, Treasurer of Ireland, 1308–14', *Analecta Hibernica* 30 (1982): 10; and Lydon, 'The Case Against Alexander Bicknor, Archbishop and Peculator', in *Ireland and the English World in the late Middle Ages: Essays in Honour of Robin Frame*, ed. Brendan Smith (Basingstoke: Palgrave Macmillan, 2009), 103–11.

38 *IEP*, 318.

39 NAI, R.C.8/14, 772–3; *CPR, 1324–7*, 250–1.

40 Philomena Connolly, 'List of Irish Entries on the Memoranda Rolls of the English Exchequer, 1307–27', *Analecta Hibernica* 36 (1995): 212–13; eadem, 'Irish Material in the Class of Chancery Warrants, Series I (C.81) in the Public Record Office, London', ibid., 145.

41 *CPR, 1327–30*, 60, 135, 139. He was paid from 12 May 1327, the day before the writ of the new king began, somewhat tardily, to run in Ireland (*IEP*, 323). For the uncertainty in Ireland after the deposition of Edward II in January 1327, see Frame, *English Lordship*, 174–6.
42 Katherine Walsh, *A Fourteenth-Century Scholar and Primate: Richard Fitz-Ralph in Oxford, Avignon and Armagh* (Oxford: Clarendon Press, 1981), 20, 79–80, 83, 110.
43 *CPR, 1330–4*, 303. Shortly after this the king added the prebend of Lusk in St Patrick's cathedral, Dublin to the various ecclesiastical benefices Bury held (ibid., 359).
44 W.M. Ormrod, 'The King's Secrets: Richard de Bury and the Monarchy of Edward III', in *War, Government and Aristocracy in the British Isles, c. 1150–1500: Essays in Honour of Michael Prestwich*, eds. C. Given-Wilson et al. (Woodbridge: Boydell and Brewer, 2008), 163–78.
45 He was appointed chief justice on 8 March and was returning to Ireland on 23 April (*CPR, 1334–8*, 389, 420). For grants and confirmations to him under the English seal between 14 March and 4 May, see ibid., 397, 409, 433 and *CFR, 1337–47*, 7, 14.
46 *CPR, 1338–40*, 151.
47 Brand, *OELP*, 54–65, chs. 6–8.
48 Statutes, *Ireland*, 408–9. Occasionally, the expectation was reinforced by their inclusion in the lists of those receiving individual summonses (H.G. Richardson and G.O. Sayles, *The Irish Parliament in the Middle Ages*, 2nd ed. (Philadelphia: University of Pennsylvania Press, 1964), 135–6, 304).
49 Hand, *English Law*, 87.
50 Two membranes from Easter 1307, containing miscellaneous business, are headed 'pleas of parliament': *CJRI*, 2: 350–5.
51 E.g., *CJRI*, 1: 8, 61, 230–1; *CJRI*, 2: 64–5, 82, 85, 103–4, 116, 133–5, 215–6, 242–3, 270–1, 290, 325–6, 502–3; *CJRI*, 3: 2–3, 3–4, 22–3, 26, 67, 76–7, 105–6, 161. Business concerning hostages was recorded on lost rolls from 13 Edw. II and 19 and 21 Edw. III: NLI, Genealogical Office, MS 190, p. 177; MS 191, pp. 305–6, 307; MS 192, pp. 11–13.
52 NAI, R.C.8/16, 354–5; *Rep. DKI*, 43: 65.
53 *Rep. DKI*, 43: 28–9; NAI, R.C.8/15, 473–7.
54 *IEP*, 461.
55 NAI, R.C.8/16, 300–6.
56 CIRCLE, Close Roll 5 Edw. III, no. 7; NAI, R.C.8/18, 603–4; NAI, R.C.8/22, 6–7, 185–6.
57 *Rotuli Scotiae*, 2 vols. (London, 1814–19), 1: 343–4.
58 The surviving lists contain only the leaders of contingents, who were of the rank of banneret or above; Ashbourne is likely to have served in that of John Darcy, the justiciar: Ranald Nicholson, 'An Irish Expedition to Scotland in 1335', *IHS* 13 (1963): 211. For the chronology, see ibid., 201–8, and Nicholson, *Edward III and the Scots, 1327–1335* (Oxford: Oxford University Press, 1965), 219–22.
59 *CFR, 1327–37*, 449; *CPR, 1334–8*, 126.
60 See J.F. Baldwin, *The King's Council in England During the Middle Ages* (Oxford: Clarendon Press, 1913), 473, for conciliar annotations of names proposed by John Darcy, the incoming justiciar, in 1328; and for an example in 1392, J.T. Gilbert, *A History of the Viceroys of Ireland* (Dublin: James Duffy, 1865), 555–6.
61 Frame, *English Lordship*, 202–3; Brand, 'Colonial Judiciary', 34–5.
62 He was a justice 1344–9 and chief justice 1352–4 (Richardson and Sayles, *Administration*, 170–1). For his career, see Simon Walker, *The Lancastrian Affinity, 1361–1399* (Oxford: Clarendon Press, 1990), 29–30, 286.

63 For what follows, see Frame, *English Lordship*, 232–61.
64 Ibid., 240 (Table 12); H.G. Richardson and G.O. Sayles, 'Irish Revenue, 1278–1384', *Proceedings of the Royal Irish Academy* 62C (1962): 87–100.
65 W.M. Ormrod, *Edward III* (London: Yale University Press, 2011), 233.
66 Paul Brand, 'Edward I and the Judges: The "State Trials" of 1289–93', in Brand, *MCL*, 103–12; N.M. Fryde, 'Edward III's Removal of His Ministers and Judges, 1340–1', *Bulletin of the Institute of Historical Research* 48 (1975): 149–61.
67 Robin Frame, 'The Justiciarship of Ralph Ufford: Warfare and Politics in Fourteenth-Century Ireland', *Studia Hibernica* 13 (1973): 10–15.
68 See, e.g., Philomena Connolly's sceptical analysis of one set of allegations: 'The Proceedings Against John de Burnham, Treasurer of Ireland, 1344–9', in *Colony and Frontier in Medieval Ireland: Essays Presented to J.F. Lydon*, eds. Terence Barry et al. (London: Hambledon Press, 1995), 57–74.
69 The earliest reference I have found to Elias as a knight dates from March 1335 (NLI, Genealogical Office, MS 191, 58). He was so addressed in the May summons to Scotland (above, n. 58), and used the style in one of his own deeds in 1336 (M.J. McEnery and Raymond Refaussé, eds., *Christ Church Deeds* (Dublin: Four Courts Press, 2001), no. 605). A grant by 'Elias de Ashbourne, knight' to 'Walter de Bermingham, knight' appears under the date '*c.*1328' in *Calendar of the Gormanston Register*, ed. James Mills and M.J. McEnery (Dublin: Royal Society of Antiquaries of Ireland, 1916), 119, but Walter's style suggests it belongs a decade or so later: during his father's lifetime he was normally known as 'Walter son of William de Bermingham' (*Cal. Gormanston Reg.*, 117–20, 122).
70 *CCR, 1337–9*, 119; Philomena Connolly, 'An Attempted Escape From Dublin Castle: The Trial of William and Walter de Bermingham, 1332', *IHS* 29 (1994): 100–8.
71 The classic discussion is J.R. Maddicott, *Law and Lordship: Royal Justices as Retainers in Thirteenth- and Fourteenth-Century England*, Past and Present supplement, 4 (Oxford: Past and Present Society, 1978).
72 *Account Roll of the Priory of the Holy Trinity Dublin, 1337–1346*, ed. James Mills (Dublin: Royal Society of Antiquaries of Ireland, 1891), 44.
73 Christ Church paid fees and gifts at the same period to William Petit, John Gernon and Hugh Brown, *narratores regis* (ibid., 45, 46, 103); while the Hospitallers at Kilmainham retained William Bosworth, keeper of the writs and rolls of the justiciar's court, and William Barlby, keeper of the writs and rolls of chancery (Charles McNeill, ed., *Registrum de Kilmainham* (Dublin: Irish Manuscripts Commission, 1932), 34, 76, 95–6).
74 Frame, *English Lordship*, 70. The links between 'absentees' and ministers of the Dublin government are discussed more generally at 66–72.
75 *Documents on the Affairs of Ireland*, no. 203. Cf. no. 212 (1347).
76 NAI, R.C.8/18, 279–80. Elias and his pledges were still making payments for his trespass in 1341–2 (TNA, E.101/241/2).
77 Bertha H. Putnam, *The Place in Legal History of Sir William Shareshull, Chief Justice of the King's Bench, 1350–1361* (Cambridge: Cambridge University Press, 1950), ch. 1; and, more generally, Anthony Musson, *Medieval Law in Context: The Growth of Legal Consciousness From Magna Carta to the Peasants' Revolt* (Manchester: Manchester University Press, 2001), 61–5.
78 Brand, 'Legal Profession in Ireland', 36–41; Brendan Smith, *Crisis and Survival in Late Medieval Ireland: The English of Louth and Their Neighbours, 1330–1450* (Oxford: Oxford University Press, 2013), 37, and the index entries for John Gernon, John Keppok, Richard Plunket, Roger and Robert Preston and Richard White, judges with Louth connections and interests.

79 The only exception I have noticed is a small parcel of land at Carrick-on-Suir, Co. Tipperary (NAI, R.C.8/21, 78), which may possibly be the unidentified Tipperary property he granted to Walter Bermingham (*Cal. Gormanston Register*, 119). His father had divested himself of interests in Cork (Brand, 'Legal Profession in Ireland', 36). Overviews of his holdings outside Dublin city may be gained from a grant of free warren made to him in 1329 (*CChR, 1327–41*, 101) and in documents relating to the debts he owed to the crown at his death (NAI, R.C.8/27, 173–5).

80 *Christ Church Deeds*, nos. 545, 605, 611, 617, 660–3, 667, 669, 670, 672, 675; 'Dublin Deeds', nos. 15d, 19d, 19f, 27–8, 44. Title deeds to certain of his Dublin properties were recorded when they were subject to an unsuccessful challenge by the prior of St John in 1342 (Eric St. John Brooks, ed., *Register of the Hospital of S. John the Baptist Without the New Gate, Dublin* (Dublin: Irish Manuscripts Commission, 1936), nos. 57, 99–101). Some of his holdings were adjacent to those of his fellow judge, John Grantchester, with whom he engaged in property transactions: *Christ Church Deeds*, nos. 596, 673; 'Dublin Deeds', nos. 27–8.

81 Charles McNeill, ed., *Calendar of Archbishop Alen's Register, c.1172–1534* (Dublin: Royal Society of Antiquaries of Ireland, 1950), 165, 166, 169, 176–8, 198.

82 Paul Dryburgh and Brendan Smith, *Inquisitions and Extents of Medieval Ireland*, List and Index Society, 320 (London: List and Index Society, 2007), no. 321.

83 *Rep. DKI*, 43: 63; 45: 55; 47: 44; 53: 49; 54: 60. These properties once belonged to Stephen Fulbourne, Edward I's treasurer of Ireland. After his fall from office in 1285, they had been leased to Dublin officials, including Elias's father (*CPR, 1313–17*, 469), in return for paying off Fulbourne's debts by light instalments.

84 CIRCLE, Patent Roll 11 Edw. II, no. 186; CIRCLE, Patent Roll 13 Edw. III, no. 15; *CFR, 1337–47*, 7, 14; *CCR, 1337–9*, 357.

85 *CPR, 1327–30*, 397, 403.

86 *CPR, 1330–4*, 309; *CFR, 1327–37*, 320.

87 Liam Price, *The Place-names of County Wicklow* (Dublin: The Dublin Institute for Advanced Studies, 1957), 319, 322.

88 NAI, R.C.27, 436, 628–30; CIRCLE, Close Roll 30 Edw. III, no. 6.

89 *Cal. Alen's Register*, 180–3, quotation at 181; for identification of places named in the grant, see Liam Price, 'The Manor of Bothercolyn', *Journal of the Royal Society of Antiquaries of Ireland* 74 (1944): 107–18.

90 *Inquisitions and Extents*, no. 244.

91 *CPR, 1334–8*, 126 (20 June 1335). He was never accused of failing to fulfil the obligation to build, and in 1366 Robert Holywood, who then held these lands, was given an allowance for having repaired a fortified house at Bothercolyn (NAI, R.C.8/29, 88–9; CIRCLE, Close Roll 40 Edward III, no. 1). Possibly Old Bawn House, a Tudor dwelling within an earlier moated site, may represent it (Margaret Murphy and Michael Potterton, *The Dublin Region in the Middle Ages: Settlement, Land-use and Economy* (Dublin: Four Courts Press, 2010), 203).

92 *CFR, 1327–37*, 449; *CPR, 1334–8*, 433.

93 K.W. Nicholls, 'Medieval Leinster Dynasties and Families: Three Topographical Notes', *Peritia* 5 (1986): 410–13; Áine Foley, *The Royal Manors of Medieval County Dublin: Crown and Community* (Dublin: Four Courts Press, 2013), 4, 14–15, 25. In 1279 these lands, with rights to timber in the forest of Glencree, had been given to John Wallop, to whom Edward I had promised thirty librates of 'wasteland' in Ireland (*CDI, 1252–84*, nos 1466, 1625–6, 1633, 2002). When they returned to the king's hands in 1295, their value was estimated, because of war and other mishaps, as only £15 (*Inquisitions and Extents*, no. 93).

94 CIRCLE, Patent Roll 32 Edw. III, no. 34. For Holywood's stormy career, see Frame, *English Lordship*, 60, 101–2; Crooks, '"Hobbes", "dogs" and politics', 125, 133.
95 NAI, R.C.8/23, 164; CIRCLE, Patent Roll 18 Edw. III, no. 9.
96 *IEP*, 363, 368, 373, 376, 395, 397, 402, 613, 620.
97 Statutes, *Ireland*, 334–41 (1342); TNA, E.101/242/5.
98 *IEP*, 402, 412, 419.
99 Ibid., 397.
100 For the conventions of royal campaigns and diplomacy in this period, see Frame, *Ireland and Britain*, ch. 14. For the leading kins, see Emmett O'Byrne, *War, Politics and the Irish of Leinster, 1156–1606* (Dublin: Four Courts Press, 2003), chs. 4–5; O'Byrne, 'Cultures in Contact in the Leinster and Dublin Marches, 1170–1400', in *Medieval Dublin* V (2004), 111–48; Christopher Maginn, 'English Marcher Lineages in South Dublin in the Late Middle Ages', *IHS* 34 (2004): 113–26, and Maginn, *'Civilizing' Gaelic Leinster: The Extension of Tudor Rule in the O'Byrne and O'Toole Lordships* (Dublin: Four Courts Press, 2005), ch. 1.
101 *Chartularies of St Mary's*, 2: 366–7.
102 Above, n. 53.
103 CIRCLE, Close Roll 29 Edw. III, no. 38.
104 CIRCLE, Patent Roll 20 Edw. III, no. 196.
105 NLI, Genealogical Office MS 191, 57–8. For this episode, see O'Byrne, *War, Politics and the Irish of Leinster*, 93, where, however, Ashbourne's leading role is not mentioned.
106 *IEP*, 380.
107 *Foedera*, 3, i, 3.
108 *PROME*, 4: 354–8.
109 *IEP*, 416.
110 *CPR, 1343–5*, 328, 330.
111 *Rep. DKI*, 54: 23, 25, 49. The three, Walter and Reginald Nerford and Robert Ryther, were all feed members of Ufford's retinue (TNA, C.260/57, no. 28).
112 Statutes, *Ireland*, 352–3.
113 *CCR, 1337–9*, 544.
114 *CPR, 1338–40*, 211.
115 *IEP*, 390, 402.
116 A family of that name held land and office on the royal manor of Saggart, which was adjacent to Tallaght (Foley, *Royal Manors of County Dublin*, 101–2).
117 CIRCLE, Close Roll 18 Edw. III, no. 206.
118 NAI, R.C.8/23, 164; CIRCLE, Patent Roll 18 Edw. III, no. 9.
119 Frame, 'Ralph Ufford', 46. He was paid from 26 June to 24 September.
120 Frame, *English Lordship*, 283–6.
121 'Dublin Deeds', no. 56.
122 NAI, MS 999/184/18, m. 37.
123 CIRCLE, Close Roll 29 Edw. III, no. 38; Close Roll 30 Edw. III, no. 6.
124 *Christ Church Deeds*, nos. 659–60. Thomas Ashbourne appears to have remained in possession of property in Dublin city at least until 1357 (ibid., nos. 662–8, 670–1, 675–6) and Robert at least until 1362 (ibid., nos. 661, 669, 672–5, 678, 690–2). For the Meath lands, see *Inquisitions and Extents*, 192.
125 NAI, R.C.8/27, 173–5.
126 'Dublin Deeds', nos. 61–4, 67–8; CIRCLE, Patent Roll 32 Edward III, nos. 73–5.
127 NAI, R.C.8/27, 356–7. In 1362, Thomas was to complain successfully that, although his father's lands had been granted to others on account of his debts, the extents were still being demanded of him (NAI, R.C.8/28, 228–30; CIRCLE, Close Roll 36 Edward III, no. 1).
128 TNA, E.101/243/12 (payments into the Dublin exchequer from Robert and John Ashbourne).

129 'Dublin deeds', no. 80.
130 *Chartularies of St Mary's*, 2: 396, where Preston is wrongly described as 'chief baron of the exchequer'.
131 *Documents on the Affairs of Ireland*, no. 218(i), at 197.
132 Peter Crooks, 'Negotiating Authority in a Colonial Capital: Dublin and the Windsor Crisis, 1369–78', *Medieval Dublin* IX (2009), 131–51, at 150.
133 Hand, *English Law*, ch. 9.
134 Ibid., 161–71. For an important discussion, see Paul Brand, 'King, Church and Property: The Enforcement of Restrictions on Alienation into Mortmain in the Lordship of Ireland in the Later Middle Ages', in Brand, *MCL*, 245–86, esp. 247–51.
135 The main bodies of legislation made in Ireland may be found in Richardson and Sayles, *The Irish Parliament*, 291–3 (1278) and Statutes, *Ireland*, 194–213 (1297), 258–77 (1310), 280–91 (1320), 374–97 (1351), 430–69 (1366). For ordinances framed in England, see Statutes, *Ireland*, 322–9 (1331), 332–63 (1342), 408–19 (1357). The distinction is in some ways deceptive; just as ordinances sent from England might be based on information from Ireland, so legislation made in Ireland might echo English enactments or reflect metropolitan attitudes and priorities. See G.J. Hand, 'The Forgotten Statutes of Kilkenny: A Brief Survey', *The Irish Jurist*, new ser., 1 (1966): 299–312; and David Green, 'The Statute of Kilkenny (1366): Legislation and the State', *Journal of Historical Sociology* 27 (2014): 236–62.
136 Hand, 'English Law in Ireland', 402.
137 Hand, *English Law*, 159–61.

8 Two jurisdictions in dispute about canonical appeals

London and Canterbury, 1375–6[1]

F. Donald Logan

Introduction

The Court of Arches was the most important church court in medieval England. It was the appellate court for the province of Canterbury, which was comprised of eighteen of the twenty-one dioceses of England and Wales. Except for the years 1321 to 1335 the medieval court sat in Cheapside in the city of London at the church of St Mary le Bow (*ecclesia beate Marie de arcubus*), from which it took its name *curia de arcubus* (Court of Arches).[2]

Appeals could come to the court either from the decision of a lower jurisdiction or from an alleged offence (*appelatio a gravamine*) of a lower jurisdiction, which could be either past or threatened. Although such appeals would usually proceed through the hierarchy of lower courts before reaching the Arches, another type of appeal could bypass all inferior courts entirely. This was an appeal to the apostolic see. Such an appeal was called a tuitorial appeal, which was, in fact, two appeals: one to the papal court for the matter being appealed and the other to the Court of Arches for protection (*pro tuicione*) for the appellant to prosecute the appeal to the pope. It was a tuitorial appeal in 1375 that gave rise to a particularly bitter dispute between the jurisdiction of the bishop of London and that of the archbishop of Canterbury.

The matter began with a visitation of St Bartholomew's Hospital in West Smithfield, London.[3] Its master, Richard Sutton, was charged with incontinence with Joan Pertenhale, a sister at the hospital. The commissioners of William de Courtenay, bishop of London, imposed on Sutton the sentence of suspension from entry to church (*ab ingressu ecclesie*), a form of personal interdict.[4] The commissioners, acting as vicars general in spirituals for Bishop Courtenay (*tunc in remotis*), were John Appleby, dean of St Paul's Cathedral; Robert Holme, chancellor of St. Paul's, and the canonist Master Adam Mottron.[5] Sutton then made a tuitorial appeal to the Court of Arches. What followed is largely recounted by Simon Sudbury, archbishop of Canterbury (1375–81), in an *intimacio* that took the form of a universal letter. It is dated 15 July 1376 and is the text presented here.[6]

Sutton's tuitorial appeal was heard by Master Nicholas Chaddesden, dean of the Arches, acting as commissary of the court in the absence of the Official. Tuition was granted, which had the effect of suspending the penalty imposed by the London commissioners for one year, during which Sutton could prosecute his appeal at the papal court. It was routine in such matters for the Court of Arches to send a letter of inhibition to the lower jurisdiction. Receipt of this inhibition caused a strong reaction. The dean of St Paul's and his co-commissioners instructed their proctor, Reginald Spaldyng, to write to Chaddesden, dean of the Arches, that he should revoke within three days the tuition granted to Richard Sutton; otherwise Chaddesden was to appear before them on the following day to give reason, if he had any, why he should not be placed under ecclesiastical censure. He refused, and excommunications were exchanged between the two parties.[7]

Precise dating of these events is not possible, but it is clear that they occurred probably late in 1375, for on 7 December 1375 security was given that Sutton would not leave England without a royal licence.[8] About five weeks later, on 13 January 1376, Sutton received royal licence allowing him to send his proctor, Nicholas Russell, to the papal court, and four days later Sutton himself was allowed by royal licence to leave England to pursue business at the papal court.[9]

Not allowing the matter to rest there, the London commissioners through their proctor, Reginald de Spaldyng, made an appeal to the apostolic see on 8 February 1376, claiming that by immemorial custom the suffragans bishop could inquire into the excesses of their subjects without the interference of the metropolitan and that, hence, the provincial court of the archbishop had no authority in this case. He further claimed that Sutton had confessed to his misdeeds.[10]

One might ask at this stage where were the archbishop of Canterbury and the bishop of London while these events were taking place. The itinerary of Bishop Courtenay is difficult to define since his register has not survived, although Dr McHardy has shown that he was probably absent at least from 10 February to 19 March 1376.[11] During these events Archbishop Sudbury was away at Bruges on a diplomatic mission. He had left England on 20 October 1375 and did not return until 31 March 1376.[12] Sudbury, a well-trained canonist, had served twelve years as an auditor at the Rota in Avignon.[13] On 17 May 1376 he sought the royal writ *de excommunicato capiendo* for the secular arm to arrest John Appleby, dean of St Paul's.[14] The bishop of London retaliated on 29 May by seeking the same writ for the arrest of Nicholas Chaddesden, dean of the Arches.[15] There is no evidence that either was captured.

In the meantime, the Good Parliament was sitting (28 April to 10 July 1376). How much that parliament played a part in what followed can only be a matter of speculation. Archbishop Sudbury recounts in this text that the bishop of London was urged to arrange a peaceful settlement in this matter.

Urging him were the Duke of Lancaster (John of Gaunt),[16] the Earl of March (Edmund Mortimer), Lord (Henry) Percy, William Wykeham (bishop of Winchester) and Adam Houghton (bishop of St Davids). Lancaster presided over the lords at this parliament, and three of the others – March, Percy and Houghton – were members of the intercommuning committee appointed at the Good Parliament probably on 9 May 1376, and ten days later Lancaster, March, Percy and Wykeham were made royal councillors.[17] The intervention of Lancaster and the others – five of the most prominent men of the kingdom – was probably crucial to settling this dispute. They obviously pressed Bishop Courtenay to have his commissioners submit. We are told that Courtenay together with the excommunicated Appleby and Mottron 'reverently humbled' themselves and begged the archbishop's forgiveness and that the latter two actually submitted on bended knees before the archbishop. They agreed that in the future they would respect the superior authority of the archbishop's court.

Whatever more general political issues might have been involved here– for example, the alleged animosity between Sudbury and Courtenay – what was essentially involved was a legal matter. The nature of the Court of Arches as an appellate court can be traced back to the middle of the thirteenth century.[18] The question at issue in this dispute was: what happens to the judgement of a lower jurisdiction when an appeal was made to a higher jurisdiction and accepted by it? If it was accepted, the law was clear: the higher court stayed the judgement of the lower court pending the decision of the higher court. Here the matter was complicated because the appeal of Richard Sutton was to the apostolic see. Routinely in tuitorial appeals, the Court of Arches would send a letter of inhibition to the lower jurisdiction protecting the appellant. The court's letter to the London commissioners announced that the court had granted tuition to Richard Sutton and stayed the action of the London commissioners for one year. The issue had been resolved in 1282, during Archbishop Pecham's time, and hundreds of such appeals had been treated in this way.[19] What happened in the Sutton case?

It might be thought that the London commissioners were unfamiliar with proper procedure in tuitorial appeals, although, whatever the backgrounds of Appleby and Roger Holme, their associate Adam Mottron was a trained canonist. They had found Sutton guilty of incontinence and punished him; they could have been so outraged by his offence that they did not want him to escape an appropriate penalty. Their outrage could have been intensified because of the alleged victim of Sutton's offence: she was Joan Pertenhale, and there happened to be a minor canon of St Paul's Cathedral with the same surname, Richard Pertenhale.[20] Whatever their motivation, it was Archbishop Sudbury who was on firm legal ground, which the Londoners at length admitted on bended knees.

As a postscript it must be mentioned that Richard Sutton apparently won his appeal, for he was still master of St Bartholomew's Hospital in 1386.[21]

Text[22]

Intimacio reuocacionis actorum et attemptatorum per decanum sancti Pauli Londonie et alios contra decanum de Arcubus Londonie et iurisdiccionem curie Cantuariensis.[23] Vniuersis presentes literas inspecturis Simon permissione diuina etc. salutem in domino sempiternam.

Vniuersitati uestre notum fieri cupimus per presentes quod, cum ex parte fratris Richardi Sutton, magistri hospitalis siue domus sancti Bartholomei in Smythfeld iuxta Londoniam, fuisset a quibusdam citacione et sentencia suspensionis ab ingressu ecclesie iniuriosis et aliis grauaminibus per magistrum Iohannem Appelby, decanum, dominum Rogerum Holme, cancellarium eccelsie Londonie, et magistrum Adam Mottron, uenerabilis fratris nostri domini Willelmi, dei gracia Londoniensis episcopi, tunc in remotis agentis, commissarios seu uicarios[24] in spiritualibus generales in hac parte, suggestis eidem fratri Ricardo, ut dixit, illatis ad sedem apostolicam et pro tuicione ad curiam nostram Cantuariensem legitime appellatum et per discretum uirum magistrum Nicholaum Chaddesden, decanum ecclesie beati Marie de Arcubus Londonie nostrumque in absencia officialis eiusdem curie nostre ad omnia et singula que ad . . .[25]

Londonensis[26] episcopi, idem magister Nicholaus decanus et commissarius noster infra triduum reuocaret sub penis grauibus ecclesiasticis et censuris latis in quibusdam pretensis et eidem magistro Nicholao penitus incognitis processibus contentis, prout dictus Reginaldus[27] asseruit, alioquin quod predictus magister Nicholaus decanus et commissarius noster sequenti die coram eisdem magistro Iohanne decano, domino Rogero et magistro Adam seu aliis incertis pretensis uicariis dicti domini Londoniensis episcopi in ecclesia Londoniensi[28] compareret propositurus causam si quam haberet quare pronunciari non deberet in penis et censuris huiusmodi incidisse, cumque eciam racione contumaciarum, offensorum et excessuum premissorum et aliorum inde secutorum per ipsos contractorum et commissorum prefati magister Iohannes decanus, dominus Rogerus et magister Adam ac dominus Reginaldus necnon dominus Iohannes Purley minor canonicus ecclesie Londoniensis ac dominus Nicholaus Wassyngbourne[29] iuste et rite suis culpis et demeritis huiusmodi exigentibus maioris excommunicacionis fuissent sentenciis auctoritate dicte curie nostre innodati et pro talibus publice nunciati ac postmodum eciam ea occasione predictus magister Nicholaus decanus et commissarius noster in prefatis censuris ecclesiasticis incidisse ipseque et nonnulli alii dicte curie nostre ministri in premissis et eciam eadem occasione excommunicati fuisse et esse cum non essent ad mandatum predictorum magistri Iohannis,[30] Rogeri et Ade commissariorum seu uicariorum generalium dicti uenerabilis fratris domini Londoniensis episcopi pretensorum et ipsius episcopi auctoritate eciam pretensa cum nulla esset aut sit in hac parte fuissent eciam nequiter et perperam nunciati, nosque cum predicta omnia tam ea uidelicet que rite et iuste per dictum magistrum Nicholaum decanum et commissarium nostrum et alios pro curia nostra Cantuariensi predicta et iurisdiccionis eiusdem conseruacione quam ea que iuniuste, perperam et inaniter contra eam eundemque magistrum Nicholaum decanum et commissarium nostrum ac alios dicte curie nostre mandatarios et ministros acta fuerunt ut prefertur debite consideracionis inspexissemus intuitu et ea prosecuti fuisse uidendissemus iuxta iuris exigenciam prima racione, tandem ad preces et frequentem instanciam incliti principis domini Iohannis dei gracia Castelli et Legionum regis illustris ducisque Lancastrie ac nobilium uirorum domini comitis Marchie et domini de Percy necnon uenerabilium fratrum nostrorum Willelmi Wyntoniensis et Ade Meneuensis episcoporum, postquam uenerabilis frater noster dominus Londoniensis episcopus magisterque Iohannes Appelby, decanus Londonie et magister Adam Mottron nobis se reuerenter humiliassent et quatenus ad eos attinebat ueniam et graciam in premissis de et a nobis humiliter et singulariter postulassent, idemque magister Iohannes Appelby decanus ueniam de commissis postulasset et in ordinacione nostra se posuisset in hac parte, nos uolentes ius et possessionem ecclesie et curie nostre Cantuariensis predicte illesa conseruare attemptataque contra ea de quibus premittitur debite et pacifice reformare omnia et singula per dictum magistrum Nicholaum decanum et commissarium nostrum aliosque dicte curie nostre mandatarios et ministros in premissis ut premittitur facta et habita iusta et legitima reputantes et humiliacionem[31] et uenie postulacionem et in ordinacione nostra posicionem predictam admisimus sic oblatas ac subsequenter ordinauimus quod prefati magister Iohannes decanus et alii subditi ac ministri eiusdem uenerabilis fratris nostri domini Londoniensis episcopi dictique magistri Iohannis decani ceterique predicti auctoritate nostra et dicte curie nostre ut prefertur excommunicati ac eciam idem dominus Londonienis episcopus nobis et dicte nostre presidentibus inhibicionibusque et mandatis debitis et consuetis eiusdem curie nostre de cetero in omnibus ut tenentur pareant, obedeant et intendant ampliusque contra ea non attemptent nec attemptari faciant aut procurent, omnia insuper et singula predicta et alia contra dictam curiam nostram et eius iurisdiccionem prefatumque magistrum Nicholaum Chaddesdene decanum et commissarium nostrum predictum, ac alios ministros et mandatarios dicte curie nostre per predictos magistrum Iohannem decanum, dominum Rogerum cancellarium, magister Adam Mottrom, dominos Reginaldum, rectorem ecclesie sancti Benedicti,[32] Iohannem Purley et Nicholaum Wassyngbourne seu alios quoscumque auctoritate seu uice pretensa dicti uenerabilis fratris nostri domini Londoniensis episcopi occasione premissa temere facta et presumpta necnon quecumque ex eis secuta tamquam erronea et de iure inualida, cassa, irrita atque nulla ac per inferiores et subditos nullam optinentes in hac parte iurisdiccionem seu potestatem legitimam in seu contra prefatam curiam nostram ipsiusque iurisdiccionem ac presidentes, ministros ac mandatarios eiusdem superius memoratos ipsorum inferiorum superiores et ab omni iurisdiccione ordinario seu delegato domini Londoniensis episcopi ac alia quacumque iurisdiccione dicte curie nostre inferiori notorie liberos et prorsus exemptos et nullatenus in premissis de consuetudine uel de iure subiectos perperam attemptata quatenus de facto processerunt auctoritate nostra ordinaria superiori reuocauimus et tenore presencium reuocamus sicque erronea, inualida, cassa, irrita, nulla attemptata et reuocata fuisse et esse decernimus et declaramus. Prefatum insuper magistrum Iohannem decanum ad peticionem dicti domini regis et ducis nomine ipsius magistri Iohannis decani et pro eo beneficium absolucionis eidem Iohanni decano tunc presenti et peticioni huiusmodi consencienti inpendi eum instancia postulantis primum et subsequenter dictum magistrum[33] Adam Mottron flexis ipsorum genibus a dictis excommunicacionum sentenciis quibus ut prefertur innodati [erant] graciose absoluimus. Ceterosque predictos dicte curie nostre auctoritate ac premissis occasione excommunicatos ab huiusmodi excommunicacionum sentenciis sic ut premittitur in eosdem latis quatenus ad nos seu officium presidentis dicte curie nostre attinet in forma iuris absoluendos fore, necnon dictis contemptoribus conuictis de peccuniarum summis in quibus occasione contemptuum suorum predictorum condempnati seu obligati fuerant remissionis graciam facere decreuimus, prefatisque magistris Iohanni decano et Ade Mottron coram nobis tunc personaliter constitutis precum instancie predictarum intuitu accedente eciam ad id consensu prefati magistri Nicholai decani et nostri in absencia officialis curie nostre predicte nuper ut prefertur commissarii ad quem protunc deberent racione sui officii predicti mulcte huiusmodi applicari remisimus. Saluo semper in omnibus iure partis aduerse fratris uidelicet Ricardi magistri hospitalis siue domus supradicte cui per premissa non intendimus derogare. Et ne premissa facta dampnata sic contra prefatam curiam nostram et ipsius iurisdiccionem dictumque magistrum Nicholaum decanum et commissarium nostrum ac mandatarios et ministros eiusdem curie ut prefertur erronnee perperam et iniuste attemptata sicque misericorditer et pacifice reformata ab aliis trahantur imposterum dampnabiliter in exemplum premissa omnia uobis intimamus et significamus per presentes sigillo nostro consignatas in fidem et testimonium premissorum.[34]

Datum Londonie quintodecimo die mensis Iulii anno domini millesimo CCCmo septuagesimo sexto et translacionis nostre anno secundo.

Notes

1 The author is in debt to David M. Smith, Karen Corsano and Daniel Williman for their much appreciated assistance with this paper.

2 For the history of the court see Logan, *Arches*, xv–xxxviii, and idem, 'The Court of Arches in the Church of Arches', in *St Mary-le-Bow: A History*, eds. Michael Byrne and G.R. Bush (Barnsley: Wharncliffe Books, 2007), 153–68.

3 For St Bartholomew's Hospital see Norman Moore, *The History of St. Bartholomew's Hospital*, 2 vols. (London: C.A. Pearson, 1918); E.A. Webb, *The Records of St. Bartholomew's Priory and of the Church and Parish of St. Bartholomew the Great*, 2 vols. (Oxford: Oxford University Press, 1921); and *VCH London*, 1: 520–5.

4 For such personal interdicts see P.D. Clarke, *The Interdict in the Thirteenth Century: A Question of Collective Guilt* (Oxford: Oxford University Press, 2007), 81–2.

5 For Appleby see *BRUO*, 1: 40–1; for Holme see *Fasti Ecclesiae Anglicanae, 1300–1541*, vol. 5, *St Paul's Cathedral*, ed. J.M. Horne (London: University of London, 1963), 18; and for Mottron see *BRUC*, 415.

6 References to this dispute can be found in Webb 1.177; Moore, 1. 592; W.L. Warren, 'A Reappraisal of Simon Sudbury, Bishop of London (1361–75) and Archbishop of Canterbury (1375–81)', *Journal of Ecclesiastical History* 10 (1959): 139–52, at 148; George Holmes, *The Good Parliament* (Oxford: Clarendon Press, 1975), 142–4; and *VCH London*, 1: 522.

7 In addition to the three London commissioners there were also excommunicated Reginald Spaldyng, their proctor, John Purly, a minor canon of St Paul's, and a certain Nicholas Wassingborne. All three were among the clergy of St Paul's in the poll-tax lists of 1381 (McHardy, *London*, nos. 148–9, 154, 156).

8 *CCR, 1374–1377*, 279.

9 Ibid., 183; *CPR, 1374–1377*, 216.

10 London Metropolitan Archives, Ms. 25, 193. Summarised in *Ninth Report of the Royal Commission on Historical Documents* (London: H.M.S.O, 1883), 44.

11 McHardy, *London*, pp. xx, 78–9.

12 Reg. Sudbury, ff. 10v, 13r.

13 *BRUO*, 3: 2218; *ODNB*, article by Simon Walker.

14 TNA, C.85/10/27 and Reg. Sudbury, f. 18v.

15 TNA, C.85/122/1.

16 He styled himself the King of Castile and Leon.

17 For these appointments see Holmes, *The Good Parliament*, ch. 5.

18 Logan, *Arches*, xix–xxii.

19 See D.L. Douie, *Archbishop Pecham* (Oxford: Clarendon Press, 1952), 192–228; and Logan, *Arches*, xxii–xxvi.

20 George Hennessy, *Novum Repertorium Ecclesiasticum Parochiale Londinese* (London: S. Sonnenschein, 1898), 60; and McHardy, *London*, no. 149.

21 N.J.M. Kerling, ed., *Cartulary of St Bartholomew's Hospital Founded 1123* (London: St Bartholomew's Hospital, 1973), 5, 175, 176, and nos. 856, 1203.

22 Reg. Sudbury, ff. 27v–28r.

23 Intimacio . . . Cantuariensis *in marg.*

24 *marg. add*: seu uicarios.

25 Part of text omitted here by the scribe, probably as a homoeoteleuton, in the interval between f. 28r–v: it would have indicated that the Court of Arches had granted tuition to Richard Sutton.

26 f. 28v.

27 Reginald Spaldyng, rector of St. Benet, Gracechurch, London, who was proctor of the London commissioners. See infra, n. 31.

28 *add. interlin:* Londoniensi.

29 Purley and Wassyngbourne are among the clergy of St Paul's in the poll tax lists of 1381 (McHardy, *London*, nos.148–9, 156).

30 *add. interlin.*: Iohannis.

31 *add. interlin.*: humiliacionem.

32 Rector of St Benet, Gracechurch, London (Hennessy, *Novum Repertorium Ecclesiasticum Parochiale Londinese*, 79).

33 *add. interlin.* ad peticionem . . . magistrum.

34 *add. interlin.*: in fidem et testimonium premissorum.

9 The outlaw in later medieval Ireland

Áine Foley

The outlaw has captured the popular imagination to a degree that few other stock characters from the medieval period – except perhaps for the wicked sheriff – have succeeded. The outlaw tales that originated in the Middle Ages continue to be popular today, and the story of that most famous of medieval outlaws, Robin Hood, continues to be told through various and diverse mediums. The medieval outlaw holds a fascination for historians too, and there is a rich historiography devoted to this topic. Except in Ireland. Here he has been largely neglected. This chapter will remedy some of that neglect. Like Robin Hood, an outlaw was a man 'whom society had placed outside the law's protection'.[1] Individuals found guilty of felonies, who were not apprehended, or who failed to turn up in court to answer the crimes levelled against them, were outlawed.[2] According to Bracton, in his *On the Laws and Customs of England*, composed in the mid-thirteenth century, the outlaw forfeited access to the law and if he returned after he was outlawed he could be executed without having to go through a judicial process. The property of an outlaw was also forfeited and anyone who had previously paid homage to an individual before they were outlawed was no longer bound by that oath.[3] Consequently, someone who was outlawed was stripped of his or her legal rights and possessions. Moreover, their friends and kinsmen were no longer allowed to associate with them. In the eyes of the law, they were invisible.

Whereas there are fewer court records surviving for medieval Ireland as compared to England, there are still enough left to confirm that the outlaw was as prominent a feature of Anglo-Irish society as he was in England. The court records of the justiciar's court provide us with the best information about outlawry in fourteenth-century Ireland. Much of this material has been lost. When the Public Record Office of Ireland [PROI], located in the Four Courts, was blown up in 1922 during the Irish civil war, all but three of the 488 medieval plea rolls were destroyed, though since then two more rolls have found their way back to the PROI.[4] Fortunately, some of these court rolls dating from 1295 to 1314 had already been published, or were in preparation for publication.[5] The National Archives of Ireland [NAI, previously the PROI] also has a substantial number of unpublished calendars,[6] and other calendars and copies of court proceedings can be found in other repositories, including the Royal Irish Academy, the National Library of Ireland, the British Library and the National Archives of the United Kingdom. Therefore, in spite of the serious loss of Ireland's medieval records, there is still much material that can offer us a glimpse into the activities of Irish outlaws. Moreover, the Anglo-Irish annals and family records, particularly the Ormond Deeds, provide additional information on outlaws. While the main focus of this chapter will be the fourteenth century, material dating from the thirteenth and fifteenth centuries will also be exploited.

The best example of a process of outlawry comes from the fifteenth century and it is contained in the Ormond Deeds. An individual had to go through a fairly lengthy process to become an outlaw. Those accused of criminal behaviour in the late Middle Ages had to be summoned to court four times, and if they did not appear after the fourth summons then they were declared outlaws. This process could take up to a year to complete.[7] This process is illustrated in the case of Thomas fitzMaurice of Kyldroght (Celbridge, co. Kildare) dating to the 1440s.[8] Between 6 February 1440 and the 8 July 1444 the sheriff of Dublin was ordered to find fitzMaurice and bring him to the king's court, but failed to do so. When he did not show up the fifth time he was summoned, fitzMaurice was outlawed. This case demonstrates how drawn out this process could be, and fitzMaurice had ample opportunity to come and defend himself. He may have been worried that the courts would treat him harshly because of the seriousness of his crimes. On 25 January 1440 he had come to Dublin with the O'Byrnes, a Gaelic sept whose main base was in modern-day co. Wicklow,[9] and had sold them bread and ale, and participated in robberies with them. A few days later on 2 February 1440 he went with the O'Byrnes to Kilgobbin, in modern-day Wicklow, and burned the wheat and corn of some of the tenants living here. Thomas fitzMaurice was clearly a notorious character whose affiliation with the Gaelic Irish would have been considered almost treasonous, albeit not that unusual.

Edmund Curtis believed that this Thomas fitzMaurice was the future seventh earl of Kildare. This theory is certainly an appealing one – an outlaw who would eventually became an earl – but the evidence supporting it is, unfortunately, flimsy. Curtis speculated that Thomas adopted the 'fitz Maurice' patronymic of the fourth earl, who died in 1390, but Maurice is a common name in late medieval Ireland, especially among the Fitzgerald family. Moreover, even though the fifth earl of Kildare did hold the manor of Celbridge,[10] and it is possible that a grandson of his born here could be called Thomas fitzMaurice of Kildroght, it is also possible that he was the earl's bastard son or grandson. It is also possible that he was no relation to the earl at all, or came from one of the many cadet lines of the Fitzgerald family. It is perhaps significant that Thomas, the seventh earl, like Thomas the outlaw, had close associations with the Gaelic Irish. The earl may even have had a Gaelic Irish wife, Dorothea (or Dorothy), daughter of Owny O'More, of Leix (Laois).[11] It appears that the earl later had this marriage annulled in order to marry his kinswoman, Joan, the daughter of James Fitzgerald, sixth earl of Desmond.[12] While both Thomases had close links with the Gaelic Irish, this is not particularly unusual because many English men, particularly in frontier zones, had relationships with the Irish. It is not enough to suggest that we are looking at one individual. It is possible that the seventh earl's first marriage to Dorothea was a youthful indiscretion, or perhaps he was attempting to come to a truce with the O'Mores. The O'Mores, living in co. Laois, were sometimes allies and sometimes enemies of the earls of Kildare. In fact, in 1513 Gerald, the eighth earl of Kildare was murdered by one of the O'Mores.[13] The outlawry of Thomas fitzMaurice were preserved among the records of the earls of Ormond. The earldom of Kildare was fiercely contested between James Butler, the fourth earl of Ormond, who was son-in-law of the fifth earl of Kildare, and Thomas, the seventh earl of Kildare and it is possible that the Ormonds kept these records in order to discredit Thomas fitzMaurice's claims to the earldom. However, men of high social status often broke the law, and even when they were outlawed it had little effect on their reputation or future careers. The methods that these men used to rehabilitate their reputations will be explored below.

While those of high social status who were English in origin could be fairly confident of a pardon if they did find themselves on the wrong side of the law, this indulgence was not extended to a significant section of the population. The issue of outlawry was a complicated one in Ireland, particularly when compared to England, because the Gaelic Irish, at least in theory, did not have access to the law because of their ethnicity. Unless they had a special dispensation, that is a grant of English law, they did not have access to the courts or the right to plead on their own behalf. Many of these Irish who were granted this dispensation probably assimilated into English society, to the extent that they were no longer recognised as being Irish.[14] There were also attempts to extend this right to all Irishmen in 1277, which was unsuccessful.[15] The Irish remonstrance of 1317 also highlighted, that in terms of access to English law, the Irish were still being left out in the cold.[16] This is not to suggest that the legal status of the Irish was comparable to that of the outlaw. The legal status of the Gaelic Irish was more comparable to that of the English villein.[17] The villein was tied to the land and did not have recourse of law, except through his lord. Naturally, the status of the Irish was more complex then this and some Irishmen who did not apply for English law actually did have access to it, or at least had as much, if not more legal rights than their English counterparts. A case in point is that of the Irish living on the royal demesne, who were tenants of the crown. The betaghs, e.g. the native Irish peasantry, living on the king's lands received royal protection and in disputes over lands they even had their rights upheld against those of Englishmen. For instance, in 1310 David Otrescan, an Irishman, protested that he had been forced out of lands on the royal manor of Saggart that had previously belonged to his father Nicholas, who was a betagh. The new resident of these lands was John Fangoner, an Englishman who had married Nicholas' granddaughter Ostina. Ostina was the daughter of John, David's brother. Fangoner argued that his wife held these lands as her inheritance at the time of her marriage and while the courts did not dispute this, David won his case. The courts were aware that as an Englishman, Fangoner was not required to carry out the customary duties associated with this landholding, but David Otrescan, as a native Irish betagh, was. It was to the king's benefit to have an Irishman hold these lands.[18] Technically, the Irish who did not have access to the common law had the same status as the unfree of medieval England and they were denied access to the king's judicial courts.[19] Even though the Irish were treated differently by the law courts – and the parliament of 1297 reference to Englishmen who were killed under the mistaken assumption that they were Irishmen does suggest that Irish lives had less value in a legal sense – I will only be examining those Irish persons who were outlawed by the king's courts.[20]

Though the majority of the Gaelic Irish population had no proper access to the law, they still could be outlawed. In 1278 Gillyce son of Cecus Orayly and Donald Mc Brady and their followers were outlawed after they burnt the vill of Kreg and killed a group of men, who appear to have been English in origin.[21] At around the same time a group of Irishmen, including Art Malachelyn and the Omalmoy family and their following were outlawed for being robbers and arsonists.[22] It is possible that the Irishmen in these cases had access to common law; if they did not, it is difficult to ascertain how being outlawed would have made much of a difference to their legal status. Some Irishmen who were outlawed were of high social status, and like their English counterparts were able to procure pardons. Around 1289 William de Barry and Gilbert le Waleis sent a petition to the crown complaining that the prior of Kilmainham, who was deputy justiciar at the time, had pardoned the outlawry of Donal Og MacCarthy, even though he had committed several robberies.[23] It is likely that he was a kinsman of the MacCarthy kings of Desmond, perhaps even a son of Donal Mór, king of Desmond at the end of the thirteenth century.[24] MacCarthy was clearly well connected and was able to behave with impunity, secure in the knowledge that he would receive a pardon, even if it was to the detriment of his English neighbours.

In 1307, Murcod Ballagh MacMurrough, son of Muiris (d. 1314), king of Leinster, was executed by David de Caunteton and Edmund le Botiller, rector of Tullow.[25] Muiris was described as 'princips Lagenie', that is, prince of Leinster, in contemporary sources. Like Donal Og MacCarthy he was of high social status. At the time of his death, Murcod was an outlaw with a price on his head. The Anglo-Irish annals reveal that Caunteton decapitated him. Since Murcod was an outlaw, once he was apprehended his captors were within their rights to execute him immediately, without going through any sort of judicial process.[26] Caunteton received a reward of twelve marks, seven shillings and eight pence for apprehending and executing Murcod.[27]

Paradoxically, David de Caunteton was himself executed two years later for rebelling against the crown.[28]

The evidence of Murcod Ballagh MacMurrough, Donal Og MacCarthy and the cases illustrated below would suggest that, like in England, the most notorious outlaws of medieval Ireland, and those who committed the most dangerous crimes, were of high social status and those who feature prominently in the records were, not surprisingly, members of the gentry class. Unlike the peasantry, the gentry had the ways and means to carry out serious acts of violence. While the peasantry stole through necessity and, perhaps, opportunity, the gentry were able to reap much larger rewards from their criminal behaviour. Many outlaws operated in gangs and were involved in robberies along the king's highway. While some members of outlaw gangs could be of low social status, the leaders were frequently members of the gentry class. John Bellamy has noted that having gentle blood was just as valued within outlaw gangs as it was in ordinary society.[29] Those of gentle blood, unlike peasants, had access to horses and were able to escape from justice into other jurisdictions, where sheriffs were loath to follow them. They could also extend their own power, or that of a kinsman or overlord, in their locality through their criminal activities.[30]

The influence an outlaw could wield in his own locality often led to the breakdown of law and order. In 1305 William fitz John was accused of committing robberies in Shanganagh near Shankill in south co. Dublin. He was such a nefarious figure that the jury who heard his case was afraid to indict him. Not only was the jury fearful of what he would do, even the sheriff admitted that he was afraid to bring this man to justice.[31] The Tyrel brothers of north co. Kildare were even more notorious and their activities drew them onto a larger political stage. When I examined the careers of the Tyrels in a previous article, I did not fully consider the political motivations of their activities as outlaws.[32] Further research has led me to the conclusion that their associations with the nobility of Ireland played an important part in their criminal behaviour. Bellamy has noted that political affiliation has been advocated as a motive for gang formation in England, but that the Coterel gang was made up of men who did not share the same political associations or inclinations.[33] However, this did not mean that they were not influenced by the political activities and intrigues of the noble class; for instance, Nicholas Coterel was an adherent of Thomas, earl of Lancaster.[34]

Members of outlaw gangs also had adversarial relationships with members of the nobility, like that between the Folville gang and King Edward II's favourite, Hugh Despenser. The Folvilles murdered one of Despenser's associates and were outlawed in Leicestershire as a result. In order to avoid being apprehended here, they moved their criminal activities to the nearby county of Lincolnshire. In 1327, after Despenser's execution and two weeks after Edward III's accession, the Folvilles were pardoned. The Folvilles returned to Leicestershire and continued to act with impunity until Roger Mortimer's fall from grace.[35] Mortimer, the earl of March, was king in all but name after the fall of Edward II. Mortimer's reign at the top was a brief one and he was quickly arrested once Edward III assumed power in 1330. Later the same year, on 29 November, Mortimer was executed in Tyburn.[36] Shortly after Mortimer's execution an order was issued to arrest members of the Folville gang and take them to Nottingham castle.[37] The order proved ineffective, but Stones does note that there appears to have been some political motivation behind the treatment of the Folville gang. They fled Leicestershire because they were clearly fearful of how Despenser would treat them for their part in the murder of his associate. However, they came back almost immediately after he was executed and they received a pardon from the Mortimer faction. When Mortimer fell from power they were out of favour once again.

Though outlaw gangs appear to have been associates of the nobility, the nobility were rarely members of these gangs themselves.[38] It is possible that they used these gangs to rob, intimidate and kill on their behalf. While members of the nobility were rarely outlawed, there was an obvious advantage to having their followers or associates do their dirty work for them. As in England, outlaws in Ireland also had connections with members of the nobility. Sir John fitz Thomas, the illegitimate older brother of Maurice fitz Thomas, the first earl of Desmond, was the leader of a notorious gang in the first quarter of the fourteenth century. Some of his activities may have been sponsored by his brother, who was not afraid to get his own hands dirty on occasion. In fact, in 1334 Ralph de Ufford, justiciar of Ireland had the earl outlawed for his rebellious activities.[39] Ufford may have been planning to take the unprecedented step of executing the treacherous earl, but he managed to slip through his fingers and eventually escaped to England. Some of his followers were not so lucky: Eustace, the son of Arnold le Poer, who will be discussed below, and William Grant were captured by the justiciar at Castle Island, co. Kerry and immediately executed.[40]

The earl's brother John fitz Thomas was described as a knight by Clyn and was still a young man when he died in 1324. Some years previously in 1319 he had burnt the vill of Athassel in co. Tipperary, which belonged to Richard Óg de Burgh, earl of Ulster.[41] This is not particularly unusual behaviour from someone of his class, but his death notice in Clyn's annals suggests that his actions were considered extreme, even for a young knight. The attack on the vill may have been motivated by the dispute between the Burghs and the Clare families, which his brother Maurice had been drawn into. The dispute originated with Edward I's grant of the lordship of Thomond to Thomas Clare, brother of the earl of Gloucester. The Burghs felt threatened by this grant because of Thomond's location between their lands in Connacht and Limerick. The Clares started to form alliances with the Geraldines of Offaly as soon as they established themselves in Thomond, which seems to have further exacerbated tensions between themselves and the Burghs, though as it turns out the support offered to the Clares by the Geraldines was minimal. The feud between the earl of Ulster and the Clares continued into the fourteenth century, when both sides supported two different contenders of the Uí Bhriain dynasty for the kingship of Thomond: Richard Clare supported Donnchad of Clann Bhriain Ruaidh and Burgh threw his support behind Muirchertach of Clann Taidgh. Eventually in 1313, Clare and the two factions agreed to split Thomond between both candidates, though this agreement fell apart as soon as Clare left for England. Marriage alliances were employed to mend the rifts between the warring factions and the future earls of Kildare and Desmond married daughters of the earl of Ulster. In spite of these alliances, Maurice fitz Thomas appears to have remained firmly on the Clare side and when Richard Clare was killed by allies of Muirchertach Ó Briain at the battle of Dysert O'Dea, in co. Clare, in 1318, Maurice went to Thomond with an army to avenge his death and install Clann Bhriain Ruaidh to the kingship. John fitz Thomas' attack on the earl of Ulster's vill at Athassel in the following year may have been part of the same dispute. Even so, it is also possible that he was acting independently, since his other activities appear to have been unrelated to his brother.[42]

On 17 May 1320 Henry Thrapston, the clerk appointed to pay the wages at the Dublin exchequer was ordered to pay the various magnates of Ireland going to Munster the substantial sum of £600 to deal with John fitz Thomas and David Barry and their followers, mainly composed of members of the Barry and Burgh families.[43] This might be related to the attack on Athassel, or other events of which there is no surviving record. Clyn's account of his death suggests that fitz Thomas was led astray by his followers. Clyn said that fitz Thomas was 'surrounded by the council of many young men, was led astray and deceived, and degenerating from the path of his military ancestors, he stood out, neither as a bulwark or a defender of the peace but an assailant'.[44] Clyn may not be the most trustworthy source in regards to the Desmonds, since his great hero Fulk de la Freigne (d. 1349), sometime sheriff of Kilkenny, had a somewhat adversarial relationship with the earl of Desmond, and had in fact profited from the earl's temporary fall from grace in the 1340s. It is possible that he exaggerated John fitz Thomas' behaviour, though the large sum of money expended on the expedition to subdue him would suggest that the administration saw him as a threat and a destabilising presence in the locality. Unfortunately, the court documents that might have documented fitz Thomas' lawless behaviour no longer survive and it is difficult to assess the extent of his crimes.

Though it is impossible to establish if John fitz Thomas was in the employ of his brother Maurice, or if he was operating autonomously of him, the outlaw Thomas Tyrel was definitely maintained by a more powerful lord: Arnold le Poer. Their close association probably began when Arnold's father Eustace was granted the manors of Oughterard and Castlewarden, which had previously belonged to Ralph Pipard.[45] Gerald Tyrel, father of Thomas, held the nearby manor of Lyons.[46] In 1310, Arnold le Poer was acquitted of the murder of John de Bonevill, and according to the annals of Dublin the deed had been done in self-defence.[47] This did not necessarily mean he was innocent however, just that he had the means to avoid the consequences of his actions. While le Poer escaped punishment for the killing of de Bonevill, Thomas Tyrel was not so lucky. Tyrel was accomplice in the murder and this involvement may appear surprising considering that, like de Bonevill, Thomas' father Gerald was a close associate of John fitz Thomas, future first earl of Kildare. Gerald served as constable of Roscommon Castle and he owed this office to his relationship with fitz Thomas.[48] He also served as seneschal of Ralph Pipard's lands in Ireland, including the manors of Oughterard and Castlewarden in co. Kildare, before they came into Eustace le Poer's hands. It is possible that Gerald continued to act as seneschal after the le Poers acquired the manors and it is likely that this is when Thomas and Arnold become associates. Thomas' brother Henry was executed in 1305 and it was at this time that Thomas was declared an outlaw; however, his outlawry did not mean that local magnates like le Poer were unwilling to use him to further their own ends.

Not only was Thomas Tyrel accused of being an accomplice in John de Bonevill's death, he was also charged with the murder of Robert le Someter, a king's serjeant in Kildare in 1311.[49] Much of Thomas' criminal activity, like that of his brother Henry, took place in or close to Oughterard and Castlewarden, and as Arnold's neighbours, the Tyrels were in a position to help him further his influence in the locality. Arnold may not have been a member of the Tyrel gang, but if they were working on his behalf in the locality he probably served as a maintainer. Maintainers were often the instigators behind the activities of some outlaws, and they received a cut of any proceeds received from these criminal activities.[50] Arnold le Poer was a particularly notorious character in early fourteenth-century Ireland and often pushed at the boundaries of the law, but he rarely found himself at the wrong side of it. Arguably, Arnold and other men of his standing were too powerful to outlaw, but by getting others to carry out illegal activities, they could ensure that they would not be implicated in any crimes.

Maintainers, who were too powerful to prosecute, would have proved useful to an outlaw gang, and the relationship was undoubtedly mutually beneficial. However, while an outlaw gang could have arguably survived without the patronage of a more powerful lord, they would have found it very hard to function without some support in the local community. The contemporary court records reveal that many men and women were punished for receiving, that is giving aid, to outlaw gangs. Unlike maintainers, receivers were usually of lower social status. While maintainers were willing participants in the illegal activities of outlaws, receivers often helped them under duress. This is illustrated in the case of a Gaelic Irishman named Oconyl who was forced to move from Kilmesantan to Tathmothan, both located on the manor of Tallaght in south-west co. Dublin, to avoid providing the notorious O'Toole sept in the Dublin mountains with food and drink. Oconyl was obviously unwilling to supply the O'Tooles because the jurors who heard his case, who were English in origin, vouched for him and confirmed that he only supplied the O'Tooles with food and drink when they were in the king's peace, and even then, it was done unwillingly. In spite of their defence, Oconyl was fined one hundred shillings.[51]

Oconyl's case was not unusual and he was not the only receiver to be given a large fine for associating with felons. An outlaw gang in the locality could prove very expensive to those who received them. Individuals or groups who harboured outlaws or who allowed criminals to escape justice could suffer heavy fines, like in 1277 when the vill of Kenlys (Kells) was fined four pounds for allowing felons to escape their custody.[52] Thomas Tyrel's brother Henry was dependent on receivers in his locality to help him carry out his many crimes and help him evade the law, and many were punished financially for giving him aid. Most of Henry's crimes were committed close to his father's manor of Lyons in north-east co. Kildare. Henry, who was executed in 1305, was described as a common robber who stole livestock, extorted money from travellers on the highway between Lyons and nearby Oughterard and committed acts of burglary in the locality.[53] One of the individuals who received Henry, whose name does not survive in the sources, was fined 100 shillings, a substantial sum at the time.[54] One of his pledges was Reginald Athgo, who probably came from Athgo in Newcastle Lyons, and it is likely the unnamed receiver came from the same place. This person was not the only one on this manor accused of receiving Tyrel, in fact, the entire settlement of Newcastle Lyons, as well as Oughterard, were fined for sheltering him.[55] It is unclear whether they were helping Tyrel willingly or under duress. Tyrel was a dangerous criminal and the local community would have had genuine reason to fear him. Nonetheless, claims in the court documents that receivers were always forced to help outlaws must be treated with scepticism since it was to their benefit to claim they were helping them against their will. Some of the residents of Lyons and other nearby settlements must have had some sympathy for him, since members of his gang came from this locality.

Outlaws not only used receivers to shelter them and provide them with food, they also used them as middle-men to hide stolen property, or sell it on. In October 1316 Roger de Finglas was executed for various crimes, including the receiving of stolen goods.[56] In 1392, when some of the monks of St Thomas' Abbey, Dublin, stole precious objects, including a cross and chalices, from the abbey, they passed them on to a goldsmith, William fitz Hugh.[57] Fitz Hugh would have been able to melt down the items, making them impossible to trace, or he could have sold the objects on to one of his contacts. It is likely that outlaw gangs, or their maintainers, would have had similar relationships with tradesmen and merchants, to help them get rid of their ill-gotten gains.

Receivers also functioned as guides to localities, particularly in places less familiar to the outlaw gangs. High-status individuals were much more mobile than peasants and were able to travel over a larger area. Moreover, a wider network of associates made it easier for them to escape and hide away from the law. The surviving records suggest that Henry Tyrel did not stray too far outside his own locality; he stayed within an area that was intimately familiar to him. On the other hand, his brother Thomas roamed further afield. John de Bonevill was murdered in Ardscull, in south co. Kildare, at some distance from Lyons.[58] It is unlikely that Thomas Tyrel was as familiar with this landscape as he was of that of north co. Kildare. The evidence of the Folville and Coterel gangs in England would suggest that outlaw gangs moved around a lot, undoubtedly looking for new opportunities to pillage and steal, as well as evade capture. Receivers with an intimate knowledge of the local terrain would have proved invaluable as guides to outlaws moving around an area which was less familiar to them. Having locals willing or compelled to help them would have widened the area where they could commit crimes. Outlaws used their own knowledge of a locality, or the knowledge of a receiver, to aid them in their criminal activity and evade the law. Oughterard, where the Tyrel brothers committed some of their crimes, was a relatively hilly area surrounded by flat land. This strategic location allowed the outlaws to survey the land for miles around, and it was also a location that was easy to defend from attack – they were able to use the landscape to their advantage. The Tyrels also positioned themselves at county boundaries, a method also employed by outlaws in England, and used the reluctance of sheriffs and seneschals to cross these boundaries to carry out their crimes.

Members of Henry Tyrel's gang also came from the vicinity of Lyons. Thomas Norreys, who shared his surname with several people who lived on the royal manors of Newcastle Lyons and Esker, had accompanied Henry on robberies, but the jury accepted the rather implausible story that Thomas had accompanied Henry under duress, even though he had been involved in other criminal activities, including horse stealing. Thomas Norreys got away without even paying a fine, but some of Henry's other followers were less lucky. Richard le Shepherd was fined the substantial sum of ten marks, though the jury conceded that he had not taken part in Henry's most serious crimes. One of Richard's pledges had the surname 'de Athgo', which suggest that he came from Athgoe Hill, located on the manor of Newcastle Lyons. It is possible Richard came from the same locality. Thomas Norreys was probably of relatively high social status; members of the Norreys family held parcels of land all around south co. Dublin and north Kildare. His social status, and the fact that all the members of the jury who heard his case would have known him well, may explain why he escaped any sort of punishment. Richard le Shepherd could have been a shepherd, his surname may have been purely descriptive. If he, like his pledge de Athgo came from Athgoe Hill, looking after sheep and other livestock would have been a likely occupation, since the land here was not suitable for tillage. Gerald Tyrel, father of Henry and Thomas, held some lands in Newcastle Lyons and Richard may have been in their employment. In fact, Maurice Tyrel, who was probably Gerald's son served as one of Richard le Shepherd's pledges and the family may have helped him pay his substantial fine.[59]

Some outlaws also had more intimate relationships with women from the locality where they committed their crimes. One of the complaints levelled against Thomas Tyrel was his abduction of the unnamed wife of Arnold le Penrys, a tenant on the royal manor of Newcastle Lyons.[60] Penrys claimed that Tyrel broke into his house and used his wife as if she was his own, bringing her with him on his travels. Though Penrys' wife is not named in this source she may be Mcnabyth, an Irishwoman, who was possibly Tyrel's concubine.[61] Unfortunately, the source that mentions her is very fragmented and it is not clear if she was involved with Tyrel or one of his associates. It was not unusual for men like Penrys, living in an area like Newcastle Lyons where there was plenty of interactions with the Gaelic Irish, to marry an Irishwoman. There are other examples of Englishmen marrying Irishwomen in the locality, like Andrew Deveneys marriage to Grathagh O'Toole.[62] If Penrys' wife was Tyrel's concubine she may have been his willing companion, but in other cases it is clear that women were with outlaws through coercion. In 1311, when Wasmayr Okenwan was accused of receiving a group of outlaws into his home, he claimed that they were sleeping with his wife and daughter and he did not do anything because he feared they would kill him.[63] Again, the names of the women are not recorded. In the same year in Waterford, Adam Osmer was accused of receiving a group of robbers led by Robert le Poer. Robert had taken Adam's daughter as his mistress and visited Adam's house against his will to talk to her. Adam claimed to be too afraid of Robert to stop him.[64] And yet again, his daughter is not named in the sources. There is no indication that any of these women wanted to be with these men, or if, like their fathers and husbands, they were afraid of them. Men were occasionally outlawed for committing violence against women. In 1278, an individual with the surname le Heywer was outlawed when he murdered Catherine Boy. He murdered her after she refused to have sex with him.[65]

As well as being the companions of outlaws, women themselves were occasionally outlawed. In 1305, on the same day Thomas Tyrel was outlawed, several other individuals were outlawed with him, including at least two women: Agnes Otyr, a Gaelic Irishwoman, and the unnamed wife of Henry Scallard of the Cruagh.[66] The nature of their crimes is unknown; the source only says that they committed divers felonies. On 19 October 1316 in Kildare Amice Louyn was outlawed for being an accomplice in the murder of John Canoun. Canoun's murderer Walter Laweles actually escaped punishment because he had paid a fine of twenty shillings.[67] Amice may have gone into hiding because she could not afford to pay a fine. While the courts were generally lenient with those who paid fines, those who could not often ended up at the end of the hangman's noose. There are multiple examples of people who had no chattels, and were presumably too poor to pay a fine, being executed. In 1295, Heyne Beket was hanged for burglary; the source records that he had no chattels.[68] A decade later in 1306, William Herbert, a common thief who also possessed no chattels, was executed.[69] In fact, the vast majority of those whose executions were recorded in the justiciary rolls had no chattels. There appears to have been less risk to those of high social status, or at least wealthy enough to pay a fine, being outlawed, because they could eventually seek a pardon, unless they were particularly notorious or had made enemies of important men, as the Tyrel brothers had.

Many individuals were outlawed for non-payment of debt. For instance, in 1375 Thomas Verdon, knight, was outlawed for not coming to court to pay a fine.[70] Presumably it would have been relatively easy for men like Verdon to have their outlawry reversed once the debt was paid. But what about those who had committed serious crimes or were members of outlaw gangs, how were they restored to grace? Some outlaws, like Henry Tyrel and John fitz Thomas of Desmond, paid the ultimate price for embarking on a life of crime and were executed, but this was a relatively unusual outcome. Thomas Tyrel was at large for several years before he was captured; when the law finally caught up with him he pleaded benefit of clergy. If someone successfully proved that they were a clergyman their case would be moved to an ecclesiastical court, where they could expect a more lenient judgement. Regrettably, Tyrel's ultimate fate is unknown. In 1278, Randolph de Nareweye fled to a church after he had murdered John Countif; Randolph claimed to have killed him in self-defence, and because he was a clerk his case was heard by the church, rather than a secular court.[71] Other individuals abjured the realm, which meant that they went to the nearest port and left the country. In 1278, when an Irishman called Kevin killed Laurence le Gardener in Dublin, he immediately abjured the realm.[72]

Some individuals were rehabilitated by doing military service. In 1402, several members of the gentry of Louth were outlawed for killing their sheriff John Dowdall and their lands were confiscated.[73] Stephen Gernon, one of those involved, had his sentence of outlawry lifted five years later in 1407, because of his good service in fighting the Welsh, under the command of the future Henry V.[74] He had to wait another few years to get his lands back and, coincidentally, a John Gernon was sheriff of Louth at the time, and he may have been instrumental in helping him reclaim his property.[75] When another John Gernon murdered Robert Athelard in 1297 he was pardoned because he went to fight in Flanders.[76] John was the son of Richard Gernon, sheriff of Louth, who was murdered during his term of office in 1311.[77] John Gernon served as sheriff himself in 1331–2, demonstrating that his previous criminal behaviour did not preclude him from this office.[78] Occasionally, men did not receive redemption until after their death. In 1374, the lands that had belonged to Edmund Butler, who was outlawed for committing various felonies against the king's peace, were restored to his widow Katherine after her marriage to Fulk, son of Patrick de la Freigne. Several parcels of land are listed in the letter close ordering their return to his widow. These included the lands of Incheroryk (Inchirourke, co. Tipperary), Finnore (Fennor, co. Tipperary), Imlagh (Emly, co. Tipperary) and Clonmel (co. Cork).[79]

Edmund Butler had extensive landholdings, and the evidence would suggest that even those of substantial means ran the risk of being outlawed. Even earls could be outlawed if they overstepped their authority, as the earl of Desmond discovered in the 1340s when he rose up in rebellion against the crown. In some instances, men suffered the ultimate punishment: Henry Tyrel was starved to death in Dublin castle, and his brother Thomas may have met a similar fate. Likewise, Murcod Ballagh MacMurrough was summarily beheaded. The sources do not say how John fitz Thomas died, but he was a young man, therefore it is likely that his end was violent as well. Members of the knightly class could be executed on occasion, English as well as Irish, but it was unusual, and in the vast majority of cases those who were outlawed were eventually rehabilitated back into normal society.

This chapter mainly focused on men of high social status who committed violent crimes and found themselves on the wrong side of the law, largely because these are the people for which the most evidence survives. Men and women of lower social status were also outlawed, but this was often because of their associations with more powerful men. While leaders of outlaw gangs often had genteel blood running through their veins, those who followed them were often of much lower social status. Some members of gangs were probably the tenants or servants of their leaders. The men and women in the local community who offered them help and sustenance, and were accused of being receivers, were also primarily low-born. Outlaws often took local women as concubines or mistresses, though in many cases it is difficult to establish how much choice these women had in the matter. Notably, many of the women involved with outlaws were Gaelic Irish – did these men feel less squeamish about forcing themselves on Irishwomen?

Deprived of the help of local communities and wealthy maintainers outlaw gangs could not have survived for very long. The records reveal that these gangs could be a major destabilising force within their various localities, but people were either too terrified or incapable of stopping them, or they proved too beneficial to their noble patrons to be stopped. Moreover, men who spent time living as outlaws, and who managed not to get killed or executed, were almost always rehabilitated. When men like Henry Tyrel were executed, it was because they had antagonised a powerful political adversary, not specifically because of the crimes they had committed. Men whose behaviour was equally as violent as Tyrel's usually went on to serve in administrative office, like that of sheriff. These men may have been dangerous and a disruptive influence, but they were also the ones who served in public office ensuring the survival of English Ireland. Though their actions were often evil, they were a necessary evil.

Notes

1 Maurice Keen, *The Outlaws of Medieval Legend*, 3rd ed. (London: Routledge, 2000), 2.

2 Susan Stewart, 'Outlawry as an Instrument of Justice in the Thirteenth Century', in *Outlaws in Medieval and Early Modern England: Crime, Government and Society, c.1066–c.1600*, eds. John C. Appleby and Paul Dalton (Farnham: Ashgate, 2009), 37.
3 *Bracton*, 2: 362–3.
4 Philomena Connolly, *Medieval Record Sources* (Dublin: Four Courts Press, 2002), 23–6.
5 *CJRI*.
6 For example, NAI, RC 7 and KB 2, and some plea rolls can also be found in RC 8.
7 A.J. Pollard, *Imagining Robin Hood: The Late-medieval Stories in Historical Context* (London: Routledge, 2004), 105.
8 Edmund Curtis, ed., *Calendar of Ormond Deeds, 1413–1509* (Dublin: Irish Manuscripts Commission, 1935), 3: 119–21.
9 For more on the O'Byrnes see Emmett O'Byrne, *War, Politics, and the Irish of Leinster, 1156–1606* (Dublin: Four Courts Press, 2003).
10 CIRCLE, PR 10 Ric. II, § 192, <http://chancery.tcd.ie/document/patent/10-richard-ii/192>.
11 Mervyn Archdall, *The Peerage of Ireland: Or, a Genealogical History of the Present Nobility of That Kingdom, by John Lodge, Esq. Revised, Enlarged, and Continued to the Present Time*, 7 vols. (Dublin; James Moore, 1789), 1: 82–3.
12 Walter FitzGerald, 'The FitzGeralds of Lackagh', *Journal of the County Kildare Archaeological Society* 1 (1894): 245–64.
13 C.W. Fitzgerald, *The Earls of Kildare and Their Ancestors: From 1057 to 1773*, 3rd ed. (Dublin: Hodges, Smith, & Co., 1858), 68.
14 A.J. Otway-Ruthven, 'The Native Irish and English Law in Medieval Ireland', in *Government, War and Society in Medieval Ireland: Essays by Edmund Curtis, A.J. Otway-Ruthven and James Lydon*, ed. Peter Crooks (Dublin: Four Courts Press, 2008), 145.
15 A.J. Otway-Ruthven, 'Select Documents VI: The Request of the Irish for English Law 1277–80', *IHS* 6 (1948–9): 261–70.
16 J.R.S. Phillips, 'The Irish Remonstrance of 1317: An International Perspective', *IHS* 27 (1990–91): 112–29.
17 J.A. Watt, 'Dublin in the Thirteenth Century: The Making of a Colonial Capital City', in *Thirteenth Century England I*, eds. P.R. Coss and S.D. Lloyd (Woodbridge: Boydell Press, 1986), 156.
18 NAI, EX 2/3, 488–9; Áine Foley, *The Royal Manors of County Dublin: Crown and Community* (Dublin: Four Courts Press, 2013), 10, 143.
19 Gwilym Dodd, *Justice and Grace: Private Petitioning and the English Parliament in the Late Middle Ages* (Oxford: Oxford University Press, 2007), 208.
20 Statutes, *Ireland*, 212.
21 There are many townlands in Ireland called Cregg, therefore it is difficult to pinpoint where this one is located.
22 NAI, 999/184/20, 56; a Matthew Omalmoy, who was fined for trespass in Wexford in 1304 is mentioned in the *Report of the Deputy Keeper of the Public Records of Ireland*, vol. 38, 100; Art Malachelyn may be the Malachelyn who was held in the king's prison in 1289, *CDI, 1285–92*, vol. 3, no. 558.
23 *CDI, 1285–92*, vol. 3, no. 817.
24 T.W. Moody, F.X. Martin and F.J. Byrne, eds., *A New History of Ireland*, vol. 9 (Oxford: Oxford University Press, 2005), 155.
25 Ballagh means 'freckled'; Richard Butler, ed., *The Annals of Ireland by Friar John Clyn and Thady Dowling* (Dublin: Dublin University Press, 1849), 18.
26 Pollard, *Imagining Robin Hood*, 106; T.A. Green, 'Societal Concepts of Criminal Liability for Homicide in Mediaeval England', *Speculum* 47 (1972): 669.
27 *CJRI, 1308–14*, 32.

28 J.T. Gilbert, ed., *Chartularies of St Mary's Abbey, Dublin* (RS, 1884–86), 2: 294.
29 John Bellamy, *Crime and Public Order in England in the Later Middle Ages* (Toronto: University of Toronto Press, 1973), 75.
30 Áine Foley, 'Violent Crime in Medieval County Dublin: A Symptom of Degeneracy?', in *Medieval Dublin X*, ed. Seán Duffy (Dublin: Four Courts Press, 2010), 221.
31 *CJRI, 1305–7*, 141.
32 See Foley, 'Violent Crime', 224–38.
33 Bellamy, *Crime and Public Order*, 75.
34 John Bellamy, 'The Coterel Gang: An Anatomy of a Band of Fourteenth-Century Criminals', *EHR* 79 (1964): 700.
35 E.L.G. Stones, 'The Folvilles of Ashby-Folville, Leicestershire, and Their Associates in Crime', *Transactions of the Royal Historical Society*, 5th series, 7 (1957): 119–21.
36 Paul Dryburgh, 'The Career of Roger Mortimer, First Earl of March (c.1287–1330)', PhD thesis, University of Bristol, 2002, p. 206.
37 Stones, 'The Folvilles of Ashby-Folville', 121; *CPR, 1330–34*, 61.
38 Bellamy, *Crime and Public Order*, 73.
39 Áine Foley, 'High-Status Execution in Fourteenth-Century Ireland', in *Fourteenth Century England IX*, eds. James Bothwell and Gwilym Dodd (Woodbridge: Boydell & Brewer, 2016), 143.
40 Bernadette Williams, ed. and trans., *The Annals of Ireland by Friar John Clyn* (Dublin: Four Courts Press, 2007), 234.
41 Gilbert, *Chartularies of St Mary's Abbey, Dublin*, 2: 360.
42 Keith Waters, 'The Earls of Desmond in the Fourteenth Century', PhD thesis, Durham University, 2004, pp. 27–31.
43 CIRCLE, CR 14 Edw. II, § 11, <https://chancery.tcd.ie/document/close/14-edward-ii/11>.
44 Williams, ed., The *Annals of Ireland*, 180.
45 *CDI, 1302–07*, §149, 57–9; A.J. Otway-Ruthven, 'The Medieval County of Kildare', *IHS* 11 (1959): 198; Foley, *Royal Manors*, 94, 157. Gerald Tyrel also held three carucates of land and twelve acres of moor on the manor of Castlewarden according to a manorial extent, TNA, SC 12/20/48 (transcribed in Paul Dryburgh and Brendan Smith, eds., *Handbook and Select Calendar of Sources for Medieval Ireland in the National Archives of the United Kingdom* (Dublin: Four Courts Press, 2005), 267–9). This document is undated, and though the catalogue assigns it to the reign of Edward III, it undoubtedly dates to before Michaelmas term 1309, by which date Gerald was deceased, NAI, EX 2/2, 404–5. The impetus to make an extent of this manor was probably the handing over of Ralph Pipard's lands to the crown. For a list of Pipard's Irish possessions see *Calendar of Ormond Deeds, 1172–1350*, 129–30.
46 Foley, *Royal Manors*, 100.
47 Gilbert, *Chartularies of St Mary's Abbey, Dublin*, 2: 294.
48 Foley, *Royal Manors*, 158.
49 *CJRI, 1308–14*, 217.
50 Bellamy, *Crime and Public Order*, 72.
51 *CJRI, 1305–7*, 503.
52 NAI, 999/184/20, 9.
53 *CJRI, 1305–7*, 477.
54 Ibid., 481.
55 Ibid., 481, 483.
56 NAI, KB 2/8, 26–7.
57 Mervyn Archdall, *Monasticon Hibernicum* (Dublin: W.B. Kelly, 1876), 48.
58 Clyn, *Annals of Ireland*, 158–9.

59 See Foley, *Royal Manors*, 162–5 for a more in depth discussion on Tyrel's followers.
60 *CJRI, 1305–7*, 477.
61 Ibid., 500.
62 Ibid., 480–1.
63 *CJRI, 1308–14*, 216.
64 Ibid., 179–80.
65 NAI, 999/184/20, 60.
66 *CJRI, 1305–7*, 480–1.
67 NAI, KB 2/8, 29.
68 *CJRI, 1295–1307*, 3.
69 *CJRI, 1305–7*, 496.
70 CIRCLE, PR 49 Edw. III, § 10, <https://chancery.tcd.ie/document/patent/49-edward-iii/10>.
71 NAI, 999/184/20, 55.
72 Ibid., 5.
73 CIRCLE, CR 9 Hen. IV, §2, <https://chancery.tcd.ie/document/close/9-henry-iv/2>.
74 Brendan Smith, 'The Murder of John Dowdall, Sheriff of Louth, 1402', in *Princes, Prelates and Poets: Essays in Honour of Katherine Simms*, ed. Seán Duffy (Dublin: Four Courts Press, 2013), 188.
75 Brendan Smith, *Crisis and Survival in Late Medieval Ireland: The English of Louth and their Neighbours* (Oxford: Oxford University Press, 2013), 16.
76 Brendan Smith, 'The Murder of Richard Gernon, Sheriff of Louth, 1311', *Journal of the County Louth Archaeological and Historical Society* 21 (1988): 391.
77 Brendan Smith, *Colonisation and Conquest in Medieval Ireland: The English in Louth, 1170–1330* (Cambridge: Cambridge University Press, 1999), 131.
78 Smith, *Crisis and Survival*, 15; Idem, *Colonisation and Conquest*, 135.
79 CIRCLE, CR 48 Edw. II, § 87, <https://chancery.tcd.ie/document/close/48-edward-iii/87>.

10 The origins and development of judicial tenure 'during good behaviour' to 1485

Ryan Rowberry[1]

Introduction

Judicial tenure, the terms by which a judge holds office, has been touted as one of the key pillars of judicial independence from oppressive executive power.[2] Judicial tenure 'during good behaviour' (*quamdiu se bene gesserit*), as opposed to the more precarious judicial tenure 'during pleasure' (*durante bene placito / quamdiu nobis placuerit)*, has customarily been viewed as a seventeenth-century legal innovation created to shield English high court judges from arbitrary removal by a meddling, overbearing monarch.[3] Drawing upon this seventeenth-century English tradition, the United States Constitution ratified in 1788 mandated that all United States federal judges would fill their offices 'during good behaviour',[4] a phrase that has come to mean that a federal judge holds office for life barring commission of a crime serious enough to warrant impeachment and conviction (typically a felony).[5] Judicial tenure 'during good behaviour' for U.S. federal judges remains a unique form of judicial office holding[6] today despite sporadic attempts to change it.[7]

Remarkably, although judicial tenure 'during good behaviour' has been a hallmark of the Anglo-American judiciary for hundreds of years, there are no comprehensive studies of its origins and development prior to the seventeenth century. Relying almost exclusively on secondary sources for their conclusions, nearly all modern scholars assume that every English monarch appointed judges to serve 'during pleasure' until the repeated clashes between the judiciary and the Stuart kings during the turbulent 1600s forced a compromise:[8] the 1701 Act of Settlement. This Act granted that 'Judges Commissions be made *Quam diu se bene Gesserint* and their Salaries ascertained and established but upon the address of both Houses of Parliament it may be lawfull to remove them'.[9] Other scholars, like George Aylmer, are acutely aware that judicial tenure 'during good behaviour' was part of a complicated, medieval administrative history but chose not to explore the topic as 'no systematic survey is available of tenure in the Middle Ages'.[10]

To my knowledge, only five scholars have attempted to examine the judicial tenure in England prior to 1600 using original records, four of them, however, in only cursory fashion.[11] The fifth, Sir John Sainty, undertook the monumental task of compiling and organising a list of all the judges of the superior courts in England from 1272–1990.[12] To populate his list, Sainty relied on previous scholars' lists of judges that were based on original records as well as the patent and close rolls produced by the royal Chancery, plea rolls of the King's Bench (KB 27) and Common Bench (CP 40) and the King's and Lord Treasurer's Remembrancers' memoranda rolls (E 159 and E 368). Using these sources, Sainty chronicled the appointments, tenures, renewals, salaries, terminations and death dates of judges from the King's Bench, Common Bench, Exchequer, the Master of the Rolls, the Vice Chancellors, the Lords Justices of Appeal in Chancery, the Judge of Probate and Divorce Courts, the Judges of the Supreme Court and the Lords of Appeal in Ordinary.[13] Sainty's published list, *The Judges of England 1272–1990*, has become the standard reference list to which one must initially turn to look for broad changes in judicial tenure in pre-Stuart England.

This is not to say, however, that a deep understanding of the origins and development judicial tenure 'during good behaviour' can be gleaned from Sainty's work. It suffers from some important limitations in this respect. The first of these is that *The Judges of England 1272–1990* is a list of information about English judges; it does not attempt to discuss reasons for changes in judicial tenure over time. Second, Sainty's study starts at the accession of Edward I (1272), ignoring the English judiciary during the long reign of Henry III (1216–72) when the courts of Common Bench, King's Bench and the Exchequer became largely separate judicial courts performing different judicial functions.[14] Third, Sainty's examinations were confined to judges sitting in the superior royal courts of England, neglecting the English judges sitting in the lordship of Ireland as well as those commissioned as forest eyre judges in England. Fourth, Sainty's narrow focus on judges in English superior courts means that he did not consider how the changing tenure of lesser court officers may have impacted the development of tenure 'during good behaviour' for judges. Finally, particularly for the fifteenth century, Sainty appears to have relied on lists of judges compiled by others rather than examining the original sources afresh, which resulted in a few inaccuracies.

Despite these limitations, scholars of the Anglo-American judiciary owe a special debt to Sir John Sainty for his pioneering undertaking. His painstaking, wide-ranging archival research was conducted before the dawn of digitised, and in some cases, searchable, primary sources.[15] And it is a lasting testament to his erudition and diligence that while *The Judges of England 1272–1990* may be added to or refined in the future, it will probably never be superseded as the standard reference listing of English judges.

The aim of this paper is to build on Sainty's work and examine the origins and development of judicial tenure 'during good behaviour' in medieval England. Using the medieval Chancery records, which record judicial appointments from the thirteenth century onward, this article will be the first to trace the rise and development of judicial tenure 'during good behaviour' from its earliest recorded instances.[16] To understand the development of judicial tenure 'during good behaviour' in medieval England, however, we must first briefly review what medieval English contemporaries considered tenure to be and how it became linked to royal offices. Thereafter, we will examine the development of tenure 'during good behaviour' for administrative offices broadly and then consider when, why and how it developed into a form of office holding for English judges in the Exchequer, Common Bench and King's Bench in both Ireland and England.[17]

Tenure and royal office in medieval England

The word 'tenure' is derived from Latin *tenere*, meaning 'to hold'.[18] Precisely how 'tenure' became linked to lands and offices in medieval England is a complex, obscure process that began with the gradual importation of inchoate Norman concepts and practices of feudal 'tenure' from 1066 onward.[19] As Professor Hyams ably pointed out, 'tenure is a long-dead metaphor which treats land as if it were an object that could be held in one's hand'.[20] In other words, 'tenure' transferred to land 'a set of images . . . which were initially intended to clarify possession and title to movable objects that could literally be held and transferred to another, or just taken "in hand"'.[21] Holding land in medieval England was, in the words of Pollock and Maitland, 'an abstraction of a very high order'.[22] Medieval landholding arrangements were supple enough to be molded 'into different individual tenures according to the kind of [land-for-service] bargain made between the (land-)lord and tenant'.[23] Such bargains typically included some form(s) of military, economic or religious service from the tenant for varying periods of time (e.g., in fee, for life, for a set term, during pleasure).[24] Over the course of the twelfth and thirteenth centuries, royal officials, lawyers and educators systematised and classified the services implicated in various land bargains into the Common Law system of tenures (known as estates) – an organisational scheme that continues to haunt first-year American law school students when they are introduced to Common Law property.[25] Indeed it is probably not a coincidence that with the rise of a professional legal class in the reign of Edward I[26] we also find the first usage of the word 'tenure' in its modern sense in a legal treatise, *Britton*, sometime around 1290.[27]

This English concept of 'tenure' also encompassed grants of feudal office from the crown, as English monarchs treated crown offices as estates of private property. As Maitland poignantly reminds us, 'jurisdiction is property, office is property, the kingship itself is property'.[28] Thus, appointment to a royal office in medieval England was 'in effect the same as a grant of land [from the king]: it conferred on the grantee an estate in the office, and (usually more important) in its emoluments', and in return the grantee agreed to perform the service required of the office.[29] In both lands and feudal office, therefore, the rights of the tenant *or* office holder were determined by the terms of the grant because both were considered property that could be alienated. Sometime in the eleventh and twelfth centuries, many offices in the king's household, like the steward or constable, were granted to magnates on terms that became hereditary (i.e., in fee), rendering such offices minimally useful to the crown in actually administering the affairs of the realm.[30] Consequently, as the expanding orbit of royal government and justice under Henry II gradually eroded older, seigniorial jurisdictions in the latter half of the twelfth and early thirteenth centuries – a transformation heralded by the creation of remarkable contemporary administrative and legal treatises, *The Dialogue of the Exchequer* and *Glanvill*[31] – newer offices like chancellor or judge emerged in the *curia regis*. These newer offices were typically staffed by *novi homines*: men of humbler rank but of greater administrative and organisational capability than the old nobility.[32] These royal officers in the *curia regis* and a growing corps of royal officials in the counties, cities and boroughs 'performed all the functions of central government of whatever kind, including of course, judicial business'.[33] And the varied tenures of their offices – 'during pleasure'; a term of years; 'for life' – reflected those non-hereditary land tenures typically granted by the king to the middling social classes.

A few illustrations from the early part of the reign of Henry III reveal that the limiting terms governing the overwhelming bulk of medieval landholding were synonymous with the terms describing the duration of various tenures of royal officers in medieval England. The majority of royal grants of land in medieval England were given with tenure 'during pleasure' (*quamdiu ei placuerit / quamdiu regi placuerit*). For example, in March 1217, the regents acting for Henry III, who was in his minority, granted the manor of Axford [Wiltshire] with all its appurtenances to Roger de Clifford to hold *quamdiu ei placuerit*.[34] Moreover, on 25 September 1241, Henry III granted P. de Sabaudia the lands of John de Warenne in Sussex and Surrey 'during pleasure' with a mandate to J. de Gatesden and Robert de Ferles 'to give him seisin of the said honor with the crops of last year'.[35] Likewise, most royal offices in the reign of Henry III were held during the king's pleasure. On 10 April 1217 Richard de Samford was appointed custodian of the forests of Chipham and Melkesham [Somerset and Wiltshire] *quamdiu ei placuerit*.[36] Peter de Rivaux, a trusted Poitevin counselor to Henry III, was appointed by the king to the 'custody of the treasurership of the Exchequer' during pleasure on 19 January 1233.[37] And on 12 May 1236, the king appointed Hugh de Bolebec 'as sheriff of the county of Northumberland' *quamdiu regi placuerit*.[38] These examples are but a few of the hundreds of grants of land and appointments to royal office 'during pleasure' inscribed on the royal Chancery rolls throughout the reign of Henry III.[39]

Of course even in the early thirteenth century not all grants of land or feudal office were held 'during pleasure'; some contained other limiting terms.[40] Royal grants of land or appointments to office for a term of years (effectively short-term leases) also occur frequently during the reign of the Henry III. Land grants for a term of years are particularly abundant. On 9 December 1225 for instance, the king granted that the men of Grimsby [Lincolnshire] could hold the village of Grimsby 'in their hand as they previously had done, for *tres annos* from Michaelmas in the ninth year.'[41] Later, on 15 November 1244, Henry III granted to the bishop of Hereford 'that notwithstanding that the five years [*v annos*] for which the king leased to him the manor of Chilteham [co. Gloucester] will expire while he [the bishop] is beyond seas by licence of the king, he shall hold that manor until his return to England'.[42] Like land, royal offices during the reign of Henry III were also leased for terms of years. On 8 December 1221, the king commissioned the royal exchange to Andre Bukerel for *tres annos* at a sum of 4000 marks.[43] And on 30 May 1234 Henry III appointed John de Plessitis 'to the custody of the castle of Devizes with the manor of Rudes [Wiltshire] pertaining to the custody' along with the 'custody of the manor of Devizes and the forest of Chippenham for ten years'.[44] Numerous other examples abound.[45]

Grants of lands and royal offices with tenure 'for life' (*tota vita sua*) are also found with regularity in records during the reign of Henry III. In 1229, the king granted the manor of Newport (co. Buckingham) to Walter de Kirkham *tota vita sua* for £40 annually.[46] And on 24 September 1242, the king granted that 'Master Richard, the queen's tailor' should hold 'for life' the 'land in Barewe and elsewhere in the county of Northumberland which Master Geoffrey, the queen's cook, had of the king's gift for life'.[47] Royal offices were also occasionally granted for life during the reign of Henry III. On 27 April 1233, the patent rolls record the 'appointment for life, of Brian de Insula to the custody of the county of York; and mandate to all persons of the county to be attending and answering unto him as sheriff'.[48] Three years later, on 28 December 1236, Henry III granted 'Aaron of York, a Jew, for life, the office of chief rabbi of all the Jews of England'.[49] And on 6 December 1265 the king granted the delightfully-named Ellis de Tingewike the 'bailiwick of the king's forest of Whittlewood and park of Hauleg [Northamptonshire]' to hold 'for life'.[50]

However, the demise of Hubert de Burgh, the earl of Kent, suggests that there was a developing sense in the early thirteenth century that certain high-level offices were beyond the king's power to grant for life.[51] On 27 April 1228 Henry III granted Hubert de Burgh the office of Justiciar of England (chief governor) 'for life'.[52] Four years later, on 11 June 1232, the king reiterated that Hubert de Burgh was to be Justiciar for life, but granted that if de Burgh was ill or away from England on the king's business, he could appoint a deputy Justiciar.[53] And on 2 July 1232 Henry III 'made an oath on the gospels and bound himself and his heirs' to uphold the grants of lands and office made to de Burgh, while Hubert swore an oath that should the king ever wish to 'invalidate the charters, gifts, grants, and confirmations' made to him that he would 'take care to impede that purpose and do all in his power to preserve the said charters inviolate'.[54] Despite these assurances, in winter 1232 Henry III petitioned Pope Gregory IX to annul his oath and revoke his grants of lands and office to Hubert de Burgh. The king claimed his oath had been extracted under duress and that his grants of land

and office 'for life' contravened his coronation oath in which he swore to 'maintain the royal rights, liberties, and dignities'.[55] The king argued that by granting Hubert de Burgh the office of Justiciar for life along with numerous lands, castles and bailiwicks to support him in this position, he had made an alienation of crown property that was prejudicial to the realm and the crown, rendering these alienations illicit.[56] Henry III's argument of illicit alienation may also have been bolstered in that his oath not to revoke his grants of life tenure to Hubert de Burgh explicitly bound his successors when it was customary for tenures to royal offices to expire on the death of the granting monarch. In any event, Pope Gregory absolved Henry III from his oath not to revoke his grants of office and lands to de Burgh, and Hubert later renounced his claims to the office of Justiciar in May 1234.[57] Following de Burgh's downfall, there was never again a Justiciar of England.

Thus far, we have spent a great deal of time analysing particular phrases defining tenure. And while some may argue against attaching too much significance to stock phrases describing tenure copied by Chancery clerks responsible for churning out thousands of written documents per year by the early thirteenth century,[58] the clerks, if they enrolled copies of letters at all,[59] appear to have been quite fastidious in delineating the different tenures applicable to particular royal offices.[60] For example, on 16 June 1232 Peter de Rivaux was appointed to multiple royal offices at the same time but held different offices by different tenures.[61] The patent roll records that the king appointed Peter to the shrievalties of Sussex and Surrey *tota vita sua*, granted him the wardenship of the royal castles at Hastings and Pevensey *tota vita sua*, but made him warden of the castle and houses at Guildford *quamdiu regi placuerit*.[62] Two weeks later the king appointed Peter as custodian of the temporalities of the archbishopric of Canterbury *quamdiu regi placuerit*.[63] Precise distinction between tenures among different royal offices can also be found in the Fine Rolls of Henry III.[64] Chancery clerks' meticulous attention to accurately copying the form of tenure attached to each royal office suggests that different forms of tenure had, in fact, salient differences to medieval contemporaries, a topic to which we will return shortly.

This deep dive into the original records of royal government in early thirteenth-century England suggests several general conclusions about the tenure of medieval royal officials. First, like grants of land in medieval England, the particular form of tenure attached to a royal office in medieval England varied according to the terms in the granting instrument. Second, while the majority of royal officers during the reign of Henry III held their positions 'during pleasure,' already by the early thirteenth century English monarchs were comfortable granting certain royal offices for a term of years or 'for life', meaning that the origins and development of these forms of tenure for royal offices likely lie in the reign of Henry II, or perhaps earlier.[65] Third, as the evidence above attests, lifetime appointments to some significant royal offices, like that of sheriff, were already present in England not long after Magna Carta. Fourth, as the story of Hubert de Burgh illustrates, the decision of the monarch to grant a high-level royal office was a weighty political decision that likely depended on the importance of the office, the monarch's power at the time, contemporary understandings of the coronation oath and what constituted crown property, and the ongoing relationship between subject and crown.

Tenure during good behaviour

But what of grants of land or royal office with tenure during 'good behaviour' (*bene gesserit*)? Unlike tenure 'during pleasure', for a term of years, or 'for life', all of which appear with frequency early in the reign of Henry III, tenure during good behaviour is noticeably different. The Charter Rolls contain, to my knowledge, no grants of land or royal office during good behaviour for the entire thirteenth century.[66] While the phrase *bene gesserit* does appear on rare occasions in the patent rolls, close rolls and fine rolls before the 1250s, it is not directly linked to holding lands or royal office.[67] Rather it seems tethered to ancient concepts of providing sureties that a certain person or people – usually prisoners, foreigners or someone run afoul of the king – would act peacefully towards the king and his subjects, a customary practice reflected in the collective, communal safeguards found in the frankpledge system which were well-known.[68]

However, the record evidence shows that in the late 1260s the phrase 'during good behaviour' enters the Chancery lexicon on permanent footing as a result of the Second Barons' War (1264–67). The Second Barons' War was a civil war led by Simon de Montfort against Henry III. Henry III triggered the conflict when he obtained a papal bull in 1261 releasing him from his oath to uphold the Provisions of Oxford (1258), short-lived sweeping governmental reforms spearheaded by de Montfort that subjugated the king to a ruling council of fifteen men and established a triennial parliament.[69] With Simon de Montfort's eventual defeat and death at the battle of Evesham on 4 August 1265, royalist forces led by Prince Edward gained the upper hand, and the war sputtered to an end with the issuance of a sort of peace agreement, now known as the Dictum of Kenilworth, on 31 October 1266.[70]

As the conflict subsided, many rebels prudently sought pardons from Henry III for their treason. Patent rolls from the mid-1260s preserve numerous copies of these pardons. These reveal that rebels were readmitted into the king's peace on a condition: they had to find sureties for their future *bene gesserit*. A typical example of such a pardon is that from 7 August 1266, which reads: 'Power to Philip Marmion to receive into the king's peace Thomas son of Alfred, Richard son of John, Richard Cok, W[illiam] son of Peter, and John son of Sweyn, provided that they find sufficient mainpernors for their good behaviour'.[71] Another pardon from 28 November 1266 reads,

> Pardon to Ralph de Sandwic[h], taken in the conflict of Evesham, of the king's indignation and rancour of mind conceived towards him by the

> occasion of the disturbance of the realm; on the mainprise of W[illiam] bishop of Bath and Wells, the chancellor, Henry Malemayns, Geoffrey de Percy and William de Faukeham for his good behaviour.[72]

Comparing the few records containing the phrase 'good behaviour' prior to the 1260s with the scores of royal pardons from the Second Barons' War containing the same phrase strongly suggests that the phrase 'good behaviour' was permanently grafted into the medieval administrative consciousness in the late 1260s. However, the requirement that rebels find sureties to pledge for their good behaviour reveals that the concept of 'good behaviour' in the 1260s remained linked to older notions of reclaiming wrongdoers into the realm through communal safeguards rather than as a condition by which one held royal office.

The precise contours of 'good' or 'bad' behaviour with respect to office holding at this time are difficult to discern. From contemporary record evidence perhaps the most that can be said is that acting with 'good behaviour' was equivalent to honouring one's oath of fealty.[73] *Bracton*, a remarkable treatise on the operations of the king's courts written by cadre of clerks and judges during the reign of Henry III, records this solemn oath of fealty. Placing his hand on the Gospels, a man stated: 'Hear this, lord N., that I will bear your fealty in life and limb, in body, goods, and earthly honor, so help me God and these sacred relics'.[74] To act with *bene gesserit*, therefore, one had to be behave faithfully toward the king 'and his heirs from henceforth,'[75] suggesting that men who acted with *male gesserit* went 'against their [oaths of] fealty' and could thereby lose their law and lands.[76] Thus, the broad spiritual and temporal obligations contained within the oath of fealty that English rebels re-swore after the Second Barons' War probably formed the initial standards for determining whether one acted with good or bad behaviour.

In its original incarnation in the mid-1260s, then, the phrase *bene gesserit* was a condition used to ensure that remitted English rebels would act faithfully toward the crown in the future. But the aging Henry III and Edward I soon applied the phrase *bene gesserit* to grants of many royal offices, gradually creating a new, expressly conditional form of tenure.[77] Perhaps wanting to clarify the type of service the king expected from royal servants, many grants of royal offices using typical forms of tenure in the late 1260s and early 1270s included the phrase 'good behaviour' as a modifier. For example on 8 October 1268, just two years after the Dictum of Kenilworth, Henry III granted Geoffrey Norman, his chaplain, the office of celebrating 'divine service at St. Margaret's in Westminster' *tota vita sua* 'so long as he be of good behaviour'.[78] And on 8 May 1271 Henry III granted that Walter of Durham and John of York should be keepers of the forest of Galtres [co. York] 'for their lives so long as they be of good behaviour'.[79] Edward I continued where his father left off, granting Roger de Hamenhal the bailiwick of the forest of Harundel 'during the king's pleasure and during good behaviour' on 7 February 1276[80] and committing the shrievalty of the 'county of Typerary, Ireland' to Walter Uncle on 2 October 1282 for ten years 'during good behaviour'.[81] The appearance of grants to royal offices that included the phrase *quamdiu se bene gesserint* immediately following a raft of royal pardons containing the same terminology strongly suggests that the upheaval caused by Second Barons' War was the primary catalyst for creating tenures for royal offices 'during good behaviour'. In doing so the crown (perhaps unknowingly) transformed a popular contemporary phrase that originally offered conditional remission to rebels into an explicit condition on royal offices designed to hold officers to their oaths of faithfulness in their future performance.[82]

While typical forms of tenure for royal offices were modified by the phrase *bene gesserit* at the end of Henry III's reign, it is only during the reign of Edward I that we find tenure *quamdiu se bene gesserint* being used as a distinct, individual form of tenure. The patent rolls record that on 2 October 1274, Edward I granted the custody of the bailiwick of the forest of Melkesham [Wiltshire] to Geoffrey de Middleton 'during good behaviour'.[83] And the close rolls state that Edward I granted Nicholas de Lenn the bailiwick of the forest of the Peak [Derbyshire] 'during good behaviour' on 23 May 1275.[84] The fine rolls also record that on 15 November 1277 Robert de Kestevene was granted the 'office of summoner in the wapentake of Wirkesworth' [Derbyshire] 'during good behaviour' for an initial fine of 100 shillings and 20 shillings annually.[85] Similar grants of royal office *quamdiu se bene gesserit* during the reign of Edward I can also be found for keepers of particular forests,[86] custodians of bailiwicks in Ireland,[87] wardens of castles,[88] custodians of county hundreds,[89] a weigher of corn,[90] a shrievalty in Ireland,[91] a custodian of the smaller piece of the seal for recognisances of debt,[92] bedelries of county hundreds,[93] custodians of castle gates,[94] tollkeepers for the weighing of lead and wools,[95] a hospital custodian[96] and butlers to the king.[97]

Edward I was also the first English monarch to extend tenure *quamdiu se bene gesserit* to ministerial offices in some of the king's courts. For example on 6 January 1280 Edward I granted Thomas de London, a clerk, the 'office of chirographer of the king's court in Ireland' with tenure 'during good behaviour'.[98] Thomas de London performed so admirably as court chirographer that he was granted the 'office of receiver in the Exchequer of Dublin' *quamdiu se bene gesserit* more than a decade later, on 30 October 1290.[99] The patent rolls also record that on 8 August 1280, Edward I granted William de Leye the office of marshal before the justices in eyre in Ireland 'during good behaviour'.[100] And on 19 June 1305, John de Seleby was granted the office of 'the usher of Exchequer of Dublin', a position paying 1.5 denarii. per day 'for life and during good behaviour'.[101] The reasons that some ministerial offices in the nascent king's courts in Ireland, not England, were the first to receive tenure *quamdiu se bene gesserit* are obscure.[102] Some of the explanation may lie in the fact that letters of appointment to offices in the king's courts in Ireland during the reign of Edward I appear to have been the joint responsibility of the Irish and English chanceries.[103] The Irish chancery may have taken the initial step of granting a ministerial court office with tenure 'during good behaviour' that was later confirmed using the same language by the English chancery. Or perhaps, Edward I was using tenure 'during good behaviour' as an incentive to attract able administrative servants to a distant English colony.[104] This is an area that would reward further study.

It is not until the turbulent reign of Edward II (1307–27) that we find appointments to ministerial court offices with tenure 'during good behaviour' in the central royal courts of England. On 28 October 1313 Edward II granted Robert de Foxton the office of chirographer of the Common Bench 'during good behaviour', an 'enlargement' of Foxton's prior royal grant to the same office 'during pleasure' on 24 March 1312.[105] Likewise, Thomas Botle's initial royal grant of the office of chief crier in the King's Bench 'during pleasure' on 7 March 1314 was enlarged to a grant of the same office with tenure 'during good behaviour' on 9 August 1320.[106] Edward II also confirmed a grant of the ushership of the Exchequer to John Dymmok on 6 December 1317 'during good behaviour'.[107] Like his father, Edward III (1327–77) appointed ministerial offices in the royal courts of England and Ireland with tenure 'during good behaviour', enlarged the tenures of some faithful court officers from 'during pleasure' to 'during good behaviour', and, in an important change, enlarged the tenures of some ministerial court officers from tenure 'during good behaviour' to either a term of years or tenure 'for life'.[108]

But what, if anything, did this new form of tenure *quamdiu se bene gesserint* mean to contemporary royal officials in the king's courts? Original sources suggest several answers. The first is unsurprising: tenure 'during good behaviour' provided enhanced security in court office over tenure 'during pleasure'. The second answer, however, is more problematic. The record evidence illustrates that medieval contemporaries viewed tenure 'during good behaviour' as inferior to tenure for a term of years or tenure for life. That is, in the *cursus honorarum* of court office holding tenures, holding an office 'during good behaviour' ranked below grants of office for a term of years or 'for life'. Precisely why this should be the case is confusing, as a grant of a court office for a term of years is of finite duration compared to a grant of a court office 'during good behaviour' that could feasibly last a lifetime. Moreover, original sources do not reveal that holding a court office with tenure for a term of years or 'for life' offered increased security over tenure 'during good behaviour' because some form of bad behaviour appears to have been a pre-requisite for removal from office for a man holding a position under any of these three forms of tenure. It may be that tenure 'during good behaviour' was viewed as a lower form of tenure because of its relatively recent development, but the most we can say with certainty is that holding a medieval court office with tenure for a term of years or 'for life' was preferable to holding it 'during good behaviour'.

Royal court officers in fourteenth-century England had a keen awareness that a heirarchy of tenures existed. A royal court official would typically begin his court service with tenure 'during pleasure' or occasionally 'during good behaviour'. Then, through faithful service and/or the influence of powerful connections, the crown might offer him a promotion: enlarging his tenure in the same office to 'during good behaviour', a term of years, or 'for life'.[109] John of Balscote, for example, was appointed to the office of chief engrosser of the Dublin Exchequer 'during pleasure' in the early 1330s, but over the course of the next decade his tenure in same office was enlarged, first to 'during good behaviour' and later to a term of ten years.[110] Similarly, Geoffrey de Say, a draper of London, was granted the office of crier of King's Bench 'during good behaviour' on 28 January 1327; shortly thereafter his grant in the same office was enlarged to tenure 'for life'.[111] Additional examples of enlargements of tenure for ministerial royal court officials abound for the reigns of Edward II and Edward III.[112] But *every* grant of tenure to royal office in medieval England – including those granted 'during good behaviour', for a term of years, or 'for life' – was tempered by the fact that an office holder's tenure automatically terminated at the death of the granting monarch.[113] The new monarch could replace the office holder, or confirm him to the same or different level of tenure.[114]

Original sources confirm that ministerial court officials holding their offices 'during good behaviour' in the reign of Edward III enjoyed more security in office than those that held 'during pleasure'. Court officials with tenure 'during pleasure' could be (and often were) removed regularly,[115] whereas those with tenure 'during good behaviour', like John de Etton (chamberlain of the Exchequer in 1340), could not be removed from office 'without just and reasonable cause whereof the king shall be certified before his removal'.[116] The exact process for providing 'just and reasonable cause' against a ministerial court officer is largely opaque, but records suggest that inquiries were held into the alleged bad conduct that resulted in a certification to the king of the accused's guilt or innocence.[117] Most of the time, however, it appears that tenure 'during good behaviour' primarily protected a ministerial court official by shielding him from the crown absent-mindedly or deliberately granting his office to someone else while he was still in it. For example, Peter de Wakefeld was appointed to be the second ingrosser of the Dublin Exchequer 'during good behaviour' on 15 March 1341.[118] A little over three years later, on 26 March 1344, the king granted the same office to John de Maydenford 'during pleasure' and Peter was removed.[119] Peter, however, petitioned the crown for redress claiming that he was removed without reasonable cause, and he was restored to his post on 6 June 1346.[120] Several other ministerial court officers in England and Ireland during the reign of Edward III thwarted similar attempts on their offices by a forgetful monarch or by powerful patrons pressuring the king to place their man in a royal court position,[121] revealing some of the challenges in staffing medieval Europe's most highly centralised, bureaucratic kingdom.[122]

Removals of ministerial court officials for 'just and reasonable causes' did happen, of course, but we rarely know much about the details. Geoffrey de Say, for example, held the office of crier in the King's Bench first 'during good behaviour' and then 'for life', but was removed on 25 June 1330 after he was found 'guilty of divers extortions in his office contrary to his oath'.[123] In another instance, John de Shordich, who held the post of chirographer of the Common Bench 'during good behaviour' and later 'for life' was removed on 1 October 1341 because he had 'borne himself ill by adhering to some rebels against the king'.[124] Shordich was pardoned a few years later and resumed his office as chirographer of the Common Bench 'for life' on 23 April 1345.[125] Ministerial court officials in the king's courts in Ireland were also removed. The appointment of Robert de Pyncebek, who held the chancellorship of the Exchequer in Dublin 'during good behaviour', was revoked on 7 June 1340 because 'he has not stayed at all in the said Exchequer or Chancery or any other of the king's courts whereby he could know how to rule the office or the condition thereof'.[126] Records reveal other removals of ministerial court officials holding office 'during good behaviour' or 'for life' when Edward III reached his majority, but the reasons for their dismissal are unclear.[127] Perhaps they joined all of the sheriffs, coroners, constables and 'other such officials' in 1330 that were removed and interrogated as to what 'oppressions' or 'grievances' they may have caused during the de facto rule of Mortimer and Isabella.[128] Although we may not know exactly what constituted *bene gesserit*, the record evidence suggests that extortion, treason and failing to report for duty constituted at least three viable causes for removing ministerial court officials with tenure 'during good behaviour' or 'for life' from office.

Original records thus suggest several conclusions about the origins and development of tenure 'during good behaviour' for non-judicial royal officials in the thirteenth and fourteenth centuries. First, drawing on language that was widely used to secure the future faithfulness of one-time rebels at the close of the Second Barons' War, the phrase 'during good behaviour' became a condition associated with holding royal offices in the late 1260s. Second, medieval contemporaries recognised tenure 'during good behaviour' to be a distinct, individual form of tenure as early as 1274. Third, from at least 1280 some ministerial offices in the king's courts in Ireland were being granted 'during good behaviour', and from the 1310s some counterparts in the central royal courts of England held their offices by the same tenure. Fourth, early in the reign of Edward III some ministerial offices in the royal courts of England and Ireland were held 'during good behaviour', while others began to be held 'for life'. Fifth, like landholding, tenure for ministerial offices in the medieval royal courts in the fourteenth century could be enlarged to a more desirable form of tenure as a reward for loyal service.[129] Sixth, royal court officials with tenure 'during good behaviour' in the early fourteenth century (if not before) experienced increased security in office over those with tenure 'during pleasure' because they could only be removed for just and reasonable causes. Seventh, extortion, treason or simply not assuming the office constituted just and reasonable causes for removing fourteenth-century ministerial court officials with tenure 'during good behaviour' or 'for life' from their positions.

Judicial tenure during good behaviour

Compared to the non-judicial officials of the king's courts, medieval judges from the Common Bench, King's Bench and Exchequer (called barons), possessed a more elevated, solemn office, as they sat in binding judgement on particular cases in particular courts.[130] The authors of *Bracton*, who were likely judges themselves, remind us of the weight and solemnity of delegated judicial office when they state that judges are to

> sit in the royal chamber, on the very seat of the king, on the throne of God, so to speak, judging tribes and nations, plaintiffs and defendants, in lordly order, in the place of the king, as though in the place of Jesus Christ, as the king is God's vicar.[131]

We have already seen that ministerial officials in the royal courts were being granted tenure 'during good behaviour' from the reigns of Edward I and his son, Edward II. But it is not until early in the reign of Edward III that we find direct evidence of judges being granted their offices under the same tenure, and only then in the distant (and often scandal-laden) courts of Ireland.[132] To my knowledge the earliest extant grant of tenure 'during good behaviour' for a royal judge was given to Master Thomas Crosse, whose original tenure as Chief Baron of the Exchequer in Ireland was enlarged from 'during pleasure',[133] to tenure 'during good behaviour' on 20 October 1335.[134] Shortly thereafter Hubert de Burgh's tenure of office as Third Baron of the Exchequer in Ireland was enlarged from 'during pleasure' to a term of four years on 13 June 1337.[135] Later that year de Burgh was transferred to the office of Chief Baron of the Irish Exchequer first 'during pleasure' and one month later with tenure 'during good behaviour'.[136] Similar grants of tenure 'during good behaviour' were given in 1340 to Robert Power (Chief Baron of the Exchequer), William Epworth (Second Baron of the Exchequer), Nicholas de Snitterby (Second Baron of the Exchequer) and in 1342 to William of Bromlegh (Second Baron of the Exchequer).[137]

In the latter half of the fourteenth century, tenure 'during good behaviour' was extended to English judges in the King's Bench and Common Bench of Ireland. In 1364, as part of the third massive reorganisation of the king's royal courts in Ireland to take place during the fourteenth century,[138] John Keppok, John de Uppyngham and Thomas Quixhull were granted tenure 'during good behaviour' on 13 February 1364 to their offices of Chief Baron of the Exchequer, Second Baron of the Exchequer and Third Baron of the Exchequer, respectively.[139] On the same day Edward III granted tenure 'during good behaviour' to Richard Whyte as Chief Justice of the King's Bench in Ireland and to Nicholas Lumbard as Second Justice of the King's Bench in Ireland.[140] Common Bench judges in Ireland had to wait until the reign of Richard II (1377–99) to enjoy this same form of tenure, when John Sotheroun was appointed Chief Justice of the Common Bench in Ireland 'during good behaviour' on 1 October 1384.[141] Precisely why tenure 'during good behaviour' was granted to English judges in Ireland starting in the fourteenth century is unclear, but it likely has to do with thinking that a more secure form of judicial office holding might assuage some the difficulties of attracting and retaining capable English men to judicial posts in a distant, unstable, hardscrabble colony.[142]

Grants of judicial offices in Ireland with tenure 'during good behaviour' continued during the reign of Henry IV (1399–1413). And during his reign we find the first judicial office in England granted with tenure 'during good behaviour'. In 1399, Henry IV again reorganised the judiciary in Ireland, appointing Richard Rede as Chief Baron of the Exchequer in Ireland, Robert Burnell as Second Baron and Hugh de Faryngton as Third Baron, all with tenure 'during good behaviour'.[143] Henry IV also appointed Stephen Bray to be Chief Justice of the King's Bench in Ireland 'during pleasure' in 1399, later enlarging his grant of that office to tenure 'during good behaviour' on 11 January 1406.[144] Roger Westwode becomes the first English judge at the courts in Westminster to be granted office with tenure 'during good behaviour' when Henry IV appointed him to be Second Baron of the English Exchequer 'during good behaviour' on 1 March 1403.[145]

The short reign of Henry V (1413–22) left little trace on forms of judicial appointment, but we do have some evidence of judicial offices in Ireland being granted with tenure 'during good behaviour'.[146] In contrast, during the turbulent reigns of Henry VI (1422–61; 1470–71) and Edward IV (1461–70), records reveal that many judicial offices in Ireland were granted with tenure 'during good behaviour',[147] and some of them, from the 1440s onward, begin to be granted 'for life'.[148]

In the mid-to-late fifteenth century, similar grants of tenure 'during good behaviour' and 'for life' were also given to judges in the English Exchequer,[149] and, for the first time, to judges in the Common Bench at Westminster.[150] On 8 July 1449 Thomas Fulthorp, who had served as a judge in the Common Bench for over a decade 'during pleasure', became the first judge in the English Common Bench to receive a grant of office 'for life'.[151] And Thomas Bryan's tenure as Chief Justice of the Common Bench was enlarged from 'during pleasure' to 'during good behaviour' on 16 February 1472.[152] Later, on 20 September 1485 the newly-crowned Henry VII (1485–1509) downgraded Bryan's appointment as Chief Justice of the Common Bench to 'during pleasure', reminding us that future monarchs were not yet bound by the terms of the grants of earlier kings.[153] But Henry VII later followed his predecessors in granting judges of the Common Bench at Westminster tenure 'during good behaviour'.[154]

Like ministerial officers in the king's courts, judges in the king's courts enjoyed greater security in office with tenure 'during good behaviour' than they did with tenure 'during pleasure'. Evidence shows that judges appointed with 'tenure during good behaviour' in some instances were able to retain their posts despite the monarch appointing a new servant to the same judicial position. For instance, John Karlell was appointed Second Baron of the Exchequer in Ireland 'during good behaviour' on 8 July 1389.[155] Perhaps due to local Irish politics, clandestine patronage pressures, or mere forgetfulness, Richard II appointed Robert Burnell to the same office also with 'tenure during good behaviour' on 24 October 1390.[156] Karlell disputed Burnell's claim to the office, and on 16 March 1391, the king revoked 'the letters patent granting by inadvertence to Robert Burnell, citizen of Dublin, the office of second baron of the exchequer in Ireland, granted previously . . . to John de Karlell . . . on trustworthy testimony of the good behaviour of the said John, who is to hold the office as granted'.[157] Judges with tenure 'for life' also enjoyed similar security in office against mistaken or deliberate royal replacements. John Cornewalshe had been appointed as Chief Baron of the Exchequer 'for life' in early October 1441. Less than a month later, Michael Gryffyn was granted the same position 'for life'. A lively tussle for the office ensued that lasted for over four years, with Cornewalshe finally being restored to office on 20 July 1446 following an English Chancery court decision.[158]

Judges with tenure 'during good behaviour' could also be removed from office for misbehaviour. But what constituted judicial misbehaviour, and therefore grounds for removal? Precise enumeration of all actions that constituted misbehaviour is not possible, but Paul Brand's work on ethical standards for medieval English judges has shown that at least since the reign of Henry III (and probably sooner) judges in the Exchequer, Common Bench and King's Bench at Westminster swore some sort of general oath that enunciated a judge's ethical obligations. By 1275, this oath was bolstered by statutory prohibitions on maintaining (i.e., supporting) pleas, cases or business in the king's courts.[159] And as a result of widespread private complaints involving judicial maintenance, abuse of power and discretion, and falsification of judicial records in which practically the entire senior judiciary of the English Exchequer, Common Bench and King's Bench was convicted, removed and punished from 1289–93,[160] Brand notes that a new form of oath was administered to judges in which the judges promised: (1) 'not to receive anything from anyone without the king's permission', excepting food and drink for the day; and (2) 'not to assent to any wrongdoing (malice) on the part of their colleagues and to attempt to prevent it as far as possible', reporting the misconduct to the king's council and then to the king himself if necessary.[161] Thus, by the late thirteenth century judicial misbehaviour could be found for one or more of the following reasons: maintenance, bribery, an abuse of power and discretion during judicial proceedings, tampering with judicial records, acting as an accomplice in a judicial colleague's wrongdoing, and failing to prevent or report a judicial colleague's wrongdoing, if known.

Extensive research into fourteenth century medieval chancery records reveals only one case that offers insight into why a judge with 'tenure during good behaviour' might be removed from office for misbehaviour.[162] Before examining this case, however, it is significant to note that Paul Brand has shown that by the reign of Edward III, royal judges in England with tenure 'during pleasure' could typically expect to remain in office barring some form showing of misconduct, while judges holding their offices 'during pleasure' in Ireland were frequently replaced at the will of the king.[163] On 16 May 1342 Edward III revoked the appointment of William de Epworth as Second Baron of the Exchequer in Ireland 'during good behaviour' because he was suspected of fraudulent dealings involving lands and donations granted by the king in Ireland.[164] Epworth was committed to the prison in Dublin castle, and the Justiciar of Ireland was ordered to send him to England to 'answer there all who wish to complain upon him'.[165] After what must have been a lengthy examination of the allegations and evidence against Epworth, 'all sinister suspicions of him' were disproved and he was restored to his office on 2 September 1348 with tenure 'during good behaviour'.[166] This case highlights the facts that allegations of misbehaviour against royal judges, such as fraud, were taken seriously by the crown, and that fraud constituted one reason for removing judges with tenure 'during good behaviour'. Perhaps more importantly, it reveals the strength of holding judicial office 'during good behaviour': after the king determined through legal process that Epworth was innocent, he was restored to his office of Second Baron of the Exchequer in Ireland with tenure 'during good behaviour' even though someone else had already replaced Epworth and had held that post for several years.[167]

In sum, medieval Chancery records reveal several conclusions about the origins and development of judicial tenure 'during good behaviour'. First, judicial tenure 'during good behaviour' was initially extended to barons of the Exchequer in Ireland in 1335, decades after the same form of tenure was granted to non-judicial court officers. Judicial tenure 'during good behaviour', therefore, did not originate *ex nihilo*; rather, it is probably better viewed as an extension of a form of royal office holding that started a generation or two earlier with ministerial officials. Second, over the course of the fourteenth century, judicial tenure 'during good behaviour' was granted to many judges serving in royal courts of Ireland – Exchequer, Common Bench and King's Bench – suggesting that this more secure form of tenure may have acted as an incentive to induce and keep capable English judges in the distant, damp, tempestuous colony. Third, tenure 'during good behaviour' or 'for life' for judges sitting in the Exchequer and at the Common Bench in Westminster did not begin until the fifteenth century. Precisely why these tenures appeared later in England is unclear. But it may have something to do with English judges wanting more security in office like their Irish counterparts, particularly during the turbulent latter half of the century. Fourth, that grants of judicial tenure 'during good behaviour' in the fourteenth and fifteenth centuries were sporadic and not universal probably reflects contemporary thought that tenure 'during good behaviour' was not a property right that should (or could) be granted to the entire judiciary, but rather was a royal gift to an individual on account of faithful service and/or relationship with the crown. Fifth, judicial tenure 'during good behaviour' provided medieval Common law judges with added stability in office. Finally, the trials, convictions, and removal of numerous thirteenth and fourteenth century judges for various types of misconduct, a specialised judicial oath developed in 1290,[168] and statutory prohibitions on certain types of judicial action from early in the reign of Edward I reveal that contours of judicial misbehaviour were already well-developed by the mid-fourteenth century.

Conclusion

This article has tilled many furrows in virgin ground; it is time now to sift what has been uncovered. Far from originating in the seventeenth century, medieval records reveal that tenure 'during good behaviour' was sometimes granted to judges in medieval Ireland and England. Such grants were themselves the culmination of a centuries-old process that eventually tethered atavistic notions of communally-enforced appropriate behaviour to feudal property principles following the Second Barons' War in the 1260s. With respect to officials in the king's highest courts, tenure 'during good behaviour' was initially granted to some ministerial court officials in Ireland in the late thirteenth century, and was then extended to some of their English counterparts in the early fourteenth century. Similarly, judicial tenure 'during good behaviour' began in the king's courts in Ireland in the fourteenth cenutry and afterwards was extended to some Exchequer and Common Bench judges at Westminster in the fifteenth century. This movement of judicial tenure 'during good behaviour' from the lordship of Ireland to England provides yet another powerful piece of evidence emphasising the important role that the king's courts in the lordship of Ireland played in the early development of the Common Law.[169]

In addition, tenure 'during good behaviour' held real value and meaning to medieval court officials and judges. Medieval judges and court officials with tenure 'during good behaviour' enjoyed increased security in office over those with tenure 'during pleasure', particularly against arbitrary or deliberate royal replacement. And by the reign of Edward III, a highly developed sense of judicial ethics existed, complete with specialised judicial oaths, statutory prohibitions on particular activities, and the knowledge of past judicial convictions, all of which could guide contemporaries in identifying judicial misconduct.[170]

Rather than creating judicial tenure 'during good behaviour', therefore, seventeenth-century legal reformers resurrected, reinterpreted and recast well-worn medieval property-holding principles to legitimise their aims.

How much these reformers knew about the medieval origins and development of judicial tenure 'during good behaviour' will remain unclear until detailed studies of judicial tenure in Tudor and early Stuart England are conducted. But it is hard to suppose that the cadre of eminent seventeenth-century English jurists, antiquarians and legal reformers, like John Selden, knew nothing about the history of judicial tenure 'during good behaviour' before their own century. Instead, it would not be the least bit surprising to find that Stuart-era legal reformers, like many before them, gazed backward for guidance and inspiration to solve contemporary problems.[171] The true innovation of the seventeenth-century judicial reformers, it seems, lies not in creating judicial tenure 'during good behaviour' but rather in extending this form of tenure to *all* judges on appointment to office. Indeed, the judicial ideas and innovations of the seventeenth century, as well as those of today, are always erected upon the foundations of the past. It is we who forget, and it is a hallmark of our honourand's career that he has helped so many to remember.

Notes

1 I presented drafts of this paper at the 50th International Medieval Conference in Kalamazoo in May 2015 and at the 2016 American Society for Legal History Conference in Toronto. I am grateful for the excellent feedback of scholars in my sessions – their insightful comments and advice were invaluable in preparing this finalised version. I am particularly grateful for the assistance and guidance of Jonathan Rose, Wendy Turner, Sasha Volokh, David Seipp, Jim Whitman, Ian Williams and Paul Brand in preparing this article. Special thanks must be extended to my good friend, Tom McSweeney, for bringing sources to my attention that I had not considered, and for his penetrating, measured criticism of a complete earlier draft. Any infelicities are mine alone.

2 See, e.g., Scott Gerber, 'William Penn and the Origins of Judicial Tenure During Good Behavior', *The Pennsylvania Magazine of History and Biography* 136 (2012): 233; J.H. Baker, *An Introduction to English Legal History*, 4th ed. (London: Butterworths, 2002), 166–7; Daniel Klerman, 'Nonpromotion and Judicial Independence', *Southern California Law Review* 72 (1999): 455; Sir William Holdsworth, *A History of English Law* (London: Methuen, 1924), 6: 234.

3 See, e.g., Paul Taylor, 'Congress's Power to Regulate the Federal Judiciary: What the First Congress and the First Federal Courts Can Teach Today's Congress and Courts', *Pepperdine Law Review* 37 (2010): 896–7; Michael Mazza, 'A New Look at an Old Debate: Life Tenure and the Article III Judge', *Gonzaga Law Review* 39 (2004): 135; Sir William Holdsworth, *A History of English Law* (London: Methuen, 1966), 1: 195.

4 U.S. Constitution, Article III, Section 1: 'The judicial power of the United States, shall be vested in one Supreme Court, and in such inferior courts as the Congress may from time to time ordain and establish. The judges, both of the supreme and inferior courts, shall hold their offices during good behaviour, and shall, at stated times, receive for their services, a compensation, which shall not be diminished during their continuance in office'.

5 U.S. Constitution, Article II, Section 4: 'The President, Vice President and all civil officers of the United States, shall be removed from office on impeachment

for, and conviction of, treason, bribery, or other high crimes and misdemeanors'. To date, only fifteen U.S. federal judges have been removed from office, the most recent in 2010 on charges of bribery and perjury. All of these federal judges were impeached by the U.S. House of Representatives, and many of them were convicted and removed by the U.S. Senate. Some federal judges, however, resigned from office after being impeached but before being convicted. See 'Impeachments of Federal Judges' www.fjc.gov/history/home.nsf/page/judges_impeachments.html.

6 During 2010–11 I served as a United States Supreme Court Fellow at the Federal Judicial Center (FJC). One of my responsibilities at the FJC was to teach foreign justices about the United States legal system and its personnel. I had the immense privilege to work with justices from 93 different countries, all of whom were astounded that U.S. federal judges held their offices 'during good behaviour' rather than for a term of years. All judges in various state courts within the United States, aside from the Rhode Island Supreme Court, serve for a term of years. Rhode Island Supreme Court justices 'shall hold office during good behavior'. *Rhode Island Constitution*, article X, section 5.

7 See *Debates on the Federal Judiciary: A Documentary History* (1787–1875), Federal Judicial Center (2013), 1: 153–65; Steven Calabresi and James Lindgren, 'Term Limits for the Supreme Court: Life Tenure Reconsidered', *Harvard Journal of Law & Public Policy* 29 (2006): 770–877.

8 See, e.g., Gerber, 'William Penn', 233–51; Taylor, 'Congress's Power', 895–7; Saikrishna Prakash, 'How to Remove a Federal Judge', *Yale Law Journal* 116 (2006): 92–103; Saikrishna Prakash, 'Removal and Tenure in Office', *Virginia Law Review* 92 (2006): 1820–3; Calabresi and Lindgren, 'Term Limits', 777, n. 32; Mazza, 'A New Look at an Old Debate', 135; Klerman, 'Nonpromotion and Judicial Independence', 455–9; William Ross, 'The Hazards of Proposals to Limit the Tenure of Federal Judges and to Permit Judicial Removal Without Impeachment', *Vanderbilt Law Review* 35 (1990): 1067; Holdsworth, *A History of English Law*, 1: 195; Ibid., 6: 232–40.

9 'William III, 1700 & 1701: An Act for the further Limitation of the Crown and better securing the Rights and Liberties of the Subject [Chapter II. Rot. Parl. 12 & 13 Gul. III. p. 1. n. 2.]', in *SR*, 7: 636–8. *British History Online* www.british-history.ac.uk/statutes-realm/vol7/pp636–638. (Italics added).

10 George E. Aylmer, *The King's Servants: The Civil Service of Charles I, 1625–1642* (London: Routledge, 1961), 107; Maitland, too, was well aware that various forms of tenure were present in medieval England, but it appears he never investigated the specific subject of judicial tenure, as he casually asserts that until the reign of William and Mary judges 'held their office *durante bene placito*'. See *The Constitutional History of England: A Course of Lectures Delivered by F.W. Maitland* (Cambridge: Cambridge University Press, 1919), 312–13.

11 (1) In his *Introduction to English Legal History*, Professor Baker devoted only a single, cryptic sentence to the history of judicial tenure 'during good behaviour' before the seventeenth century. Perhaps simply wanting to indicate that other forms of judicial tenure aside from judicial tenure 'during pleasure' existed prior to the seventeenth century, he states: 'Bryan C[hief] J[ustice of the] C[ommon] P[leas] had (perhaps uniquely) received a judicial patent *quamdiu se bene gesserint* in 1472, and the majority of the barons of the Exchequer after 1450 were given tenure in like terms'. Baker, unfortunately, does not give citations for either of these claims. See Baker, *An Introduction to English Legal History*, 167; (2). In his examinations of the Irish judiciary from their beginnings through the reign of Edward III, Paul Brand states that there 'are no examples during this period of appointments made during good behaviour or for life'.

See Paul Brand, 'The Birth and Early Development of a Colonial Judiciary: The Judges of the Lordship of Ireland, 1210–1377', in *Explorations in Law and History: Irish Legal History Discourses, 1988–1994*, ed. W.N. Osborough (Dublin: Four Courts Press, 1995), 21 n. 86; (3). Just over a century ago Charles McIlwain published a twelve-page essay on the history of English judicial tenure before the 1701 Act of Settlement using unpublished Chancery patent rolls as evidence. While his essay demonstrates that Plantagenet and Tudor monarchs sporadically granted judicial tenure 'during good behaviour' to the barons of the Exchequer prior to the rule of the Stuart kings, the majority of the essay is dedicated to the development of judicial tenure 'during good behaviour' in the seventeenth century, and the entire essay is bereft of citations making it difficult to proof his assertions. See C.H. McIlwain, 'The Tenure of English Judges', *The American Political Science Review* 7 (1913): 217–29; (4). As an incidental byproduct of his pioneering research into the origins and functions of the medieval Exchequer, Thomas Madox, revealed that early fourteenth-century medieval barons of the Exchequer – royal officials appointed to adjudicate on financial matters affecting the crown – held their offices 'during pleasure'. See Thomas Madox, *History and Antiquities of the Exchequer of the Kings of England*, 2nd ed. (New York: Greenwood Press, 1969; reprint of the 1769 edition), 2: 56–62.

12 Sir John Sainty, *The Judges of England 1272–1990: A List of Judges of the Superior Courts*, Selden Society Supplementary Series, vol. 10 (London: Selden Society, 1993), ix.

13 Ibid., vii–viii, xvii–xix. It should also be noted that Sainty stated that he owed 'a special debt to Paul Brand who made most valuable comments on the lists for the period 1272–1327', a sentiment which, I surmise, can be echoed by virtually all scholars of the medieval English judiciary. See ibid., ix.

14 C.A.F. Meekings and David Crook, *King's Bench and Common Bench in the Reign of Henry III*, Selden Society Supplementary Series, 17 (London: Selden Society, 2010), 26–9.

15 Digital pictures of original manuscripts and legal records related to medieval and early modern England may be accessed freely at the AALT; British History Online also contains digitised, searchable databases to thousands of pages of printed primary records relevant to Anglo-American legal history. See www.british-history.ac.uk/. The Fine Rolls, copies of agreements to pay the king a sum of money for a specified concession, for the reign of Henry III (1216–72) have also been digitised and are freely searchable. See www.finerollshenry3.org.uk/home.html

16 Published Chancery record evidence for this paper comes from the following: *RCh*; *CChR*; *CFR* https://familysearch.org/search/catalog/show?availability=Family%20History%20Library; *RLP*; *CPR* (http://sdrc.lib.uiowa.edu/patentrolls/search.html); *CCR* (www.british-history.ac.uk/); *RLC*; *ROF*; the AALT; all unpublished documents cited are preserved in TNA unless otherwise stated.

17 The reason that judges of the forest are not included in the list of English judges to be examined is that, while I have discovered two instances of forest eyre judges being appointed 'for life' early during the reign of Edward II (1307–27), these men appear to have never acted in a judicial capacity in cases of vert and venison because only one forest eyre was called late in the reign of Edward II. See *CPR, 1307–1313*, 1: 73, 183; Jane Winters, 'The Forest Eyre, 1154–1368', PhD thesis, King's College London, 1999, 22–4.

18 Oxford English Dictionary Online: 'Tenure', www.oed.com/view/Entry/199286?rskey=fRztfC&result=1#eid

19 'Instead the most sensible conclusion about the development of Norman feudal tenure may be that by 1066 a set of developing but unsystematized feudal

practices existed in Normandy, which were introduced into England by its Norman conquerors'. See Emily Tabuteau, 'Definitions of Feudal Military Obligations in Eleventh-Century Normandy', in *On the Laws and Customs of England: Essays in Honor of Samuel E. Thorne*, eds. Morris S. Arnold et al. (Chapel Hill: University of North Carolina Press, 1981), 19.

20 Paul Hyams, 'Notes on the Transformation of the Fief Into the Common Law Tenure in Fee', in *Laws, Lawyers and Texts: Studies in Medieval Legal History in Honour of Paul Brand*, eds. Susanne Jenks, Jonathan Rose and Christopher Whittick (Leiden: Brill, 2012), 22.

21 Ibid. The symbolic and physical roles that 'hands' played in medieval land tenure can readily be seen in the ceremonies of homage and feoffment with livery of seisin. For a brief, excellent examination of the vocabulary of landholding in northern France at this time see, Thomas McSweeney, 'Property Before Property: Romanizing the English Law of Land', *Buffalo Law Review* 60 (2012): 1145.

22 P&M, 1:239.

23 Hyams, 'Notes on the Transformation', 22. In the memorable words of Maitland, 'tenure implies service'. See P&M, 1:243.

24 For an excellent overview of the various forms of service performed by tenants in exchange for land, see J.M. Kaye, *Medieval English Conveyances* (Cambridge: Cambridge University Press, 2009); see also P&M, 1:232–96.

25 Reynolds argues that the widespread institution of feudal relationships in England was largely a product of 'the increasingly bureaucratic government and expert law that began to develop from about the twelfth century'. See Susan Reynolds, *Fiefs and Vassals: The Medieval Evidence Reinterpreted* (Oxford: Oxford University Press, 1994), 479; See also Hyams, 'Notes on the Transformation', 41–8.

26 See Brand, *OELP*, 158–60.

27 See Hyams, 'Notes on the Transformation', 46, note 95; Professor Hyams also points out that for most of the thirteenth century contemporaries did not use the term 'tenure' but rather 'tenementum' when referring to the physical holdings themselves. See ibid., 46.

28 P&M, 1: 230. See also Aylmer, *The King's Servant*, 106.

29 McIlwain, 'The Tenure of English Judges', 218. The emoluments for a judge in the central royal courts – King's Bench, Common Bench, Exchequer – were many. They included, among other things, robes, royal salary, a share in fees levied by the courts for writs (typically 1 denarius per writ issued), wine, deer and a benefice from the royal gift if the judge was clerk, or for lay judges, wardships and escheats. See generally C.A.F. Meekings and David Crook, *King's Bench and Common Bench in the Reign of Henry III*, Selden Society Supplementary Series, vol. 17 (London: Selden Society, 2010), 67–8, 130, 145, 278; Ralph Turner, *The English Judiciary in the Age of Glanvill and Bracton c. 1176–1239* (Cambridge: Cambridge University Press, 1985), 51–64; For a general explication of the development of judicial robes see J.H. Baker, 'A History of English Judges' Robes', *Costume* 12 (1978): 27; For specific grants of robes see *CCR, 1272–9*, 1: 484; *CCR, 1346–1349*, 8: 20, 125, 194, 445; *CCR, 1349–1354*, 9: 562; For information about the standard medieval royal salary for King's Bench and Common Bench judges (which the crown often paid in a dilatory fashion) see *CCR, 1272–1279*, 1: 503–4; For the 1 denarius judges portion of judicial writs see *CFR, 1347–1356*, 6: 89; *CFR, 1356–1368*, 7: 26, 55; For wine see *CPR, 1354–1358*, 10: 513; For deer see *CCR, 1288–1296*, 3: 175, 238; For wardships see *CPR, 1338–1340*, 4: 106; *CFR, 1347–1356*, 6: 55; *CPR, 1354–1358*, 10: 513.

30 See McIlwain, 'The Tenure of English Judges', 218–19; for general information about grants of land in fee see Kaye, *Medieval English Conveyances*, 59–133.

31 The *Dialogue of the Exchequer* (*Dialogus de Scaccario*) was a medieval administrative treatise on the practice and procedures of the English Exchequer written by Richard Fitz-Nigel, Lord Treasurer to Henry II, sometime in the late 1170s or early 1180s. See Richard Fitz-Nigel, *Dialogus de Scaccario*, ed. and trans. Emilie Amt and S.D. Church (Oxford: Clarendon Press 2007), 1–194; Glanvill, or more appropriately, *The Treatise on the Laws and Customs of the Realm of England Commonly Called Glanvill* (*Tractatus De Legibus et Consuetudinibus Regni Anglie qui Glanvilla Vocatur*) is exactly what its name claims: it is a treatise on the laws and customs of the realm of England written sometime between 1187–89 by a man (or men) with vast legal expertise in the king's court of the Exchequer. The work is commonly called Glanvill after Ranulf de Glanvill, Justiciar to Henry II in the 1180s, but its author(s) is more than likely a royal clerk who attended court during the 1180s and 1190s. See *Glanvill*; John Hudson argues that one of *Glanvill*'s great achievements was the 'working out the interrelationship and consequences of legal norms' within a secular legal context in late twelfth-century England. See John Hudson, 'From the *Leges* to *Glanvill*: Legal Expertise and Legal Reasoning', in *English Law Before Magna Carta*, eds. Stefan Jurasinski, Lisi Oliver and Andrew Rabin (Leiden: Brill, 2010), 221–49.

32 Turner, *The English Judiciary*, 65–107; McIlwain, 'The Tenure of English Judges', 219; For general information about the decline of seigniorial justice in the face of expanding royal justice, see Baker, *An Introduction to English Legal History*, 12–34; Joseph Biancalana, 'For Want of Justice: Legal Reforms of Henry II', *Columbia Law Review* 88 (1988): 433–42, 534–6; S.F.C. Milsom, *Historical Foundations of the Common Law*, 2nd ed. (London: Butterworths, 1981), 11–36; J.E.A. Jolliffe, *The Constitutional History of Medieval England* (London: Adam and Charles Black, 1937), 204–17; P&M, 1: 136–73.

33 McIlwain, 'The Tenure of English Judges', 219.

34 *CPR, 1216–1225*, 1: 42 ('*Dominus rex concessit, quamdiu ei placuerit, Rogero de Clifford manerium de Axeford cum pertinenciis suis, quod fuit Radulfi de la Bruere, qui est cum inimicis suis, et mandatum est omnibus militibus, libere tenentibus et aliis de manerio illo, quod ei in omnibus sint intendentes et respondetes*').

35 *CPR, 1232–1247*, 3: 258.

36 *CPR, 1216–1225*, 1: 55 ('*Dominus rex commisit Ricardo de Samford forestam de Chipham et de Melkesham, custodiendam quamdiu ei placuerit. Et mandatum est Johanni Marescall quod custodiam illiam ei in pace tenere permittat*').

37 *CPR, 1232–1247*, 3: 8.

38 Ibid., 3: 145.

39 For various grants of land 'during pleasure' during the reign of Henry III see e.g., *CPR, 1216–1225*, 1: 39, 82, 59, 65, 128, 279, 327, 374, 493; *CPR, 1225–1232*, 2: 89, 121, 178, 313, 316; *CPR, 1232–1247*, 3: 195, 253, 366, 385, 422, 424, 425, 498, 499; *CPR, 1247–1258*, 4: 25, 43, 45, 86, 145, 184, 244; *CPR, 1258–1266*, 5: 451, 458, 469, 467; *CPR, 1266–1272*, 6: 173, 642; *RLC*, 2: 6, 88; For grants of various royal offices 'during pleasure' during the reign of Henry III see e.g., *CPR, 1216–1225*, 1: 82, 146, 327, 333, 378, 428, 466, 473; *CPR, 1225–1232*, 2: 66, 92, 178, 180, 226, 270, 313, 314, 316, 322, 431, 434, 486; *CPR, 1232–1247*, 3: 25, 47, 50, 58, 142, 173, 284, 476; *CPR, 1247–1258*, 4: 11, 42, 165, 223, 366, 499; *CPR, 1258–1266*, 5: 27, 65, 143, 163, 195, 420, 501; *CPR, 1266–1272*, 6: 25, 30, 85, 297, 392, 652.

40 One interesting form of limited tenure that deserves further exploration concerns the Land of the Normans (*terra Normannorum*). These are lands in the Channel Islands or the Norman mainland that were confiscated by the English crown from Anglo-Normans who had entered the service of the king of France

following the loss of Normandy in 1204. Both John and his son, Henry III, were careful to grant out those lands again on an interim basis with phrases like 'to hold until the land of England and Normandy be one or the king restore the said land to the right heirs of his free will or by a peace'. *CChR, 1226–1257*, 1: 324; see also J.A. Everard and J.C. Holt, *Jersey 1204: The Forging of an Island Community* (London: Thames & Hudson, 2004), 127–31. I owe this idea and reference to Professor Tom McSweeney.

41 C 60/24 m. 9 (9 December 1225).

42 *CPR, 1232–1247*, 3: 445. For other grants of land from the king for a term of years see, e.g., C 60/25 m. 11 (10 January 1227); C 60/28 m. 12 (5 December 1228); C 60/28 m. 9 (23 March 1229); C 60/32 m. 8 (4 January 1233); C 60/35 m. 9 (18 May 1236); C 60/58 m. 17 (4 December 1260); *CPR, 1216–1225*, 1: 144, 195, 368, 508; *CPR, 1225–1232*, 2: 31, 51, 63, 107, 202 226, 236, 325; *CPR, 1232–1247*, 3: 47, 83, 149, 193, 334, 479; *CPR, 1247–1258*, 4: 73, 93, 268, 322, 454, 477, 504; *CPR, 1258–1266*, 5: 87, 576, 577, 653; *CPR, 1266–1272*, 6: 12, 179, 185, 401, 407.

43 *CPR, 1216–1225*, 1: 322; ('*Sciatis quod commisimus et concessimus Andree Bukerel cambium nostrum Anglie cum omnibus pertinenciis suis, habendum et tenendum a festo Sancti Hyllarii, anno regni nostril vi, in tres annos sequentes completes, pro iiii mille marcis*').

44 *CPR, 1232–1247*, 3: 51.

45 For other appointments to office for a term of years see, e.g., C 60/23 m. 1 (22 October 1225); C 60/35 m.9 (18 May 1236); C 60/54 m. 7 (April 20, 1257); *CPR, 1225–1232*, 2: 31, 51, 202; *CPR, 1232–1247*, 3: 146, 212; *CPR, 1247–1258*, 4: 64, 69, 133, 220, 457, 550; *CPR, 1258–1266*, 5: 5, 71, 87, 148, 208, 233; *CPR, 1266–1272*, 6: 6, 468.

46 *CPR, 1225–1232*, 2: 314. ('*Rex concessit Waltero de Kirkeham manerium suum de Neuport cum pertinenciis tenendum ad firmam tota vita sua, reddendo inde per annum ad Scaccarium regis xl libras blancas*').

47 *CPR, 1232–1247*, 3: 326; For other grants of land 'for life' in the reign of Henry III, see e.g., C 60/22 m. 5 (31 October 1224); C 60/29 m. 6 (22 April 1230); C 60/33 m. 8 (12 March 1234); *CChR, 1226–1257*, 1: 49, 54, 277, 280, 331; *CPR, 1216–1225*, 1: 280; *CPR, 1225–1232*, 2: 190, 323, 406, 407, 433; *CPR, 1232–1247*, 3: 46, 87, 144, 147, 474; *CPR, 1247–1258*, 4: 40, 47, 54, 83, 149, 316, 326, 387, 529, 618; *CPR, 1258–1266*, 5: 465, 523, 642; *CPR, 1266–1272*, 6: 15.

48 *CPR, 1232–1247*, 3: 15.

49 *CChR, 1226–1257*, 1: 225.

50 *CPR, 1258–1266*, 5: 525; For other appointments to royal office 'for life' in the reign of Henry III see, e.g., C 60/30 m. 5 (18 April 1231); C 60/31 mems. 3–4 (27–28 June 1232); C 60/32 m. 5 (27 April 1233); *CChR, 1226–1257*, 1: 163; *CPR, 1225–1232*, 2: 439, 455, 460, 486, 489, 490, 500; *CPR, 1232–1247*, 3: 41, 42, 88, 100, 139; *CPR, 1247–1258*, 4: 46, 178, 457; *CPR, 1258–1266*, 5: 140, 143, 217, 261, 556, 567, 639; *CPR, 1266–1272*, 6: 5, 18, 503, 676, 680; *RLC*, 2: 175.

51 For an excellent brief biography of Hubert's life see F.J. West, 'Burgh, Hubert de, Earl of Kent (*c*.1170–1243)', *ODNB*; online ed., Jan 2008 [www.oxforddnb.com/view/article/3991].

52 *CChR, 1226–1257*, 1: 74.

53 Ibid., 156.

54 Ibid., 164–5.

55 F.M. Powicke, 'The Oath of Bromholm', *EHR* 56 (1941): 535–8.

56 Ibid., 537–8.

57 *CCR, 1234–1237*, 3: 509; *CPR, 1232–1247*, 3: 48.

58 For the dramatic increase in volume of documents produced by the Chancery in the late twelfth and early thirteenth century see David Carpenter, *Magna Carta* (London: Penguin Books, 2015), 160; Michael Clanchy, *From Memory to Written Record: England 1066–1307*, 2nd ed. (Oxford: Basil Blackwell, 1993), 57–62.

59 Paul Brand noted that only twice during Henry III's reign did the English Chancery bother to record the appointments of justices to the English Bench; but appointments of justices in eyre were more frequently enrolled. See Brand, 'The Birth and Early Development of a Colonial Judiciary', 15 and note 55.

60 Poor clerical work could have very real consequences, a hard fact that an attorney, Thomas de Scotland, learned in 1335. Scotland's name was accidentally listed by the 'carelessness of a clerk in the [Common] Bench' as the attorney for William de Joueby in a case involving land in Yorkshire. When the Common Bench justices asked Scotland if he was de Joueby's attorney and he denied it, he was promptly imprisoned in the Fleet. The king eventually 'pardoned the said Thomas his imprisonment' and allowed him to continue practising as an attorney. *CPR, 1334–1338*, 3: 127.

61 For a brief, potted biography of Rivaux see Nicholas Vincent, 'Rivallis, Peter de (*d.* 1262)', *ODNB*; online ed. [www.oxforddnb.com/view/article/23688].

62 *CPR, 1225–1232*, 2: 486.

63 Ibid.

64 See e.g., C 60/31 m. 1 (21 October 1232); this is a memorandum stating that John of Hulcote is appointed sheriff of Oxfordshire *quamdiu regi placuerit* but exempting from his purview the custody of the manor, houses and appurtenances at Woodstock along with the castle of Oxford and its mill and meadow, all of which were previously granted to Geoffrey de Crowcombe *tota vita sua*.

65 Occasional references to landholding *quamdiu domino regi placuerit*, for a term of years, or *tota vita sua* in the reign of King John support the likelihood that these same landholding forms of tenure were extended to royal officials before the thirteenth century. For tenure *quamdiu domino regi placuerit* see, e.g., *ROF*, 119; For landholding for a term of years see, e.g., ibid., 206; For landholding *tota vita sua* see, e.g., ibid., 435.

66 *RCh*; *CChR*, Henry III: vol. 1 1226–1257; Henry III: vol. 2 1257–1300.

67 There is one case of the phrase 'during good behaviour' potentially being linked to a grant of office, but it is probably a scribal mistake. The patent rolls record that in April 1231 Henry III granted Ela, countess of Salisbury, the county of Wiltshire to hold *quamdiu bene se gesserit*. However, an additional grant a few paragraphs later in the patent rolls states that Ela made a fine with the king for 200 marks to hold the county of Wiltshire and the castle of Salisbury *tota vita sua*. The corresponding entry for this grant also appears on the fine rolls, and there it is also written that Ela would hold the castle of Salisbury and the county of Wiltshire *tota vita sua*. While grants of land and office at this time were often held 'for life', I have not found any other grants of land or office held 'during good behaviour' until the 1270s. Thus, I assume that the initial description of Ela's tenure in the patent rolls is a clerical error. See *CPR, 1225–1232*, 2: 431; C 60/30 m. 5 (18 April 1231).

68 See e.g., *RLP*, 54; *CPR, 1216–1225*, 1: 288–289; *CPR, 1225–1232*, 2: 106, 247; *CPR, 1232–1247*, 3: 59; *CPR, 1247–1258*, 4: 12, 532, 553; *CPR, 1258–1266*, 5: 309; For an excellent history of the surety of the peace and how they relate to the writs *De Minis* and *Supplicavit*, see Susanne Jenks, 'Writs *De Minis* and *Supplicavit*: The History of the Surety of the Peace', in *Laws, Lawyers, and Texts: Studies in Medieval Legal History in Honour of Paul Brand* (Leiden: Brill, 2012), 253–77; for the interplay between custom and law in thirteenth-century England see Paul Brand, 'Law and Custom in the English Thirteenth Century

Common Law', in *Custom: The Development and Use of a Legal Concept in the Middle Ages*, eds. Per Andersen and Mia Munster-Swendsen (Copenhagen: DJØF, 2009).

69 To place the rise and fall of the Provisions at Oxford within their proper historical context see, J.R. Maddicott, 'Magna Carta and the Local Community 1215–1259', *Past & Present* 102 (1984): 25–65; F.M. Powicke, *King Henry III and the Lord Edward: The Community of the Realm in the Thirteenth Century*, 2 vols. (Oxford: Clarendon Press, 1947), 343–56; for text of the Provisions of Oxford see Stubbs, *Charters*, 378–406; the striking parallels of Henry III's papal pardon releasing him from the Provisions of Oxford and King John's release from Magna Carta in 1215 through papal intervention are obvious.

70 The Dictum of Kenilworth was drafted by a royally-appointed committee of four prelates and eight laymen who were 'to suggest changes to the policy of total disinheritance of the Montfortians which would conciliate the revels and help re-establish domestic peace'. The text of the Dictum of Kenilworth is innovative: it reestablished monarchical supremacy and provided that the lands of the king and his loyal followers taken by the rebels were to be returned, and that rebels would not be banished, killed or disinherited, but could ransom their lands from the king for set amounts depending on the severity of their rebellion. Provisions of the Dictum of Kenilworth were later incorporated into the Statute of Marlborough on 19 November 1267. The Statute of Marlborough is considered by some to be the oldest piece of statute law that has not been fully repealed, as the version of the Magna Carta that remains in force dates from 1297. For the Dictum of Kenilworth see Paul Brand, *Kings, Barons and Justices: The Making and Enforcement of Legislation in Thirteenth-Century England* (Cambridge: Cambridge University Press, 2003), 185–6; *SR*, 1: 12–18; *Sources of English Constitutional History*, ed. and trans. Carl Stephenson and F.G. Marcham, rev. ed. (London: Harper & Row, 1972), 149–50; for the Statute of Marlborough (1267) see Brand, *Kings, Barons and Justices*, at 184–204, 453–83; *SR*, 1: 19–25.

71 *CPR, 1258–1266*, 5: 624.

72 *CPR, 1266–1272*, 6: 12; for examples of other pardons to rebels on condition of 'good behaviour' see e.g., *CPR, 1258–1266*, 5: 311, 515, 560, 572, 587, 592, 603, 604, 606, 613, 615, 621, 632, 638, 647, 666, 669, 670; *CPR, 1266–1272*, 6: 8, 10, 11, 12, 14, 16, 17,19, 20, 22, 26, 31, 34, 35, 36, 46, 62, 64, 73, 75, 80, 86, 95, 148, 157, 188, 199, 237, 238, 286, 298, 362, 375, 501, 543, 596.

73 Fealty is derived from the Latin *fidelitas*, meaning 'faith' or 'faithful'; for a general discussion of the relationship and differences between homage and fealty see P&M, 1: 296–307.

74 *Bracton*, 2: 232.

75 *CPR, 1258–1266*, 5: 647 ('Whereas Edward the king's son has admitted into the king's peace the men of the hundred of Kokesfeld as is contained in his letters patent; the king accepting this at the instance of his said son, has remitted to them his indignation and rancor of mind conceived towards them for any trespasses against him done by them in the time of the late disturbance and admitted them into his grace and peace, so that they be faithful to him and his heirs from henceforth'.) For a similar letter patent see ibid., 547.

76 See *CPR, 1266–1272*, 6: 16 ('Admission to the king's peace of Roger Godbert and William his brother; and pardon to them of all their trespasses and forfeitures in the time of the late disturbance on condition of their good behaviour; and grant to them that the lands which they hold now shall not incur loss thereby provided that they stand to the award of Kenilworth with regard to their lands which the king has given to others. And if they offend against their fealty again, their bodies shall be at the king's will, and their lands shall fall

(*incurrantur*) to the king and his heirs for ever'.) For similar letters patent linking a breach of fealty to bad behaviour see *CPR, 1258–1266*, 5: 445, 455, 588, 609, 615; *CPR, 1266–1272*, 6: 11.

77 I use the term 'expressly' here because to some extent it is implied in all previous tenures – in fee, during pleasure, for a term of years, for life – that the tenant would act faithfully to the lord or else forfeit his holding.

78 *CPR, 1266–1272*, 6: 261.

79 Ibid., 534; for grants of other royal offices under the same terms in the reign of Edward I see *CPR, 1272–1279*, 1: 417, 434; *CPR, 1281–1292*, 2: 381; *CPR, 1301–1307*, 4: 15; *CFR, 1272–1307*, 1: 120, 236, 325; *CCR, 1302–1307*, 5: 273.

80 *CCR, 1272–1279*, 1: 268; for grants of other royal offices under the same terms in the reign of Edward I see *CPR, 1272–1279*, 1: 223; *CCR, 1279–1288*, 2: 259; *CFR, 1272–1307*, 1: 271.

81 *CFR, 1272–1307*, 1: 169; for grants of other royal offices under the same terms in the reign of Edward I see *CFR, 1272–1307*, 1: 177; *CPR, 1292–1301*, 3: 492.

82 We know little about specific oaths of office sworn by non-judicial royal officers at this time. Contemporary evidence suggests that all royal officers had to take an oath that they would execute the office with faithfulness before starting their position. But the exact language of these oaths is elusive. See e.g., *CPR, 1247–1258*, 4: 637; *CPR, 1292–1301*, 3: 105; *CPR, 1301–1307*, 4: 471; *CCR, 1272–1279*, 1: 446; *CCR, 1279–1288*, 2: 121–2; *CFR, 1307–1319*, 2: 51; *CCR, 1339–1341*, 5: 8.

83 *CPR, 1272–1279*, 1: 58.

84 *CCR, 1272–1279*, 1: 172.

85 *CFR, 1272–1307*, 1: 88.

86 *CCR, 1272–1279*, 1: 155, 444; *CFR, 1272–1307*, 1: 41, 120; *CPR, 1281–1292*, 2: 31; *CPR, 1301–1307*, 4: 4, 5.

87 *CCR, 1272–1279*, 1: 404, 538.

88 *CFR, 1272–1307*, 1: 92.

89 *CPR, 1272–1279*, 1: 366; *CFR, 1272–1307*, 1: 124.

90 *CPR, 1281–1292*, 2: 236; *CFR, 1272–1307*, 1: 227.

91 *CPR, 1272–1279*, 1: 128.

92 *CPR, 1301–1307*, 4: 332.

93 *CFR, 1272–1307*, 1: 148; *CPR, 1281–1292*, 2: 470.

94 *CPR, 1272–1279*, 1: 369; *CPR, 1292–1301*, 3: 356.

95 *CFR, 1272–1307*, 1: 450; *CPR, 1301–1307*, 4: 330.

96 *CPR, 1281–1292*, 2: 386.

97 *CPR, 1292–1301*, 3: 408; *CPR, 1301–1307*, 4: 74.

98 *CPR, 1272–1279*, 1: 360.

99 *CPR, 1281–1292*, 2: 392.

100 *CPR, 1272–1279*, 1: 394.

101 *CCR, 1302–1307*, 5: 273.

102 For the development of the English judiciary in Ireland from their beginnings to the end of the reign of Edward III see Brand, 'The Birth and Early Development of a Colonial Judiciary', 1–48.

103 Ibid., 15–16.

104 Ibid., 24–5.

105 *CPR, 1307–1313*, 1: 448; *CPR, 1313–1317*, 2: 31.

106 *CPR, 1313–1317*, 2: 91; *CPR, 1317–1321*, 3: 500.

107 *CPR, 1317–1321*, 3: 63.

108 (1) For ministerial offices in the Common Bench granted with tenure 'during good behaviour' or 'for life' in the reign of Edward III see, e.g., *CPR, 1327–1330*, 1: 94; *CPR, 1330–1334*, 2: 36, 262, 308, 398; *CPR, 1340–1343*, 5:

292, 378, 535, 560; *CPR, 1343–1345*, 6: 458; *CPR, 1348–1350*, 8: 411, 467; *CPR, 1350–1354*, 9: 200, 409; *CPR, 1354–1358*, 10: 3; *CPR, 1361–1364*, 12: 99, 499; *CPR, 1370–1374*, 15: 199; *CPR, 1374–1377*, 16: 372.

(2) For ministerial offices in the King's Bench granted with tenure 'during good behavior' or 'for life' in the reign of Edward III, see, e.g., *CPR, 1327–1330*, 1: 1, 3, 166, 198, 542; *CPR, 1343–1345*, 6: 263; *CPR, 1354–1358*, 10: 147; *CPR, 1361–1364*, 12: 82, 499; *CPR, 1364–1367*, 13: 223.

(3) For ministerial offices in the English Exchequer granted with tenure 'during good behaviour' or 'for life' in the reign of Edward III see e.g., *CPR, 1327–1330*, 1: 8, 103, 365; *CPR, 1338–1340*, 4: 448.

(4) For ministerial offices in the Common Bench of Ireland granted with tenure 'during good behaviour' or 'for life' in the reign of Edward III see e.g., *CPR, 1327–1330*, 1: 188, 550; *CPR, 1330–1334*, 2: 44, 192; *CPR, 1338–1340*, 4: 478; *CPR, 1340–1343*, 5: 429, 460; *CPR, 1343–1345*, 6: 482; *CPR, 1348–1350*, 8: 229.

(5) For ministerial offices in the King's Bench of Ireland granted with tenure 'during good behaviour' or 'for life' in the reign of Edward III see e.g., *CPR, 1327–1330*, 1: 419, 546, 550; *CPR, 1330–1334*, 2: 564; *CPR, 1334–1338*, 3: 28; *CPR, 1361–1364*, 12: 468.

(6) For ministerial offices in the Exchequer of Ireland granted with tenure 'during good behavior' or 'for life' in the reign of Edward III see e.g., *CPR, 1327–1330*, 1: 8, 143, 332, 451, 546; *CPR, 1330–1334*, 2: 44, 123, 423; *CPR, 1334–1338*, 3: 57, 175, 309; *CPR, 1338–1340*, 4: 314, 317, 441, 532; *CPR, 1340–1343*, 5: 31, 158, 501; *CPR, 1345–1348*, 7: 467; *CPR, 1348–1350*, 8: 433; *CPR, 1350–1354*, 9: 234; *CPR, 1354–1358*, 10: 467; *CPR, 1361–1364*, 12: 468; *CPR, 1364–1367*, 13: 376, 399; *CPR, 1367–1370*, 14: 119.

109 I have found no instances where ministerial royal court officials obtained a grant of office 'for life' that was later extended to tenure 'in fee'.

110 *CPR, 1330–1334*, 2: 423; *CPR, 1334–1338*, 3: 412; *CPR, 1338–1340*, 4: 334.

111 *CPR, 1327–1330*, 1: 1, 3.

112 For enlargements of tenure for ministerial court offices in the royal courts during the reigns of Edward II and Edward III see, e.g.,: (1) Robert de Foxton, chirographer of the Common Bench, see *CPR, 1307–1313*, 1: 448; *CPR, 1313–1317*, 2: 31; *CPR, 1327–1330*, 1: 94; 500; (2) Luke de Burgh, attorney for the king in Common Bench – *CPR, 1330–1334*, 2: 27, 262; (3) Thomas de Brembre, chirographer of the Common Bench – *CPR, 1343–1345*, 6: 534; *CPR, 1348–1350*, 8: 467; (4) Hugh de Segrave, crier in Common Bench – *CPR, 1350–1354*, 9: 409; *CPR, 1354–1358*, 10: 3; (5) Thomas Botle, chief crier in the King's Bench – *CPR, 1313–1317*, 2: 91; *CPR, 1317–1321*, 3: 500; (6) William la Marche, crier of the King's Bench – *CPR, 1327–1330*, 1: 538, 542; (7) Nicholas de Tewkesbury, office in Exchequer formerly held by Nicholas de Acton – *CPR, 1327–1330*, 1: 103; (8) John de Leicester, chamberlain of the Exchequer – *CPR, 1327–1330*, 1: 181, 365; (9) William de Gloucester, chirographer and keeper of the writs and rolls Common Bench, Ireland – *CPR, 1334–1338*, 3: 462; *CPR, 1338–1340*, 4: 58; (10) Nicholas de Balygavern, chirographer and keeper of the writs and rolls Common Bench, Ireland – *CPR, 1340–1343*, 5: 7, 34, 478; (11) William de Boseworth, keeper of writs and rolls Kings Bench, Ireland – *CPR, 1327–1330*, 1: 316, 419, 546; (12) Robert Power, chancellor of the Exchequer, Ireland – *CPR, 1334–1338*, 3: 122, 309, 405; (13) Robert de Salkeld, second chamberlain of the Exchequer, Ireland – *CPR, 1334–1338*, 3: 57, 170; *CPR, 1343–1345*, 6: 55; (14) Hugh de Burgh, treasurer of the Exchequer, Ireland – *CFR, 1337–1347*, 2: 137, 164; (15) William de Brawode, chancellor of the Exchequer, Ireland – *CPR, 1327–1330*, 1: 39, 332, 451.

113 Grants of tenure to royal office, including ministerial offices in the king's courts, expired on the demise of the crown until Parliament passed the Commissions and Salaries of Judges Act in 1760. See Commissions and Salaries of Judges Act, 1 George III c. 23 (1760).

114 For example, see the confirmation of Robert de Foxton, chirographer to the Common Bench in 1327, see *CPR, 1327–1330*, 1: 94.

115 For instance on 28 October 1331 Peter de Wetewang, who held the office of chirographer and keeper of the writs and rolls for the Common Bench in Ireland 'during pleasure', was removed in favour of Nicholas Balygavernan, who was granted the same office 'during good behaviour' at the request of the Bardi. See *CPR, 1330–1334*, 2: 76, 77, 192.

116 *CPR, 1338–1340*, 4: 314, 317, 448; See also *CPR, 1338–1340*, 4: 314, 317.

117 See, e.g., *CPR, 1327–1330*, 1: 538; *CPR, 1338–1340*, 4: 532.

118 *CPR, 1340–1343*, 5: 441.

119 *CPR, 1343–1345*, 6: 220.

120 *CPR, 1345–1348*, 7: 120.

121 Brand has shown that the initiative behind the appointment of William le Deveneys as a justice of the Dublin Bench in October 1312 lay with le Deveneys himself or with his 'friends in England' rather than with the crown. See Brand, 'The Birth and Early Development of a Colonial Judiciary', 18–19.

122 See e.g., (1) Peter de Wakefeld protecting his office of second ingrosser of the Exchequer, Ireland for a second time: *CPR, 1354–1358*, 10: 467; (2) Geoffrey de Say protecting his office of crier in the King's Bench: *CPR, 1327–1330*, 1: 1, 3, 198, 241; (3) Walter de Mauny protecting his office of marshal of the King's Bench: *CPR, 1343–1345*, 6: 263, 264; *CCR, 1349–1354*, 9: 430; (4) William Bette protecting his office of usher of the Exchequer, Ireland: *CPR, 1340–1343*, 5: 501; (5) Nicholas Balygavern protecting his office of chirographer and keeper of the writs and rolls for the Common Bench, Ireland: *CPR, 1334–1338*, 3: 462; *CPR, 1338–1340*, 4: 22, 197, 313, 315, 478; (6) John de Evesham protecting his office of second chamberlain of the Exchequer, Ireland: *CPR, 1348–1350*, 8: 433; *CPR, 1350–1354*, 9: 234; *CPR, 1354–1358*, 10: 261; (7) Robert de Salkeld protecting his office of second chamberlain of the Exchequer, Ireland: *CPR, 1334–1338*, 3: 57, 170.

123 *CPR, 1327–1330*, 1: 1, 3, 538.

124 *CPR, 1330–1334*, 2: 36, 308, 398; *CPR, 1340–1343*, 5: 292.

125 *CPR, 1343–1345*, 6: 458.

126 *CPR, 1338–1340*, 4: 317, 532.

127 See, e.g., (1) Richard de Foxton, chirographer of the Common Bench during the reign of Edward II held his office first 'during pleasure' and then for life 'during good behaviour'. It appears, however, that de Foxton was removed from his position by skullduggery (or confusion) during the transition from Edward II's reign to that of Edward III, with Roger Mortimer and his steward, Richard de Haukeslowe, playing a role. Foxton continued to fight for his office, but eventually surrendered his patent on 11 June 1332. See *CPR, 1307–1313*, 1: 448; *CPR, 1313–1317*, 2: 31; *CPR, 1327–1330*, 1: 2, 94; *CPR, 1330–1334*, 2: 36, 281, 308; E 175/2/216 mem. 3d. (November 1330); (2) John de la Bataille held the office of chirographer and keeper of the writs and rolls in the Common Bench, Ireland 'during good behaviour', but was removed for some unknown reason 24 August 1330. De la Bataille was later reinstated to his post with the same tenure. See *CPR, 1327–1330*, 1: 188, 550; *CPR, 1330–1334*, 2: 44.

128 See 'Edward III: November 1330, C 65/2, mm.7–5', no. 21 in *PROME, British History Online* www.british-history.ac.uk/no-series/parliament-rolls-medieval/november-1330-c-65.

129 On 1 May 1257 Henry III enlarged his mother's tenure to the manor of Fakenham from a grant 'for life' to a grant giving her power to 'bind, pledge, lease,

or assign the manor to whom she will, for fifteen years after her death'. *CPR, 1247–1258*, 4: 552; On 25 July 1282 Edward I extended a 'grant of life into a grant of fee simple' of some land to his servant, Thomas le Trevr'. See *CPR, 1281–1292*, 2: 31. These are but a few of the numerous examples of land tenure extensions that abound in the medieval Chancery records.

130 It is well to remember here that the Exchequer 'had a dual function: to audit the accounts of Crown debtors and to adjudicate upon actions between subjects'. H.G. Richardson and G.O. Sayles, *The Administration of Ireland 1172–1377* (Dublin: I.M.C., 1963), 42.

131 *Bracton*, 2: 20.

132 For scandals in the Irish Exchequer in the reigns of Edward I, Edward II and Edward III, see Richardson and Sayles, *The Administration of Ireland*, 47–8.

133 *CPR, 1334–1338*, 3: 122.

134 Ibid., 175.

135 Ibid., 462.

136 Ibid., 520, 539.

137 *CPR, 1338–1340*, 4: 542; *CPR, 1340–1343*, 5: 20, 28, 127, 158, 488, 511.

138 Paul Brand has noted the restructuring of the king's Irish courts in 1311 and in 1351. See Brand, 'The Birth and Early Development of a Colonial Judiciary', 39; Likewise, Richardson and Sayles note a reorganisation of the Irish judiciary in 1232 which they claim 'reflects the processes by which the position of the justiciar in England was undermined'. See Richardson and Sayles, *The Administration of Ireland*, 21–4.

139 *CPR, 1361–1364*, 12: 468.

140 Ibid.

141 *CPR, 1381–1385*, 2: 463; Richard II also continued to appoint some judges from the Exchequer in Ireland with tenure 'during good behaviour'. See (1) Thomas Bache, Chief Baron of the Exchequer in Ireland: *CPR, 1381–1385*, 2: 168; *CPR, 1389–1392*, 4: 72; (2) John de Karlell, Second Baron of the Exchequer in Ireland: *CPR, 1389–1392*, 4: 390; (3) Robert Burnell, Second Baron of the Exchequer in Ireland: *CPR, 1389–1392*, 4: 313; I have been unable to find any appointments to the King's Bench in Ireland with tenure 'during good behaviour'.

142 Brand's work on the judiciary in Ireland shows that numerous judicial appointments to positions in Ireland in the reigns of Edward II and Edward III were ineffective due to a general reluctance to serve in the English colony. See Brand, 'The Birth and Early Development of a Colonial Judiciary', 21–5; Richardson and Sayles also note the reluctance of king's servants to serve in posts in Ireland. See Richardson and Sayles, *The Administration of Ireland*, 17–21.

143 *CPR, 1399–1401*, 1: 113.

144 *CPR, 1399–1401*, 1: 120; *CPR, 1405–1408*, 3: 106.

145 *CPR, 1401–1405*, 2: 202.

146 On 26 January 1423 Henry VI confirmed the grant of James Cornewalshe as Chief Baron of the Exchequer in Ireland 'during good behaviour' made by his father, Henry V, on 24 April 1421. See *CPR, 1422–1429*, 1: 75; On 14 June 1423 Henry VI also confirmed the grant of Richard Bernyngham, Second Baron of the Exchequer in Ireland 'during good behaviour' made by Henry V on 26 April 1421. See *CPR, 1422–1429*, 1: 88.

147 (1) James Cornewalshe, Chief Baron of the Exchequer, Ireland: *CPR, 1422–1429*, 1: 75; (2) Richard Bernyngham, Second Baron of the Exchequer, Ireland: *CPR, 1422–1429*, 1: 88; (3) Thomas Darby, Second Baron of the Exchequer, Ireland: *CPR, 1436–1441*, 3: 179; (4) William de Tynbegh, Chief Justice of the Common Bench, Ireland: *CPR, 1422–1429*, 1: 99.

148 (1) Michael Gryffyn, Chief Baron of Exchequer, Ireland: *CPR, 1441–1446*, 4: 7; *CCR, 1441–1447*, 4: 104, 352–3; C 1/13/288 (1445–1446); (2) William

Sutton, Third Baron of the Exchequer, Ireland: *CPR, 1441–1446*, 4: 392; (3) John Cornewalshe, Chief Baron of the Exchequer, Ireland: *CPR, 1441–1446*, 4: 352–3, 410, 455; C 1/13/288 (1445–1446); (4) John Blakeney, Chief Justice of Common Bench, Ireland: *CPR, 1436–1441*, 3: 184; (5) Robert Dovedall, Chief Justice of Common Bench, Ireland: *CPR, 1446–1452*, 5: 23; *CPR, 1461–1467*, 1: 21; (6) James Alleyn, Chief Justice of King's Bench, Ireland: *CPR, 1446–1452*, 5: 72; (7) Nicholas Bernewell, Chief Justice of the King's Bench, Ireland: *CPR, 1453–14601*, 6: 350; (8) Barnabas Bernewell, Second Justice of the King's Bench, Ireland: *CPR, 1461–1467*, 1: 11.

149 See, e.g., (1) Peter Arden, Chief Baron of the Exchequer: *CPR, 1446–1452*, 5: 180; reconfirmed by Edward IV on 20 June 1461 *CPR, 1461–1467*, 1: 94; (2) John Durem (Holm), Baron of the Exchequer: *CPR, 1446–1452*, 5: 235; See also Sainty, *The Judges of England*, 90, 105.

150 I have not discovered any grants of tenure 'during good behaviour' or 'for life' for King's Bench judges in England during the thirteenth through fifteenth centuries. Sainty may well be correct in his estimation that all King's Bench judges until 1632 held their offices 'during pleasure'. Sainty, *The Judges of England*, 20.

151 *CPR, 1436–1441*, 3: 238; *CPR, 1446–1452*, 5: 267; Sainty's observations that 'until 1640 tenure [for judges on the Common Bench] was during pleasure' will need to be updated in light of this. See Sainty, *The Judges of England*, 57.

152 *CPR, 1467–1477*, 1: 258, 315; *CPR, 1477–1485*, 1: 9.

153 *CPR, 1485–1494*, 1: 7.

154 (1) John Fisher, Judge in Common Bench: *CPR, 1494–1509*, 2: 253; (2) Thomas Frowyk, Chief Justice of Common Bench: *CPR, 1494–1509*, 2: 299; (3) John Kyngesmyll, Judge in Common Bench: *CPR, 1494–1509*, 2: 354. Again, Sainty's observations on the tenure of Common Bench judges needs to be revised in light of this new information. See Sainty, *The Judges of England*, 43, 57.

155 *CPR, 1389–1392*, 4: 83.

156 Ibid., 313.

157 Ibid., 390; William de Epworth, Second Baron of the Exchequer in Ireland with tenure 'during good behaviour' in the 1340s was also protected in his office by this tenure from the appointment of Nicholas de Snitterby to the same office. See *CPR, 1340–1343*, 5: 20, 28, 127.

158 See *CPR, 1441–1446*, 4: 7, 352–3, 410, 455; *CCR, Henry VI, 1441–1447*, 4: 104; C 1/13/288 (1445–1446).

159 Paul Brand, 'Ethical Standards for Royal Justices in England, c. 1175–1307', *University of Chicago Law School Roundtable* 8 (2001): 240–6.

160 Ibid., 250–65.

161 Ibid., 274. Along with this new judicial oath, some new procedures were implemented to try and punish those who falsely accused royal judges of misbehaviour. See ibid., 274–8.

162 Stephen Bray's appointment as Chief Justice of the King's Bench 'during good behaviour' on 11 January 1406 was revoked by Henry IV on 28 January 1406, but not for misbehaviour. In this case Henry IV had tried to enlarge Bray's original appointment to that office 'during pleasure' to tenure 'during good behaviour', but the king had forgotten that he had given the power to 'appoint and remove all officers and ministers of the king [in Ireland] not having estate in fee or for life' to his son, Thomas Lancaster, the Justiciar) of Ireland. With Thomas' assent, Bray was later reappointed as Chief Justice of the King's Bench in Ireland 'during pleasure' on 6 February 1407. See *CPR, 1399–1401*, 1: 120; *CPR, 1401–1405*, 2: 456; *CPR, 1405–1408*, 3: 106, 145, 285.

163 See Brand, 'Ethical Standards for Royal Justices in England', 246–55; Brand, 'The Birth and Early Development of a Colonial Judiciary', 41–6; Of course, and handful of judges in Ireland with tenure 'during pleasure' did get removed

due to misconduct. See Brand, 'The Birth and Early Development of a Colonial Judiciary', 38–40.

164 *CPR, 1340–1343*, 5: 127, 432; *CCR, 1341–1343*, 6: 367.

165 *CCR, 1341–1343*, 6: 367.

166 *CPR, 1348–1350*, 8: 144.

167 Ibid.; Medieval English kings also occasionally rehabilitated royal judges and non-judicial court officers who had been convicted of misconduct, allowing them to serve again in judicial or other important positions, suggesting that monarchs were more concerned with efficient administration of the realm than small-scale corruption of capable court officers. See Brand, 'Ethical Standards for Royal Justices in England', 274, 278–9; Richardson and Sayles, *The Administration of Ireland*, 17–18.

168 Fortescue informs us that by the first quarter of the fifteenth century a judge's oath included 'among other things that he will do justice without favour, to all men pleading before him, friends and foes alike, that he will not delay to do so even though the king should command him by his letters or by word of mouth to the contrary. He shall swear also that he will not receive from anyone except the king any fee or other pension, or livery, nor take any gift from any pleaders before him, except food and drink of no great price'. Sir John Fortescue, *De Laudibus Legum Anglie*, ed. and trans. S.B. Chrimes (Cambridge: Cambridge University Press, 1942), 127.

169 Paul Brand's scholarship has done much to elucidate the important, but often unrecognised, role that Ireland played in the development of the early Common Law: 'The statements of English law sent to Ireland in the 1220s and 1230s may well have played a part in the development of the common law not only in Ireland but also in England. The need to state clearly what the English rule was may, paradoxically, have helped to create a single fixed rule in England: and, as has been seen, at least one of these statements – the 1236 mandate on parcenry – found its way into English collections of statutes as the *Statutum Hibernie de Coheredibus*. That the Irish connection continued to be of some importance for the literature of the early common law – and, therefore, for the Common Law as a whole – is shown by the main manuscript tradition of the early fourteenth century pleading manual, *Novae Narrationes*, which clearly descends from an archetype produced in the lordship of Ireland. Discussion of the literature of the early common law must, it seems, therefore, bear in mind that the Common Law was the legal system not just of England but also of the lordship of Ireland, since the process of transmission of English law to Ireland was a significant factor in the creation of literature of the early common law.' Paul Brand, 'Ireland and the Literature of the Early Common Law', *The Irish Jurist* n.s. 16 (1981): 113, reprinted in Brand, *MCL*, 445–64.

170 Enforcing stringent penalties against judicial misconduct, however, was not always to the crown's advantage. See Brand, 'Ethical Standards for Royal Justices in England', 278–9.

171 Charlemagne and Henry II looked to Roman law for principles of governance. See Charles J. Reid, Jr., 'A Brief Account of Western Constitutional History: Raoul Van Caenegem's An Historical Introduction to Western Constitutional Law', *Emory Law Journal* 46 (1997): 791–805.

11 'Et Subridet etc.'

Smiles, laughter and levity in the medieval Year Books

Gwen Seabourne

According to a report of *W v Robert*, a 1440 Common Pleas debt case,[1] during discussion of procedural issues, one of the judges, William Paston, smiled or laughed: *et subridet etc*. This is far from being the only reference to smiling, laughing or joking in the medieval Year Books.[2] Such inclusions raise several questions. Perhaps most obviously, we could ask why a judge might have laughed (or smiled) in court. In addition, it is worth considering why such behaviour might have been deemed worthy of mention in a law report. As this paper will seek to demonstrate, such references to smiling and laughter, along with the wider body of apparently 'light' or humorous verbal content found in these reports – wordplay, whimsy and jokes – have much to contribute to a variety of areas of scholarship. For the legal historian, they have particular value in illuminating medieval common lawyers' perceptions of themselves, each other and their world, while they are also clearly relevant to those working in medieval history and literature, and, more widely in philosophy, psychology and literature, who are engaged in debate about the nature and meanings of smiles, laughter and humour, and their portrayal.

The Year Books, which are to be considered here, include reports of some of the cases argued in the central courts of common law at Westminster, and in other sessions, from the thirteenth to the sixteenth century.[3] They do contain inaccuracies, as legal historians are aware.[4] In addition, even where the reports' text has not become distorted, it is not possible to know whether what appears in the reports represents what was actually said or done in court. While some earlier commentators took the written words more or less at face value,[5] it is clear that they cannot be taken to represent 'the truth, the whole truth, and nothing but the truth'. Those who made the reports picked and chose between cases, to decide which were worthy of a report at all, and they were at least selective in what they reported in any given case. They may have tidied up or altered for effect what was actually said and done, as we can see from the fact that, in some instances, there are different versions of the same case.[6] Reporters did not see or present themselves as objective, comprehensive, neutral recorders of cases unfolding before them, feeling free to insert their own queries, criticism and comments.[7] The implication of all this for this investigation is that, while there is no evidence to suggest that the Year Books comprise deliberate or thoroughgoing fiction, we cannot be sure that Paston did smile in a particular case in 1440, or that, if he did, he, or others, did not do so elsewhere without the fact being noted. Nevertheless, it is still worth asking why a judge *might* have done so in such a situation, and also why reporters chose to include such material, alongside the drier aspects of legal rule and procedure.[8] A point is being made when 'light' material is included. This paper will make suggestions as to what the point might have been.

Interpretation of smiles, laughter and levity

The words used for smiles and laughter are the Latin *ridet* and *subridet, ridendo* and *subridendo*, and there is occasional use of the related but more loaded *derisus*. There is room for debate on the meaning to be ascribed to the laughter/smiling words: when we read that a judge *ridet* or *subridet*, are we to imagine smiling (of a natural 'Duchenne' type, or the 'non-Duchenne' aggressive smile), chuckling, laughing, guffawing or something else, and what mood or emotion is to be understood as having prompted this behaviour? It is generally agreed that feelings behind smiles and laughter may range from nervousness to merriment to aggression.[9] It is important to be alive to the very different ways in which these words can be read.

These laughter/smiling terms are set down in Latin, in contrast to the usual Anglo-Norman French of the rest of the report. Although this linguistic change is not peculiar to comments on smiles and laughter, since other 'stage directions' and summarised speech, as well as queries and comments by the reporter are also rendered in Latin,[10] it is significant. Movement between languages in a variety of medieval texts has been the subject of considerable interest in recent years, and a deliberate design behind this 'code switching' has often been suggested. In the context of the Year Book reports, this linguistic change both draws attention to the content after the 'switch', and also emphasises the participation, the selection of the reporter, separating the report into two distinct (sets of) voices: the participating lawyers and judges (who are reported speaking in French) and the Latin-writing reporter.[11]

As well as the 'stage directions' for smiling or laughter, the reports contain a number of apparently humorous remarks said to have been made, usually by judges, during the course of a case: an array of witticisms, word-play, jokes and sarcastic put-downs.[12] Although this 'verbal humour' category is more difficult to delineate than the laughter/smiling material, since what was meant to be humorous or light may be elusive, [13] uncertainty as to identification of all instances of humour or levity should not prevent analysis of instances which are relatively uncontroversial.

How is this reported smiling, laughter and levity to be read? Scholarly work from several areas puts forward a number of theories as to why people may find material humorous, and why they laugh, and on the connected issue of the consequence or functions of smiles, laughter and humour. Theoretical explanations are often divided into 'the superiority theory, the incongruity theory and the relief theory', explaining humour, laughter and smiling as expressions of perceived superiority to some other person or defined group of others (superiority theory), as a release of formerly suppressed energy (relief theory), or as a response to a perceived incongruity between what is expected and what we are actually told (incongruity theory).[14] There have also been attempts to formulate a single over-arching theory of humour, perhaps the best known being that of Bergson, which suggests laughter to be behaviour 'directed by some against others in order to rectify the overly rigid behaviour that has temporarily disrupted the natural elasticity of life'.[15] Work which has taken as its focus the consequence or function of smiles, laughter and humour may stress their role in improving social relations, reducing tension and promoting group cohesion,[16] in marking or reinforcing divisions between an in-group and outsiders, in subverting hierarchies, or in defending against a perceived threat.[17] It may also argue for the conscious and deliberate use of smiles, laughter and humour as matters of display or performance of emotion for political ends and the creation of a particular image.[18] Such work clearly has something to contribute to the study of levity in legal records, and vice versa. As will become apparent, a number of these theories and interpretations are helpful to our understanding of the Year Book reports of smiles, laughter and humour.

It should also be borne in mind that, while those coming to the Year Books from a background in modern legal practice or academia may see incongruity in the inclusion of judicial or lawyerly smiles, laughter and levity in a law report, scholars of the medieval period, familiar with the ludic images in the margins of even the most sacred texts,[19] (and having left behind the idea of the medieval period as one of unremitting solemnity),[20] are less likely to be surprised by the fact that legal texts should include such material, though they might not have appreciated the interest of the light content in legal sources, and its relevance to their work.[21]

Levity, humour and the developing legal profession

Some of the reported smiling, laughter and humour of lawyers directed towards their opponents in court might be seen as an attempt to gain superiority,[22] but the most obvious manifestations of superiority-based levity and humour is that directed by judges against the lawyers pleading before them. At times, pleaders who have displeased the judges are simply reported to have been told off, without detectable humour.[23] At other times, however, wittier judicial criticisms are reported. Sarcasm and a proverbial expression can be seen in *Michael de Meldoun's Case* (1305): Howard J asks Serjeant Scrope, who is making a plea which the judge regards as contradicting itself, whether he will 'have the egg and the halfpenny too'.[24] Staunton JCP engages in gentler mocking in a report from 1311 when he tells Serjeant Miggele that, if Miggele should find a case in the rolls supporting his assertion, Staunton would give him his hood.[25] In *Edmund of Reynham's Case* (1345) Stonor CJCP tells Serjeant Greene: 'you are as hot on this as if you were right' and 'you would have to be more learned than God to prove that', both rather creative put-downs.[26] In the same year, the same judge reportedly expressed amazement that the same serjeant, appearing before him, made out that he knew everything in the world 'and he was only a young man'.[27] Several decades later, Martin J reportedly made a rather elegant metaphorical put-down, saying, 'I see well that Serjeant Rolf has breakfasted well today, for it seems to me he has dined on (or swallowed) an error'.[28]

Professor Brand noted an interesting late-thirteenth-century put-down, in which a judge, John of Mettingham, reportedly compares a man pleading before him with a stupid and/or disreputable woman in a fabliau-like story which was, no doubt, regarded as humorous. The situation in court was that a party had accepted the homage of another party, but was trying to avoid the implications of this acceptance. Metthingham told this lawyer that, in doing this, he was similar to 'the young lady who took money to be fucked (*fotu*) and then repented and went back to the young man who had fucked her', asking him to take back his money and 'unfuck' her, because she regretted what had happened.[29] This bawdy comparison of a male lawyer to the foolish woman of the tale clearly served to heap layers of ridicule upon the man being criticised.

In another interesting early instance, we read of general derision and laughter at the poor pleading of a serjeant. In *Simon of Berton v Walter* (1306), it is noted that one of the lawyers, Serjeant Nicholas Laufare, was laughed at (*derisus*) by the court for an answer given during the pleading process: he made a plea, the judges thought it unsuitable, and mocking laughter ensued.[30]

It can be argued that there was a change in the Year Books' portrayal of the atmosphere in court over the course of the fourteenth century. This was the contention of Plucknett, who contrasted the early reports, and particularly those of the reign of Edward II ('the gayest of lawbooks'), with the more stolid versions of Richard II's day. In his view, a change in reporting style came about in the third quarter of the fourteenth century.[31] Some of the judges' remarks in the earlier law reports, noted above, may be taken as suggestive of a degree of ill temper rather than simple 'gaiety' in judge-lawyer relations, but a change of tone over time can certainly be detected. This could be explained by developments within the legal profession. The early Year Book period was also a formative period for the legal profession, and specifically for the beginning of the judiciary being drawn from the ranks of those who had formerly pleaded cases in the courts of common law, the forging of a path from serjeant to judge, rather than these two branches remaining separate.[32] It is not inconceivable that such restructuring, and the new structure in itself, with somewhat blurred lines between judges and the serjeants who might one day join them on the bench, precipitated assertive judicial behaviour, reinforcing superiority of status through ridicule of those pleading in court. The use of laughter and humour to bolster the position of those in authority has been studied in particular in relation to medieval kings, with discussions of the trope of the *rex facetus*, present in chronicle and narrative images of kings from several Western realms, in which royal power was emphasised through the king's wit, laughter and joking.[33] Might one see in remarks from the Year Books such as those mentioned above either the reality or the image of the *judex facetus*, an office-holder asserting himself through levity, in a developing professional world?

The incidence of humour, laughter and smiles in the Year Books is in some ways similar to results seen in modern work on the dynamics of organisations. In a classic study of senior and junior members of staff at an American psychiatric institution, by R.L. Coser, for example, senior staff make jokes about the juniors who will one day replace them, but the reverse is not true (or at least juniors do not make jokes about their superiors whilst in their presence).[34] Similarly, there is little evidence in the Year Books of 'subversive' use of humour, in court, against hierarchical superiors:[35] pleaders do not ridicule judges, though some trace of the slightly inferior teasing or joking about the slightly superior may, perhaps, be seen in remarks between serjeants at different levels of seniority,[36] and between judges of different ranks.[37] Tension between individuals and between groups and attempts to assert superiority do not ever seem to have been the whole story relating to reports of laughter, smiles and humour, however. A playful mood in the early fourteenth-century courtroom is hinted at by the use of a nickname for a judge.[38] There is also a 'clubby' light-heartedness in the reported use of serjeants or judges in hypotheticals, seen from the earliest reports onwards, as when we read of a serjeant imagining vouching William of Bereford, judges imagining conducting land deals with other judges, and judges joking about serjeants refusing money or being involved in an assault.[39] Reports of laughter and levity might indicate cross-generational solidarity within the legal profession, with the humour of previous judges recalled.[40] Later case reports also featured non-confrontational humour: the size and age of serjeants, or their names, is reported as a subject for mild joshing in *Abbot of Tore's Case* (1443); there was a certain self-mocking in mentioning money and lawyers; and status-based humour, emphasising the lofty position of common law judges, is evident in a tongue-in-cheek suggestion that the Chief Justice of Common Pleas is a 'servant'.[41]

A particularly friendly atmosphere is suggested in some of the examples of smiling involving Thomas Littleton (d. 1481), a serjeant who would go on to become a judge and famous (though not notably humorous) legal writer.[42] He was reported smiling or laughing on more than one occasion, and also raising smiles from the judges. These may be seen as showing the friendly nature of judges' banter with a distinguished serjeant, or, more generally, as showing a collegial, relatively relaxed atmosphere between those with different roles and ranks.[43]

It would appear that both benign and aggressive meanings can be understood from the smiles, laughter and humour reported to have been seen and heard in court. If, as I suggest, we can see a trend of less aggressive, superiority-bolstering uses of humour, laughter and sarcasm from judges towards pleaders, that may be taken to suggest a period of some anxiety, or uncertainty as to how to behave within the new professional structure, in the late thirteenth and earlier fourteenth centuries, followed by a period of greater collegiality, particularly in the fifteenth century.[44] The portrayal of Paston's smiling or laughing behaviour in *W v Robert* fits into this more relaxed atmosphere. He is commenting on the pleas made in the case, noting an apparent oddity,[45] but these is no aggression or insult directed towards counsel. The case was a long-running dispute, with areas of real difficulty, and the atmosphere portrayed is one of relaxed and pleasant debate, some distance from the scene of the early Year Books.

Play and display

Some of the light material demonstrates a particular playful atmosphere in court.

Ludic imagery can be seen in some case reports. In *Bank v Maulevere* (1378), for example, Serjeant Hanmer is shown likening a case to a game of chess.[46] The pleasure of argument is mentioned in a case of 1522.[47] Lawyers might be shown taking a literary turn, as can be seen in Serjeant Laufare's possible poem in a case of 1304, rhyming couplets about the consequences of adultery and elopement (1309), on confiscation of property (1441), and on hunting (1520).[48] Judges are seen joking about parties and legal proceedings themselves, as in the case of one judge's tale of a knight who won a case despite being asleep and not a party, and another judge's description of the way in which champions for trial by battle used to be treated.[49]

A playful tone can be seen even in relation to death and execution. A parable concerning execution is told by Bereford in a replevin case,[50] and Scot alluded to execution in an apparently humorous tale of mishaps in another case.[51] In discussing a suicide, use was made of a rhyming couplet.[52] Spigurnel JKB, when told an accused thief was dead, is reported to have said 'It's as well for him that he is!'.[53] Wychyngham JCP, in *Anon* (1365), is noted to have said that if the defendant in the case had waited until he had been beheaded (as threatened) he would have been too late to make a deed.[54] The funny side of beheading was also seen in a report of a case of 1457 which noted, with comic understatement, that the plaintiff would have suffered 'mischief and inconvenience' if his head had been cut off by the rebels in the Cade rebellion.[55] Reports of such 'gallows humour', although it may seem crude to the modern reader, were in tune with contemporary literary sources, which have a number of examples of hanging or beheading games and humour relating to corpses.[56]

In a legal world which focused intently on language and exploiting variance and ambiguity, it is not surprising that puns and plays on words are to be found in the Year Books. In 1306, for example, Serjeant Toutheby is shown making a play on the word 'volee'.[57] We see Bereford playing with the several meanings of 'gross' in 1312,[58] and there are several other examples of puns or plays upon words in court in the fifteenth century.[59]

Proverbs appear particularly in the speeches of judges. Those which might be classed as humorous include 'Where you have a man you also have a lord', and 'Did you never see one hunt in a park and another had the deer?'.[60] Proverbs were familiar from the Bible, were prevalent in medieval literature, and their use was a recommended rhetorical technique.[61] Some proverbial sayings found in Year Books follow Biblical examples.[62] There are also a number of examples of expressions amounting to 'I would not give a fig for . . . ', or 'is not worth a fig', though the preferred hypothetical trifle is a strawberry.[63] A particular favourite proverb in the Year Books concerned the legal position of a child born within marriage: the presumption that the husband of the child's mother was the child's father was supported by the earthy expression 'whoso bulleth my cow, the calf is always mine'.[64] Others are more-or-less recognisable ancestors of surviving proverbs, such as the impossibility of having one's cake and eating it, and the observation that some people, given an inch, take a mile, and that one ought not to put the 'cart before the oxen'.[65]

Display of knowledge can also be seen in the inclusion of Bible references, which often appear to be used with an interestingly light tone. The church organisations in York and Canterbury are likened to Jews and Samaritans who will have no dealing with one another, an allusion to John 4:9.[66] More than one judge alluded to Matthew 14:31, 'O thou of little faith, wherefore didst thou doubt', to tease serjeants not prepared to take the risk of making a particular plea.[67] It is unclear whether Serjeant Mutford's 'Blessed be the womb that bare thee', to Mettingham after a favourable judgment, is to be read as serious sycophancy or as humour.[68] Exaggerated horror is seen in the fairly frequent use of 'God forbid' by judges and serjeants,[69] and light is made of the word heresy.[70] In addition, lawyers and judges frequently swear by God, St James or St Nicholas.[71]

There are also some references to secular literature. I have noted the similarity between one judge's story and a fabliau.[72] In addition, there are allusions to more famous literary traditions. In one report of *Frank Scoland's Case* (1313), in the Eyre of Kent, a serjeant described his opponent's argument as irrelevant, comparing it to a 'tale of Roland and Oliver',[73] and, in 1429, another serjeant used a line from a Robin Hood ballad, in order to ridicule as irrelevant the pleading of his opponent.[74] Also on display are a knowledge of logic terminology, and the rhetorical technique of *reductio ad absurdum*, the latter of which in particular injects a light note into Year Book discussions.[75]

Educational function – memory enhancement and a wide concept of legal study

It is generally agreed that the Year Books had an educational function.[76] Some of the light material discussed in this paper might be classed as enhancing the learning of legal rules and procedure, and it could also help with legal education in a much wider sense than this, including courtroom etiquette, tactics and 'gamesmanship'.

Light content of the sort discussed might have been included for the reporter's own amusement, or the entertainment of others. It has provided entertainment for lawyers of succeeding generations: famously, Serjeant Maynard is said to have 'had such a relish of the old year-books that he carried one in his coach to divert him in travel, and said he chose it before any comedy'.[77] It could be argued that making the content entertaining would also have enhanced the likelihood of remembering a case. Medieval common law education included a large amount of memory-work, as can be seen from surviving manuscripts containing mnemonics to aid this process.[78] Laughter or amusement had been noted at least as far back as Horace as a good way of remembering things.[79] The use of levity in education was known elsewhere in the medieval world: one might cite the reported jokes of a lecturer in surgery, humour in the syllogisms of Peter Abelard, or the inclusion of humour in the work of those engaged in the broader educational task of preaching.[80] The Year Books' reports of laughter and mockery may, therefore, have been included at strategic points, to give particular notice of what were understood to be bad pleading mistakes, much as a visual cue, such as a pointing finger, might be included in other medieval records, to highlight the most important matters. The Year Book reporters' playful choice of fictitious names in some cases,[81] like the practice in *Novae Narrationes* of naming several people with the names of animals,[82] may also have been calculated to enhance memory.

It is not always obvious to the modern reader why certain mistakes or conduct might have been highlighted by noting that they gave rise to laughter or smiles. Why, for example, might Laufare's pleading in *Simon of Berton v Walter* (1306) have been worthy of the reported derision? It might be that the individual plea Laufare made was seen as inept,[83] but the strength of the (reported) response might also be explained by the accumulation of irritations presented to the court by this particular serjeant. There had already been heated exchanges with the judges, and the mocking laughter may be an instance of the judges combining in opposition to a serjeant who has annoyed them. This reported ridicule might make other pleaders think twice before attempting such a plea again, or before trying the patience of the judges.

In addition to acting as markers or reminders of important mistakes or innovations, some of the various quips and smiles might have been included as hints about the use of humour as a tactic for pleading in court, teaching etiquette or 'gamesmanship' as well as technically correct pleading. A pleader might be shown play-acting to feign confidence in his own case, when, in fact, he knew that he was on somewhat shaky ground.[84] As with the pedagogical use of humour, its tactical use goes far back in the rhetorical tradition, and it is not unlikely that there was some influence, direct or mediated, from those classical sources which were accessible to medieval scholars.[85]

As we have seen above, lawyers were sometimes portrayed taking the opportunity to show off their wit, literary knowledge or familiarity with academic learning or techniques, perhaps to impress or gain favour with the court. More clearly falling under the heading of 'gamesmanship' appear to be those instances of serjeants shown smiling to suggest confidence in their own position. For example, Serjeant Catesby is reported to have smiled when telling his opponents that they should proceed with the plea they had signalled that they were planning to use.[86] At times, serjeants appear to be using smiles and humour when on difficult ground. Thus, Serjeant Rolf laughs at his opponent's client as he mocks him in *Caunt's Case* (1430). The case concerns sale of allegedly unwholesome wine, and Rolf, laughing, derides the opposing party as a mere 'wine drawer' who knows nothing about wine and its quality. He is attempting to argue that the plaintiff was not in a position to know whether or not the wine was wholesome, and the ridicule is an attempt to 'put down' the opposition, probably by suggesting his inferiority to the serjeants and judges, as well as the more arguably relevant suggestion that he cannot prove his case. Rolf's laughter and put-down were strictly unnecessary, for the task in hand was to arrive at an issue, and the issue Rolf was feeling towards at this point was 'The wine was wholesome at the time of sale'. His conduct appears to have been an attempt to bolster his (possibly shaky) case by belittling his opponent's client.[87]

Clearly, 'performance' came to be an essential part of being a lawyer. A profession in which one gained status through performance – where one became a serjeant by performing a count, a barrister by performing in a moot – is likely to have been one which paid attention to physical attitudes, to gestures, to how words were spoken, as well as to the essentials of legal doctrine.[88] In such a world, the inclusion of quips and 'stage directions' may have seemed natural, and instructive.[89] Inclusion in the reports of such material also fits in well with a world in which the written word was often intended as much for aural as for visual consumption.[90]

As well as having a role in instructing lawyers in correct doctrine and advantageous conduct, we may also conclude that there was, in some of the inclusions of 'light' material, an element of promotion or reinforcement of particular images of the courts of common law and prominent individuals working there. Some of those present in court are, perhaps, emphasised as 'characters' – cantankerous, erudite, witty, urbane or hapless. Note, for example, the special emphasis in early fourteenth-century reports on the often cantankerous humour attributed to Sir William Bereford, Chief Justice of the Common Bench, (d. 1326),[91] and the more playful smiling and wit of several fifteenth-century judges, noted above, all of which seems to be rather removed from Fortescue's portrayal of judges as *viros graves*,[92] and at odds with Bakhtin's view of 'serious' official or learned culture.[93] In addition, a possible explanation for the noting of derision in *Simon of Berton v Walter* (1306) is that Laufare was seen, or was being built up by the reporter as a particularly hapless pleader.[94] As we have seen, smiles are frequently noted in reports relating to serjeant Littleton. The 'character-construction' view of the reports is also supported by the well-known fact that some lawyers might be given a prominent role in reports of a particular case despite the fact that they were demonstrably absent from the event itself.[95]

Whatever may have been the intention of those including levity and humorous remarks in the reports, they did in fact contribute to the collective memory of the profession, with regard to law, procedure and individual characters. The choices made in including this material in reports shaped ideas of the world of the medieval common law for many generations of lawyers, legal historians and historians.[96]

'Outgroup' humour: women, foreigners, the lowly

Directing humour at 'outgroups' is one of the standard examples of the 'superiority theory' of humour, and having a shared 'other' as the butt of a joke in court might serve to bolster cohesion amongst the lawyers and judges. It will be no surprise that there is a certain amount of humour involving both foreigners and women, particularly the latter. We see also some instances of disdain for lower social orders and of negative attitudes towards the clergy. Nevertheless, some of the humour involving 'outgroups' is as suggestive of anxiety as it is of superiority.

It is not surprising to find misogynist humour, such as Cavendish CJ's famous reported remark about women of thirty wanting to look eighteen, making it impossible for men to assess their age, references to 'shrews' getting their come-uppance, and Paston JCP's reported smiling remarks in a case of 1441, when discussing the hypothetical case of a man about to rape one's wife.[97] There are also more elaborate bawdy stories with misogynist elements. One, mentioned above, was told by Mettingham at the end of the thirteenth century.[98] Meant as a criticism of a male lawyer, this story, which bears more than a passing resemblance to well-known fabliau types,[99] also serves to criticise women as foolish and perhaps immoral. Somewhat similarly, in the replevin case of *John the Cooper of T v Isolde widow of Richard Ildok* (1312), Bereford is reported as having told a story concerning a young woman who was asked by a vallet whether she was a virgin, and, in response, said 'make trial, make trial'. The judge used this during an attempt to encourage a party to try out a plea he was hesitating to make.[100] The tale suggests a negative attitude to women – again, on the grounds of foolishness and immorality. This story, and its inclusion, however, also raise interesting issues concerning gender and legal hierarchy, for Bereford, who intends to encourage boldness of pleading in the serjeant, is effectively cast as the (forward or foolish) young woman in the story, and the serjeant as the timid or uncertain male partner.[101] What layers of complexity, misogyny and gender insecurity lie behind such an inclusion?

Bereford is reported to have made a joke about nuns and wives the same year, though this also has undertones about male inadequacy.[102] Margery had married Roger, but, subsequently, he had allowed her to become a nun. Twenty years later, she had come back to the secular world and to her husband. The spouses brought novel disseisin concerning lands in Middlesex. Margery came in ordinary clothes rather than a nun's habit. She was allowed to appoint an attorney to act for her. Then it was objected that she was a nun, so should not be involved in matters of temporal property, and should not be heard. The argument on her side, however, was that the court had accepted her as a litigant when they had let her appoint an attorney, so that this could not now be challenged. Bereford announced that in the (absurd) event that 'all the nuns in England had come in that way, we should have let them appoint attornies', by which he meant that the court could not be expected to check up on everyone, and that the fact that she had been allowed an attorney was not sufficient to defeat the defendant's challenge to her as a proper person to sue in the courts of common law. Eventually, Margery was excommunicated for having left the abbey, which brought things to an abrupt end. Bereford apparently said to Roger that if he had proved that she was his wife, then he had a nun for a wife, presumably mocking Roger's inability to fulfil the proper masculine role.

A degree of gender insecurity is evident in possibly humorous reported statements about women being less amenable to their husbands than in the past, and the suggestions that a woman may be the master of her husband.[103] Humour concerning women, and its combination of misogyny, insecurity and occasional admiration, is much discussed amongst literary scholars,[104] and the Year Books are ripe for examination in this context.

Foreigners appear in a few reported remarks. The idea that 'a Frenchman' might get his land is reportedly used by Hertford J in *Adam v B* (1294) as a ridiculous idea.[105] There is a possible joke or pun involving the similarity between 'Scottish' and 'stockfish': *Copley v Anon* (1470).[106] There is no particular mocking of the Irish or Welsh,[107] but the people of Norfolk are the object of Yorkshireman Fairfax J's amusement when he (reportedly) said, *ridendo*, that they were full of wiles and disinclined to lay out money.[108]

Another matter for quip and humorous observation is social status, perhaps another area of insecurity in the social-climbing world of the legal professions,[109] and one which can be seen to have come to the fore in the late fourteenth and fifteenth century, prompting, or as a result of, sumptuary legislation of 1363 and 1413 legislation on the descriptive 'additions', included in writs.[110] In *Caunt's Case* (1430), for example, Serjeant Rolf, *ridendo & protestando*, mocks his client's opponent as a mere 'wine drawer', ignorant about wine,[111] and, in *Anon* (1436), in a discussion of whether a cook is or is not a 'gentleman', Juyn JCP jokes that the masters of the royal kitchen would be aggrieved by being described as 'cooks'.[112]

Churchmen are another group treated with a certain levity, and even disrespect, in the reports. Some judges reportedly used sarcastic humour towards or about them. Bereford CJ alluded to the greed or craftiness of churchmen,[113] a tardy Ordinary was asked by Friskeney J where he had been sleeping, and Mowbray JCP told a bishop to 'go to the devil without day'.[114] Priests are treated as proverbially lecherous, and there is some joking relating to unchaste priests and women even in a replevin case which seems to have nothing to do with either.[115] The church organisations in York and Canterbury are likened to Jews and Samaritans who will have no dealing with one another, an allusion to John 4:9.[116] This light or disrespectful attitude has obvious parallels with literary depictions of venial, lecherous clergymen, but might also be read as owing something to the prickliness of a new profession, asserting itself against a more established one.

Conclusion

It has long been known to legal historians that the Year Books contain a number of reports of smiles, laughter and levity, though they have not generally done more than note the incidence of such inclusions and enjoy them. Those from other fields of scholarship have not yet expended much energy on exploring this light or humorous content in legal texts. As has been outlined here, however, this material has much to offer both legal historians and other scholars. The fact that reporters took an active role in constructing events, personalities and the culture of the courts, rather than simply recording what happened, is evident from the inclusion of this material, and this paper has made some preliminary suggestions as to the reasons for including it. As humour, laughter and smiles are complex phenomena,[117] and as the sources discussed cover a long period of time and produced by several different hands, the 'light' material under discussion cannot be reduced to having only one purpose or meaning; but this article has suggested some interpretations of what such inclusions show with regard to the world-view of medieval common lawyers, and to contemporary ideas of professional education, the image and self-image of judges and lawyers. It is to be hoped that these preliminary explorations will encourage others to continue work on the Year Books as literary productions or texts, lying in the intriguing area of 'interplay between medieval reading . . . and orality',[118] and as evidence for history of humour and emotion, despite their sometimes forbidding subject matter and their acknowledged problems, the better to enrich both legal history and other areas of study.

Notes

1 *Seipp* 1440.012; YB Pasch. 18 Hen. VI pl.9 f.10a–11b.
2 A number of Year Book reports mention that a judge laughed or smiled, or, less frequently, that a lawyer pleading in court did so. See, e.g., *Seipp* 1306.191rs; YB Mich. 34 Edw. I pl 24, YB 33–5 Edw. I, RS 31 part A vol. 5, 324–7. *Seipp* 1440.012, YB 14 Hen. VI pl. 51, f. 15a–b. *Seipp* 1443.021, CP Hil. 21 Hen. VI pl. 21 f 33b–34a; *Seipp* 1411.003, 12 Hen. IV pl.3 f.12b–13b; *Seipp* 1462.024, YB Trin. 2 Edw. IV pl. 1, f. 10a–10b, *Seipp* 1481.051, YB 21 Edw. IV pl. 20. f. 26a–b; *Seipp* 1443.021, YB Hil. 21 Hen. VI pl. 21 f 33b–34a; Paul Brand, *Observing and Recording the Medieval Bar and Bench at Work; The Origins of Law Reporting in England* (London: Selden Society, 1999), 6–8.
3 See, e.g., *EELR I*, introduction; F.W. Maitland, 'Of the Year Books in General', in *Year Books of 1 and 2 Edward II*, SS 17 (London: Quaritch, 1903), ix–xx; J.H. Baker, *Introduction to English Legal History*, 4th ed. (London: Butterworths, 2002), 178–82 and 192–3; E.W. Ives, 'The Purpose and Making of the Later Year Books', *LQR* 89 (1972): 64–86, at 64; David J. Seipp, 'The Law's Many Bodies and the Manuscript Tradition in English Legal History', *JLH* 25 (2004): 74–83; Paul Brand, 'Inside the Courtroom: Lawyers, Litigants and Justices in England in the Later Middle Ages', in *The Moral World of the Law*, ed., Peter Coss (Cambridge: Cambridge University Press, 2000), 91–112, at 92–3.
4 This is particularly true of the printed 'black-letter' Year Books: see, e.g., Maitland, 'Of the Year Books', xxi; E.W. Ives, *The Common Lawyers of Pre-Reformation England: Thomas Kebell: A Case Study* (Cambridge: Cambridge University Press, 1983), ch. 7; *EELR I*, cxix–cxx.
5 Bolland was confident that 'The words . . . come to us straight from life, true to life, true to sound'.: W.C. Bolland, *The Year Books* (Cambridge: Cambridge University Press, 1921), 24; Maitland, 'Of the Year Books', xv–xvii; Edward Manson, 'Scenes in Court From the Year Books', *LQR* 10 (1894): 63–7, Thomas Lund, *The Creation of the Common Law: The Medieval Year Books Deciphered* (Clark, NJ: The LawBook Exchange, 2015).
6 See, e.g., varying versions of the *Waltham Carrier's Case* (1321): two reports have a pithy remark that 'for a cartload of hay, we will not [change the law]', while another has the equivalent speech in more general words: Helen M. Cam, ed., *Eyre of London 1321*, SS 86 (London: Quaritch, 1969), 286. See also *EELR I*, 128, 171–2.
7 One reporter likens brothers who had settled their dispute to Herod and Pilate: *Seipp* 1284.050ss; *EELR III*, 141–2.
8 See Brand, *Observing and Recording*, 9–21; *EELR I*, introduction. Note also that this article will proceed on the basis of the spirited case for using the printed Year Books in legal historical research made in Seipp, 'The Law's Many Bodies', 74–83.
9 See Brand, 'Inside the Courtroom', 105. Interpretations of smiles and laughter, medieval and modern, have been offered by those working in several different areas. See, e.g., Jacques Le Goff, 'Rire au Moyen Age', *Cahiers de centre de recherches historiques [En ligne]* 3 (1989), http://ccrh.revues.org/2918 at 12; Colin Jones, *The Smile Revolution in Eighteenth Century Paris* (Oxford: Oxford University Press, 2014), 3; Lucy Perry and Alexander Schwarz, eds., *Behaving Like Fools: Voice, Gesture and Laughter in Texts, Manuscripts and Early Books* (Turnhout: Brepols, 2012); D.-R. Moser, 'Lachkultur des Mittelalters?': Michael Bachtin und die Folgen Seiner Theorie', *Euphorion: Zeitschrift für Literaturgeschichte* 84 (1990): 89–111; Albrecht Classen, ed., *Laughter in the Middle Ages and Early Modern Times: Epistemology of a Fundamental Human Behavior, Its Meaning and Consequences* (Berlin: De Gruyter, 2010);

Siegrid Schmidt, 'Sebastian Brant's Ship of Fools and Its Woodcuts', in Perry et al., *Behaving Like Fools*, 91; Paul Ekman and Wallace V. Friesen, 'Felt, False and Miserable Smiles', *Journal of Nonverbal Behavior* 6 (1982): 238–52; Jon E. Roeckelein, *The Psychology of Humor: A Reference Guide and Annotated Bibliography* (Westport, CT: Greenwood Press, 2002); Joseph Polimeni and Jeffrey P. Reiss, 'The First Joke: Exploring the Evolutionary Origins of Humor', *Evolutionary Psychology* 4 (2006): 347–66; Jerry Palmer, *Taking Humour Seriously* (London: Routledge, 1994); Lothar Fietz, Joerg O. Fichte and Hans-Werner Ludwig, eds., *Semiotik, Rhetorik und Soziologie des Lachens* (Tübingen: Max Niemeyer, 1996); John Morreall, *Comic Relief* (Oxford: Wiley-Blackwell, 2009); R.L. Coser, 'Laughter Among Colleagues', *Psychiatry* 23 (1960): 81–95; N. Butler, 'Joking Aside: Theorizing Laughter in Organizations', *Culture and Organization* 21 (2015): 42–58. On the history of emotions, see, e.g. Barbara H. Rosenwein, 'Thinking Historically About Medieval Emotions', *History Compass* 8 (2010): 828–42; Michael Champion and Andrew Lynch, eds., *Understanding Emotions in Early Europe* (Turnhout: Brepols, 2015); Peter King, 'Emotions in Medieval Thought', in *The Oxford Handbook of Philosophy of Emotions*, ed., Peter Gildie (Oxford: Oxford University Press, 2010), 167–88; Jutta Eming, 'The Discussion of Emotion in the Study of Medieval Literature', *Journal of Literary Theory* 1 (2007): 251–73; Simo Knuuttila, *Emotions in Ancient and Medieval Philosophy* (Oxford: Oxford University Press, 2004), chs. 3 and 4; Peter N. Stearns and Carol Z. Stearns, 'Emotionology: Clarifying the History of Emotions and Emotional Standards', *AHR* 90 (1985): 813–36.

10 *Seipp* 1311.072ss, YB Hil. 4 Ed. II pl. 58 (winking).

11 See, e.g. J.H. Baker, 'The Three Languages of the Common Law', *McGill Law Journal* 43 (1998): 5–24, at 5. Paul Brand, 'The Languages of the Law in Later Medieval England', in *Multilingualism in Later Medieval Britain*, ed., D.A. Trotter (Woodbridge: Boydell and Brewer Press, 2000), 63–76; Herbert Schendl, 'Linguistic Aspects of Code-switching in Medieval English Texts', in idem, 77–92, at 79; Jocelyn Wogan-Browne et al., eds., *Language and Culture in Medieval Britain: The French of England c.1100-c.1500* (Woodbridge: Boydell and Brewer, 2009).

12 See Brand, 'Inside the Courtroom', 111.

13 *Mirror of Justices*, xlviii; Classen, *Laughter*; Schmidt, 'Sebastian Brant's Ship of Fools', 93.

14 See, e.g., John Morreall, ed., *The Philosophy of Laughter and Humour* (Albany, NY: SUNY Press, 1987); John Morreall, *Taking Laughter Seriously* (Albany, NY: SUNY Press, 1983); Simon Critchley, *On Humour* (London: Routledge, 2002), 2–3; Herbert Spencer, 'On the Physiology of Laughter', *Macmillan's Magazine* (1860): 395–402; Sigmund Freud, *Jokes and Their Relation to the Unconscious* (London: Penguin Books, 1976).

15 Butler, 'Theorizing Laughter in Organizations', at 43; Henri Bergson, *Laughter: An Essay on the Meaning of the Comic*, trans. Cloudesley Brereton and Fred Rothwell (*Le Rire*, Paris: F. Alcan, 1900; reprint, Rockville, MD: Arc Manor, 2008).

16 Alan W. Gray, Brian Parkinson and Robin I. Dunbar, 'Laughter's Influence on the Intimacy of Self-disclosure', *Human Nature* 26 (2015): 28–43; A.J. Chapman, 'Social Aspects of Humorous Laughter', in *Humour and Laughter: Theory, Research and Applications*, eds. A.J. Chapman and H.C. Foot (London: Wiley, 1976), 155–85.

17 See, e.g., Jones, *The Smile Revolution*, 7; Ekman and Friesen, 'Felt, False and Miserable Smiles'; E. Hatfield, J.L. Cacioppo and R.L. Rapson, 'Emotional Contagion', *Current Directions in Psychological Sciences* 2 (1993): 96–9; J.E.

Roeckelein, *The Psychology of Humor: A Reference Guide and Annotated Bibliography* (Westport, CT: Greenwood Press, 2002). There are disagreements as to the evolutionary purposes of such behaviour: Joseph Polimeni and J.P. Reiss, 'The First Joke: Exploring the Evolutionary Origins of Humor', *Evolutionary Psychology* 4 (2006): 347–66; J. Carty and Y. Musharbash, eds., 'You've Got to Be Joking: Anthropological Perspectives on Humor and Laughter', special issue of *Anthropological Forum* 18 (2008); Jerry Palmer, *Taking Humour Seriously* (London: Routledge, 1994); John Morreall, *Comic Relief* (Oxford: Wiley-Blackwell, 2009); Robin Tapley, 'On Morreall: A Failure to Distinguish Between Play and Humour', *Journal of Value Inquiry* 47 (2013): 147–62. Those looking at humour within stratified societies or organisations have stressed the 'subversive' use of humour against hierarchical superiors. See, e.g. Mary Douglas, *Implicit Meanings: Essays in Anthropology* (London: Routledge, 1975), 98; Sharon Bolton, 'A Bit of a Laugh: Nurses' Use of Humour as a Mode of Resistance', in *Questioning the New Public Management*, eds. Mike Dent, John Chandler and Jim Barry (Aldershot: Ashgate, 2004), 177–89.

18 See, e.g. Rosenwein, 'Worrying About Emotions in History', 823; Jacques Le Goff, 'Une enquête sur le rire', *Annales* 52 (1997): 449–55. Gerd Althoff, 'Ira Regis: Prologomena to a History of Royal Anger', in *Anger's Past: the social uses of an emotion in the Middle Ages*, ed. Barbara H. Rosenwein (Ithaca, N.Y.: Cornell University Press, 1998), ch.5.; Penelope Nash, 'Reality and Ritual in the Medieval King's Emotions of Ira and Clementia', in *Understanding Emotions in Early Europe*, eds. Michael Champion and Andrew Lynch (Tournhout: Brepols, 2015), 251–71. Michael Clanchy, 'Law and Love in the Middle Ages', in *Disputes and Settlements: Law and Human Relations in the West*, ed. John Bossy (Cambridge: Cambridge University Press, 1983), 47–67; P. Jones, 'The Sublime and the Ridiculous: Laughter, Sovereignty and Sanctity at the Court of Henry II', PhD diss., New York University, 2014, ch.1; Jennifer Carpenter, 'Positive Emotion in the 13th C: The Emotional World of Goswin of Bossut', in *Understanding Emotions in Early Europe*, 171–90; Peter Jones, 'Preaching Laughter in the Thirteenth Century: The Exempla of Arnold of Liège (d. *c.* 1308) and His Dominican Milieu', *Journal of Medieval History* 41 (2015): 169–83; Jeannine Horowitz and Sophia Menache, *L'Humour en chaire: le rire dans l'Eglise médiévale* (Geneva: Labor et Fides, 1994); idem, 'Le rire au quotidien dans la société médiévale au miroir de la prédication', paper given at the Tenth International Congress of Humour, Paris, University of Paris VIII, July 1992; Palmer, *Taking Humour Seriously*, 44; Laurence Moulinier, 'Quand le Malin fait l'esprit: le rire au Moyen Age vu depuis l'hagiographie', *Annales* 52 (1997): 457–75; L.E. Felsen, 'Medieval Monks: Funnier Than You Thought', in *Misconceptions About the Middle Ages*, eds. S.J. Harris and B.L. Grisby (New York: Routledge, 2008), 70–5; Sandra M. Hordis and Paul Hardwick, eds., *Medieval English Comedy* (Turnhout: Brepols, 2007); Paul Ruggiers, ed., *Versions of Medieval Comedy* (Norman: University of Oklahoma Press, 1977); H. Braet, G. Latré and W. Verbeke, eds., *Risus Mediaevalis: Laughter in Medieval Literature and Art* (Leuven: Leuven University Press, 2003); L.R. Perfetti, *Women and Laughter in Medieval Comic Literature* (Ann Arbor: University of Michigan Press, 2003); A.P. Tudor and A Hindley, eds., *Grant Risee? The Medieval Comic Presence: Essays in Memory of Brian J Levy* (Turnhout: Brepols, 2006); Philippe Menard, *Le Rire et le Sourire dans le Roman Courtois en France au Moyen Age 1150–1250* (Paris: Université, 1969); T.D. Arner, 'No Joke: Transcendent Laughter in the "Teseida" and the "Miller's Tale"', *Studies in Philology* 102 (2005): 143–58. Note the contrast with former ideas of the 'emotionally childlike' Middle Ages, with its 'violent, public, unashamed' display of emotions: Johan Huizinga, *The Waning of the Middle Ages*, trans. F.J. Hopman (New York: E. Arnold, 1924).

An important, though disputed, idea of medieval laughter is that of Bakhtin, who saw it as linked to the carnivalesque, undermining or suspending hierarchy: Mikhail Bakhtin, *Rabelais and His World*, trans. Hélène Iswolsky (Cambridge, MA: MIT Press, 1968; Bloomington: Indiana University Press, 1984), 10; Chris Humphrey, *The Politics of Carnival: Festive Misrule in Medieval England* (Manchester: Manchester University Press, 2001).

19 See, e.g., Michael Camille, *Image on the Edge: The Margins of Medieval Art* (London: Reaktion Books, 1992; 2004).

20 See, e.g. Le Goff, 'Une enquête sur le rire', 449–55; Horowitz and Menache, *L'humour en chaire*; Felsen, 'Medieval Monks'; M.W. George, 'An Austere Age Without Laughter' in *Misconceptions About the Middle Ages*, 183–7; Braet, Latré and Verbeke, eds., *Risus Medievalis*; J.S.P. Tatlock, 'Medieval Laughter', *Speculum* 21 (1946): 289–94; Helen Adolf, 'On Medieval Laughter', *Speculum* 22 (1947): 251–3.

21 Scholars of medieval literature have drawn upon legal sources in their interpretation of literature, but literary analysis of those legal sources has been less common: see, e.g. R.F. Green. 'Medieval Law and Literature', in *The Cambridge History of Medieval English Literature*, ed. David Wallace (Cambridge: Cambridge University Press, 1999), 407–31; Emily Steiner and Candace Barrington, *The Letter of the Law: Legal Practice and Literary Production in Medieval England* (Ithaca: Cornell University Press, 2002); V.C. Hunt Thomas, 'Piers Plowman, Legal Authority and the Law of Subject Status', PhD diss., Washington University, 2012. For the effective use of legal texts in connection with the study of other emotions, see, in particular, Rebecca McNamara, 'The Sorrow of Soreness: Infirmity and Suicide in Medieval England', *Parergon* 31 (2014): 11–34, Rebecca McNamara, 'The Law on Feeling: Finding Emotions in Medieval English Legal Texts', paper from the *Sourcing Emotions in the Medieval and Early Modern World Conference*, University of Western Australia, Perth, June 2013.

22 See, e.g., *Seipp* 1481.051, YB Pasch. 21 Edw. IV pl. 20 f. 26a–b; *Seipp* 1481.047, YB Pasch 21 Edw. IV pl. 16 f. 25b. *Seipp* 1430.083, YB Mich. 9 Hen. VI pl. 37 f. 53b.

23 See, e.g., Weyland snapping at a lawyer before him that 'On my faith, what you say is neither well said nor true', in *EELR I*, case 1287.5; YB 21 & 22 Edw. I RS 31.2, p 224; *Seipp* 1312.017ss; YB Hil. 5 Edw. II pl. 17.

24 *Seipp* 1305.017rs; YB Hil. 33 Edw I pl. 17; Maitland, 'Of the Year Books', ix–xx, xv; *Seipp* 1311.269ss, YB Mich. 5 Edw. II pl. 22.

25 *Seipp* 1311.106ss, YB Pasch. 4 Edw. II pl. 16.

26 *Seipp* 1345.015rs YB Hil. 19 Edw. III pl. 15; and 1344.271 YB 18 Edw III Lib. Ass pl. 16.

27 *Seipp* 1345.018rs, YB Hil. 19 Edw III pl. 18.

28 *Seipp* 1426.027; YB Pasch. 4 Hen. VI pl. 11 f. 23b–24b. See also earlier cases, in which a judge suggests that a party or serjeant is 'having a laugh' or making fun of the court: *Seipp* 1346.122 rs, YB Trin. 20 Edw. III pl.1; *Seipp* 1384.020am, YB Pasch. 7 Ric. II pl. 4.

29 Brand, 'Inside the courtroom', 111 (his translation), BL MS Add 35116 f.186v. See below note 96 for parallels in fabliaux.

30 *Seipp* 1306.191rs, YB Mich. 34 Edw. I pl 24. *Derisus* is also seen in *Seipp* 1413.014, YB Hil. 14 Hen. IV pl. 14 f. 17a–b, in relation to Serjeant Skrene's strained pleading. Some early non-legal writing suggests that courts could be places for mocking laughter: *Lawsuits*, 1: 174.

31 T.F.T. Plucknett, ed., *Year Books of Richard II: 13 Ric II, 1389–1390* (London: Spottiswoode, Ballantyne and Co., 1929), xiv–xvi.

32 See, e.g. Paul Brand, 'The Serjeants of the Common Bench in the Reign of Edward I: An Emerging Professional Elite', in *Thirteenth Century England*

VII, eds. Michael Prestwich, Richard Britnell and Robin Frame (Woodbridge: Boydell and Brewer, 1999), 81–102; Paul Brand, 'Edward I and the Judges: the State Trials of 1289–93', in *Thirteenth Century England I*, eds. P.R. Coss and S.D. Lloyd (Woodbridge: Boydell and Brewer, 1986), 31–40, reprinted in Brand, *MCL*, 103–12; Paul Brand, 'The Origins of the English Legal Profession', *LHR* 5 (1987): 31–50, reprinted in Brand, *MCL*, 1–20; Brand, *Observing and Recording*, 12; Bereford was an early example of a pleader in the courts of common law rising to be a judge, in the 1290s: A. Harding, Bereford [Barford], Sir William, d. 1326, justice', *ODNB*.

33 See, e.g., Jacques Le Goff, 'Rire au moyen age', http://ccrh.revues.org/2918; R.J.W. Evans, *The Humour of History and the History of Humour*, Dacre Lecture, 2011 (Oxford: Dacre Trust, 2012), 10; A.M. Frutos, 'La palabra en la ocasión: Alfonso V como rex facetus a través del Panormita', *e-Spania* 4 (2007); J.M. Pujol, 'Jaume I: *rex facetus*: notes de filologia humoristica', *Estudis Romanics* 25 (2003): 215–36; Theresa Hamilton, *Humorous Structures of English Narratives, 1200–1600* (Newcastle: Cambridge Scholars Publishing, 2013), 56; David Carpenter, 'The Sense of Humour of King Henry III', www.finerollshenry3.org.uk/content/month/fm-11–2011.html; Palmer, *Taking Humour Seriously*, 25. The considered use of displays or performances of emotion for political ends has been discussed, generally with regard to kings, and often with regard to anger or sorrow rather than smiles and laughter: see, e.g., Althoff, 'Ira Regis', in *Anger's Past*, ch.5.; Nash, 'Reality and Ritual', in *Understanding Emotions*, 251–71. Clanchy, 'Law and Love'.

34 R.L. Coser. 'Laughter Among Colleagues', *Psychiatry* 23 (1960): 81–95; Butler, 'Theorizing Laughter'.

35 See above, note 17.

36 See, e.g., *Seipp* 1488.036; YB Mich. 4 Hen. VII pl. 1, f. 15b–17a: Serjeant Kebell, not yet a king's serjeant himself, joshes Serjeant Vavasour, who has reached that rank, about what king's serjeants have to do to earn their fee.

37 *Seipp* 1443.021, YB Hil. 21 Hen. VI pl. 21 f. 33b–34a, which reports a mocking attitude in Hankford (JCP 1398–1413) towards his superior, Thirning (CJCP 1396–1413). Hankford is also reported smiling or laughing as he states (*ridendo dixit*) that the King's Bench judges cannot or do not make mistakes. The smile/laugh here indicates the judge's doubt that his words are literally true, although they acknowledge a 'legal truth' about the position of the King's Bench in relation to the Common Pleas: *Seipp* 1409.049, YB Mich 11 H IV pl 38 f 16b–17a.

38 Hervey de Stanton was, apparently known as 'Hervy le Hasty': *Seipp* 1309.222ss; SS 19, 200.

39 *EELR I*, 1284.2, 1284.9; *RS 31.2* 598; 1284.12, 1284.15, 1286.1, 1287.9, 1289.7; *Seipp* 1440.090, YB Mich. 19 Hen VI pl. 72 f. 34b–35a; *Seipp* 1441.007, YB Hil. 19 Hen. VI pl. 7 f. 50 a-b; *Seipp* 1294.083rs, YB Mich. 22 Edw I pl. 83.

40 *Seipp* 1330.665ss, YB Hil. 4 Edw. III pl. 21.

41 *Seipp* 1443.045; YB Pasch. 21 Hen. VI pl. 23 f 46a–48a. See also *Seipp* 1443.101, YB Mich 22 Hen. VI pl. 42 f. 23b–24a; *Seipp* 1456.060, YB Mich. 35 Hen. VI pl. 6 f. 5a–b; *Seipp* 1456.003, YB Hil. 34 Hen. VI pl.3 f. 25b–26b; *Seipp* 1425.021. YB Hil. 3 Hen. VI pl. 21 f.31b.

42 See, e.g., J.H. Baker, 'Sir Thomas Littleton, d. 1481, Justice and Legal Writer', *ODNB*; J.H. Baker, *The men of court 1440-1550: a prosopography of the Inns of Court and Chancery and the Courts of Law*, SS Supplementary series vol. 18, 2 vols. (London: Selden Society, 2012), 2: 1021.

43 *Seipp* 1462.026; YB Trin. 2 Edw. IV pl. 3 f. 11b; *Seipp* 1462.059, YB Mich. 2 Edw. IV pl. 32 f. 27a–28b. See also *Seipp* 1462.024, YB Trin. 2 Edw. IV pl. 1

f. 10a–b. Creative pleading on the part of a serjeant might be greeted with a judicial smile or laughter, as in another case of 1462 which featured a smile or laughter by Moyle JCP, apparently showing appreciation of creative pleading: *Seipp* 1462.027, YB Trin. 2 Edw. 4 pl. 4 f. 11b–13a. Clearly, the argument being made was unusual, as Moyle said he had not seen it outside moots. Seipp notes the 'light, humorous tone' and courtesy of the whole report and wonders whether this is because the claimant was Serjeant Littleton's mother. In *Seipp* 1462.036, YB Mich. 2 Edw. IV pl. 9, Littleton is reported smiling when, after a break in the case, he produces a statute which he thinks will help his client. Littleton's argument was dismissed by the court – so the smiling here might indicate an attempt to bolster a weak argument, in this case an argument based on a statute which did not apply in the circumstances. Possibly similar is the smiling in the same year by Serjeant Laken, whose client had lost a debt case, as he asked Danby CJCP not to arrest his client: *Seipp* 1462.045, YB Mich. 2 Edw. IV pl. 18 f. 21b.

44 There might be some distortion due to the tastes and influence of the reporters, but since these men were also members of the legal profession, we would not expect their tastes to be significantly out of line with the views and ideals of the profession as a whole.

45 He makes the point that there appear to be two 'first deliveries'.

46 *Seipp* 1378.007am, YB Trin 2 Ric II pl 7; a metaphor echoed by Maitland's invocation of the Ruy Lopez opening: Maitland, 'Of the Year Books', xv.

47 *Gervys v Cooke* (1522); SS 119, 122. *Seipp* 1522.014ss.

48 *Seipp* 1304.160rs, YB Mich. 32 Edw. I pl. 14; *Seipp* 1309.193ss, YB Mich. 3 Edw. II pl. 43; *Seipp* 1441.028, YB Pasch 19 Hen. VI pl. 1 f. 62a–65a.; SS 119, 16, *Filloll v Assheleygh* (1520).

49 *Seipp* 1330.665ss, YB Hil. 4 Edw. III pl. 216; *EELR III*, SS 122, 118–19. Brand, SS 123, xxix doubts the reality of this case.

50 J.M. Kaye, ed., *Placita Corone*, SS Supplementary series vol. 4 (London: Selden Society, 1966), xxxviii; *Seipp* 1309.169ss, YB Mich. 3 Edw. II pl. 19, 19ss 116–118; *Seipp* 1310.152ss, YB Mich. 4 Edw. 2, pl. 11, 22 SS, 64–70.

51 *Seipp* 1337.101rs, YB Mich. 11 Edw. III pl. 38; *Seipp* 1429.003, YB Mich. 8 Hen. VI pl. 9 f. 3b–4b.

52 *Seipp* 1441.028, YB Pasch 19 Hen. VI pl. 1 f. 62a–65a. On the background to this phrase, see Ernst Kantorowicz, *The King's Two Bodies: A Study in Medieval Political Theology* (Princeton: Princeton University Press, 1957), 174–7. One version of the report of *Alice de S v Robert Fox*. SS, 19: 145, *Seipp* 1309.193ss, YB Mich. 3 Edw. II pl. 43 includes a Latin couplet on the consequences on dower of adulterous elopement.

53 *Seipp* 1313.310ss, YB 6 Edw. II Corone 154.

54 *Seipp* 1365.102, YB Mich. 39 Edw. III pl. 28 f. 28a–b.

55 *Seipp* 1457.006, YB Hil. 35 Hen. VI pl. 6 f. 44b–45b. See also a joke about an infant's body not being severable – perhaps a reference to the judgement of Solomon (I Kings 3: 16–27): a Bible story likely to have appealed to medieval judges – *Seipp* 1411.055, YB Hil. 14 Hen. IV pl. 55 f. 37a.

56 See, e.g., Derek Brewer, 'The Comedy of Corpses in Medieval Comic Tales', in *Risus Mediaevalis*, 11–30; Walter Haug, 'Schwarzes Lachen: Überlegungen zum Lachen an der Grenze zwischen dem Komischen und dem Makabren', in *Semiotik, Rhetorik und Soziologie des Lachens*, 49–64 ; Guillemette Bolens, 'Traditions of Similated Folly, in the *Canterbury Interlude* and *Tale of Beryn*', in *Behaving Like Fools*, 15–46, at 31; 'Mankind' in *Medieval Drama: An Anthology*, ed. Greg Walker (Oxford: Blackwell, 2000), 258–79, at 271–3; Lucy Perry, 'Don't Make Me Laugh! Fooling Around in *Sir Gawain and the Green Knight*', in *Behaving Like Fools*, 277–95.

57 *Seipp* 1306.157rs, YB Trin. 34 Edw. I pl. 59.
58 *John the Cooper of T v Isolde widow of Richard Ildok* (1312) *Seipp* 1312.017ss, YB Hil. 5 Edw. 2 pl.17, 31 SS 84–95. Bereford plays with the words 'gros' in the sense of fat (or pregnant?), in a numismatic sense and the legal idea of homage 'in gross', and 'grille' (thin).
59 See, e.g., *Seipp* 1429.001, YB Hil. 7 Hen. VI pl. 1 f. 18b–19a; *Seipp* 1443.042, YB Pasch. 21 Hen. VI pl. 20 f. 43a–b; *Seipp* 1431.027, YB Pasch. 9 Hen. VI pl. 5 f. 2a–b; *Seipp* 1442.049, YB Pasch. 20 Hen. VI pl. 28 f. 30b; *Seipp* 1442.059, YB Trin. 20 Hen. VI pl. 7 f. 37a; *Seipp* 1456.036, YB Trin. 34 Hen. VI pl. 3 f. 43a–b; *Seipp* 1456.069, YB Mich. 35 Hen. VI pl. 15 f. 10a–b.
60 *Seipp* 1286.010ss, YB Mich. 14 Edw. I pl.2; *Seipp* 1496.019, YB Pasch. 11 Hen. VII pl. 4 f. 19b–20b; Brand, *Observing and Recording*, 8. Additional proverbs or maxims: *Seipp* 1307.025rs, YB Hil. 35 Edw. I pl. 25; *EELR II*, p 251, 1286.7; *Seipp* 1463.009, YB Mich. 3 Edw. IV pl. 8 f. 12b–15a; *Seipp* 1454,045, YB Mich. 33 Hen. VI pl. 9 f. 32b–34a; *Seipp* 1309.129ss, YB 2 Edw. II pl. 129; *Seipp* 1344.226rs, YB Mich. 18 Edw. III pl. 64.
61 Grace Frank, 'Proverbs in Medieval Literature', *Modern Language Notes* 58 (1943): 508–15, at 508; W.A. Pantin, 'A Medieval Collection of Latin and English Proverbs and Riddles From the Rylands Latin MS 394', *Bulletin of the John Rylands Library* 14 (1930): 81–114; W.W. Skeat, *Early English Proverbs, Chiefly of the Thirteenth and Fourteenth Centuries, With Illustrative Quotations* (Oxford: Clarendon, 1910).
62 See the suggestion by a serjeant that someone has fallen into a pit which he himself has dug: *Seipp* 1294.088rs, YB Mich. 22 Edw. I pl. 88, *YB 21 & 22 Edw. I RS 31.2*, 448 S – an idea found at several points in the Bible: see, e.g. Ps. 7:16, Prov. 26:27, Sirach 27:29. See also a serjeant telling his opponent that he would not have judgment before Gabriel has blown his horn: *Seipp* 1406.087, YB Trin. 7 Hen. IV pl. 26 f. 19b. This allusion comes from a wider tradition, as the Bible does not specify Gabriel as the musician in this context: see, e.g. David Keck, *Angels and Angelology in the Middle Ages* (Oxford: Oxford University Press, 1998), 65, 170–1; A. Angel, 'Gabriel: Judaism', in *Encyclopedia of the Bible and its Reception*, eds. Christine Helmer et al., vol. 9 (Berlin: De Gruyter, 2014), 859.
63 See *Seipp* 1317.114ss, YB Mich. 11 Edw. II pl. 10; *Seipp* 1317.122ss, YB Mich. 11 Edw. II pl. 8; *Seipp* 1317.153ss, YB Mich. 11 Edw. II pl. 49; *Seipp* 1329.082, YB Trin. 3 Edw. III pl. 5 f. 22a–23a.
64 *Seipp* 1304.027rs, YB Hil. 32 Edw. I pl 27; *Seipp* 1307.020rs, YB Hil. 35 Edw. I pl. 20; *Seipp* 1406.013, YB Hil. 7 Hen.IV pl. 13 f. 9a–b; *Seipp* 1440.003, YB Hil. 18 Hen VI pl. 3 f. 30b–34b; P&M, 1: 422; John Barton, 'Nullity of Marriage and Illegitimacy in the England of the Middle Ages', in *Legal History Studies*, ed. Dafydd Jenkins (Cardiff: University of Wales Press, 1975), 40; Paul Hyams, 'The Action of Naifty in the Early Common Law', *LQR* 90 (1974): 326–50; *LHP*, 243, no. 77, 2a.
65 *Seipp* 1305.017rs, YB Hil. 33 Edw. I pl. 17; *Seipp* 1310.045ss, YB Pasch. 3 Edw. II pl. 10; *Seipp* 1310.152ss, YB Mich. 4 Edw. II pl. 11; *Seipp* 1334.049, YB Pasch. 8 Edw. III pl. 9, f. 20b–23a. In one case, the reporter felt obliged to explain the relevance to the law of the proverb 'One does not know of what metal a bell is made until it has been hit', reportedly quoted by Hankford JCP: *Seipp* 1409.077, YB Mich. 11 Hen. IV pl. 66 f. 34b–37a.
66 *Seipp* 1481.074, YB Mich. 21 Edw. IV. pl. 6 f. 44b–49b.
67 *Seipp* 1333.016; YB Hil. 7 Edw. III pl. 16 f. 7b–8a; *Seipp* 1346.225rs, YB Mich. 20 Edw. III pl. 32; *Seipp* 1459.068, YB Mich. 38 H 6 f. 5 pl. 14 (CP). A.J. Horwood, ed., *Year Books 21 & 22 Edw. I*, xi. Note also the use of this phrase by a serjeant in *Seipp* 1390.023am, YB 13 Ric. II p. 154; John H. Baker and

S.F.C. Milsom, *Sources of English Legal History: private law to 1750* (London: Butterworths, 1986), 267. Note the more respectful use of Biblical authority in *Seipp* 1520.003ss, YB Trin. 12 Hen. VIII pl. 3.

68 *Seipp* 1294.083rs, YB Mich. 22 Edw. I pl. 83. Luke 11:27, Ave Maria.

69 See, e.g., *Seipp* 1309. 212ss; 1310.099ss; 1400.007; 1429.090; 1436.043; 1436.072; 1440.100; 1440.107; 1442.059; 1456.058; 1456.087; 1478.033; 1481.060; 1481.069; 1481.087; 1489.034.

70 *Seipp* 1302.103rs; YB 30 Edw. I pl. 58.

71 RS YB 20 Edw. III part I, 104; RS YB 15 Edw. III, p. 158 no 55; RS YB 20–21 Edw. I vol 31.1, 220. RS YB 21 & 22 Edw. I, p. xi, 211 also notes a lawyer swearing 'by his hood'.

72 See above, note 29.

73 *Seipp* 1313.407ss, YB 6 Edw. II, Atteinte pl.5. SS 24, 182. See also *Seipp* 1310.009ss, YB Hil. 3 Edw. II pl. 9. For the song of Roland and the influence of French literature in England, see, e.g. Rosalind Field, 'Romance in England, 1066–1400', in *The Cambridge History of Medieval English Literature*, 152–78, 154, 165.

74 *Seipp* 1429.051, YB Pasch. 7 Hen. VI pl. 45 f. 37b.

75 *Somer v Sapurton* (1428), *Seipp* 1429.009; YB Mich. 7 Hen. VI pl. 9. f. 5a–7; SS 51, 38–44 (pl. 13). Seipp notes the presence of logic terminology. We see in reports the idea that someone might be enfeoffed to the use of Salisbury Plain or the moon': *Seipp* 1467.049, YB Mich. 7 Edw. IV pl. 11 f. 16a–18b. See also the example of an impossible contract – in which a man tries to bind himself to pay money if he is unable to make the Tower of London come to Westminster: *Seipp* 1310.229ss, YB Mich. 4 Edw. II pl. 88.

76 Paul Brand, 'Courtroom and Schoolroom: The Education of Lawyers in England Prior to 1400', *Bulletin of the Institute of Historical Research* 60 (1987): 147–65, reprinted in Brand, *MCL*, 57–75; Brand, 'Inside the Courtroom', 112.

77 Bolland, *The Year Books*, 2; title pages of Selden Society Year Books series.

78 J.H. Baker, *Legal Education in London 1250–1850* (London: Selden Society, 2007), 7; J.H. Baker, *Catalogue of English Legal MSS in Cambridge University Library* (Woodbridge: Boydell and Brewer, 1996), xxvii–xxix.

79 See, e.g. Horace, *Epistles*, Lib. II, Epist. I, lines 262–3; Jonathan Waterlow, 'Sanctioning Laughter in Stalin's Soviet Union', *History Workshop Journal* 79 (2015): 198–214; *Educational Philosophy and Theory* vol. 46, no.2 (2014), special issue, *Humor, Laughter and Philosophy of Education*.

80 L.M. Paterson, 'Military Surgery: Knights, Serjeants and Raimon of Avignon's Version of the *Chirurgia* of Roger of Salerno', in *The Ideals and Practice of Medieval Knighthood II*, eds. Christopher Harper-Bill and Ruth Harvey (Woodbridge: Boydell and Brewer, 1988), 117–46, at 119; Paul Kershaw, ch. 8 in Halsall, *Humour, History and Politics*.; Robert of Basevorn, *Ars Praedicandi*, translated in James Murphy, *Three Medieval Rhetorical Arts* (Berkeley: University of California Press, 1971), 212.

81 For example, we find a series of Adams, and one Adam and Eve pairing in cases in one set of reports: *RS YB 20–21 Edw I*, *passim* and 392.

82 SS 80, 328.

83 The case concerned a distraint against Simon, which was allegedly contrary to the Statute of Marlborough 1267, st. 52 H III, c 15. Walter's serjeant admitted that he had made a distraint, but pleaded that this had been done as bailiff, for arrears owed to his lord, so that it had not been contrary to the law. The pleading by Laufare, for Simon, which caused derision was that the distraint was not taken for the cause alleged by Walter's side but for another cause. The court was happier to have an issue concerned with whether sums of money were owed.

84 See below, note 87.

85 See, e.g., Stefan Seeber, 'Medieval Humour? Wolfram von Eschenbach's Parzifal and the Concept of the Comic in Middle High German Romances', *The Modern Language Review* 109 (2014): 417–30, at 421–2; Chris Holcomb, *Mirth-making the Rhetorical Discourse on Jesting in Early Modern England* (Columbia, SC: University of South Carolina Press, 2001), 44–5; John Morreall, 'Philosophy and Religion', in *The Primer of Humor Research*, ed. Victor Raskin (Berlin: De Gruyter, 2008), 211–43; J.M. Martin, 'Cicero's Jokes at the Court of Henry II of England', *Modern Languages Quarterly* 51 (1990): 144–66.

86 *Seipp* 1481.051, YB Pasch. 21 Edw. IV pl. 20 f. 26a–b.

87 *Seipp* 1430.083, YB Mich. 9 Hen. VI pl. 37 f. 53b; Baker and Milsom, *Sources*, 56.

88 J.H. Baker, *The Third University of England* (London: Selden Society, 1990), 8, 9, 16–17.

89 For the 'dramatic' side of law reporting, including mention of crying, sighing, smiling, laughter, use of props and gestures, see Brand, 'Inside the Courtroom', 105–7. For Year Book references to anger and annoyance, see, e.g., *Seipp* 1311.106ss, YB Pasch. 4 Edw. II pl. 16; *Seipp* 1534.033, YB Trin. 26 Hen. VIII pl. 26 f. 5b; *Seipp* 1348.135, YB Mich 22 Edw. III pl 25 f. 13a; *Seipp* 1481.001, YB Hil. 20 Edw. IV pl. 1 f. 16a–17a; *Seipp* 1355.186ass, YB 29 Edw. III Lib. Ass. pl. 8 f 57a–b; *Seipp* 1384.037am, YB Mich. 8 Ric. II pl. 8.

90 M.T. Clanchy, *From Memory to Written Record England 1066–1307*, 2nd ed. (Oxford: Blackwell, 1993), 216 and ch. 8; Alberto Manguel, *A History of Reading* (New York: HarperCollins, 1996) ch. 2; Brand, 'Courtroom and Schoolroom'.

91 Note here Paul Brand, 'Judges and Judging 1176–1307', in *Judges and Judging in the History of the Common Law and Civil Law From Antiquity to Modern Times*, eds. Paul Brand and Joshua Getzler (Cambridge: Cambridge University Press, 2012), at 19, 21, 25. See also Bereford's digression, lamenting changes in legal procedure, and marital power, over time: *Seipp* 1312.017SS, YB Hil 5 Edw. II, pl.17.

92 Sir John Fortescue, *De Laudibus Legum Anglie*, ed. and trans. S.B. Chrimes (Cambridge: Cambridge University Press, 1942), 116; Brand, 'Courtroom and Schoolroom'.

93 Johan Verbrerckmoes, 'What About Medieval Humour? Some Historiography', in *Risus Mediaevalis*, 1–10, at 7; Bakhtin, *Rabelais*.

94 On Laufare, see J.H. Baker, *The Order of Serjeants at Law* (London: Selden Society, 1984), 150, 522. This was not the only occasion on which this serjeant was criticised in reports for his poor pleading: elsewhere he was said to have 'pleaded badly' and 'pleaded too feintly'. *Seipp* 1305.075rs, YB Pasch. 33 Edw. I pl. 50; *Seipp* 1307.015rs YB Hil. 35 Edw. I pl. 15; *Seipp* 1309.177ss YB Mich. 3 Edw. II pl. 27, *Seipp* 1310.039ss, YB Pasch. 3 Edw. II pl. 4; *Seipp* 1310.171ss, YB Mich. 4 Edw II pl. 30; *Seipp* 1311.305ss, YB Mich. 5 Edw. II pl. 58; *Seipp* 1312.002ss, YB YB Hil. 5 Edw. II pl. 2.

95 See, e.g., Ives, *Common Lawyers*, 148.

96 See, e.g. *Seipp* 1309.129ss, YB 2 Edw. II pl 129 (remembering a judicial *bon mot*) and *Seipp* 1443.021, YB Hil 21 H VI pl 21 f 33b–34a (recalling judicial laughter). Perhaps the most striking line of reference is that for the line 'Robin Hood in Barndale stood', which Professor Seipp has traced in varying forms from *Seipp* 1429.051, through *Witham v Barker* (1608) Yelverton 147, 148 80 ER 99 (reported as *Metham v Barker* (1608) 1 Brownlow and Goldesborough, 203; 123 ER 761; *Earl of Pembroke v Green and Bostocke* Littleton 223, 225 124 ER 218, 219 (CP 1629); *Read v Dawson* 2 Modern 139, 140, 86 ER 987 988 (CP 1676); *Stanhope v Dawson* 2 Lutwyche 1428, 1434 125 ER 788, 791 (1704), *Lambert v Stroother* Willes 218, 221 125 ER 1140, 1141 (CP 1740);

R v Cotton, Parker 112, 133, 145 ER 729, 735 (KB 1751). See T.H. Ohlgren, *Robin Hood, the Early Poems, 1465–1560: Texts Contexts and Ideology* (Newark: University of Delaware Press, 2007), 212. Likewise, the 'good way to be rid of a shrew' humour of Juyn CJCP in *Seipp* 1436.047, YB 14 Hen. VI. pl. 47 f. 14a was recalled in *Seipp* 1478.026; YB Pasch. 18 Edw. IV pl. 20 f. 4a) and repeated n *Smith v Ash* 1 Croke 58, Hil. 2 Car (I), Hutton 86, 123 ER III9; in *Manby v Scott* 1 Mod. 136, 86 ER 788 Trin. 15 Car. II, Hyde J. See also YB 21 & 22 Edw I RS 31.2, xi.

97 *Seipp* 1376.012, YB Hil. 50 Edw. III pl. 12, f. 5b–6a. For criticisms of women's use of cosmetics for deception of men, see, e.g. Georges Duby, *Women of the Twelfth Century: Eve and the Church*, trans. Jean Birrell, vol. 3 (Chicago: University of Chicago Press, 1998).

For 'shrews', see note 96 above. Paston J's smile or laugh when saying, in a trespass case of 1441 that one would be justified in beating somebody attempting to defile one's wife (to protect 'one's most dear companion') is hard to link with the subject matter of the case: *Seipp* 1441.032, YB Pasch. 19 Hen. VI pl. 5 f. 65b–66a. There might also be humour in the common pleading technique of a serjeant identifying himself with the party he is representing (as noted in Brand, 'Inside the courtroom', 111), if that party was a female, as in YB 20 Edw. III part I, p. 280.

98 BL MS Add 35116 f.186v, translated in Brand, 'Inside the courtroom', 111. See above, note 26.

99 See, e.g. 'Le héron', in *Eighteen Anglo Norman Fabliaux*, Anglo-Norman Text Society, Plain Texts series, vol. 14, eds. Ian Short and Roy Peacey (London: Anglo-Norman Text Society, 2000), 31–3; Darren Hopkins, 'The Original Tale of the Sparrow-hawk', *Monatshefte* 98 (2006): 505–23. In the fuller story, the varlet has sex with the woman again, to 'unfuck' her, and she returns the payment.

100 *Seipp* 1312.017ss, YB Hil. 5 Edw. II pl. 17, 31 SS 84–95. Note also Bereford's reported gratuitous introduction of a tale involving a brothel in a trespass case: *Paris v Page, Seipp* 1308. 1308.003ss, YB Pasch. 1 Edw. II pl. 1.

101 This may seem a rather ill-fitting joke, since the main bone of contention is whether particular legal rights are whole and indivisible, or not. There is, perhaps, some further sexual humour in the mention of rights being 'in gross' or not, which might indicate pregnancy. It is all complicated by the fact that this is a case with multiple reports, and only one has Bereford's joke in it.

102 *Seipp* 1312.140ss, YB Trin. 5 Edw. II pl. 21.

103 *Seipp* 1336.045, YB Pasch Edw. III pl. 9 f.17b; *Seipp* 1345.104rs, YB Trin. 19 Edw. III pl. 5. See also *Seipp* 1506.017, YB Hil. 21 Hen. VII pl. 17 f. 13a–b for apparent humour concerning a woman riding behind a justice on a horse. See also the comment, in the context of alleged rape, that it is 'marvellous' that a child can be engendered without the consent of both parties': *Seipp* 1313.299ss; SS 24, p. 111; Samuel E. Thorne and John H. Baker, eds., *Readings and Moots at the Inns of Court in the Fifteenth Century*, SS vol. 105 (London: Selden Society, 1989), 2: 275.

104 See, e.g. Perfetti, *Women and Laughter*; Antònia Carré, 'The Mirror (1460) by Jaume Roig: Misogyny, Misogamy and Laughter', *Studi Medievali*, ser.3, 50 (2009): 203–29; S.M. Hordis, 'Gender Anxiety and Dialogic Laughter in Malory's Morte Darthur', in *Medieval English Comedy*, 145–70.

105 *Seipp* 1294.183rs, YB Mich. 22 Edw. 1 pl. 183, YB 21 & 22 Edw I RS 31.2, 618 For the poor state of Anglo-French relations at this time: see, e.g. Michael Prestwich, *Edward I* (London: Methuen, 1988), ch.15.

106 *Seipp* 1470.006, YB Hil. 9 Edw. IV pl.5 f. 49a. This case seems to be *William Copley and Margaret or Margery his wife v. Henry Daubere recently mercer*

of London (1470) CP 40/834 m. 23, concerning the goods of Margaret's late husband, John Grenefeld. If this identification is correct, a 'light' mood might be explained by the fact that the case involved people well known to the court: William Copley was chief prothonotary of the Common Pleas, and John Grenefeld was a serjeant at law: Ives, *Common Lawyers*, 464; Baker, *The Order of Serjeants at Law*, 45; Baker, *Men of Court*, 1: 519–20.

107 See, e.g. Andrea Ruddick, *English Identity and Political Culture in the Fourteenth Century* (Cambridge: Cambridge University Press, 2013), ch. 3, especially at 142.

108 *Frankessh v Bokenham* (1490), Baker and Milsom, *Sources*, 622–3; KB 27/915 m.27, SS, 115: 27. For regional antagonism, see H.M. Jewell, *The North-South Divide: The Origins of Northern Consciousness in England* (Manchester, Manchester University Press, 1994), especially chs. 2 and 3. On medieval thought about Norfolk, see Naomi Riches, *The Agricultural Revolution in Norfolk*, 2nd ed. (London: Frank Cass, 1967), 36; *Anonymi Petroburgensis Descriptio Norfolciensium* and refutation by John of St Omer, in *Early Mysteries and Other Latin Poems of the Twelfth and Thirteenth Centuries*, ed. Thomas Wright (London: Nichols and Son, 1838), 93–8; 99–106.

109 See, e.g., Ives, *Common Lawyers*, especially at 410.

110 Statute of Additions 1413; see, e.g., Peter Coss, *The Origins of the English Gentry* (Cambridge: Cambridge University Press, 2003), 4, 216–38.

111 *Seipp* 1430.083, YB Mich. 9 Hen. VI pl. 37 f. 53b; CP Mich 9 H VI pl 37 f. 53b.

112 *Seipp* 1425.021. YB Hil. 3 Hen. VI pl. 21 f.31b; *Seipp* 1436.051 YB 14 Hen. VI pl. 51 f. 15a–b.

113 *Seipp* 1310.152ss, YB Mich. 4 Edw. II pl. 11.

114 *Seipp* 1321.130ss, YB 14 Edw. II Corone pl. 15; *Seipp* 1369.116 YB Mich 43 Edw III pl. 43, f. 33b–34a.

115 *Richard Gervys's Case* (1522), 119 SS 108, at p. 115. See, e.g., Jerónimo Méndez, 'The bad behaviour of friars and women in medieval Catalan fabliaux and Chaucer's Cantebury Tales', *Skepsi* 3 (2010): 52–63.

116 *Seipp* 1481.074, YB Mich. 21 Edw IV. pl. 6 f. 44b–49b.

117 Classen, *Laughter*, 4.

118 D.H. Green, 'Orality and Reading: The State of Research in Medieval Studies', *Speculum* 65 (1990): 267–80, at 277; Brand, 'Courtroom and Schoolroom', 155, 158, 164.

12 Men of law and professional identity in late medieval England

Anthony Musson

The last quarter of the twentieth century witnessed an explosion of academic concern for the history of the legal profession in England. Essays and monographs on the 'rise' of legal practitioners across the chronological spectrum (from the Middle Ages to the nineteenth century) re-energised perspectives on the development of its different branches and provided a platform for an historical re-assessment of the profession in action.[1] Revisionist work on its origins was spearheaded by Paul Brand in a seminal article 'The Origins of the English Legal Profession',[2] later expanded into a more comprehensive study of the same title,[3] which was in some ways responding to the gauntlet laid down a decade previously by Robert Palmer in a similarly entitled article.[4] While Brand's work was in some ways a corrective of the somewhat anachronistic argument initially adopted by Palmer,[5] in fact both approached the subject from very different angles, stressing particular facets and characteristics they saw as defining the nascent profession or 'professionalism'.[6]

Examining the nature of legal professional identity in light of this and subsequent research in the fields of legal and social history, this paper assesses what contemporaries (and historians have) understood by 'men of law' and how lawyers themselves perceived their own status within the profession. In so doing it focusses on the paradoxes of the legal hierarchy, the ambiguities in terminology, deliberate refusal of promotion and attempts both to mask professional status and obscure social origins. Drawing on diverse legal, literary and visual sources (including wills, tomb effigies, memorial brasses), it aims to recapture lawyers' professional identities (including their self-representation) by exploring the interface with their private personas. Evaluating evidence from the mid-thirteenth to the late fifteenth centuries both within and outside the immediate professional legal world, it demonstrates the importance of adopting a holistic view in order to provide a balanced assessment of the evolution of the profession.[7]

Terminology

Views on what constitutes the legal profession (and whether it is indeed a single profession)[8] differ. Scholars have followed particular paths, partly because of the perspectives and agendas adopted initially, partly as a result of the nature of the sources examined, their availability and intelligibility, and the comparative abundance (or paucity) of information yielded.[9] Researchers have been able to build incrementally on earlier work and new perspectives or more interdisciplinary approaches have led to revisions or refinements to previous stances.[10] In terms of the evolution of the legal profession and 'professionalism', much has depended upon whether a narrow view has been adopted: one that focusses predominantly on the elite, the well-defined and measurable activities of the serjeants-at-law and higher judiciary and those whose practice was largely focussed on the Westminster courts.[11] Studies of leading lawyers, such as William Bereford, Geoffrey le Scrope, William Shareshull and Thomas Kebell,[12] and legal dynasties, such as the Scropes, Stonors, Willoughbys, Thorpes and Townsends, have further enriched perspectives on the development of the legal profession, but again primarily from the point of view of those at the apex of the hierarchy.[13] By contrast, other historians have advocated a broader perspective, one that explores the whole spectrum of the legal profession and incorporates the activities of men of law in the provinces. They identify as a key dynamic in its growth men who were not only acting as attorneys in the central courts, but who were employed in a variety of roles as local officials (e.g. stewards, bailiffs, under-sheriffs, coroners, town clerks) and those involved (either judicially, administratively or in a representative capacity) in the assizes, gaol deliveries, peace sessions and the shire, hundred, urban and manorial courts.[14]

The dichotomy that has emerged for legal historians, therefore, lies in the extent of the legal profession in the Middle Ages and thus to whom the term lawyer or 'man of law' can justifiably be applied. Is the legal profession (as a profession) solely the clearly differentiated elite? Did 'man of law' equally refer to those outside the charmed circle? Was there an over-arching, all-embracing single legal profession, albeit one comprising a spectrum of practitioners (men of law)? If the latter, a further concern is how far down the scale should the term be stretched and whether all constituents merit the label 'professional'? Both Brand and Palmer offer definitions or tests for what to their minds constitutes the hallmark of a 'professional lawyer': possession of legal knowledge or expertise, a willingness to offer legal advice or services to others and an expectation of remuneration (what Donahue terms 'the classic sociological definition of a profession'),[15] further measured by the proportion of time devoted to professional activities, the amount gained financially from legal service and the length of time the practitioner has been engaged in such work.[16] Arguably, though, their definition does not necessarily take into account medieval patterns of work and service or the multiple occupations that contemporaries (even those within the established elite) balanced.[17] Did an astute and intelligent individual earning a living from less than full-time involvement in legal activities (in a strict sense) make him any less part of the legal profession?

Social historians have viewed the activities of men of law from the opposite end of the telescope and brought another perspective to the debate. Charting the rise of the gentry as a social class and examining the composition and functioning of lordly affinities within county communities, they have adopted a more inclusive approach.[18] Lawyers' capacity for social mobility is seen as a catalyst in the formation of the gentry class and their professional relationships an integral part of their own identity.[19] The men of law amongst the earl of Warwick's annuitants, for example, are referred to as 'professionals' to distinguish them from members of the gentry, though there is nevertheless some overlap between them, making identification 'a difficult and somewhat subjective exercise'.[20] Since every large landowner relied on lawyers for advice and assistance, increasingly so given the growing complexity of estate management, it made sense both to have a core of salaried staff with 'a sound working knowledge of the law' (some of whom were retained for long periods of time) as well as those who could be brought in for specific cases on a more short-term basis. Indeed, the 'legal element' of the duke of Buckingham's council in the 1440s apparently 'all . . . possessed the highest qualifications'.[21]

These sets of views are not irreconcilable if the question is looked at holistically. Royal, lordly, civic or ecclesiastical service in a legal and administrative capacity or on judicial commissions (of oyer and terminer, gaol delivery and as justices of the peace and members of the 'quorum') provided vital experience and connections for those who later went on to be serjeants and judges as much as those who did not go on to ascend the professional ladder.[22] Indeed, some magnates (and kings) were keen to advance the careers of 'promising lawyers' making service to the crown, the church or in a lord's affinity a significant starting point for ambitious men of law.[23] In a more multi-dimensional model, the legal profession is a dynamic entity in which practitioners should be viewed both diachronically and synchronically: the careers and fortunes of individuals and particular cohorts can thus be examined at a fixed point or over a more extended timeframe. It is not the ranks or positions that are definitive or important as such, but the fact that men of law are distinguished and united by technical know-how and a common ethos, irrespective of the level at which they operate or the point at which they are viewed (captured) within the profession.

In this respect lawyers' self-representation of their professional status should also be acknowledged and brought into the equation. It can be seen to an extent in their wills and testaments,[24] but more overtly observed in monumental inscriptions. These are an important signifier of the way in which law as a profession or calling was gaining greater recognition and legitimation within the culture of funerary epitaphs, but confirmation, too, of what individuals within the profession regarded as important markers of status. They provide details of rank, affiliations or explanations of the post they held in service of the king or a local magnate – what they (or their family) considered necessary (or fitting) for posterity. Robert Thorp (d.1372), for example, is remembered on his memorial (formerly extant in Peterborough Abbey) purely as 'cancellarius domini regis Angliae', his highest post, but one he held for little over a year.[25] For others their legal reputation was clearly important: John Rede (d.1404), is recorded as 'quondam serviens [ad legem][26] domini Regis' on his brass at Checkenden (Oxon), while John Edward's brass in Rodmarton (Gloucs) recalls him as being 'famosus apprenticius in lege peritus' at his death in 1461.[27] The breadth of service and honourable connections is revealed in the case of William Estfield (d. 1386), who is referred to as 'steward of the lordship of Holderness and the honour of Tickhill with Queen Philippa and of the lordship of Hatfield with Edmund, duke of York' at Tickhill (Yorks).[28]

With an expansion in the opportunities open to lawyers during the fifteenth century, the tendency to note major (and even minor) offices and their royal or magnate connection becomes more noticeable: William Hudesfield (d.1499) was remembered as Attorney-General to King Edward IV, and of the Council to King Henry VII and Justice of Oyer and Terminer.[29] John Darrell (d.1438) was steward to the Archbishop of Canterbury according to his brass at Little Chart (Kent); Robert Constable (d.1454) is noted on his memorial at Bossall (Yorks) as having been chancellor of Durham; while Henry Unton (d. 1470) is recorded as chirographer in the court of common pleas on his brass at Sculthorpe (Norfolk).[30] Nicholas Rody (d.1458), steward and counsel to the collegiate church of St Mary's Warwick requested that his memorial should bear the inscription 'Pray for the sowle of Nicholas Rody sumtyme steward of this towne'.[31] Former steward of York Minster, Miles Metcalfe, desired burial in the Minster in 1486 and wanted his monumental inscription to reflect the fact he had served the city as recorder. Someone also decided to mention his service to the Duchy as a Justice at Lancaster.[32] Some practising lawyers who had attended Oxford or Cambridge equally regarded their degree as a significant marker of status and included the qualification on their memorial. William Crofton (d.1480) records both his BCL and membership of Gray's Inn on his brass at Trottescliffe (Kent).[33] The monumental inscription thus had an important function in communicating professional identity, providing a veritable curriculum vitae for the on-looker.

The ambiguity and confusion over terminology is something that contemporaries, too, recognised and (in typical medieval fashion) perpetuated. From fourteenth- and early fifteenth-century legislation and petitions it is apparent that 'man of law' was a phrase used without special differentiation when referring to lawyers generally.[34] In particular, the term is used to describe the preferred appointments to the 'quorum' of the peace commission and other posts where legal knowledge is insisted upon (such as the justices of labourers). In the case of the 'quorum' (and gaol delivery/oyer and terminer commissions) the men of law are predominantly county-based lawyers with the addition of senior lawyers from the central courts (serjeants, king's serjeants) serving on the assize circuits.[35] The term is also employed in the royal ordinance of 1372 in respect of lawyers (*gents de ley*) elected to parliament as knights of the shire.[36] Indeed, the men of law returned to parliament were characterised as typically those who were legal advisors to important men in the county; they were therefore well connected and drew up or advised on parliamentary petitions.[37] It is further used in a generalised way to describe the personnel chosen to conduct special inquiries[38] as well justifying conduct. Thomas, earl of Lancaster, for example, in a petition to the king (1319–22), explained he had acted on the advice of 'gents de ley'.[39] The parliamentary writs of 1404, by prohibiting the election of any apprentices or any other men of law (*aut apprenticius sive aliquis alius homo ad legem*),[40] equally indicate that 'men of law' was a catch-all term.[41] As a phrase, 'homme de ley' can also be observed in the fourteenth century in the identification of specific individuals who are clearly provincial lawyers.[42] William Ellis, for example, retained by the abbot of St Augustine's Canterbury for judicial hearings in Sandwich in 1380 and briefly king's attorney in the court of common pleas (1380–1), is described as 'homo legis' in the Poll Tax returns of 1380.[43] Another county-based practitioner, John Lopynford, who appeared as an attorney in the court of common pleas in the 1380s[44] and built up a practice in Devon representing clients at the Exeter assizes and in the central courts,[45] is identified as 'homme de ley a Honnington' (Honiton).[46]

Application of the term by contemporaries in other documents or scenarios, however, demonstrates things were not quite so straightforward. When applied in specific instances, the phrase 'man of law' could be regarded as synonymous with 'sergeant'. For example, William de Miggele, who was a serjeant-at-law (called in 1309),[47] is described as 'homme de ley' in the response to a petition of 1320 appointing certain 'faithful and suitable justices' to an oyer and terminer commission.[48] While there was no statutory stipulation until 1340 that assize justices had to be serjeants,[49] the link was made in a petition of Edward II's reign concerning the holding of assizes in Northumberland. It was assumed that Robert Barton,[50] even though he was not a serjeant-at-law, was nevertheless of similar status to William Denum, who was, since both men were described as 'gents de lei'.[51] Moreover, the language of both a parliamentary petition of 1384 concerning 'men of law' (*homme de loi*) acting as assize justices in their own home counties and the resulting legislation of the same year demonstrates the two were interchangeable since 'man of law' can only be referring to those who were not otherwise members of the judiciary, in other words, sergeants.[52] This is backed up by literary evidence: the poet, John Gower in *Mirour de l'omme* refers to both 'sergants du loy' and 'gens du loy' in a way that implies he understood the terms were similar and interchangeable,[53] while William Langland's reference in *Piers Plowman* to 'men of lawe . . . that pleteden' may be an elaboration of their role, but similarly suggests the two could be synonymous.[54] The ambiguity is also highlighted in the character of the 'Sergeant of the Law' in *The Canterbury Tales*. Ostensibly Chaucer's pilgrim can be understood in very specific terms, but his subsequent address by the Host as 'Man of Law'[55] may underline the fact that the two could be regarded as synonymous, or in turn expect the audience to regard him as a representative of the legal profession in general.[56]

The elasticity of the term 'man of law' in the fourteenth century has been regarded as problematic, especially if one is trying to gauge the scope of the legal profession on the basis of the extent of legal knowledge required.[57] There is no reference in Brand's or Palmer's prerequisites to particular educational requirements or formal levels of attainment. This may of course reflect the fact that there were no qualifications as such available in the common law in this period (unlike the degrees in Roman civil law and canon law available in the universities).[58] Although there was physical provision for students (from the early fourteenth century) to observe the law in action in the Westminster courts and for demonstrating legal erudition in the nascent Inns of Court (from at least the 1340s), it was probably practical skills, innate ability and a good reputation that demonstrated legal acumen before membership of the Inns came to be an inherent marker of being 'learned in the law' (*juris peritus*).[59] While evidence of legal training or details of membership of the Inns (and thus evidence of access to their legal learning) is extremely sparse before the early fifteenth century,[60] the close relationships between members of the legal fraternity employed in the courts themselves (including the clerks), in baronial affinities, ecclesiastical institutions and civic centres, strongly suggests the acquisition of pragmatic legal literacy through a combination of private reading and practical experience enhanced by mentoring and coaching from other lawyer.[61] These intangible relationships can be glimpsed in the appointment of feofees and executors, in the geographical proximity of houses,[62] and in the gifts made in wills.[63]

Professional advice was sought in connection with numerous legal undertakings, transactions and contentious issues, be they marriage arrangements, property deals, inheritance matters, contracts, personal injury or damage to property. Even though there are sometimes clear stipulations in contemporary documents that men 'knowing the law' are required,[64] it is difficult to get a clear sense of how learned or well-equipped they needed to be or what status of practitioner was intended. In 1380 William Gilbert specified in a petition that he wanted errors in the judgment of his plea of debt corrected by 'les justices, sergeantz et autres *apris de la ley*',[65] suggesting that other lawyers (of unspecified rank) were deemed competent in addition to the justices and serjeants-at-law. In his will, provincial lawyer Richard de Flore (d.1427) advised his wife and child simply to find 'a wel lerned man of the lawe' to ensure the property he had left to them remained intact,[66] but does not otherwise specify what precisely he had in mind. Moreover, slightly different terminology is employed at times and though the meaning is probably the same, it is not clear whether emphasis should be placed on the finer linguistic nuances. As might be expected, in relation to certain judicial posts appointees were required (or desired) to be sufficiently knowledgeable (or skilled) in the law and of good reputation (*sufficialment apris de la ley e de bon condicion*),[67] and similarly for the office of recorder (*sachaunt de la ley et de bon fame*).[68] Requests for matters to be heard by or set before men described as 'sages de la ley'[69] may imply people with skill or training ('wise') in the law were envisaged. Parliamentary input on the composition of the peace commissions in 1352 equally recommended 'les plus loialx et sages de la ley', suggesting not only the most trustworthy, but those proficient in the law. It is significant, however, that an unofficial abstract of the statute of Westminster of 1361 (concerning peace commissions), drawn up in about 1362, substitutes 'sages de la ley' for 'hommes de ley' in the text. This phrase is open to interpretation: while it could mean that rather than appointing ordinary 'men of law' (in the broad sense), more knowledgeable persons were desired; or another reading of this alteration might be that it was not considered necessary for appointees to the 'quorum' of the peace commission to be an *homme de ley* (in the narrow sense), rather someone knowledgeable in the law.[70]

Arguably differentiation within the hierarchy was based predominantly on the nature of the legal practice, the type of work undertaken, clientage and its location. Indeed, some distinctions can be made on the grounds of the specialised nature of the legal work (requiring a higher degree of legal knowledge or a particular skill) over more generalised practice. In 1316 Robert Darcy contested the extent of his knowledge of the law when he disingenuously tried to wriggle out of responsibility for an error in the record and process of a plea of trespass. Although he had served on numerous royal commissions, Darcy maintained that unlike his colleague, William de la Launde who was an 'home de lay',[71] he was only an 'homme d'armes' and so not learned in the law (*ne savoit les lays*). Presumably he was trying to claim that he was not expected to have training or formal qualification if he was a knight rather than a lawyer. The argument did not carry sufficient weight as the fact that he was the designated senior justice meant the responsibility was his.[72] Lack of formal training or recognised legal status did not absolve royal justices from liability for mistakes. But there were frequent overlaps between the tasks carried out by personnel otherwise differentiated by their function or office held, thus making in some cases the construction of strict professional hierarchies problematic.[73] The basic bifurcation of responsibility to the client between attorney and pleader, for example, could be regarded as a significant distinction, but as Nigel Ramsay warns: 'categorization of lawyers by or within the type of legal activity in which they were principally engaged – that is as pleader and attorney – can produce false distinctions.'[74] For example, John de Codyngton describes himself in a petition of 1337 as 'an apprentice of the king's court and attorney'.[75] Equally, someone could be an attorney in the court of common pleas or king's bench, yet, as in the case of John Fleming (of Exeter) also appear for clients in the local courts.[76] William Eyre (d.1509) clearly represents himself as an all-rounder: on his memorial at Great Cressingham (Norfolk) he establishes initially that he is *legis peritus* ('learned in the law'), but adds that he was sometime a member of the quorum of the peace commission of Suffolk and Norfolk, an attorney in the court of common pleas and later a bencher of the Middle Temple.[77]

Moreover, as the legal records and other documentation reveal, men with legal know-how were called upon to give advice and write or interpret legal documents for clients occupying every level of the social hierarchy (including the unfree).[78] These were people for whom local practitioners were the first port of call.

> At the bottom was a proletariat of local legal officials, land agents, professional courtkeepers and hommes d'affaires, men miles away from and below Westminster Hall, but at once the most numerous and, for the mass of the population, the only lawyers who mattered.[79]

Aside from drawing up petitions and legal instruments, town clerks and scriveners acted as feofees and represented clients in arbitrations in the same way as other legal professionals higher up the 'food chain'.[80] From what little evidence about them can be gleaned from the records, we know that they are there,[81] but as the late Christopher Brooks found in his influential study of the Elizabethan legal profession, the lower echelons comprised (then as earlier) 'an extremely diverse group of men who defy easy categorisation or definition'.[82] The terminology is confusing and often misapplied, but only serves to underline the breadth and depth of the legal profession.

Refusal of legal promotion

The complexity of the picture of professional identity is further revealed by the fact that at all levels of the hierarchy there were lawyers who, in spite of the financial incentives and professional distinction that might accrue, never ascended the professional ladder when the opportunity arose. For a group stereotypically concerned with status, men of law from a variety of backgrounds nevertheless eschewed promotion to the higher judiciary, the order of serjeants-at-law or becoming a bencher in their Inn of Court. In some cases this was as a result of circumstances beyond their control: John Bowes was stricken by illness and had to be replaced as recorder of London just as his legal career was taking off,[83] while Alexander Anne (senior) expired before he could assume the coif.[84] For others, it was because they deliberately refused to take promotion, preferring (for whatever reason) to remain at their existing station.

Promotion to the higher judiciary, for example, set holders of the office at the apex of the profession. Yet, although Sir John Fortescue (chief justice of King's Bench under both Henry VI and Edward IV) paints a picture of the idyllic life of a royal justice,[85] in practice the work entailed a considerable amount of travel, statutory limitations on the way that they could earn income and frequent arrears of payment by the crown.[86] Accession to the bench brought the potential for royal recognition and greater responsibility (as chief justice of one of the higher courts), but also exposed justices to the vagaries of politics and the whims and idiosyncrasies of the monarch.[87] Dismissal of the judiciary *en masse* in 1289 and 1341 and attainder for treason of the chief justice and six other judges by the Merciless Parliament of 1388 (those providing answers to Richard II's 'Questions to the Judges' issued the previous year) highlighted the jeopardy of collective responsibility.[88] Equally, while high-profile 'sackings' of individuals (or their sudden resignations) such as William Thorp (1350), Henry Green (1365) and William Gascoigne (1413) to take but a few, undoubtedly affected the attitude of the judiciary of the time, the hazards and precariousness of office clearly lived on in the institutional memory.[89]

Given these drawbacks, it is a wonder that leading serjeants risked their fees and their necks by becoming justices. For some, their lack of promotion may have derived from recognition by the crown (and chief justices where consulted) that it would be inappropriate either because of their personality or on account of their political or religious affiliations.[90] If tipped for the judiciary it was probably not political or easy to refuse, but some may have deliberately resisted elevation either through a lack of ambition on their part or because they preferred the more lucrative, comparatively unfettered life of a serjeant.[91] One of the drawbacks may also have been the timing and speed of promotion since elevation to the judiciary too soon after call to the coif evidently brought difficulties in accruing sufficient income to buttress the resulting drop in fees. Having been raised to the bench only two years after becoming a serjeant, William Ayscough was particularly incensed in this respect, maintaining in a petition to Henry VI that:

> by which makyng Justice all his Wynnings that he sholde have hade in the said office of Sergeant and alle the fees that he had in England weere and be cessed and expired fro hym to his grete empoverysshyng for they weere the grete substance of his lyvelode.[92]

Even so, in spite of the prestige attached to the coif, a number of lawyers chosen to become serjeants, did in fact prefer to avoid the call to the degree. Indeed, Thomas Rolf's portrayal in serjeant's robes on his memorial at Gosfield in Essex belies his initial refusal to accept the summons to assume the coif.[93] In light of the stereotypical view of lawyers as concerned only with status and advancement, as the 'fees and robes' of which Chaucer's *Serjeant of the Law* is in receipt implies,[94] refusal of the opportunity to adopt the coif might seem strange, especially since (as noted above) it usually guaranteed business and secured them personal recognition. Indeed, over the course of the fourteenth century, a narrowing of the numbers of serjeants practising had led to a growing exclusivity of the role, effectively forming an elite. From the 1370s to the late 1390s, for example, the number eligible to practise stood at an average of eight per annum, a rate of decline of 82 per cent if measured from the end of Edward I's reign, underlining both the honour and prestige attached to elevation to serjeant-at-law and the level of royal or judicial control exercised over admissions.[95]

An obvious reflection of this and evidence of some concern attached to it is observable in the crown's resort to monetary penalties for those who sought to avoid the honour, just as it did with men deemed eligible to assume knighthood.[96] While it may not have been considered a problem initially, the fluctuating level in the penalty threatened by the king's council demonstrates the shortfall in recruits must have been appreciated and intended to deter those nominated from refusing. Introduced at £5 in the 1370s, the fine increased to £100 a decade later. The amount liable to be paid was raised to 500 marks in 1412, before reaching an astronomical £1000 three years later. The swingeing increase in the level underlined royal displeasure in the face of group refusals and continued avoidance.[97] The committal of three of the defaulting serjeants-elect, John Barton, junior; John Hals and William Wynard, to the Tower of London in 1412 and the summoning of further defaulters before parliament in 1417 strongly suggests the king (or members of his council overseeing royal policy and the operation of the courts in his name) took the matter extremely seriously. According to the explanation given at the time, the Crown considered their lack of co-operation as endangering the administration of royal justice and the smooth running of the courts given the number of 'suits, actions and causes which have been submitted and are pending in his courts do not make as good progress as they used to make, because there are so few serjeants at law there'.[98]

Although the apprentices summoned before parliament put forward 'certeins causes et maters' (of which unfortunately there is no further detail in the record)[99] one of the primary reasons for reluctance to assume the estate may have been the 'grete expenses and costes' associated with the call ceremony, as William Ayscough vociferously complained.[100] Even though he went ahead with his own creation in 1438,[101] the giving of gold rings and provision of a sumptuous feast (for which those called usually pooled their resources) could certainly set a serjeant back £100 or more, with the need to recoup it in earnings subsequently.[102] A further disincentive may have been the assumption of other judicial and public duties, such as undertaking diplomatic missions or riding the assize and gaol delivery circuits. The latter, though technically limited by legislation of 1340 to central court justices and king's serjeants, in practice also ensnared some senior serjeants-at-law.[103] Many apprentices-at-law it seems preferred to work in a comparatively less high-powered atmosphere and resisted the call accordingly. William Wynard and John Barton are notable examples in this respect and may have valued more highly their civic responsibilities, regional practices and provincial life-style. Wynard steadfastly refused promotion, preferring to remain as recorder of Exeter until his death in 1442.[104] The acceptance by John Barton, senior, of the recordership of London at the time of his call (1415) may similarly have provided sufficient excuse to gain exemption from the coif.[105] His brother, John Barton junior, steward of St Alban's Abbey (c.1408–29) and one of the earl of Warwick's legal advisors (and on his council) from 1417 must have been extremely reluctant to relinquish his private practice to be able to maintain such stout resolve in the face of the financial and custodial penalties meted out by the Crown before he, too, obtained an exemption.[106]

By the mid-fifteenth century there may have been more liaison between the crown and potential serjeants in advance of election to the order, reducing tensions. But even though there were fewer outright defaulters, exemptions were still sought. While the coif was not a bar to being retained by lordly, civic or ecclesiastical patrons, the cases of John Heydon, Thomas Burgoyne and Thomas Young, who were excused the call in 1442,[107] suggest the time-consuming nature of service with a range of patrons (to say nothing of the financial attractions) may have influenced their response. Having been recorder of Norwich, Heydon's service to the duchy of Lancaster, William de la Pole, duke of Suffolk and Norwich Cathedral, among others, brought him a lucrative practice within East Anglia.[108] Similarly, Burgoyne, undersheriff of London was retained (among others) by the duke of Buckingham as a member of his 'councel lerned'.[109] Candidature for the office of recorder seems to have provided a reasonable excuse. Young, having been appointed recorder of Bristol only a year before his call, in fact managed to put off the coif for another twenty-one years.[110] Guaranteeing an income and civic status, it was increasingly attractive to men of law, though a balance between civic duties and other responsibilities clearly had to be weighed up by those called to the coif and presented an ethical challenge for those promoted to the bench.[111] There were also other legitimate reasons behind the failure to take up the degree. In the case of Roger Huswife, who ceased practising in 1424, it was not a lack of ability or desire for financial wealth, but a change in vocation. Having declined the honour of joining the order of serjeants-at-law, he decided to go into the priesthood instead.[112]

Reluctance and outright refusal to accept promotion within the hierarchy of the legal profession appears strange to modern sensibilities in light of the ambition to succeed required of medieval lawyers. It was perhaps contrary, too, to the expectations that contemporaries had of the legal profession, both inside and outside it. Gower envisaged that serjeants would give gold at their call ceremony, but then be able to recoup the expenditure by reaping the rewards of legal practice thereafter.[113] It is unlikely the reluctance to ascend was purely a financial consideration. The preponderance of refusals to join the coif occur in the later fourteenth and early fifteenth centuries may possibly be linked to the hostilities and uncertainties of these years. During a period when both serjeants and those elevated from their ranks to the judiciary had a prominent role in parliament and were often at the forefront of political events, it would not be surprising to find the legacy of the Peasants' Revolt (which had witnessed such violence to lawyers), the problems created by Richard II's tyranny and the challenges of Henry IV's reign engendering a good measure of reluctance.[114]

Fusion of professional and social status

Identity equally derived from the fusion of professional status and social recognition. In the mid-fifteenth century Fortescue claimed (somewhat idealistically) that 'there is scarce a man learned in the law to be found in the realm who is not genteel or sprung of gentle lineage'.[115] The prestige that attached to the elite body of serjeants-at-law has parallels to other ceremonial forms outside the legal world that are significant for gauging perceptions of the honour and value of this rank. The creation of a serjeant bore close resemblance to the ceremonies associated with assuming knighthood and even the writs of summons bear a striking similarity both to those commanding attendance at parliament as a lord and to the writs ordering the take-up of knighthood. The word 'creation' itself added lustre to the call and underlined that this was not an ordinary appointment to office. Although the ceremonial has some parallels with the formation of guilds and mysteries and with admissions to the church, especially the 'profession' of monks, it is knighthood that draws most similarities.[116] This is noticeable in the elaborate nature of the accompanying feast, which according to Fortescue rivalled a coronation banquet and lasted a week.[117] The ritual and ceremony associated with becoming a serjeant also engendered a sense of community amongst the leading lawyers and over time bred a particular sense of tradition that in turn leant it specialness and exclusivity.

In spite of the redolent associations with knightly rank, serjeants-at-law of the late medieval period were not accorded full social equality. The use of the phrase *status et gradus servientis ad legem* in the writ of the call may theoretically have been equated with an 'estate' (in social terms), but in spite of Fortescue's contention that it was ('*nedum gradus sed et status*'),[118] the coif did not in the minds of (non-legal) contemporaries confer the prized honour of *dignitas*, nor convey the markers of gentility.[119] Unlike the civilian tradition, which (following Bartolus) held that doctors of law were knights through their legal endeavours, there was no equivalent of *seigneurie* or *chevalerie ès lois* for common law practitioners.[120] While they were equated with barons and knights for taxation purposes, this may have reflected an economic rather than social parity. Even though 'serjeant' was used as an addition when required under the Statute of Additions of 1413 (which declared that all parties in original lawsuits must henceforth state their 'Estate, or Degree, or Mystery')[121] and the elaborate call ceremony emulated that of the knight's, it was not until the mid-sixteenth century that a shift occurred in the concept of dignity, enabling the degree of serjeant-at-law to be regarded as comparable with knighthood, certainly in terms of precedence accorded them. Summons from the king to the order of the coif was then recognised as a mark of both professional and social prestige that could be coveted by lawyers.[122]

To an extent, however, a merging of the two cultures had already begun once laicisation of the judiciary was underway during Edward I's reign, thereby enabling rewards for service to be more temporal in essence and focus.[123] From the early fourteenth century professional achievement became entwined with social elevation through the common practice of raising lawyers to knightly rank on promotion to the bench.[124] By Edward III's reign, royal patents to assume knighthood (*l'ordre de chivaler de nos*) were accorded almost automatically to judges appointed to the higher courts of king's bench or common pleas and in some cases to the chief baron of the exchequer.[125] This connection, once initiated, was more or less maintained in order to emphasise and display (both inwardly to the profession and outwardly to the world) the honour and importance of serving the king in high judicial office.

Even the award of knighthood brought differentiation and its own marks of distinction. Letters to the clerk of the royal wardrobe concerning delivery of their apparel demonstrate that the level of knighthood accorded royal justices varied. Robert de Scardeburgh, for example, was appointed a knight bachelor (*bachelier*),[126] whereas William Shareshull was accorded the greater prestige of banneret.[127] Knights banneret were typically senior knights that carried a square banner in the field, commanded a contingent of troops, and had usually distinguished themselves in battle. It was recognised as a slightly higher level of social gradation, though clearly not all recipients of the honour had achieved this militarily.[128] While Chief Justice Geoffrey le Scrope (knighted in 1326), perhaps unusually for a lawyer had gained a reputation as a jouster and soldier,[129] it is unlikely that Robert Charleton, elevated to knight-banneret in 1389 having been appointed chief justice of common pleas the previous year (without previous experience as puisne judge), had seen military action. Some judges, among them John Shardlow (in 1332), William Hankford (in 1399) and Thomas Littleton (in 1475),[130] were even awarded the accolade of being dubbed as knights of the Bath. This was one of the elaborate ceremonial orders of chivalry, advancement to which seems to have occurred in conjunction with various royal ceremonies and was thus a personal accolade from the sovereign in gratitude for the debt of service.[131] Robert Danby, William Yelverton and John Markham were dubbed at Edward IV's coronation in 1461; Walter Moyle and John Needham at that of his queen, Elizabeth Woodville, in 1465. Even if, unlike their military counterparts, lawyers promoted to the higher orders of knighthood had not performed heroic deeds on the battlefield, they enjoyed heightened prestige and status amongst leading men of the realm as well as participating (albeit vicariously) in 'grete worshippe of Knyghthood' and the bonding chivalric ethos.[132] For some men of law, absorption of the knightly image and its honour was in turn reflected in their chosen mode of commemoration:

knight-banneret Henry Scrope (d.1336) was shown in armour on his tomb at Easby Abbey (Yorks) rather than wearing judicial robes.[133]

Knighthood conferred a level of social distinction but the various duties that knights were expected to perform as part of the community of the shire (in terms of local office holding, attending parliament and serving on special commissions and juries), in addition to which there was the expense of the ceremonial *abdoument* and maintaining the status of a knight itself, potentially placed an unwelcome burden on recipients.[134] Even in the sixteenth century Thomas Elyot complained that he had been 'rewarded with the order of knighthood, honourable and onerous, having much less to live on than before'. It is not surprising, therefore, that from the thirteenth century onwards a number of men chose to seek exemption from shire duties as well as avoid becoming knights.[135]

Distraint to knighthood provides an indication of a man of law's substance within a particular county. Richard Choke, for example, appointed a justice of the court of common pleas in 1461, was found by a royal commission of 1465 to have land of at least £40 in Somerset, but had not yet assumed knighthood, which he duly rectified.[136] Even though assessments may not reflect the true value of estates held,[137] some men of law had clearly reached significant income levels. Robert Hill of Spaxton, steward for various landowners in Devon and Somerset and retained for his legal counsel by the earl of Devon, was assessed for tax purposes in 1412 as having income from land of around £140.[138] Yet, displaying perhaps a sense of inverse snobbery, Hill refused to take up knighthood when ordered to do so, paying a fine of £3 as a result.[139] Other lawyers exhibited a similar desire not to have the hollow honour, among them apprentice-at-law John Edwards, who was distrained at 54s 4d (and is not shown in armour on his brass)[140] and erstwhile recorder of Bristol, Thomas Young (at 66s 8d), both in Henry VI's reign.[141]

Ironically some lawyers went to the trouble to secure respite from assuming knighthood only to be compelled to take it up at the behest of the crown a few years later on promotion to the bench. For example John Bousser, Walter Friskeney, Robert Malberthorpe, Edmund Pashley, Gilbert Toutheby and Geoffrey le Scrope were all distrained for refusing knighthood at various times during Edward II's reign prior to their elevation to the judiciary.[142] Similarly a number of Yorkshire lawyers were distrained *en masse* (John Vavasour, Thomas Metcalf, William Fairfax, Edward Remayne, Brian Palmes and William Thwaites), only some of whom capitulated.[143] Thomas Rolf's argument against assuming knighthood made in the Exchequer in 1430 was that he had been enjoined to assume the coif under pain of £1000 on the first occasion (1415) and then 500 marks on the second (1417). Having finally capitulated, he was created serjeant in 1418 and had since then occupied and exercised that estate and degree.[144] This same argument may have been the reverse of John Barton junior's claim for respite from becoming a serjeant made around the same time, which may have been allowed because he had been elected to parliament as knight of the shire for Buckinghamshire in 1417.[145]

Knighthood was not the only marker of social status linked to the profession. According to the 1379 Poll Tax levies, the broad group of apprentices-at-law were, for economic purposes at least, explicitly differentiated 'each according to his estate' by the imposition of three graduated levels of payment.[146] The sum of 40s was payable by 'each . . . great apprentice of the law', similar to that expected of serjeants, which equated with the level for knights. The second category comprised 'other apprentices who follow the law', men such as John Dronsfeld of Monk Bretton (Yorks), who were taxed at 20s, which put them alongside 'bachelors and esquires who by statute ought to be knights'.[147] Finally 'other lesser apprentices', a group that seems to have included Thomas Frisby (probably the same man who eventually became a serjeant in 1401)[148] and attorneys such as William Ellis (see above), were on a level with 'esquires of lesser estate'. Judging by the sums paid by individuals displaying the rank was equivalent to that of franklin, an ambivalent figure in the late fourteenth century, but one who was socially aspirant and probably typified the status of county-based men of law.[149] The new title of 'gentleman', which became a demarcation of gentility in the early fifteenth century through the Statute of Additions (1413), took some time for acceptance, but seems to have been adopted by men of law, particularly those connected with the Inns of Court, who added 'of London' to their status.[150]

While Fortescue was undoubtedly exaggerating when claiming that every man of law possessed the genteel lineage or other attributes of gentility, he was nevertheless reflecting a seismic change in the status genuinely accorded or at least aspired to by 'men of law'. Conversely it was the legal profession that had become the chosen route for the sons of knights and esquires to the extent that William Worcester, writing in the fifteenth century, lamented that instead of taking up arms in pursuit of the chivalric ethos, they 'lerne the practique of law or custom of lande, or of civil matier'.[151] Those already possessing social status were seeking to further their position through the law.

Obscuring identity

A man's identity first and foremost was encapsulated in his name, which at best might reveal pedigree and connections, suggest his family's occupation or geographical location, or at worst betray lowly status and origins. Attempts were made by some men of law to disguise their humble background by adopting an alias or more suitable surname. John Heydon, for example, during the course of his career adopted the surname Heydon from the village his family came from, but was formerly known as John Baxter.[152] A different surname could also promote a new identity, one untainted by less prestigious family associations or that could highlight a particular wing of the family. Thomas Littleton chose (or was perhaps required as part of her marriage settlement) to take his mother's maiden name, rather than his father's name of Westcote (which his brothers used).[153] Richard son of John Craddock of Newtown in Montgomeryshire reinvented himself as Richard Newton when he became a serjeant-at-law in 1425,[154] while Richard Willoughby I's father adopted the name Willoughby from the village of the same name in which his grandfather, Ralph Bugge (d.c.1248), a Nottinghamshire merchant, had cobbled together a manorial estate and settled it on his son.[155]

Another method of influencing impressions, particularly posthumous ones, was by employing visual signifiers on funerary monuments such as particular modes of dress, heraldic devices or other forms of outward display. Men of law, however, appear to have adopted ways of avoiding revealing their professional identity. A number of memorials to fourteenth-century judges represent them in armour rather than in legal costume. Richard Willoughby I (d.1326) lies in effigy in the church at Willoughy in the Wolds, as does Henry Hambury (d.c.1350) at Hanbury (Staffs), while Roger Hillary (d.1356) was also shown in armour in a brass at Walsall (Staffs).[156] It is not as though they did not have knightly status or possess armour, as both Willoughby and Hillary (among others) bequeathed it to their sons, who were also lawyers (and namesakes).[157] However, given that there are extant effigies to other contemporaries such as John Stonor (d. 1354) at Dorchester Abbey and John Stowford (d.1359) at West Down (Devon) portraying them quite similarly in judicial costume, this would appear to be a deliberate choice on their (or their families') part. Given contemporary beliefs in the hereafter, though, we should not think it so unusual if the judges who were portrayed as knights in death considered themselves to be members of the 'whole collectivity of knighthood', which flourished in heaven as it did on earth.[158]

Although the order of serjeants-at-law had developed its own professional identity, very few of the serjeants (who had not been promoted to the judiciary) can be identified by their full legal attire before that to Thomas Rolf, dating from around the mid-fifteenth century. Indeed, the extant memorials suggest the sculptors were not entirely *au fait* with the iconography associated with the profession or it was not stipulated to them in precise enough terms. While the coif might be expected to be a key visual signifier,[159] it is absent from the brass of John Rede (d.1404) at Checkendon (Oxon) and the effigy of Thomas Frisby (d.1408) at Flamstead (Herts).[160] Nor does the retrospective brass at Cople (Beds) commemorating Nicholas Rolond (dating about a century after he was active in c.1310) bear the coif or other professional attributes. Indeed, only two effigies of fourteenth-century serjeants, John Trevaignon at Trent (Dorset)[161] and Nicholas Gour at Pembridge (Heref), are depicted wearing coifs. Moreover, the effigy of serjeant-at-law Henry Power at Limington (Som), datable to about 1345, has no discernible markings of his professional status.[162] Conversely, the effigy of John Cockayne (d.1372), who lies in the family chapel at Ashbourne (Derbs) and is depicted wearing a coif, would suggest deliberate portrayal of legal rank. He was professionally active in the service of the duchy of Lancaster in his native Derbyshire, but there is no evidence surviving indicating he was ever called to the order of serjeants-at-law.[163] The coif (and mantle) may imply legal status or be an iconographic nod towards the fact that he was a serjeant-elect or considered to be worthy of call, but had refused. On the other hand, it may simply be an attribution introduced by the sculptors, unaware of the precise distinctions or as a result of copying from a model elsewhere.[164]

Some men of law who had been knighted preferred to be commemorated in armour, thereby disguising their legal prowess. Sir Thomas Skelton (d.1416), a leading apprentice and chief steward of the Welsh and southern parts of the duchy of Lancaster has a memorial brass in armour in the church at Hinxton (Cambs).[165] Sir William Huddesfield (d.1499), buried in the church of Shillingford St George (Devon) had ample legal qualification, having been attorney general to Edward IV and recorder of Exeter 1483–4, but his emblazoned tabard and armour (complete with spurs, gauntlets and helmet) emphasise his links with the nobility through his second wife, Katherine Courtenay.[166] John Mordaunt (d.1504) is buried in armour reflecting his genuine military service (having fought against the Scots in 1484 and on the side of Henry VII at the Battle of Stoke Field in 1487) and elevation to knighthood a year before his death.[167] It belies, however, his distraint to knighthood several years before and his legal appointments as serjeant-at-law, king's serjeant and chief justice of Chester.[168] More of an enigma is John Barton, the younger (d.1434). Having refused to obey the writ of summons to assume the degree of serjeant, probably on the basis of his election to parliament as a knight of the shire, a position he held five times in all (1414–23), he is commemorated by effigy in the church of Thornton (Bucks) not in lawyers' robes, but in armour, even though he was not technically a knight. Ironically, having achieved exemption from the coif, this attempt to obscure his legal background equally masks the fact that his widow was forced to sell the majority of Barton's six manors in the county to pay off his debts. Her burial in the church alongside him twenty-two years later combined with re-foundation of the chantry he had endowed in the church may thus have provided an opportunity to re-commemorate him posthumously (in a memorial with twin alabaster effigies) as a lordly benefactor emphasising his political and social rather than his legal standing.[169]

A desire to celebrate both knightly and legal status is suggested by an unusual fusion of funerary imagery evident in the case of several fifteenth-century men of law. Sir William Yelverton, for example, a justice of the king's bench, is shown on his brass at Rougham (Norfolk) not only attired in armour, but also wearing a judicial mantle over it. Similarly, the effigy of Sir John Portington, justice of common pleas, in the family chapel at Eastrington (Yorks), although damaged, reveals armour under his cloak. The iconographic melange may have been a conscious decision or accidental as a result of confusion in the mind of the artist over their attributions. Unfortunately, in both cases the memorial inscription is missing. Although about ten years and several hundred miles separates the two images, the earliest example of this combination of social and professional memorialisation is in the incised effigial slab to Hugh Hercy (d.1455) at Grove (Notts). Although he was not knighted, Hercy, who came from an established gentry family, is dressed in armour, but also somewhat incongruously wears the distinctive hat denoting his legal standing.[170]

Memorial brasses to men of law such as Robert Constable at Bossall (Yorks), John Leventhrope at Sawbridgeworth (Herts), Robert Ingleton at Thornton (Bucks) and Robert Staunton (Castle Donington) also depict an armoured figure, but the deceased is an esquire rather than a knight.[171] These were men who had not attained knighthood, but who as esquires, had appropriated the honour of this effigial attire. Taken up by lesser gentry for their memorials from the late fourteenth century onwards, its use signified a fluidity and redefinition in the ranks of the elite.[172] It was employed by lawyers to play down the fact they owed their landed estate to their professional know-how by confirming their standing in their locality. This is notable in the case of Thomas Playter (d.1479), a bencher and later governor of Lincoln's Inn and a legal adviser to Sir John Fastolf. He is memorialised by a brass at Sotterley (Suffolk) where he is dressed in armour and described as an esquire. Acquisition of the lordship of the manor of Sotterley appears to have clinched his social standing and gave him the iconographic license to appear in armour. As Colin Richmond puts it: 'with Sotterley he became a Suffolk gentleman. Manor, house, advowson and church put his gentility beyond question; he had established himself'.[173]

Whether or not they were entitled to be shown wearing it is another matter. Portrayal in armour was clearly not restricted to the armigerous, as Henry Unton's Sculthorpe brass reveals: he is described as 'gentilman'.[174] Although widely accepted by the mid-fifteenth century as signifying an entitlement to arms, the link between military service and social status was not a strong one. Indeed, many professionals styling themselves 'gentlemen' may have adopted coats of arms on their own authority, though in the case of Robert Whitgreve, the accolade was genuinely a gift from the Duke of Buckingham.[175]

The desire to be represented in armour is particularly ironic and redolent of pretension in the case of those who had sought exemption from the burdens of knighthood. William Finderne, for example, sought exemption in 1441, yet is posthumously portrayed wearing armour in an elaborate memorial brass at Childrey, the gilding on which serves to define his surcoat and bring out (when illuminated by candles or sunlight) the heraldic devices emblazoned on it and thereby further emphasise his assumed status.[176] John Harewell's effigy at Wootton Wawen (Warws.) depicts him as a knight, even though he vociferously argued in 1392 against his appointment as county coroner on the grounds that the statute of Westminster required men for this position to be drawn from the 'lawful and wisest knights' and he himself did not have this distinction.[177]

Differences in the attire in which men of law chose to be commemorated can be explained partly as attempts to avoid revealing their social origins. Portrayal in legal clothing, on the one hand, could effectively hide an obscure or lowly background by placing the focus on professional achievement. This would be obvious, too, from the accompanying inscription. Portrayal in 'civilian' clothing,[178] as opposed to armour or legal robes, on the other hand, could not only obscure an individual's legal background (as the route to social mobility) but also blurred social distinctions.[179] While the choice of memorial format, medium and size indicate some were affluent, others show they were perhaps of more modest means.[180] The choice of civilian attire for commemoration may have arisen because they had not achieved sufficiently high professional rank or did not consider themselves members of the landed gentry.[181] Although some esquires chose to portray themselves in armour, William Eyre and others preferred to be depicted in furred robes corresponding to the dress of merchants with whom those local lawyers practising in towns may have shared ideals and ambitions.

Conclusion

The poet, John Gower, characterised the legal profession as the fourth estate, recognising (albeit in his moralising work) that men of law formed a clearly identifiable grouping after the traditional three: knights, clergy and peasants.[182] This paper has examined the broad spectrum of individuals comprising the legal profession, highlighting the need to avoid too narrow a perception of lawyers. It also urges caution in assuming that all lawyers followed the same career path. Combining the various studies that have informed the structure and composition of what may be referred to generally as the legal profession, it is possible to perceive, therefore, that it comprised an amorphous group of men with varying levels of legal knowledge and ability, who had practices that operated on different levels and on a national, regional or purely local scale, but were united by motivation to succeed and their shared ethos and common identity as 'men of law'. As such they formed a community of practitioners engaged in matters of law and justice and together assisting (and no doubt fuelling) society's demand for legal services in an age of expanding legislation, litigation and legal documentation.

> The wide gap between an apprentice who pleaded in Westminster Hall and a petty lawyer who kept a manorial court is obvious, yet in subsuming all common lawyers under one label, popular usage was recognising a vital fact about the profession, its unity.[183]

If a lawyer's sense of identity was dictated in the first instance by his status within the hierarchy of the legal profession, this again is by no means straightforward to analyse. Paradoxically, some men of law refused professional accolades, preferring to accept them only at a time of their own convenience, if ever. Professional identity was also affected by social origins and perceived status in society. Like an individual's career, however, social status should not be viewed purely at one single moment in time, but over a period and was influenced not only by financial benefits, but by external factors such as marriage and political fortunes. The aspirations and pretensions of individuals influenced their outlook, while the social mobility afforded by legal practice led to a blurring of lines and deliberate confusion of identities.[184] Although self-representation can sometimes be a guide, this too can be shown to be subject to misleading and ambiguous elements.

Analysis of the complex trajectories of members of the legal profession and their relationships within society can help us to understand more about who these men of law were, how they operated and how they interlinked not only with the traditional estates (some of whom they derived from or ended up joining), but those within the merchant class and equally within the broad spectrum of the legal profession. The work that Paul Brand has done and inspired over the years has greatly facilitated this. It is up to succeeding generations of historians (of whatever hue) to continue the quest. As Sir John Baker succinctly put it:

> As we uncover more evidence, and try to sift out what is useful, we are simultaneously relating it to our older questions and formulating new ones, until now and again we see enough light to propose some answers. We never produce final answers, but we help to take the general understanding forward. It is a collective exercise.[185]

Notes

1 E.W. Ives, *The Common Lawyers of Pre-Reformation England* (Cambridge: Cambridge University Press, 1983); J.H. Baker, *The Legal Profession and the Common Law* (London: Hambledon Press, 1986) [though some of the essays in this collection appeared far earlier]; C.W. Brooks, *Pettyfoggers and Vipers of the Commonwealth: The Lower Branch of the Legal Profession in Early Modern England* (Cambridge: Cambridge University Press, 1986); W.R. Prest, *The Rise of the Barristers: A Social History of the English Bar, 1590–1640* (Oxford: Clarendon Press, 1986).

2 *Law and History Review* 5 (1987): 31–50; reprinted in Brand, *MCL*, 1–20.

3 Brand, *OELP*.

4 R. Palmer, 'The Origins of the Legal Profession in England', *Irish Jurist*, n.s., 11 (1976): 126–46.

5 See also the distortions pointed out by Peter Coss in 'Knighthood and the Early Thirteenth Century County Court', in *Thirteenth Century England II*, eds. P.R. Coss and S.D. Lloyd (Woodbridge: Boydell Press, 1988), 45–58.

6 Palmer adjusted his stance slightly in his later work: R. Palmer, *The County Courts of Medieval England, 1150–1350* (Princeton, NJ: Princeton University Press, 1982).

7 This paper draws on research carried out for 'Lawyers in Society, 1258–1558' a project funded by the UK Economic and Social Research Council.

8 Sir John Baker asked this in the early 1980s: 'When we contemplate lawyers as a whole, we are bound to wonder whether these diverse men of law can properly be regarded as constituting a single profession' (*Legal Profession*, 76).

9 The scarcity of information on the internal workings of the profession before the records of the Inns of Court start becoming available in the fifteenth century has naturally focused attention on later periods. A valuable prosopographical almanac has been constructed for the period from the mid-fifteenth to the mid-sixteenth centuries on the basis of surviving documentation: *The Men of Court 1440 to 1550: A Prosopography of the Inns of Court and Chancery and the Courts of Law*, ed. Sir John Baker, Selden Society Supplementary Series, 18 (London: Selden Society, 2012).

10 For personal approaches see: Sir J. Baker, 'Reflections on "Doing" Legal History', in *Making Legal History: Approaches and Methodologies*, eds. A. Musson and C. Stebbings (Cambridge: Cambridge University Press, 2012), 7–17; and P. Brand, 'Editing Law Reports and Doing Legal History: Compatible or Incompatible Projects?' in ibid., 18–29.

11 P. Brand, 'The Serjeants of the Common Bench in the Reign of Edward I: An Emerging Professional Elite', in *Thirteenth Century England VII*, eds. M. Prestwich, R. Britnell and R. Frame (Woodbridge: Boydell Press, 1999), 81–102; *The Order of Serjeants at Law*, ed. J.H. Baker, Selden Society Supplementary Series, 5 (London: Selden Society, 1984); *Readers and Readings in the Inns of Court and Chancery*, ed. J.H. Baker, Selden Society, Supplementary Series, 13 (London: Selden Society, 2000).

12 C.P. Cottis, 'Sir William de Bereford, c.1250–1325', unpublished B.Litt diss., University of Oxford, 1958; E.L.G. Stones, 'Sir Geoffrey Le Scrope, Chief Justice of the King's Bench, 1324–1338', unpublished PhD thesis, University of Glasgow, 1950; B.H. Putnam, *The Place in in Legal History of Sir William Shareshull* (Cambridge: Cambridge University Press, 1950); Ives, *Common Lawyers.*

13 C.E. Moreton, *The Townsends and Their World: Gentry, Law and Land in Norfolk c. 1451–1551* (Oxford: Clarendon Press, 1992); E. Noble, *The World of the Stonors: A Gentry Society* (Woodbridge: Boydell Press, 2009); M.R. Bloom, 'The Careers of Sir Richard II de Willoughby and Sir Richard III de Willoughby, Chief Justice of the King's Bench (1338–1340) and the Rise of the Willoughbys of Nottinghamshire', unpublished DPhil thesis, University of Oxford, 1985; B. Vale, 'The Scropes of Bolton and Masham, c.1330–c.1450: A Study of a Northern Noble Family With a Calendar of the Scrope of Bolton Cartulary', unpublished D.Phil thesis, University of York, 1987; R. Kinsey, 'Legal Service, Careerism and Social Advancement in Late Medieval England: The Thorpe's of Northamptonshire, c. 1200–1391', unpublished D.Phil thesis, University of York, 2009. See also D.J.M. Higgins, 'Judges in Government and Society in the Reign of Edward II', unpublished D.Phil thesis, University of Oxford, 1986.

14 E.W. Ives, 'The Common Lawyers in Pre-Reformation England', *Transactions of the Royal Historical Society*, 5th series, 18 (1968): 145–63; R.C. Palmer, 'County Year Book Reports: The Professional Lawyer in he Medieval County Court', *English Historical Review* 91 (1976): 776–801; N. Ramsay, 'What Was the Legal Profession?', in *Profit, Piety and the Professions in Later Medieval England*, ed. M. Hicks (Gloucester: Alan Sutton, 1990), 62–71; N. Ramsay, 'Scriveners and Notaries as Legal Intermediaries in Later Medieval England', in *Enterprise and Individuals in Fifteenth Century England*, ed. J. Kermode (Stroud: Alan Sutton, 1991), 118–31; A. Musson, *Public Order and Law Enforcement: The Local Administration of Criminal Justice, 1294–1350* (Woodbridge: Boydell Press, 1996); T. Haskett, 'Country Lawyers: The Composers of English Chancery Bills', in *The Life of the Law*, ed. P. Birks (London: Hambledon Press, 1993), 9–24; A. Musson, *Medieval Law in Context: The Growth of Legal Consciousness From Magna Carta to the Peasants' Revolt* (Manchester: Manchester University Press, 2001); S.J. Payling, 'The Rise of

Lawyers in the Lower House, 1395–1536', *Parliamentary History* 23 (2004): 103–20; D. Youngs, *Humphrey Newton (1466–1536) an Early Tudor Gentleman* (Woodbridge: Boydell Press, 2009); K. Bevan, 'Clerks and Scriveners: Legal Literacy and Access to Justice in Late Medieval England', unpublished PhD thesis, University of Exeter, 2013.

15 C. Donahue, Jr. 'The Legal Professions of Fourteenth-Century England: Serjeants of the Common Bench and Advocates of the Court of Arches', in *Laws, Lawyers and Texts: Studies in Medieval Legal History in Honour of Paul Brand*, eds. S. Jenks, J. Rose and C. Whittick (Leiden: Brill, 2012), 227.

16 Brand, *OELP*, vi; Palmer, *County Courts*, 89.

17 Ives, *Common Lawyers*, 12–16, 20; M. Tompkins, '"Lets Kill All the Lawyers": Did Fifteenth-Century Peasants Employ Lawyers When the Conveyed Customary Land?', in *Identity and Insurgency in the Late Middle Ages*, ed. L. Clark (Woodbridge: Boydell Press, 2006), 83–5; *Concepts and Patterns of Service in the Later Middle Ages*, eds. A. Curry and E. Matthew (Woodbridge: Boydell Press, 2001).

18 P. Coss, *The Origins of the English Gentry* (Cambridge: Cambridge University Press, 2003); C. Rawcliffe, *The Staffords, Earls of Stafford and Dukes of Buckingham, 1394–1521* (Cambridge: Cambridge University Press, 1978); S. Walker, *The Lancastrian Affinity, 1361–1399* (Oxford: Clarendon Press, 1990); S.J. Payling, *Political Society in Lancastrian England* (Oxford: Oxford University Press, 1991); C. Carpenter, *Locality and Polity: A Study of Warwickshire Landed Society, 1401–1499* (Cambridge: Cambridge University Press, 1992); E. Acheson, *A Gentry Community: Leicestershire in the Fifteenth Century, c.1422–1485* (Cambridge: Cambridge University Press, 1992); H. Castor, *The King, the Crown and the Duchy of Lancaster, 1399–1461* (Oxford: Oxford University Press, 2000).

19 Professional interaction can be explored through the correspondence preserved for certain families: e.g. *The Plumpton Letters and Papers*, ed. J. Kirkby, Camden Society, 5th series, 8 (1996); *Kingsford's Stonor Letters and Papers, 1290–1483*, ed. C. Carpenter (Cambridge: Cambridge University Press, 1996); *The Paston Letters and Papers of the Fifteenth Century*, eds. N. Davis, R. Beadle and C. Richmond, 3 vols. (Oxford: Oxford University Press, 1971–2005).

20 Carpenter, *Locality and Polity*, 267 especially n.23.

21 Rawcliffe, *Staffords*, 75. These included serjeants-at-law, apprentices and other men of law.

22 E.W. Ives, 'Promotion in the Legal Profession of Yorkist and Early Tudor England', *Law Quarterly Review* 75 (1959): 348–63; N. Ramsay, 'Retained Legal Counsel, c.1275–c.1475', *Transactions of the Royal Historical Society*, 5th series, 35 (1985): 95–112; P. Brand, 'Stewards, Bailiffs and the Emerging Legal Profession in Later Thirteenth Century England', in *Lordship and Learning: Studies in Memory of Trevor Aston*, ed. R. Evans (Woodbridge: Boydell Press, 2004), 139–53; A. Musson and W.M. Ormrod, *The Evolution of English Justice: Law Politics and Society in the Fourteenth Century* (Basingstoke: Macmillan, 1999), 62–8; P. Tucker, *Law Courts and Lawyers in the City of London, 1300–1550* (Cambridge: Cambridge University Press, 2007), 240–71.

23 Rawcliffe, *Staffords*, 159–60; M.J. Bennett, *Community, Class and Careerism: Cheshire and Lancashire Society in the Age of Gawain and the Green Knight* (Cambridge: Cambridge University Press, 1983); G. G. Astill, 'Advancement Through Seignorial Service: The Case of Simon Pakeman', *Transactions of the Leicestershire Archaeological Society* 54 (1978–9): 14–25.

24 Though these can sometimes be uninformative and are generally somewhat prosaic.

25 London, British Library, MS Additional 71474 f. 121r (Sir William Dugdales' *Book of Monuments*); Kinsey, 'Thorpes' 21, 40–2. He had been chief justice of common pleas for 15 years (1356–71).

26 These words are defaced.
27 M. Stephenson, *A List of Monumental Brasses in the British Isles* (London: Headley Brothers, 1926), 155, 401.
28 Stephenson, *Monumental Brasses*, 560.
29 Stephenson, *Monumental Brasses*, 94–5.
30 S.R. Glynne, *Notes on the Churches of Kent* (London: J. Murray, 1877), 157; Stephenson, *Monumental Brasses*, 364, 544.
31 Exchequer, Treasury of Receipt, Ancient Deeds Series A, E 40/4653 (will of Nicholas Rody).
32 *Testamenta Eboracensia IV*, ed. J. Raine, Surtees Society, 53 (1869), 9.
33 Stephenson, *Monumental Brasses*, 263.
34 Musson and Ormrod, *Evolutioni*, 56–7.
35 E. Powell, 'The Administration of Criminal Justice in Late Medieval England: Peace Sessions and Assizes', in *The Political Context of Law*, eds. R. Eales and D. Sullivan (London: Hambledon Press, 1987), 55–6; S. Walker, 'Yorkshire Justices of the Peace, 1389–1413', *English Historical Review* 108 (1993): 291–8.
36 *PROME*, Parliament of April 1372; *SR*, I. 394); K.L. Wood-Legh, 'Sheriffs, Lawyers and Belted Knights in the Parliaments of Edward III', *English Historical Review* 46 (1931): 381. Its intention was not so much to discriminate against lawyers as to guard against abuses of the position of shire representative. 'Men of law' ought not to come to parliament as representatives because, as 'attorneys for private individuals', they 'procure and cause to be put forward in parliament many [private] petitions in the name of the commons'.
37 Musson and Ormrod, *Evolution*, 149–51.
38 For example where two men of law (*duo legis homines*) were assigned to enquire by whom a fishing weir was erected in the River Wye causing damage to boats and fishing (SC 8/124/6176).
39 TNA, Public Record Office, Special Collections, Ancient Petitions, SC 8/234/ 11689.
40 *Report From the Lords Committees Touching the Dignity of a Peer of the Realm* (London, 1829), IV, 792.
41 Arguably 'apprentice-at-law', too, was another ambiguous classification in being a general term applied to those below the level of serjeant: J.H. Baker, The *Legal Profession and the Common Law: historical essays* (London: Hambledon Press, 1986), 88–9; Baker, *Men of Court*, I, 14–15.
42 Given the sparseness of information on some individuals, it may provide their only formal identification as lawyers (e.g. Robert de Leeds – SC 8/192/9592; John Mulys – SC 8/47/2331; James Belers – SC 8/23/1107A).
43 *History of Parliament: House of Commons, 1386–1421*, eds. J.S. Roskell, L. Clark and C. Rawcliffe, 4 vols. (Stroud: Allen Sutton, 1992), 3:11–12. He was MP for Canterbury five times between 1382 and 1395.
44 For example: TNA, Public Record Office, CP 40/484 m.209d (Somerset pleas).
45 *History of Parliament, 1386–1421*, 3: 627–8. Lopinford was MP for Tavistock in 1411.
46 SC 8/231/11518.
47 Baker, *Serjeants*, 151.
48 SC 8/87/4333.
49 14 Edward III, st. 1 c.16 (*SR*, I. 287); A. Musson, 'Centre and Locality: Perceptions of the Assize Justices in Late Medieval England', in *Law, Governance and Justice: New Views on Medieval Constitutionalism*, ed. Richard W. Kaeuper (Leiden: Brill, 2013), 224–5. The legislation stipulated king's serjeants, but in practice some serjeants joined the justices of the central courts on circuit.
50 A 'professional royal official' with judicial experience on commissions of assize, gaol delivery and oyer and terminer (1316–32): C.M. Fraser, 'Cumberland and

Westmorland Lay Subsidies for 1332', *Transactions of the Cumberland and Westmorland Archaeological Society* 66 (1966): 132–3.

51 SC 8/65/3205.

52 *PROME*, Parliament of November 1384; 8 Richard II, c.2 (*SR*, II, 36); Musson, 'Centre and Locality', 229–30.

53 John Gower, 'Mirour de l'Omme or Speculum Hominis', in *The Complete Works of John Gower: The French Works*, ed. George C. Macaulay (Oxford: Clarendon, 1899), ll. 24421, 24180.

54 William Langland, *The Vision of Piers Plowman: A Critical Edition of the 'B' Text*, ed. A. V. C. Schmidt (London: J. M. Dent, 1978), VII: 39.

55 In the 'Introduction' to the Man of Law's Tale (II: 33) in *The Riverside Chaucer*, ed. L.D. Benson, 3rd ed. (Oxford: Oxford University Press, 1987).

56 For a more detailed analysis of Chaucer's treatment of this pilgrim see: A. Musson, 'The Sergeant-at-Law', in *Historians on Chaucer: The General Prologue of the Canterbury Tales*, eds. S. Rigby and A. Minnis (Oxford: Oxford University Press, 2014), 206–26.

57 Coss, *Origins*, 244–5.

58 Baker, *Men of Court*, I, 14; J.A. Brundage, *The Profession and Practice of Medieval Canon Law* (Aldershot: Ashgate, 2004), I, VII–VIII. However, there was no stipulation about the degree of legal expertise required for judges of the *ius commune*. 'Men without formal legal training could act as judges, provided they knew the law': R.H. Helmholz, 'Magna Carta and the Ius Commune', *University of Chicago Law Review* 66 (1999): 346–7 (quotation at 347).

59 P. Brand, 'Legal Education in England Before the Inns of Court', in *Learning the Law: The Teaching and Transmission of Law, 1150–1900* (London: Hambledon Press, 1999), 51–84; P. Brand, *Observing and Recording the Medieval Bar and Bench at Work*, Selden Society Lecture (London: Selden Society, 1999); *Readings and Moots of the Inns of Court in the Fifteenth Century*, eds. S.E. Thorne and J.H. Baker, Selden Society, 71 and 105 (London: Selden Society, 1954–90).

60 M.J. Bennett, 'Provincial Gentlefolk and Legal Education in the Reign of Edward II', *Bulletin of the Institute of Historical Research* 57 (1984): 203–7; P. Brand, 'Courtroom and Schoolroom: The Education of Lawyers Prior to 1400', *Historical Research* 60 (1987): 145–65; reprinted in Brand, *MCL*, 57–76.

61 Musson, *Medieval Law in Context*, 67–9, 120–4; Ramsay, 'Legal Profession', 68–9; Youngs, *Humphrey Newton*, 42–6; P. Coss, *The Foundations of Gentry Life: The Multons of Frampton and Their World, 1270–1370* (Oxford: Oxford University Press, 2010), 209–29.

62 In the fourteenth century Robert Thorp lived at Longthorp, which is only about 15 miles from John Knivet at Southwick; from the fifteenth century, the Tremayle, Hody and Gurney families, among whose male off-spring could be counted justices of king's bench, serjeants-at-law and recorders of Bridgewater and Bristol respectively, lived in a trio of houses within a few miles of each other near Cannington (Som).

63 Wills of various county practitioners reveal ownership of law books, which they in turn passed on to their family or colleagues. For example: Devon man of law John Prescott (d.1412) bequeathed 'all his books on the law of the land' to Walter Northcote, while his colleague, Thomas Raymond, recorder of Exeter (d.1418) left a *Nova Statuta de Lege* to fellow lawyer, Thomas Norris. (*The Register of Edmund Stafford, A.D. 1395–1419*, ed. F.C. Hingeston (London: G. Bell, 1886), 400, 419).

64 Magna Carta c.45 (1215) had emphasised that only justices who knew the law of the land (*qui sciant legem regni*) ought to be appointed, although this stipulation was omitted in subsequent versions.

65 SC 8/19/912.

66 *The Fifty Earliest English Wills in the Court of Probate, London AD 1387–1439*, ed. F.J. Furnivall, EETS, 88 (London, 1887), 64.
67 Justice of North or South Wales: SC 8/145/7250.
68 Recorder of York: *York Memorandum Book Part I, 1376–1417*, ed. M. Sellers, Surtees Society, 120 (1912), 40.
69 SC 8/145/7221 (William Upton); SC 8/22/1060 (Joan Windsor).
70 Musson and Ormrod, *Evolution*, 57.
71 Launde was called as a serjeant in 1316: Baker, *Serjeants*, 153.
72 SC 8/296/14770. Conversely, John Codyngton managed to avoid an order to attend the admiral attired as a 'man at arms' on account of testimony that he was an attorney (SC 8/12/580).
73 For example: A. Musson, 'The Role of Amateur and Professional Judges in the Royal Courts of Late Medieval England', in *Judicial Tribunals in England and Europe, 1200–1700: The Trial in History*, eds. M. Mulholland and B. Pullan (Manchester: Manchester University Press, 2003), 37–57.
74 Ramsay, 'What Was the Legal Profession?' 66.
75 SC 8/12/580.
76 Baker, *Men of Court*, 22 n74.
77 Stephenson, *Monumental Brasses*, 330; Baker, *Men of Court*, I, 653.
78 From the formulation of their complaints, legal advice must have been given to unfree tenants petitioning the king or their lord: see J.F. Nichols, 'An Early Fourteenth-century Petition From the Tenants of Bocking to Their Manorial Lord', *Economic History Review* 2 (1929–30): 300–7; Tompkins, '"Lets Kill All the Lawyers", 73–88.
79 Ives, *Common Lawyers*, 20.
80 A. Musson, 'Arbitration and the Legal Profession in Later Medieval England', in *Law and Legal Process: Substantive Law and Procedure in English Legal History*, eds. D. Ibbetson and M. Dyson (Cambridge: Cambridge University Press, 2013), 60. Arguably, they should be regarded as part of the legal profession: see Bevan, 'Clerks and Scriveners'.
81 Sir John Baker makes the point that 'Little or no work has been done on these lowly men of affairs; until it is, we can do no more than guess at their social and intellectual characteristics': *Legal Profession*, 88. This is now being addressed.
82 C.W. Brooks, *Pettyfoggers and Vipers of the Commonwealth: The 'Lower Branch' of the Legal Profession in Early Modern England* (Cambridge: Cambridge University Press, 1986), 12.
83 S.J. Payling, 'Bowes, John (*c*.1383–1444)', *ODNB*; online ed., Jan 2008 [0-www.oxforddnb.com.lib.exeter.ac.uk/view/article/92981]
84 *History of Parliament, 1509–58*, 93–4; Baker, *Men of Court*, 15 n.22; Baker, *Serjeants*, 162.
85 Sir John Fortescue, *De Laudibus Leges Anglie*, ed. S.B. Chrimes (Cambridge: Cambridge University Press, 1942), 126.
86 *SCCKB*, IV, xxii–xxv; Ives, *Common Lawyers*, 304–5, 322–3. Judicial salaries were put on a better footing during the fifteenth century with higher increments and a share of court fees payable in addition to their regular payments as assize justices (*SCCKB*, VII, xv; Ives, *Common Lawyers*, 323).
87 Judges owed their position to the king (*judices non habentur nisi per regem*): Musson, *Medieval Law in Context*, 58–61. See also P. Brand, 'Chief Justice and Felon: The Career of Thomas Weyland', in *The Political Context of Law*, eds. R. Eales and D. Sullivan (London: Hambledon Press, 1987), 27–47, reprinted in Brand, *MCL*, 113–34.
88 P. Brand, 'Edward I and the Judges: State Trials of 1289–93', in *Thirteenth Century England I*, eds. P.R. Coss and S.D. Lloyd (Woodbridge: Boydell Press, 1986), 31–40, reprinted in Brand, *MCL*, 103–12; N.M. Fryde, 'Edward III's

Removal of his Ministers and Judges, 1340–1', *Bulletin of the Institute of Historical Research* 48 (1975): 159–61; T.F.T. Plucknett, 'Impeachment and Attainder', *Transactions of the Royal Historical Society*, 5th series, 3 (1953): 145–58.

89 J.R. Maddicott, *Law and Lordship: Royal Justices as Retainers in Thirteenth and Fourteenth Century England*, Past and Present Supplement, 4 (Oxford: Past and Present Society, 1978), 48–51, 84–5; Baker, *Serjeants*, 285 (speech of the chief justice at the serjeants' feast of 1521 recalling the Gascoigne's removal).

90 Ives, 'Promotion in the Legal Profession'; M. Jurkowski, 'Lawyers and Lollardy in the Early Fifteenth Century', in *Lollardy and the Gentry in the Later Middle Ages*, eds. M. Aston and C. Richmond (Stroud: Sutton, 1997), 155–82.

91 Among others, William Fifhide (created serjeant, 1354, d.1361) and Richard Jay (created serjeant 1486, d.1493/4), for example, as well as the better documented Thomas Rolf and Thomas Kebell, never became royal judges: Baker, *Serjeants*, 511, 520, 521, 534.

92 S. Lysons, 'Copies of Three Remarkable Petitions to King Henry the Sixth With that King's Sign Manual, Preserved Among the Records in the Tower; With a Schedule annexed to one of them, containing an Account of the Robes provided for the Royal Colleges of our Lady of Eton, and of our Lady and St. Nicholas of Cambridge' *Archaeologia* 16 (1812): 3–8.

93 See below for further discussion.

94 *Riverside Chaucer*, 28 (General Prologue: I. 317).

95 See calculations of Donahue in 'Legal Professions', 233–5.

96 Distraint to knighthood was a phenomenon observable from the thirteenth century: see M. Powicke, *Military Obligation in Medieval England: A Study in Liberty and Duty* (Oxford: Clarendon Press, 1962); P. Coss, *Lordship, Knighthood and Locality: A Study in English Society, c.1180-c.1280* (Cambridge: Cambridge University Press, 1991).

97 Baker, *Serjeants*, 28–30. Five called in February 1415 defaulted, while these and a further four did the same when new writs were issued in July of the same year (ibid., 160–1).

98 *CCR, 1409–13*, 372 (25 October); *PROME*, Parliament of 1417 (*'suites, matiers, et causes eiantz et pendantz en ses courts, n'eussent si bone esploit come ils soloient avoir, par cause de si petit nombre qe y fuit des serjeantz de la ley*).

99 *PROME*, Parliament of 1417. The transcription erroneously names one of the apprentices summoned as John Ivin (*recte* John Juyn).

100 Lysons, 'Three Remarkable Petitions', 3–4.

101 Baker, *Serjeants*, 162.

102 Baker, *Serjeants*, 99. Fortescue considered the sum of expenditure to be as much as £266 13s 4d.

103 Musson, 'Centre and Locality', 224–8. During Richard II's reign a third of assize commissioners had this status: Baker, *Serjeants*, 36 n.5.

104 Baker, *Men of Court*, II, 1645–6 (Wenard). He was extolled by John Hooker as: 'A Man . . . Very Well Learned in the Laws of the Realm' (*The Chronicle of Exeter, 1205–1722*, ed. T. Gray (Exeter: Mint Press, 2005), 41.

105 *History of Parliament, 1386–1421*, 2: 138–40.

106 *History of Parliament, 1386–1421*, 2: 140–42.

107 The text of Heydon's exemption as enrolled on the patent rolls (C 66/455 m.19) is provided in Baker, *Serjeants*, 261.

108 Anthony Smith, 'Heydon, John (*d.* 1479)', *ODNB*, online ed., Jan 2008 [0-www.oxforddnb.com.lib.exeter.ac.uk/view/article/52787]

109 Rawcliffe, *Staffords*, 158, 219.

110 Thomas Young received a writ to assume the coif again (on pain of a £1000 fine) a year after relinquishing being recorder of Bristol (1441–62), having also served as MP for Bristol on ten occasions between 1435 and 1456: J.T. Driver,

'Parliamentary Burgesses for Bristol and Gloucester, 1422–1437', *Transactions of the Bristol and Gloucestershire Archaeological Society* 74 (1955): 113–15. Like Burgoyne he was also retained by the duke of Buckingham (Rawcliffe, *Staffords*, 221, 238).

111 J. Lee, 'Urban Recorders and the Crown in Late Medieval England', in *The Fifteenth Century III: Authority and Subversion*, ed. L. Clark (Woodbridge: Boydell Press, 2003), 163–77.

112 Baker, *Serjeants*, 34, 162; *Registrum Cancellarii*, ed. H.E. Salter, Oxford Historical Society (1932), I, 24.

113 Gower, 'Mirour de l'Omme', ll. 24385–92. See also: B. Vale, 'Profits of the Law and the "Rise" of the Scropes: Henry Scrope (d. 1336) and Geoffrey Scrope (d. 1340), Chief Justices of England to Edward II and Edward III', in *Profit, Piety and the Professions*, ed. Michael Hicks (Stroud: Alan Sutton, 1990), 91–102; P.J. Jefferies, 'Profitable Fourteenth-Century Legal Practice and Landed Investment: The Case of Judge Stonor, *c.* 1281 to 1354', *Southern History* 15 (1993): 18–35.

114 A. Harding, 'The Revolt Against the Justices', in *The English Rising of 1381*, eds. R.H. Hilton and T.H. Aston (Cambridge: Cambridge University Press, 1984), 165–93; N. Saul, *Richard II* (London and New Haven: Yale University Press, 1997); *The Reign of Henry IV: Rebellion and Survival, 1403–1413*, eds. D. Biggs and G. Dodd (York: York Medieval Press, 2008).

115 Fortescue, *De Laudibus*, 118.

116 Baker, *Serjeants*, 17–20.

117 Fortescue, *De Laudibus*, 122; Baker, *Serjeants*, 99.

118 Fortescue, *De Laudibus*, 120; Baker, *Serjeants*, 49–50.

119 N. Saul, *For Honor and Fame: Chivalry in England, 1066–1500* (London: Bodley Head, 2011), 170–7.

120 For a discussion of this phenomenon see 'The Ethos of the Legal Profession – Honor and Loyalty' (forthcoming).

121 1 Henry V c.5.

122 Baker, *Serjeants*, 34–5, 49–50.

123 Maddicott, *Law and Lordship*, 17–18.

124 Higgins, 'Judges in Government and Society', 192.

125 For example: Robert Sadington (1337), Humphrey Starkey (1483).

126 TNA, Public Record Office, Exchequer, King's Remembrancer: Accounts Various, E 101/386/55.

127 E 101/386/16, /386/18.

128 P. Coss, 'Knighthood, Heraldry and Social Exclusion in Edwardian England', in *Heraldry, Pageantry and Social Display in Medieval England*, eds. P. Coss and M. Keen (Woodbridge: Boydell Press, 2002), 66–7.

129 *The Controversy Between Sir Richard Scrope and Sir Robert Grosvenor in the Court of Chivalry, A.D. MCCCLXXV-MCCCXC: A Transcript of the Original Roll*, ed. N.H. Nicolas (London: Samuel Bentley, 1832), e.g. 142–3 (Aton), 144–6, (Rither) 162 (Eynsford).

130 Jens Röhrkasten, 'Shardlow, Sir John (*d.* 1344)', *ODNB;* online ed. [0-www.oxforddnb.com.lib.exeter.ac.uk/view/article/25203]; Roger Virgoe, 'Hankeford, Sir William (*c.*1350–1423)', *ODNB;* online ed. Jan 2008 [0-www.oxforddnb.com.lib.exeter.ac.uk/view/article/12196]; J.H. Baker, 'Littleton, Sir Thomas (*d.* 1481)', *ODNB;* online ed. May 2007 [0-www.oxforddnb.com.lib.exeter.ac.uk/view/article/16787].

131 F. Pilbrow, 'The Knights of the Bath: Dubbing to Knighthood in Lancastrian and Yorkist England', in *Heraldry, Pageantry and Social Display*, ed. Coss and Keen, 196–7, 199–201.

132 Pilbrow, 'Knights of the Bath', 198–9, 216–17.

133 Nicolas, *Scrope and Grosvenor*, 222.
134 Coss, *Origins*, 98; N. Saul, *Knights and Esquires: The Gloucestershire Gentry in the Fourteenth Century* (Oxford: Oxford University Press, 1981).
135 S.L. Waugh, 'Reluctant Knights and Jurors: Respites, Exemptions and Public Obligations in the Reign of Henry III', *Speculum* 58 (1983): 937–86.
136 E 198/4/37 m. 11 (5 Edward IV).
137 Estates were notoriously undervalued for taxation purposes, but particularly in relation to *Inquisitions Post Mortem* – though see the balanced critique in M. Holford, '"Notoriously Unreliable": *The Fifteenth Century Inquisitions Post Mortem: A Companion*, ed. M. Hicks (Woodbridge: Boydell Press, 2012), 117–44.
138 BL, Additional Roll 64320; *Feudal Aids*, VI, 514; *History of Parliament, 1386–1422*, 3: 373–5.
139 E 198/4/34 (dated only *temp Henry IV*).
140 E 159/234 m. 4d (1457–8).
141 E 159/234 m. 7d (1457–8). Unusually, Young remained unknighted even though later, having accepted the coif, he became a justice of common pleas (1467–71) and of King's Bench (1475–7): Baker, *Men of Court*, 2: 1736–7.
142 TNA, Public Record Office, Chancery, Chancery Miscellanea, C 47/1/8 mm. 14–15, 26, 30–1.
143 E 198/4/19 (16 Henry VII); E 198/4/26 (1 Henry VIII). The latter two were only included in the first and second distraints respectively. Redmayne was listed, but recorded as dead (*mortuus est*) by the time of the second one.
144 TNA, Public Record Office, Exchequer, King's Remembrancer: Memoranda Rolls and Enrolment Books, E 159/207 m.14d (printed in Baker, *Serjeants*, 258–9). The expedition of 1430–1 for which new knights were required may in Rolf's mind have harked back to Henry V's reign and the days of Agincourt when he and other serjeants-elect made their stand.
145 Barton's exemption – TNA, Public Record Office, Chancery, Patent Rolls, C 66/400 m.25 (printed in Baker, *Serjeants*, 260).
146 *PROME*, Parliament of April 1379; C. Fenwick, *The Poll Taxes of 1377, 1379, and 1381*, ed. C. Fenwick, 3 vols (Oxford: Oxford University Press, 1998–2005), 1: xv.
147 *Poll Taxes*, ed. Fenwick, 3: 343.
148 *Poll Taxes*, ed. Fenwick, 1: 554; Baker, *Serjeants*, 160.
149 N. Saul, 'The Social Status of Chaucer's Franklin: A Reconsideration', *Medium Aevum* 52 (1983): 10–26; P. Coss, 'The Franklin', in *Historians on Chaucer*, eds. Rigby and Minnis, 233–41.
150 Coss, *Origins of the Gentry*, 216; Carpenter, *Locality and Polity*, 45–6, 75–7; Ives, *Common Lawyers*, 17–18.
151 William Worcester, *The Boke of Noblesse*, ed. J.G. Nichols (London: Roxburghe Club, 1860), 77–8.
152 Anthony Smith, 'Heydon, John (*d.* 1479)', *ODNB*; online ed. Jan 2008 [0-www.oxforddnb.com.lib.exeter.ac.uk/view/article/52787]
153 J.H. Baker, 'Littleton, Sir Thomas (*d.* 1481)', *ODNB*; online ed. May 2007 [0-www.oxforddnb.com.lib.exeter.ac.uk/view/article/16787]
154 Henry Summerson, 'Newton, Sir Richard (*d.* 1448)', *ODNB*; online ed. [0-www.oxforddnb.com.lib.exeter.ac.uk/view/article/20063]
155 Bloom, 'Willoughbys', 7–19.
156 C. Blair, 'The Date of the Early Alabaster Knight at Hanbury', *Church Monuments* 7 (1992): 3–18; Stephenson, *Monumental Brasses*, 445–6; Saul, *English Church Monuments*, 274.
157 Oxford, Bodleian, MS Dodsworth 90 fol. 58 (Willoughby); London, Lambeth Palace Library, Register of Archbishop Islip fol.121 (Hillary).

158 Coss, 'Knighthood', 64–5.
159 A connection between standards of behaviour and wearing the coif is explicitly made in a petition brought against sergeant-at-law William Paston by Juliana Herbard in 1426 which claims that he has forfeited the 'coif of truth with appurtances of clothing', which are 'a sign to be known as a just man': TNA, Special Collections, Ancient Petitions, SC 8/169/8449–50; A. Musson with E. Powell, ed. and trans., *Crime, Law and Society in the Later Middle Ages* (Manchester: Manchester University Press, 2009), 227–8.
160 N. Saul, 'The Early Fifteenth-Century Monument of a Serjeant-at-Law in Flamstead Church (Hertfordshire)', *Church Monuments* 27 (2012): 7–21.
161 Trevaignon actually rose to become a justice of common pleas, but this is not reflected in his memorial.
162 He has a sword at his side, though this normally symbolises 'lordship'.
163 Saul, *English Church Monuments*, 243–4.
164 Ibid., 277–8.
165 *History of Parliament, 1386–1422*, 4: 380–2.
166 Stephenson, *Monumental Brasses*, 94–5; Saul, *English Church Monuments*, 278–9.
167 Henry Summerson, 'Mordaunt, Sir John (*d.* 1504)', *ODNB*; online ed. Sept 2011 [0-www.oxforddnb.com.lib.exeter.ac.uk/view/article/19165].
168 E 159/278 (1500) where he is described as 'serjeant-at-law' in the entry; Baker, *Serjeants*, 526.
169 *History of Parliament 1386–1422*, 2: 142.
170 Saul, *English Church Monuments*, 282.
171 Stephenson, *Monumental Brasses*, 50, 195, 275, 544.
172 Saul, *For Honour and Fame*, 164–6.
173 C. Richmond, 'The Expenses of Thomas Playter or Sotterley, 1459–60', *Proceedings of the Suffolk Institute of Archaeology and History* 35 (1981): 43.
174 Stephenson, *Monumental Brasses*, 364.
175 Rawcliffe, *Staffords*, 80, 221.
176 Stephenson, *Monumental Brasses*, 17; Saul, *English Church Monuments*, 286–7.
177 *CCR, 1392–6*, 10.
178 This is the term used by historians to describe those not wearing armour and should not be confused with those qualified in Roman civil law who are usually termed 'civilians'.
179 Identification can be hindered where there is no memorial inscription.
180 Monumental brasses to the latter men are usually comparatively small and many are similar in design. Effigies and incised slabs are sometimes more detailed and of high quality (see Saul, *English Church Monuments*, 238–40).
181 Saul, *English Church Monuments*, 371.
182 Gower, 'Mirrour l'homme', ll 24806–8.
183 Ives, *Common Laywers*, 20.
184 A. Musson, 'Legal Culture: Medieval Lawyers' Aspirations and Pretensions', in *Fourteenth Century England III*, ed. W.M. Ormrod (Woodbridge: Boydell Press, 2004), 16–30.
185 Baker, 'Reflections', 16.

13 Legal services for the poor in the early common law

David J. Seipp

Paul Brand's 1992 book *The Origins of the English Legal Profession* wrested every bit of evidence from the plea rolls of the king's courts and manuscript reports of cases on the formation and practice of England's secular legal profession. All that could be said about whether thirteenth- and early fourteenth-century lawyers volunteered or felt compelled to offer their legal services for poor litigants who could not afford to pay their usual fees Brand summed up in two sentences on page 104:

> By the 1290s the justices in eyre were probably assigning serjeants to the service of poor clients and perhaps requiring them to provide gratuitous services. In a bill presented in the 1292 Shropshire eyre a complainant who claimed to be poor asked the justices to 'grant' him a serjeant, 'so that his right is not lost'.

In hopes that there may be more to say about this question down through the early sixteenth century, I offer this contribution in tribute to the friendship and generosity that Paul has shown to me over many years.

By way of contrast, the *other* lawyers of thirteenth- and fourteenth-century England, canon lawyers in the ecclesiastical courts, had a rich literature about whether and how they should donate their services to the poor, or be compensated by the broader public for doing so. James Brundage wrote a wonderful little article in 1988 about legal aid for the poor in medieval Europe.[1] He summarised the abundant writing of canon lawyers and canon law teachers in the thirteenth through fifteenth centuries about the duty of bishops to give justice to widows, orphans, the poor, and the oppressed – and the duty of legally-trained clerics to represent and advocate for such persons.

The common lawyers of England left far less written evidence about their aspirations or activities on behalf of the poor. They were secular-minded laymen without university educations. As Brand has told us, they grew into a profession at the same time the canon lawyers did, in the thirteenth century. These common lawyers probably knew about the canonists' pronouncements about a moral and professional duty to donate services to the poor. Many of the Church's decrees and commentaries on this duty originated in the British Isles.[2] By the late thirteenth century, common lawyers must have known too that a person without legal counsel stood little chance of prevailing in the king's courts of common law. An early twelfth-century text, the *Leges Henrici Primi*, recommended that an accused person should obtain counsel and that no law should forbid this, but counsel in this context meant advice of family and friends, not the services of a professional expert.[3] In the thirteenth century and after, however, English common law rapidly became an elaborate, highly technical enterprise. If one side had a professional pleader, the other side was at a severe disadvantage without one. When poor people sought redress in the king's courts or were themselves prosecuted, their need for professional advocacy must have been obvious.

Kings of England long regarded the provision of justice to be one of their principal duties. Statutes as early as 1275 promised 'that common right be done to all, as well poor as rich, without respect of person'.[4] Keeping the large number of poor people quiescent was a concern of the royal establishment. In 1196 in London, one William Fitz-Osbert, called Longbeard, described in Roger de Hoveden's chronicle as a lawyer (*legis peritus*), called himself a spokesman for the poor (*advocatus pauperum*) and advocated that the rich contribute their proportionate share of taxation. Richard I's justiciar, Hubert Walter, Archbishop of Canterbury, had William arrested and hanged with eight associates.[5] His London followers, who numbered in the tens of thousands, treated his corpse, gallows, and blood as relics and circulated reports of miracles.[6] The king's justices preferred that any advocate for the poor should represent individual paupers in their suits in the king's courts, and not embolden them, as Fitz-Osbert had done, to seek to intervene in governmental policy.

The evidence that Brand presented of poor litigants begging for appointment of counsel came from royal courts known as eyres. In the thirteenth century the king's justices presided during four terms per year in Westminster Hall. They also traveled around from county to county in eyres. Nearly all of the lawsuits that began in Westminster Hall originated by writ and were costly to file. In the traveling eyre, on the other hand, the king's justices replaced the county court during their visit and would receive informal complaints called bills. Among the bills presented to the king's justices on their eyres in the 1290s, a few petitioners explicitly mentioned their inability to pay for professional advocacy. Among the bills selected by Selden Society editor William Craddock Bolland from the Shropshire Eyre of 1292 and the Staffordshire Eyre of 1293, John Feyrewin added in his request for justice, 'I have not a halfpenny to spend on a pleader'.[7] William, son of Hugh of Smethumilne, prayed for a remedy and said, 'I am so poor that I can pay no counter' (meaning lawyer).[8] Alan, son of Alan Plotman, told Justice John of Berewyk that he and his mother Alice 'are poor folk' and begged him to 'grant them a serjeant for them, so that they lose not their right, for the sake of the Queen's soul'.[9] What these petitioners all needed, but were too poor to afford, were the professional skills of an advocate, called variously in this period a pleader, a narrator, a counter, or a serjeant, and in later centuries, a barrister.

The records do not say whether any of these poor petitioners got lawyers, but William Bolland thought 'the mere fact of the application being made is a fair proof that counsel were assigned to plead the causes of people too poor to pay any fees'.[10] Paul Brand also relied upon this 1292 bill for his tentative conclusion, quoted above, that justices in eyre were 'probably' answering these petitions by assigning serjeants to serve the poor complainants and 'perhaps' requiring them to do so without compensation.[11]

The king's courts made other provisions for the poor. Poor plaintiffs did not have to pay the usual fees to purchase writs from the chancery.[12] They did not have to find the usual 'pledges' for prosecuting their suits.[13] Year Book reports bear out this relief for the poor from some of the expenses of litigation. In a Cornwall Eyre in 1302, a defendant who was fined for a false claim had his fine remitted because he was poor.[14] In the same eyre, a defendant was fined for having put forward a false denial of the plaintiff's suit. The plaintiff's attorney asked the court to forgive the defendant's fine, 'for he is poor'. Justice Berewyk commended the plaintiff's attorney for his gesture, but ordered the sheriff to take pledges from the plaintiff's attorney for the defendant's fine.[15] Readers of this report took warning that their charitable impulses might cost them dearly, and the ironic twist that one who sought to be generous with someone else's money would himself pay a heavy price became a recurrent theme in Year Books and later case reports.[16] In the same Cornwall Eyre of 1302, two 'poor widows' were reported suing by bill, one with a serjeant arguing her case against two serjeants retained by her defendant.[17]

The central courts at Westminster also heard of poor litigants. In 1307 in Westminster, when a King's Serjeant advised a plaintiff to retake the disputed land on his own, Serjeant Willoughby argued that the plaintiff was a poor man who needed the court's assistance to vindicate his rights.[18] In 1309, a serjeant begged the court to clarify what estate his client had, because his client was poor and knew no law. The opposing serjeant replied, 'It is because he knows no law that he has retained you, and it is for you (his counsel) to say at his peril what estate he ought to claim.' Chief Justice Bereford agreed that it was for the poor litigant's counsel to assert his legal claim, not for the court to figure it out.[19] In the same year, a serjeant pleaded that his client, a plaintiff, was so poor that he did not have the wherewithal to live, so it would be a hardship to him if the defendants were permitted to delay his suit. This plea of poverty did not prevent the delay.[20] Serjeant Hedon pleaded the poverty of a woman who intervened on the defendant's side in a case in Common Pleas, again with no discernible effect.[21] Chief Justice Bereford recalled in a case of 1310 that a few decades earlier a poor woman had traced her claim in a way that did not advance her cause. The whole court had taken pity on the poor woman, Bereford recalled, but could not help her because of the way she had pleaded.[22] Perhaps the point of Bereford's story was that if she had gotten better legal advice, she could have pleaded differently and won. These Year Book cases and the dozen that follow from the succeeding century do not indicate whether serjeants were assigned to represent the parties they described as poor, whether they donated their services, or whether someone else paid the fee to represent the poor litigant as an act of charity. Some cases do not mention whether poor litigants had counsel, and a few cases made clear that poor litigants lacked counsel.

In Parliament in January 1315, a petition of the commons to the king and his council complained that 'the poor people of the land who have to plead in the king's courts' faced great harm and disinheritance at the hands of conspirators who maintained false suits and corrupted jurors.[23] An example of this complaint came in a Year Book case of 1322. A poor man who had been maimed was brought to the bar of King's Bench. In the previous year the poor man had sued a defendant who had struck the poor man's hand off. The poor man had sued him and was awarded £40 compensation. But a jury, perhaps bribed by or in fear of the defendant, had assessed goods of the defendant as being worth £40 that were in fact worth less than £7. The poor man prayed a remedy. The court considered whether they could extend a statute to make the jurors answerable for their overvaluation of the defendant's goods.[24]

Under Edward III, courts seemed less reluctant to grant occasional concessions to poor litigants. In 1330, a poor woman who had first brought a faulty writ and had failed to prosecute her lawsuit was later represented by a serjeant and was allowed to begin her suit again with a better writ, despite her earlier nonsuit.[25] In 1333 and 1337, a poor woman defendant 'without counsel' and a poor plaintiff who did have a serjeant pleading on his behalf both got the court's assistance in presenting their cases.[26] In 1341, Chief Justice Hillary said that poor plaintiffs who could give nothing would not be forced to find pledges for their suits.[27] In 1343, a poor man sued an attorney who had conspired with a sheriff to forge court documents depriving the man of his land. Although the attorney had concealed his forgery well, the court got him to confess the truth of the poor man's claim, awarded damages, and adjudged the guilty attorney to prison.[28] But a year later a Year Book reported a poor woman plaintiff who lacked counsel, pleaded badly, and saw her case dismissed by Chief Justice Hillary when better pleading could have avoided this outcome.[29] In the same year a poor female defendant and a poor male plaintiff both had serjeants speaking for them. The woman's outcome was not recorded but the man lost.[30] Parliament in the mid-1340s prescribed the oath of the king's justices to 'do equal law and execution of right to all his subjects, rich and poor, without having regard to any person'.[31] In 1346, Chief Justice Hillary refused to reverse the nonsuit of a poor plaintiff who had a serjeant speaking for him, because a poor plaintiff could thereby harass the same defendant forty times over.[32] No serjeant was recorded speaking for another poor plaintiff who was also nonsuited in the same year and also lost his chance to reopen his suit.[33] In 1352, a poor woman plaintiff had both a serjeant and an apprentice lawyer speaking for her, and she won.[34] If there is a lesson in all these early fourteenth-century cases, it is that litigants rich or poor were much better off if they had counsel, but that the court could and sometimes did intervene to prevent or reverse an injustice caused by poverty and lack of legal counsel.

In the reign of Richard II, Justice Skipwyth said that it was an act of charity for the court to allow a poor plaintiff to amend his writ rather than to quash the writ for a clerical error.[35] A poor woman recovered against a knight.[36] And Chief Justice Belknap came to the aid of another poor plaintiff who lacked counsel.[37] Perhaps the most revealing record from the end of the fourteenth century came, however, not from the Year Books, but from a legal opinion preserved in the public records. Three plaintiffs petitioned to the king's council in 1397 claiming a manor. The council referred their petition to four serjeants. The petition alleged that the plaintiffs could not afford the cost of a long action at common law, and that to deny them justice because they were poor was 'against law and conscience'.[38] The parties presented evidence and arguments through serjeants and apprentices to eight royal justices. The plaintiffs lost. 'Since the plaintiffs could afford serjeants to act for them', the Selden Society editor concluded, 'the allegation of poverty was on its face a fiction'.[39] He did not imagine that serjeants could have been assigned or could have donated their services to impoverished litigants.

By the late fourteenth century, pleading had become more and more complicated, litigation more and more expensive, and outcomes more and more subject to interference by powerful lords. By then, petitioners who were too poor to secure a remedy at common law had started to seek the direct assistance of the Chancellor, bypassing the ordinary courts of common law entirely in favor of the new equity jurisdiction of Chancery.[40] It became standard form in petitions to the Chancellor for 'your poor orator' humbly to beseech a remedy 'for God and in way of charity'.[41] Some of these petitioners undoubtedly claimed poverty as a convenient fiction.

Meanwhile, popular literature condemned lawyers for not providing services to the poor. William Langland's *Vision of Piers Plowman* (c. 1370) envisioned lawyers who refused to plead unless they were paid:

> There hovered an hundred in caps of silk,
> Serjeants they seemed who practised at Bar,
> Pleading the law for pennies and pounds,
> And never for love of our Lord unloosing their lips.
> You might better measure the mist on the Malvern hills,
> Than get a "mum" out of their mouth unless money were showed.[42]

London Lickpenny, a poem from the early fifteenth century, was a 96-line ballad to the lack of legal services for the poor. A Kentish countryman went to 'King's Bench', 'Common Place', and 'the clerks of the Chancery' but learned in every court, from every lawyer, judge, and clerk that 'for lack of money, I might not speed'.[43] Here are a few bits of 'London Lickpenny':

> Fast to Westminster-ward I went
> To a man of law, to make my complaint.
> I said, "For Mary's love, that holy saint,
> Have pity on the poor, that would proceed.
> I would give silver, but my purse is faint."
> For lack of money, I may not speed . . . .
> Unto the Common Place I went then
> Where sat one with a silken hood,
> I did him reverence as I ought to do
> And said of all my goods, by north and south,
> I am defrauded with great falsehood;
> He would not give me a "mum" of his mouth.
> For lack of money, I may not speed . . . .
> In all Westminster Hall I could find never a one
> That for me would do, though I should die.

Mum and the Sothsegger, another early fifteenth-century poem, repeated that the poor litigate in vain, that it would not benefit a poor man to plead with a great man, for 'law lies much in lordship' and 'poor men's plaints penniless abate'.[44] Langland, *Lickpenny*, and *Mum and the Sothsegger* do not prove much. They tell us that many people in late medieval England heard and believed that lawyers were greedy and that legal services were priced out of their reach. The same could be said of early twenty-first-century Britain or America. The question remains: does the silence of our sources for the thirteenth and fourteenth centuries mean that English common lawyers ordinarily donated their services to poor litigants with deserving cases, or that more likely they did not?

Fifteenth-century evidence is more abundant and more positive. At the outset of the new century, Serjeant Rede pleaded on behalf of a poor plaintiff, called him 'my client', but didn't use the first person plural form of address that he and every other serjeant used in nearly all Year Book reports.[45] In the Rolls of Parliament for October 1423, the lords of the king's council provided that the King's Serjeant, a senior lawyer named to plead for the king, should 'be sworn truly and plainly' to give 'assistance and good advice' to the poorest suitor whose bill of complaint came before the Clerk of the King's Council each day, 'without taking anything from him, on pain of discharge from his office'.[46] This provision was repeated verbatim as an Article of the King's Council in the Rolls of Parliament in 1429.[47] There were two King's Serjeants at any one time between 1420 and 1426, three between 1427 and 1429, and one or two thereafter to 1439, but no records are known to have survived naming any particular King's Serjeant as having been sworn to give assistance and good advice to the poorest suitor of the day. This order of the royal council concerned only cases brought before the council by petition. It only provided for counsel to be assigned to the single poorest petitioner whose complaint came to the council on any particular day. It was compulsion from the highest authority in the land, not the voluntary charity of a lawyer who proffered advice to a needy litigant. And it attached a punishment of disbarment for refusal to give advice to a poor litigant for free.

Scotland had passed a similar statute a few months later, in March 1424, that if any poor creature who for lack of cunning or expense could not follow his cause, the king for the love of God should ordain that the judge before whom the cause should be determined purvey and get a lawful and wise advocate to follow such poor creature's cause.[48] Again the command came from on high, but now for all litigants too poor to pursue their lawsuits, not just for the poorest individual on a particular day before a particular tribunal.

In 1425 a serjeant sued his client for his fee, and to prevent the client from simply swearing that he owed nothing – a gambit called 'wager of law' – the serjeant tried to get himself into the position of those who could not refuse to serve any prospective customer.[49] Serjeant Pole showed to the Justices that a serjeant could be compelled by law to be of counsel to any person. Nevertheless, the client whom the serjeant was suing was permitted to wage his law. A retainer voluntary on both sides was sufficiently different from compulsory service, or assignment of counsel.[50]

In 1431 and thereafter, the issue was maintenance. Interference in the lawsuit of another, called maintenance, was a longstanding problem of the early common law. By the fifteenth century, the loser of a lawsuit could then sue those who had maintained his opponent in the original lawsuit. Judges had to draw lines marking out what was legitimate assistance and what was unlawful maintenance. Justice Martin in 1431 said that a master could maintain his servant's lawsuit, that one blood relative could maintain another's litigation, and that 'I can give gold or silver to one who is poor to maintain his plea, if he himself cannot because of his poverty, and this is not maintenance contrary to law'.[51] Serjeant Markham and Justice Paston continued the point in another maintenance case in 1442. It is lawful, said Markham, to ask and desire one learned in law to be of counsel with another person, because this is only an act of charity. And Paston said that one can give money to the counsel of poor people, and this is justifiable.[52] Serjeant Arderne repeated this point in 1443, that if I give charity to one who has a suit, giving him money to pursue his suit by my own hand, or by the hand of my servant, this is no maintenance.[53] Another serjeant or justice said in 1443 that in a writ of Maintenance it was a good plea to say that he who was supposed to have been maintained was a poor man, and had nothing himself to defend the suit that a plaintiff had brought against him, and that one should not be sued for maintenance who of his charity gave the poor man 20 shillings, because this was lawful for everyone.[54] These positions were strongly contested by other serjeants and justices who took the contrary view that anyone meddling in another's lawsuit without a close family or employment relationship was guilty of maintenance. Nevertheless, we see that there were lawyers who could imagine that donating legal services to the poor was an act of charity to be applauded.

In 1471, in the Court of Common Pleas at Westminster, Chief Justice Bryan, in the midst of an argument about how to sue a serjeant in that court, said that if a serjeant declined to plead for a poor man when the court assigned him to do so, the justices could refuse to hear him plead for anyone.[55] Jenney, the serjeant being sued in that case, recalled that he saw William Cheyne, Chief Justice of the Court of King's Bench around 1430, require serjeants to be of counsel in a plea that was before him, and if they would not do so he would forbid them to plead for anyone else in King's Bench.[56] Justice Littleton agreed that a chief justice could well do that.[57] A canon lawyer might have quoted civilian and canonist texts for the same principle.[58] This Year Book passage led William Holdsworth to observe that if litigants 'were too poor to employ counsel the court could and did assign counsel to assist them'[59] and that 'from a very early period', serjeants 'might be required by any of these courts' of common law or chancery 'to plead for a poor man'.[60]

In 1475, a short Year Book note tells us that, by the advice of the Justices of Common Pleas, one John Brown, a court clerk, was chosen to be the prothonotary for the poor in that court, and if any poor man wanted to swear to him that he was not able to pay for the entry of his pleas in the rolls, then Brown was to enter the pleas without taking anything for his labor.[61] Older evidence shows that courts did not charge poor litigants the usual fees. Court clerks often filled the position of attorneys for litigants, accepting their authorization to take legally binding steps in litigation when the parties could not attend court sessions, and these clerks took compensation for doing so. Poor litigants could not afford attorney fees, and this 1475 appointment represented an attempt of the principal common law court to remedy the situation. In late 1483 or early 1484, a clerk named John Harington was appointed by the king's council 'for his good service before the lords and others of the council, especially in the custody, registration, and expedition of bills, requests, and supplications of poor persons'.[62] Harington may have handled this attorney function for poor petitioners to the Council, again without the usual compensation from them.

From 1476 or 1477 we have a letter to Sir William Plumpton from his London agent, reporting about helping a woman's suit against some defendants, presumably at Plumpton's request. The agent wrote that Guy Fairfax, a king's serjeant, 'said openly at the bar that he knew so, verily, they [the defendants] were not guilty [and] that he would labour their deliverance for alms, not taking a penny'.[63] Plumpton's London agent then engaged another serjeant and an apprentice to be the woman's counsel. Such chance survivals of private letters show that a web of personal relationships provided connections between poor litigants and wealthy patrons or generous neighbors who might pay for their legal counsel.

Alongside the ordinary courts of common law, a special court developed in the 1480s and 1490s to deal specifically with petitions from poor people. A draft ordinance of 1491 required the poorest suitors' petitions to be heard first and required the king's serjeants to represent paupers without taking any fee, upon pain of losing their office if they refused.[64] Members of the king's council who were assigned to deal with these petitions became established, by 1493, as the Court of Requests, also known in its early decades as the 'Court of Poor Men's Causes'. This court offered quick and summary justice for poor plaintiffs and for members of the king's household, and soon attracted wealthier litigants. In November 1509, there was discussion in Star Chamber before the two chief justices, other judges, and lawyers of a proposal that this Court of Requests and other new courts be abolished, leaving all to sue in the king's courts at Westminster and assigning counsel to poor litigants without paying any fees.[65]

Lawyers' services for the poor in the courts of common law were put on a new footing in 1495. Parliament provided in that year that poor persons could petition to plead *in forma pauperis* in all courts of record without the payment of any court fees, and provided further that the Chancellor and Justices should assign to such poor persons attorneys and learned counsel who should give their counsels without taking any reward.[66] As noted above, Scotland had passed a similar statute seven decades earlier in 1424.[67] Immediately after the English statute of 1495, we read in a Year Book report that one of the busiest serjeants, Thomas Kebell, 'came to the bar and put to the justices that he was at issue for a poor man, and prayed their discretion'.[68] In 1534, the lord of a manor complained to the Chancellor that in a case begun in the 1490s one of his tenants 'was admitted *in forma pauperis*' in Common Pleas to protest an inclosure 'and had assigned to his counsel four serjeants at the law and his attorney to give him counsel, without paying any fees for the same'.[69] The lord who had to pay for his lawyers thought that his poor tenant had been given an unfair advantage.

Providing legal counsel to the poor became a sign of virtue. An early biographer of Thomas More wrote that 'when he was a private lawyer' in the early 1500s, 'he would take no fees of poor folks, widows, or pupils'.[70] Thomas Wolsey, chancellor from 1515 to 1529, was said to 'make the lawyers plead gratis for all poor men'.[71] In 1575 the lords of the King's Council, 'taking great compassion' for a petitioner's poverty, were 'moved to help' him so far as they might by law, and so 'earnestly required' two serjeants to consider his case on such evidence and witnesses as he could show, and to return their opinions and advice, so that the Council could give him the most comprehensive remedy they might by law.[72] Sixteenth- and seventeenth-century records show the Lord Chancellor and the king's justices appointing senior serjeants as counsel for *in forma pauperis* litigants, not the newest barristers.[73] On the other hand, it was said of Thomas Egerton, Lord Ellesmere, chancellor from 1603 to 1617, that he was never suspected of seeking vulgar praise by becoming counsel for the poor.[74] Seventeenth-century plays featured lawyer characters running away or scheming to avoid their obligations to 'do justice for nothing' *in forma pauperis*.[75]

From the sixteenth century, we have the earliest surviving speeches by Chief Justices to lawyers entering the Order of Serjeants. Serjeants should 'be as glad to tell the poor man the truth of the law for God's sake as the rich man for his money'.[76] 'By doing for the poor for nothing you cannot but win much good name and fame and praise and thanks at the hands as well of God as man'.[77] 'As you should have one tongue for the rich for your fee, as a reward for your long studies and labours, so should you also have another tongue as ready without reward to defend the poor and oppressed'.[78] 'Your heart and hand must be ready for the relief of the poor'.[79] These scattered cases, statutes, administrative orders and speeches are my only documentary evidence of a professional duty to serve the poor. They come late and are accompanied by ongoing complaints that lawyers never fulfilled that duty. Proverbs from the sixteenth and seventeenth centuries repeat Langland and *London Lickpenny*: 'Who would have law, must have money', 'Little money, little law', 'No fee, no law',[80] down to Shakespeare's King Lear, whose fool's advice was 'like the breath of an unfee'd lawyer, you gave me nothing for't'.[81]

Do the Year Book report of 1471 and the 1495 statute point to a new duty where previously English lawyers had felt none? Or do they indicate the formal recognition of what had already been a longstanding informal practice of charitable provision of legal services for the poor? I think that there are some general features of the early common law that bear on this question.

Official records of the common law courts, the plea rolls, do not record the wealth of plaintiffs and defendants. Legal rules were meant to apply to all, regardless of poverty or wealth. It would not have been relevant to any legal issue for a court clerk to write down that a party was poor, too poor to pay his or her lawyer. The lack of direct positive evidence before the late fifteenth century – even anecdotal evidence – is not all that surprising.

Year Book reports of cases litigated from the late thirteenth century onward name serjeants who pleaded on behalf of widows, criminal defendants, and persons alleged to be villeins – the sort of people we doubt could pay the usual fees. Serjeants pleaded cases involving a single acre of freehold land or the return of one cow wrongfully sequestered – the sort of stakes for which we wouldn't expect people to undertake expensive litigation. Often the Year Books show two, three, or more serjeants all making arguments for the same party in cases for small stakes. I have long been led to suspect that some of these lawyers were volunteering their arguments to the court – kibitzing if you will – without expectation of payment for their advocacy.

Thus far all the cases considered have been civil pleas. Criminal matters were less frequently reported in the Year Books, but there were hundreds of such cases. In private prosecutions called 'appeals', criminal defendants were never forbidden to retain counsel if they could afford to do so.[82] In indictments brought on behalf of the king, a rule eventually developed prohibiting counsel from arguing matters of fact on behalf of a defendant, but Year Book cases in the fourteenth and fifteenth centuries show serjeants and apprentices speaking for indicted defendants and raising matters of fact.[83] This strongly suggests that there was then no rule against such advocacy. So does a 1352 case that mentioned that a defendant indicted for felony was 'without counsel of law'. The defendant put forth a charter of pardon, but it was defective. The court did not order the defendant to be hanged immediately, but instead remitted him in custody so that he could sue for a better pardon from the king, 'on better advice of the Justices'.[84] In 1464, the court ordered the sheriff to find counsel for a criminal defendant who refused to plead either guilty or not guilty, thereby leaving the court at an impasse.[85] As in civil cases, the king's justices noticed when a litigant's poverty worked a severe disadvantage, and responded often not by assigning counsel, so far as we can tell, but rather by relieving poor litigants of some of the consequences of their situations. As Christopher St. German wrote in 1530, the judges would instruct an indicted defendant, and so order him that he should run into no jeopardy by his mispleading, because it would be unreasonable for the law to prohibit one who stood in jeopardy of his life that he should have no counsel and then to drive him to plead according to the strict rules and formalities of the law, which he did not know.[86]

Sometime in the sixteenth century or later, lawyers were prohibited from acting for criminal defendants indicted by the king, at least as to matters of fact. Legal historians have assumed that this rule applied in the thirteenth through fifteenth centuries as well. Some have supposed further that even if there had been no prohibition, most criminal defendants were too poor to have afforded legal counsel, so that, in the words of S.F.C. Milsom, 'crime has never been the business of lawyers'.[87] I have written elsewhere that there are 172 criminal cases in the Year Books, some from every decade between 1300 and 1500, in which named lawyers spoke as counsel.[88] Lawyers spoke for the defence in 123 of these reports and for private prosecutors or the king in 109. Whether or not felony defendants usually had lawyers, acquittal rates were quite high by current standards, over 50 percent in some gaol delivery rolls. In the three reports suggesting that judges prevented lawyers from speaking for criminal defendants, I find that the only prohibition was an extremely narrow one, requiring that an accused felon speak the initial plea of guilty or not guilty in person, without anyone speaking for him or her.[89] Despite the probability that many criminal defendants had no money to spend on lawyers and the fact that convicted felons would lose all the lands and goods they ever held, my conclusion was that English common lawyers viewed criminal law as part of the body of rules they were supposed to master and part of the work they were supposed to do. I can find no category of 'poor people's cases' on the plea rolls of the courts of common law that is notable for its absence from the lawyers' Year Books.

When lawyers pleaded cases involving very small stakes and defended accused felons, we may suspect that either lawyers were serving without payment or that somebody else was paying the fees. A fight over a single acre of land or a single cow might often have been the 'test case' for a much larger dispute, a fight between rich lords waged by proxy through their poor tenants, with the rich lords paying counsel fees.[90] Relatives, neighbors, and friends might have found legal counsel for poor litigants. A very early twelfth-century source, the *Leges Henrici Primi*, seems to indicate that lords were expected to support their tenants in court.[91] Bishops might have fulfilled their duty to provide justice for the poor by paying for serjeants in the secular courts out of church funds. Fifteenth-century cases show that masters could not be prosecuted for the common law crime of maintenance (meddling in strangers' lawsuits) when they paid for counsel for their servants or tenants.

A further consideration bearing on this question is the relatively low cost of legal counsel in these centuries. Sources from the 1290s onward reveal that some lawyers received annual retainers from wealthy clients to handle all of their cases, and perhaps also cases of their dependants and the recipients of their charity. But the usual arrangement was a one-time payment for an individual case, and from the 1290s onward the standard lawyer's fee appears to have been 40 pence (three shillings fourpence, or 10 groats).[92] By way of comparison, the lowest amount of damages that could be claimed in a writ of trespass in the king's courts was 40 shillings, 12 times the standard lawyer's fee. In a Year Book report of 1452, Serjeant Moyle stated that if no certain sum of money was promised to a serjeant for his services, he should have 40 pence by common right, and an attorney 20 pence.[93] Herman Cohen, E.W. Ives, and C.W. Brooks, historians of the legal profession, have found many instances of counsel fees of 40 pence in the fifteenth and sixteenth centuries – at least for one consultation or one day's appearance in court.[94] Shakespeare made it a proverb, 'as fit as ten groats is for the hand of an attorney'.[95] This standard fee persisted through centuries of inflation. In most of the surviving accounts of litigation expenses from the late fifteenth century, counsel fees typically totaled to less than half of the amount of fees paid to the chancery for writing out and to the court for enrolling the writs necessary for various stages of the litigation.[96] Lawyers made their money on high volume, not high fees.

Proposals were made in the mid-sixteenth century to eliminate lawyers' fees entirely. The king could use confiscated monastery wealth, *The Complaynt of Roderyck Mors* (1545) suggested, to pay stipends to every man of law who pleaded at the bar in any of his high courts, so that all suitors should pay nothing for counsel or for his pleading, and every lawyer should take no penny from any man, upon pain of losing his right hand and being banished from pleading forever. Thereby the poor should be heard as well as the rich, and each lawyer might live 'like a lawyer, and not like a lord, as they do with such goods as they have gotten by robbing the poor'.[97]

A proposal of 1534 for 'conservators of the commonweal' also advocated modest salaries for lawyers replacing fees paid by clients.[98] In the sixteenth century, it did not seem inconceivable that the relatively modest expense of fees to barristers and attorneys could be replaced by salaries from the king.

A reason that lawyers' fees were so low was that lawyers spent relatively little time on a typical case. Pleading was the heart of the lawyers' expertise, and pleading took place prior to the trial and so prior to the full development of facts. Lawyers in the Year Books bluffed and blustered mainly by posing hypothetical arguments and drawing upon analogies to well-settled points. Each common law court heard the pleading of several cases in a single day.[99] Trials before juries also took very little time, and counsel often were not present at trials.[100] It would not have been a great sacrifice for an English common lawyer to donate his services for a poor litigant in need of his help, if he had otherwise a steady practice of paying clients.

What can we conclude? There is very little evidence that English common lawyers gave their services freely to poor people before the statute of 1495 required them to do so. On the other hand, there is no proof that they did not. The question of legal services for the poor in the early common law remains an interesting one because of what it tells us about ourselves, our assumptions concerning the constants of human nature, our own altruism or cynicism, and our expectation of sincerity or hypocrisy in others.

Should we presume that lawyers would never have given away their expertise? Jurists of ancient Rome, we are told, gave their advice to anyone who approached them and never took fees,[101] and advocates only began accepting fees in the first century AD.[102] Why might medieval lawyers have given free to the poor what they charged other clients for doing? Charity would be one reason, and another reason might well have been a strong notion of fairness – procedural fairness. The early common law held out few promises for the poor. Substantive fairness – fairness in the distribution of the world's wealth – was not a principle that the secular courts embraced. Rather, the common law's promise of fairness was entirely procedural, a promise of the equal application of abstract rules to rich and poor alike. When one party to a transaction had an action to enforce it, but the other did not, this principle of procedural fairness was violated.[103] When one side had a lawyer to make the proper legal arguments and the other side did not, this too may have seemed a denial of fundamental fairness. If one side in an adversarial contest is unrepresented, lawyers today will feel an impulse to make the arguments – devil's advocate arguments, if you will – for the side that is not being upheld. Long before a medieval lawyer got his first paying client, he honed his skill by mooting, by arguing knotty hypothetical cases against fellow students of the law. One can imagine a Londoner getting a little free legal advice by finding a group of law students in the courtyard of an Inn of Court and asking them how his own legal difficulty would be argued. Even if medieval English lawyers had only this love of argument for argument's sake, it would be enough of a reason for them to have donated their services to the poor litigant who could not pay them. Of one final point I can be more certain: Paul Brand has counseled this poor scholar with generosity, kindness, and a love of argument for argument's sake time and again through more than three decades, and I contribute this paper in thanks to him for this.

Notes

1 James A. Brundage, 'Legal Aid for the Poor and the Professionalization of Law in the Middle Ages', *JLH* 9 (1988): 169–79.
2 William of Drogheda, John of Acton, William Lyndwood. See idem.
3 *LHP*, ch. 46, 4, p. 157; ch. 48, 1, p. 159; ch. 49, 3a, p. 163; p. 356, s.v. consilium (anonymous text, c. 1114).
4 Westminster I (1275), 3 Edw. 1, ch. 1 (*SR*, 1: 26); repeated in 1 Edw. 3 (1327), stat. 2, ch 14.
5 *Lawsuits*, 2: 687, 693 (no. 644 D).
6 The fullest account was from William of Newburgh, *Historia Rerum Anglicarum*, bk. 5, ch. 20. A more sympathetic view was in *Matthaei Parisiensis, monachi sancti Albani, Chronica majora*, ed. H.R. Luard, RS, 57 (1872–83), 2: 418. See Derek Keene, *ODNB*, s.v. William fitz Osbert.
7 *Select Bills in Eyre*, 6, bill 11 (joe nai dener ne mayl pur pleyter).
8 Ibid., 47, bill 72 (ie su si poure ke ie ne alower nule Countour).
9 Ibid., 21, bill 35 (Shropshire Eyre 1292) (pur ceo ke il sount pouerus priunt pur deu cher sire si vos plest ke vos les grantez un seriant pur eus issint ke lour dreyture ne seyt pas perdue pur lalme la Reyne).
10 Ibid., xlviii.
11 Brand, *OELP*, 104.
12 P&M, 1: 194. On court fees and other litigation costs reduced or remitted for the poor, see A.J. Musson, 'Social Exclusivity or Justice for All?: Access to Justice in Fourteenth-Century England', in *Pragmatic Utopias, 1200–1630*, eds. R. Horrox and S. Rees-Jones (Cambridge: Cambridge University Press), 136–55.
13 *Britton*, 1: 299; *Fleta*, 77 (fol. 33), 222 (fol. 85d); *Mirror of Justices*, 14; Irton's Case, Pasch. 15 Edw. 3, pl. 8, RS 7–11 (CP) (1341.057rs). Year Book citations are to my database, www.bu.edu/law/seipp.
14 *Bodmyn v. Beatone*, 30 Edw. 1, pl. [41], RS 141–143 (Cornwall Eyre) (1302.086rs).
15 *Tovyn v. William*, 30 Edw. 1, pl. [45], RS 147–149 (Cornwall Eyre) (1302.090rs). See William Thomas Charley, *The Legal Profession* (London: W. Ridgway, 1873), 106.
16 In Paston's Case, Pasch. 5 Edw. 4, Long Quinto pl. [8], fol. 5a–6b (Exch. Ch.) (1465.040), it was recounted that a sheriff had falsely returned that a poor prior had 'nothing' that could be sold to pay the fine the prior owed; the sheriff was himself fined heavily for this. In Stanton v. Gate, Mich. 2 Ric. 3, pl. 22, fol. 9b–11a (Star Ch., Exch. Ch.) (1484.022), a similar story was told that Chief Justice Hengham, at some time between 1301 and 1309, had taken pity on a very poor man and had erased the enrollment of a 13s. 4d. fine against him; for this erasure the Chief Justice was himself fined 800 marks, the money used to build a clock house for Westminster Hall and furnish it with a clock. This was the story repeated in later centuries, e.g. Edward Coke, *Institutes of the Laws of England* (London: M. Flesher 1644), 4: 255; Anon., 1 Salkeld 257, 91 Eng. Rep. 225–226 (KB 1700); Rex v. Wilkes, 4 Burrow 2527, 2567, 98 Eng. Rep. 327, 350 (KB 1770); Edward Foss, *Biographica Juridica* (London: J. Murray 1870), 339.

17 Wymond's Case, 30 Edw. 1, pl. [82], RS 199 (a) (1302.127rs), Sjt Kyngeshemede for plaintiff widow; Anon., 30 Edw. 1, pl. [87], RS 203 (a) (Cornwall Eyre) (1302.132rs).
18 Prior of Kenilworth's Case, Pasch. 35 Edw. 1, pl. [1], RS [467] (CP) (1307.038rs), Sjt Toutheby also spoke on the poor plaintiff's side.
19 *Brauneby v. Cokesale*, 2 Edw. 2, pl. 14, SS, 17: 62–65 (CP) (1309.014ss), Sjt Toutheby for poor defendant, Sjt Herle for the plaintiff. In three manuscripts of this case, the poor plaintiff was a woman; in two manuscripts, a man.
20 Llewellyn's Case, 2 Edw. 2, pl. 75, SS, 17: 150 (CP) (1309.075ss).
21 Anon., 2 Edw. 2, pl. 86, SS, 17: 164 (CP) (1309.086ss); also reported at 4 Edw. 2, addit. pl. 11 (c), SS, 42: 191 (CP) (1311.236ss).
22 *Scaldeford v. Abbot of Vaudey*, Mich. 4 Edw. 2, pl. 3, SS, 22: 30–34 (version IV at 33–34) (1310.144ss). Bereford CJCP also showed sympathy for the poor in Venour v. Blund, Mich. 4 Edw. 2, pl. 51, SS, 22: 157–162 (1310.192ss) and in Randolf v. Bavent, Hil. 4 Edw. 2, pl. 48, SS, 26: 106–110, SS, 42: 191 (1311.048ss).
23 1 Rot. Parl. 289a (1315).
24 Burdon's Case, Pasch. 15 Edw. 2, pl. [7], fol. 464 (b) (KB) (1322.021).
25 Anon., Mich. 4 Edw. 3, pl. 60, fol. 54b (1330.154).
26 Anon., Trin. 7 Edw. 3, pl. 1, fol. 23b–24a (CP) (1333.066); Anon., Pasch. 11 Edw. 3, pl. [10], RS 67–69 (CP) (1337.025rs).
27 Irton's Case, Pasch. 15 Edw. 3, pl. 8, RS 7–11 (CP) (1341.057rs).
28 Anon., Mich. 17 Edw. 3, pl. 27, RS 139–141 (CP) (1343.168rs).
29 Anon., Trin. 18 Edw. 3, pl. 45, RS 407 (CP) (1344.146rs).
30 Anon., Mich. 18 Edw. 3, pl. 86, RS 347–349 (1344.248rs); Anon., 18 Edw. 3, Lib. Ass. pl. 6, fol. 58a–58b (Assize) (1344.261ass).
31 Oath of the Justices, 18 Edw. 3, stat. 4, SR, 1: 305 (1344); Ordinance for the Justices, 20 Edw. 3, ch. 1, *SR*, 1: 303 (1346).
32 Anon., Trin. 20 Edw. 3, pl. 48, RS 57 (1346.169rs).
33 Winchester's Case, 20 Edw. 3, Lib. Ass. pl. 12, fol. 71b–72a (Assize) (1346.320ass).
34 Anon., 26 Edw. 3, Lib. Ass. pl. 2, fol. 119a–119b (Assize) (1352.066ass).
35 *Frances v. Malmain*, Trin. 6 Ric. 2, pl. 37, Ames 50–51 (1382.037am).
36 Windsor's Case, Mich. 6 Ric. 2, pl. 11, Ames 72–73 (1382.049am).
37 *Wallegh v. Smyth*, Mich. 8 Ric. 2, pl. 44, Ames 170 (1384.074am). Belknap allowed the poor plaintiff to deny the defendant's title generally without denying it specifically.
38 *Gardian v. Catesby*, K.R. Exchequer Miscellanea (E. 163), 6/46, Appendix VI in *Select Cases in the Court of King's Bench*, vol. 7, ed. G.O. Sayles, SS, 88: lxv–lxvi (1397).
39 *Select Cases in the Court of King's Bench*, vol. 7, xlv.
40 W.P. Baildon, ed., *Select Cases in Chancery*, SS, 10 (London: Quaritch, 1896), xxiii, 41 (case 37), 47 (case 43), 77 (case 80), 134–135 (case 139); George Spence, *The Equitable Jurisdiction of the Court of Chancery* (London, 1846), 1: 351 (order of 13 Ric. 2 apparently establishing a tribunal for the very poor not able to sue at common law).
41 *Select Cases in Chancery*, 23, 47, 48, 56, 59, 63, 92, 100, 111, 122, 123.
42 William Langland, *The Vision of Piers Plowman*, Prologue (Part II), lines 210–25, trans. D. and R. Attwater (London: Sheed and Ward, 1959), 6.
43 'London Lickpenny', in *Medieval English Political Writings*, ed. J.M. Dean (Kalamazoo: Medieval Institute Publications, Western Michigan University, 1996), 223 (from British Library MS Harley 542, fols. 102r–104r). Also in E. Hammond, 'London Lickpenny', 20 *Anglia* 404–20 (1898), reprinted in Eleanor Hammond, ed., *English Verse between Chaucer and Surrey* (Durham, NC: Duke University Press, 1927), 238–9.

44 *Mum and the Sothsegger* ll. 1577–1584, ed. Mabel Day and Robert Steele, EETS (o.s.) (London: H. Milford, 1936), 199.

45 Anon., Mich. 2 Hen. 4, pl. 43, fol. 8b–9a (1400.043).

46 4 Rot. Parl. 201b (no. 17) (1423); *PROME*, 10: 85 (Item, that the clerc of the [king's] counsail be sworn that every day that the counseill sitteth on ony billes bitwyx partie and partie, that he shall, as fer as he can, aspye which is the porest suyturs bille, and that first to be redd and answered; and the kings sergeant to be sworne trewly and plainly, to yeve the poor man that for suche is accept to the counsail, assistense and trewe counsaill in his matere so to be suyd, wyth oute eny good takyng of hym, on peyne of discharge of ther office.); Harris Nicolas, ed., *Proceedings and Ordinances of the Privy Council* (London: Eyre and Spottiswoode, 1834), 3: xix, 150, 217; Margaret Hastings, *The Court of Common Pleas in the Fifteenth Century* (Ithaca: Cornell University Press, 1947), 79.

47 4 Rot. Parl. 344 (no. 27, item 15) (1429), *PROME*, 10: 393–4.

48 Act 1424, c. 45; in William Alexander, *An Abridgement of the Acts of the Parliaments of Scotland*, 12 Mar. 1424, c. 24 (Edinburgh: A. and C. Black 1841), vol. 1, p. 8: 'gif thar be ony pur creatur that for defalt of cunnyng or dispense can nocht or may nocht folow his cause the king for the lufe of god sall ordaine that the Juge before quham the caue suld be determyt purvay and get a lele and a wyse aduocate to folow sic pur creaturis cause And gif sic cause be obtenyt the wrangar sall assyth bath the party scathit and the aduocatis costis and trauale', quoted in C.N. Stoddart, 'A Short History of Legal Aid in Scotland', *Juridical Review* 24 (1979): 170. See John Finlay, 'Ethics, Etiquette, and the Early Modern Scots Advocate', *Juridical Review* 2 (2006): 147; idem, *Men of Law in Pre-Reformation Scotland* (East Linton: Tuckwell Press, 2000), 82–6.

49 Wager of law enabled a defendant to deny that he owed a debt to the plaintiff by swearing this and finding eleven oath-helpers who would swear that they believed the defendant. When the defendant incurred a debt in such a way that the plaintiff could not refuse to transact with the defendant, the defendant was not allowed to wage his law.

50 Serjeant Pole's Case, Hil. 3 Hen. 6, pl. 26, fol. 33 (CP) (1425.026); also reported at Mich. 21 Hen. 6, pl. 6, fol. 4a; Brooke, Ley gager 45 (CP) (1442.102).

51 *Rothewel v. Pewer*, Hil. 9 Hen. 6, pl. 17, fol. 64a–64b (CP) (1431.017).

52 *Pomeray v. Abbot of Buckfast, Mich.* 21 Hen. 6, pl. 30, fol. 15b–16b; Brooke, Maintenance pl. 14 (CP) (1442.126).

53 *Pomeray v. Abbot of Buckfast*, Mich. 22 Hen. 6, pl. 7, fol. 5a–7a (CP) (1443.066).

54 Anon., Mich. 22 Hen. 6, pl. 54, fol. 35a; Brooke, Maintenance pl. 17 (CP) (1443.113), probably not a speech by Serjeant Prysot, to whom it is attributed in the Year Book, because it ran contrary to the arguments he made for the plaintiff in this case.

55 *Paston v. Jenney*, Trin. 11 Edw. 4, pl. 4, fol. 2b, 3a; SS, 64: 189–190 (CP) (1471.004): *si un Serjeant ne voile estre de counsaile icy ove un pouer home par nostre assignement, nous ne luy poyoms faire non Serjeant, car il ad ceo nosme donne par le Roy, mes nous poioms luy estrange del barre, issint que il ne serra resceu de pleade, &c.* See James Manning, *Serviens ad legem* (London: Longman, 1840), 40–1, 232–3. The same point is made by Chief Justice Matthew Hale in Deakins v. Scroggs, 1 Freeman 389, 89 Eng. Rep. 289; 3 Keble 441, 84 Eng. Rep. 812 (KB 1674).

56 *Paston v. Jenney* at 3b: *Jeo voy mon master Cheine chief justice de Bank le roy venir en cest court, et require les Serjeants d'estre de councell en un plee que fuit devant luy, et s'ils ne voillent il voilloit avoir forjuge eux de pleder en Bank le Roy.*

57 Ibid. (*Bene potuit*).

58 Cod. J. 2.8.14; William of Drogheda, *Summa aurea*, c. 33 (c. 1239), ed. Ludwig Wahrmund (Innsbruck: Wagner, 1914); Guillaume Durand, *Speculum Juris* bk. 1, pt. 4, p. 253 (1271) (Frankfurt, 1668); Herman Cohen, *A History of the English Bar and Attornatus to 1450* (London: Sweet & Maxwell, 1929), 567–8.
59 W.S. Holdsworth, *A History of English Law*, 3rd ed. (London: Methuen, 1923), 2: 478.
60 Ibid., 491.
61 Anon., Trin. 15 Edw. 4, pl. 2, fol. 26b; Brooke, Fees pl. 5, Officer pl. 15 (1475.015). See Manning, *Serviens ad legem*, 41; Hastings, *Court of Common Pleas*, 124–6. Hastings doubted that John Browne, third prothonotary from 1476 to 1480, was the clerk to whom the Year Book note referred.
62 J.F. Baldwin, *The King's Council in England During the Middle Ages* (Oxford: Clarendon Press, 1913), 435, citing Calendar of Patent Rolls, 1 Ric. 3, p. 413.
63 Thomas Stapleton, ed., *Plumpton Correspondence* (London: J.B. Nichols and Son, 1839), 35.
64 Sir John Baker, *The Oxford History of the Laws of England, 1483–1558* (Oxford: Oxford University Press, 2003), 203; M.M. Condon, 'An Anachronism with Intent?: Henry VII's Council Ordinance of 1491/2', in *Kings and Nobles in the Later Middle Ages*, eds. R.A. Griffiths and James Sherborne (Gloucester: Sutton, 1986), 236, 247, art. 15.
65 Baker, *Oxford History of the Laws of England*, 194, citing BL MS. Lansdowne 639, fol. 28.
66 Statute 11 Hen. 7, ch. 12, *SR*, 2: 578 (1495) 'A mean to help and speed poor persons in their suits' (the headnote reads: 'An Acte to admytt such persons as are poore to sue in formâ paup[er]is and a sidenote reads: and Counsel and Attorneys assigned to them'.) ('And that the' seid Chaunceller for the same tyme being shall assigne . . . also lerned Councell and attorneyes for the same, without any rewarde taking therfor . . . [T]he Justices ther [afore the King in his Benche] shall assigne to the same pou[re] p[er]sone or p[er]sones Councell lerned by their discrecions which shall geve their Councelles nothing taking for the same'.).
67 See text at note 48 above.
68 Anon., Trin. 11 Hen. 7, pl. 1, fol. 23a (CP) (1496.030).
69 *Selby v. Mulsho*, SS, 25: at 319, lix (Star Chamber 1534) (in a case that was litigated from 1494 to 1538).
70 John Hoddesdon, *The History of the Life and Death of Sr. Thomas More* (London, 1662), 85.
71 Sebastian Guistinian, 1519, in *Calendar of State Papers Relating to English Affairs in the Archives of Venice* (London: Longman, 1867), 2: 556–65.
72 J.R. Dasent, ed., *Acts of the Privy Council of England*, new series (London: H.M.S.O, 1894), 9: 60–1.
73 W.J. Jones, *The Elizabethan Court of Chancery* (Oxford: Clarendon Press, 1967), 326–7; W.R. Prest, *The Rise of the Barristers: A Social History of the English Bar, 1590–1620* (Oxford: Clarendon Press, 1986), 22. Perhaps senior serjeants with well-established practices could better afford to give gratuitous counsel.
74 Lord Campbell, *Lives of the Lord Chancellors*, 4th ed. (London: J. Murray, 1856), 2: 380.
75 E.g., Thomas Middleton, *The Phoenix*, act 1, scene 6, lines 50–6; James Drake, *The Sham Lawyer*, sig. C1r; William Wycherley, *The Plain Dealer*, in E.F.J. Tucker, '*Ignoramus* and Seventeenth-Century Satire of the Law', *Harvard Library Bulletin* 19 (1971): 314, 327–8.
76 John H. Baker, *The Order of Serjeants at Law* (London: Selden Society, 1984), 292 (from MS. Harl. 160, fol. 192v, reign of Henry VIII): 'be as glad to tel the poure man the truth of the law for God's sake as the riche man for his monye'.

77 Ibid. at 293: 'And by doinge for the poure for nothinge ye cane not but wine much good name and fame and prayse and thanke at the handes as well of God as man'.

78 The Lord Chief Justice's Speech, Popham 45, 79 Eng. Rep. 1163 (KB 1594) (Popham CJKB).

79 Jones, *The Elizabethan Court of Chancery*, 323 (citing G.W. Sanders, *Orders of the High Court of Chancery* (1845), 2: 1035) (Hatton LC).

80 Morris P. Tilley, *Dictionary of the Proverbs of England in the Sixteenth and Seventeenth Centuries*, L125, 372; *Oxford Dictionary of English Proverbs*, 3rd ed., 447 (citations include: 'Wo Wytt haue law, must haue monye' (c. 1460); 'Lytle mony lytle lawe' (c. 1550); 'Thou are akinne to the Lawyer, thou wilt doo nothing without a Fee' (c. 1581); 'No fee, no lawe' (1597); 'A Lawyer will not pleade but for money' (1661); 'A man may as well open an Oister without a knife, as a Lawyers mouth without a fee' (1618); 'A Lawyer's tongue runs glib when he's fed [fee'd?]' (1618); 'A Lawyers lips are lockt without a fee' (1657)).

81 William Shakespeare, *King Lear* 1:4:128–9 (1605–06): 'This [advice] is nothing, fool. – Then 'tis like the breath of an unfee'd lawyer. You gave me nothing for't'. Also 'Here's a fish hangs in the net like a poor man's right in the law, 't will hardly come out'. Shakespeare, *Pericles*, scene 6, lines 158–160.

82 *Britton*, 1: 84–5; Christopher St. German, *Doctor and Student*, dialogue 2, ch. 48, ed. T.F.T. Plucknett and J.L. Barton, SS, 91: 285.

83 David J. Seipp, 'Crime in the Year Books', in *Law Reporting in Britain*, ed. Chantal Stebbings (London: The Hambledon Press, 1995), 23–6.

84 Anon., 26 Edw. 3, Lib. Ass. pl. 46, fol. 129b, Fitzherbert, Office del Court pl. 34 (1352.110ass).

85 *Armethorpe v. Eypton*, Pasch. 4 Edw. 4, pl. 16, fol. 11a–12a (Nottingham Assize and Gaol Delivery) (1464.021).

86 St. German, *Doctor and Student*, dialogue 2, ch. 48, SS, 91: 285.

87 S.F.C. Milsom, *Historical Foundations of the Common Law* (London: Butterworths, 1969), 374.

88 Seipp, 'Crime in the Year Books', 22.

89 Ibid., 25.

90 An example is the litigation described in David J. Seipp, 'Jurors, Evidences, and the Tempest of 1499', in *"The Dearest Birthright of the People of England": The Jury in the History of the Common Law*, eds. John W. Cairns and Grant McLeod (Oxford: Hart, 2002), 75–92.

91 *LHP*, 57.8: 178.

92 Brand, *OELP*, 104.

93 Tailour's Case, Mich. 31 Hen. 6, pl. 1, fol. 8b–10a (1452.020); Hastings, *Court of Common Pleas*, 76.

94 Cohen, *History of the English Bar*, 381; E.W. Ives, *The Common Lawyers of Pre-Reformation England* (Cambridge: Cambridge University Press, 1983), 299, 303, 304; C.W. Brooks, *Pettyfoggers and Vipers of the Commonwealth* (Cambridge: Cambridge University Press, 1986), 233.

95 William Shakespeare, *All's Well That Ends Well* 2:2:22 (1601). A slang term for an attorney in the eighteenth century was a 'six-and-eightpence', twice the medieval fee. Francis Grose, *A Classical Dictionary of the Vulgar Tongue* (London, 1785).

96 Ives, *Common Lawyers of Pre-Reformation England*, 320.

97 Henry Brinklow, *The Complaynt of Roderyck Mors* (1545), ch. 9, ed. J. Meadows Cowper, EETS, e.s., 22 (London, 1874; repr., Oxford: Oxford University Press, 2001), 23–4.

98 Alan Harding, *A Social History of English Law* (Baltimore: Penguin Books, Inc., 1966), 244.

99 See Hastings, *Court of Common Pleas*, 29–35 ('A Day in Court').

100 See ibid., 204–5; R.B. Pugh, 'The Duration of Criminal Trials in Medieval England', in *Law, Litigants and the Legal Profession*, eds. E.W. Ives and A.H. Manchester (London: Royal Historical Society, 1983), 104–8; J.H. Langbein, 'The Criminal Trial Before the Lawyers', *University of Chicago Law Review* 45 (1978): 274–5. I have no reason to think that civil trials lasted notably longer than criminal ones.

101 W.W. Buckland, *A Text-Book of Roman Law From Augustus to Justinian*, 3rd ed., revised by Peter Stein (Cambridge: Cambridge University Press, 1966), 21; H.F. Jolowicz, *Historical Introduction to the Study of Roman Law* (Cambridge: Cambridge University Press, 1967), 91; Bruce W. Frier, *The Rise of the Roman Jurists* (Princeton: Princeton University Press, 1985), 255; J.A. Crook, *Legal Advocacy in the Roman World* (London: Duckworth, 1995), 43.

102 Adolf Berger, *Encyclopedic Dictionary of Roman Law* (Philadelphia: The American Philosophical Society, 1953), 352, s.v. advocatus; J.M. Kelly, *Roman Litigation* (Oxford: Clarendon Press, 1966), 48 n.1.

103 See, e.g., Doige's Case, Trin. 20 Hen. 6, pl. 4, fol. 34a–35b, SS, 51: 97–101 (Exch. Ch.) (1442.056).

Index

www.ingramcontent.com/pod-product-compliance
Ingram Content Group UK Ltd.
Pitfield, Milton Keynes, MK11 3LW, UK
UKHW022014180926
475701UK00003B/357
9780367594367